Autonomous Public Bodies and the Law

ELGAR MONOGRAPHS IN CONSTITUTIONAL AND ADMINISTRATIVE LAW

Series Editors: Rosalind Dixon, *University of New South Wales, Australia,* Susan Rose-Ackerman, *Yale University* and Mark Tushnet, *Harvard University, USA*

Constitutions are a country's most important legal document, laying the foundation not just for politics, but for all other areas of law. They allocate power among different levels and branches of government, record and promote a society's shared values, and protect the rights of citizens. Countries around the world are adopting written constitutions, though what defines a constitution is evolving to include a variety of sources beyond canonical texts, such as political conventions, statutes, judicial decisions and administrative law norms.

This cosmopolitan monograph series provides a forum for the best and most original scholarship in constitutional and administrative law, with each book offering an international, comparative or multi-jurisdictional approach to this complex and fascinating field of research.

Titles in the series include:

Political Technology and the Erosion of the Rule of Law
Normalizing the State of Exception
Günter Frankenberg

Constitutional Sunsets and Experimental Legislation
A Comparative Perspective
Sofia Ranchordás

Constitutionalism and Religion
Francois Venter

The Arab Spring
An Essay on Revolution and Constitutionalism
Antoni Abat i Ninet and Mark Tushnet

American Judicial Power
The State Court Perspective
Michael L. Buenger and Paul J. De Muniz

Citizen Journalists
Newer Media, Republican Moments and the Constitution
Ian Cram

Against the New Constitutionalism
Tamas Gyorfi

Autonomous Public Bodies and the Law
A European Perspective
Stéphanie De Somer

Autonomous Public Bodies and the Law

A European Perspective

Stéphanie De Somer

Postdoctoral Researcher, FWO Flanders, University of Antwerp, Belgium and an academic advisor (Of Counsel) for law firm Van Olmen & Wynant, Brussels, Belgium

ELGAR MONOGRAPHS IN CONSTITUTIONAL AND ADMINISTRATIVE LAW

Edward Elgar PUBLISHING

Cheltenham, UK • Northampton, MA, USA

Published by
Edward Elgar Publishing Limited
The Lypiatts
15 Lansdown Road
Cheltenham
Glos GL50 2JA
UK

Edward Elgar Publishing, Inc.
William Pratt House
9 Dewey Court
Northampton
Massachusetts 01060
USA

A catalogue record for this book
is available from the British Library

Library of Congress Control Number: 2016959925

This book is available electronically in the **Elgar**online
Law subject collection
DOI 10.4337/9781785364686

MIX
Paper from
responsible sources
FSC® C013604

ISBN 978 1 78536 467 9 (cased)
ISBN 978 1 78536 468 6 (eBook)

Typeset by Columns Design XML Ltd, Reading
Printed and bound by CPI Group (UK) Ltd, Croydon, CR0 4YY

Contents

Preface

On 23 June 2016, the majority of the voters in a referendum decided that the UK should cease to be a Member State of the European Union. The precise conditions under which this 'Brexit' will take place were still unclear in July 2016, when the manuscript of this book was submitted to the publisher. They will probably remain so for some time. An important part of this book, however, studies the influence of EU law on the phenomenon of autonomous public bodies. Four EU Member States were selected to study the impact of EU obligations on the creation of autonomous public bodies on national constitutional and administrative law. The UK is one of them.

The UK's decision to leave the Union does not make this book or its conclusions with regard to the UK irrelevant or invalid.

First of all, the UK will remain an EU Member State until all the necessary formalities have been fulfilled. Until then, it has to comply with EU law.

Secondly, it is possible that the UK will remain a member of the European Economic Area (EEA). Most of the EU legislation discussed in Chapter 2 of this book has EEA relevance and will remain applicable to the UK if it remains in the EEA. Even if this is not the case and the UK would pursue a so-called 'hard Brexit', the UK Government has declared its intention to convert the 'acquis communautaire', wherever practical and appropriate, into domestic law, at least until Parliament has had the time to consider which elements of that law to keep.[1]

Thirdly, this book contains an analysis of how UK law has dealt with the constitutional objections against autonomous public bodies in general, apart from the context of EU influence. Chapter 3 discusses how each of the four national legal systems examined in this book have recently launched initiatives to overcome these constitutional objections and – most importantly – the democratic concerns that go hand in hand

[1] White paper 'The United Kingdom's exit from and new partnership with the European Union' (February 2017), 9: *https://www.gov.uk/government/uploads/system/uploads/attachment_data/file/589191/The_United_Kingdoms_exit_from_and_partnership_with_the_EU_Web.pdf.*

with the creation and empowerment of autonomous public bodies. For the UK, substantial attention is paid to the goals, technique, contents and effects of the Public Bodies Act 2011, which is compared with the framework legislation on autonomous public bodies issued in the Belgian region of Flanders and in the Netherlands. This analysis remains relevant regardless of the question whether and to what extent EU law applies to the UK. The development of general legislative frameworks on autonomous bodies has long been advocated by legal doctrine in various European legal systems. UK law offers an interesting example of how such framework legislation can be designed, which may inspire other European legislatures.

Finally, central to this book is the question whether and to what extent the EU is imposing on its Member States a model of administrative organization that is contrary to national constitutional traditions with regard to the democratic embedment of executive authorities. An argument put forward by many 'Brexiteers' was that of the democratic deficit of the EU and especially its (alleged) disregard for the will of national parliaments and their politically responsible Governments. The EU is often depicted as a purely technocratic legal order. The study contained in this book reveals that EU legislation is increasingly imposing a similar model of governance on its Member States, by obliging them to entrust the implementation of substantive EU law obligations to administrative bodies that enjoy a substantial degree of political autonomy. Thus, EU legislation diverts power from central government institutions, which are responsible to elected representatives. Requirements like these contribute to the perception that the EU promotes undemocratic decision making by curbing the influence of national democratic actors. This book contains recommendations as to how the valid concerns behind these EU requirements can be reconciled with the national concerns about the political and democratic accountability of autonomous public bodies. The discourse used by the 'leave campaign' in the UK demonstrates that reflections on the democratic nature of EU governance are long overdue and should once again focus on more traditional accounts of democracy, linked to political legitimacy and accountability to elected representatives.

This book takes into account developments up to June 2016.

Acknowledgements

I dedicate this book to Professor Ingrid Opdebeek for her support, encouraging words and above all her kindness, which have made my work so much more agreeable.

Thanks are due to the various other academics with whom I have had interesting debates on the topic of autonomous public bodies, and especially to Professor Pierre-Olivier de Broux, Professor Patricia Popelier, Professor Richard Rawlings, Professor Steven Van Garsse and Professor Sjoerd Zijlstra.

Thanks also go to the reviewers appointed by Edward Elgar and to the series editors for their useful comments and suggestions.

Thanks to my colleagues at the University of Antwerp, for making the university such a pleasant working environment for me, and to my friends who have supported me throughout the process.

My husband, Cedric, himself a lawyer, often volunteered to hear my arguments and ideas before I put them on paper. I thank him for his honest opinions and for being the wind beneath my wings in all my endeavours.

My parents and other family members (especially Bobonne Kiel, Ata, Tiny, Vincent and Caroline) deserve my sincere gratitude for offering me the opportunities to pursue my dreams and for their continuous belief in me.

Finally, with this book, I hope to honour my grandmother, Tie Van Cappellen or Bobonne Kampelaar, who passed away a week before I finished this manuscript. May she rest in peace.

Abbreviations

AAI (France)	Autorité administrative indépendante
ALB	Arm's length body
APB	Autonomous public body
API (France)	Autorité publique indépendante
Awb (Netherlands)	Algemene wet bestuursrecht (General Act administrative law)
BWHI (Belgium)	Bijzondere Wet Hervorming Instellingen (Special Act on the Reform of Institutions)
CC (France)	Conseil Constitutionnel
DPA	Data protection authority
ECHR	European Convention on Human Rights
ECJ	European Court of Justice
ECtHR	European Court of Human Rights
Eerste Kamer (Netherlands)	First Chamber of the Dutch Parliament
EPA (France)	Établissement public administratif
EPIC (France)	Établissement public industriel et commercial
EVA (Flanders)	Extern verzelfstandigd agentschap
GwH (Belgium)	Grondwettelijk Hof (Belgian Constitutional Court)
IRA	Independent regulatory authority
IVA (Flanders)	Intern verzelfstandigd agentschap
KDBB (Flanders)	Kaderdecreet bestuurlijk beleid
KWZBO (Netherlands)	Kaderwet zelfstandige bestuursorganen
NDPB (UK)	Non-departmental public body
NHRI	National human rights institution
NPM	New Public Management
NRA	National regulatory authority

OECD	Organisation for Economic Co-operation and Development
PBA (UK)	Public Bodies Act
PBB (UK)	Public Bodies Bill
Quango (UK)	Quasi-autonomous non-governmental organization
TEU	Treaty on the European Union
TFEU	Treaty on the Functioning of the European Union
Tweede Kamer (Netherlands)	Second Chamber of the Dutch Parliament
Vl. Parl. (Vlaams Parlement) (Flanders)	Flemish Parliament
ZBO (Netherlands)	Zelfstandige Bestuursorgaan

1. Introduction

1. ADMINISTRATION AT A DISTANCE: SETTING THE SCENE

> In area after area of public life, elected government is being replaced by appointive government. Those who are elected count for ever less ... ; those who are appointed count for ever more.[1]

A model of administrative organization that nearly all developed states have to some extent adopted in the 21st century is that of administration through entities that are part of the governmental organization chart, but function with a certain degree of autonomy vis-à-vis elected government. For the purpose of this study, these entities will be referred to as autonomous public bodies (APBs).

The 'depoliticization' of the administration in favour of APBs has been an ongoing evolution in Western states ever since the aftermath of World War II. The creation of APBs has often been inspired by the goal of bringing more expertise (in a technocratic or broader, experience-related sense) to the administration. This has given rise to a tension between two values that are of central importance to the functioning of the government today. On the one hand, there is expertise, as in informed and knowledge-based decision making. On the other hand, there is the primacy of elected leaders, who take responsibility for government actions. This tension will be central to the ideas and proposals developed in Chapter 5 of this book.

In the 21st century, however, 'depoliticization' is no longer exclusively about giving sufficient leeway to appointed experts, even if, in the end, it is indeed mostly non-elected experts who populate the boards of APBs. Many of the more recent initiatives of depoliticization indeed have other roots and are inspired by considerations that are more radical. It cannot be overlooked that, somehow, to some people and in an increasing number of contexts, 'politics' seems to have become a 'dirty word'. What is 'political' is most likely negotiated in back rooms, done in an

---

[1] Stuart Weir, 'Quangos: Questions of Democratic Accountability' (1995) 48(2) Parliam Aff 306, 321.

incompetent way or surrounded by scandal and suspicion, the arguments of the sceptics say. This is even so to the extent that it sometimes feels awkward or inappropriate to associate politicians with something as sacred as (representative) democracy.

Nonetheless, there was a time when it was taken for granted in Western politics that democratic government relied on the elected representatives of the people, who were the only authorities entitled to constrain people's individual freedoms. For the acquisition of these rights, barricades had been raised and (civil) wars had been fought. They were not to be the subject of limitations and compromise unless for very good reasons, in the public interest. Only the representatives of the people, appointed after free and fair elections, could define this public interest and decide on rules, measures and actions to achieve it. In Western societies, people regard it as self-evident that others should respect their liberal rights and that private parties cannot impose obligations on each other without their mutual permission. This power of making unilateral, binding decisions is monopolized by the state, which is ultimately under the supervision of elected government. These assumptions, derived from the political philosophy of thinkers such as Locke and Rousseau, are seldom made explicit. However, when we think of the reasons why we accept state authority in general, we inevitably end up referring to the democratic mandate that we have entrusted our political leaders with. The title 'representative of the people' inspires respect and reliability. In any case, it sounds a lot more august than 'politician'. Nevertheless, it is obvious that all elected representatives *are* politicians and it is precisely because they have a particular view on a desirable future and development of the *polis* that they have been elected by their voters. Considering that politics and politicians constitute a representative democracy, the increasing feeling of distrust towards them – in general, as a category – indeed seems peculiar.

Whether the result of rational trade-offs between competing values or of a sheer aversion vis-à-vis all that is labelled 'political', depoliticization is a fact for many parts of the administration today. Moreover, it is more than a political reality. In the past decades, it has also had an impact on public *law* and more precisely on the law of administrative organization. In recent years, many parts of government administration have deliberately been insulated against political influence and this has been translated in their legal status. Autonomy (or 'independence') of politicians is increasingly regarded as a 'quality label' for public sector institutions. Numerous public organizations that enjoy various degrees of political autonomy have been established and entrusted with often far-reaching powers in order to execute public missions. Not infrequently, they are responsible for large amounts of public expenditure. These organizations constitute the object of study of this book.

APBs are anything but a recent phenomenon in (Western) Europe. Many of them were established in the years following World War II,[2] when the welfare state made its entrance and the government's radius of action enlarged. Later, in the 1980s, characterized as an 'era when the *Zeitgeist* has been anti-political',[3] the theories of New Public Management (NPM) resulted in an increase of the number of APBs. Roughly, NPM promoted the idea that rational and efficient management always requires the fulfilment of the same principles and conditions, regardless of whether an entity operates inside or outside the public sphere.[4] Disaggregation of large administrations and the increase of the responsibility of the top management were among the most important principles of NPM.[5]

Promoted by the proponents of neoliberalism, also referred to by eponyms such as 'Thatcherism' or 'Reaganism', NPM resulted in ambitious programmes of reorganization. Hierarchy and centrality of government bureaucracies, two key features of the Weberian model, were regarded as the main impediments to administrative efficiency. 'Hierarchical control, it was argued, has fostered over-centralisation, with time-consuming referral of decisions to more senior levels, reluctance to take risks and insensitivity to local conditions.'[6] The creation of a number of separate (often specialized) units of government and the decrease of detailed, day-to-day political control were deemed the proper remedies. Managers had to be given autonomy and were to be held accountable on the basis of the final results achieved, rather than on grounds relating to their methods, procedures and day-to-day decisions.

The central panacea of these reforms being 'less government', it is at first sight surprising that they have stimulated the creation of such a large

---

[2] See e.g. Luc F M Verhey, 'British Agencies: Surveying the Quango State' in Tom Zwart and Luc Verhey (eds), *Agencies in European and Comparative Law* (Intersentia 2003) 19, 22.

[3] Johan P Olsen, 'Democratic Government, Institutional Autonomy and the Dynamics of Change' (2009) 32(3) West European Politics 439, 443.

[4] ibid 442; Gavin Drewry, 'The Executive: Towards Accountable Government and Effective Governance?' in Jeffrey Jowell and Dawn Oliver (eds), *The Changing Constitution* (Oxford University Press 2011) 187, 196.

[5] See e.g. Richard Mulgan, *Holding Power to Account: Accountability in Modern Democracies* (Palgrave Macmillan 2003) 153.

[6] ibid 152.

number of administrative bodies. Notwithstanding important liberalization and privatization projects, achieved under the flag of these same politico-economic movements, the public task has hardly diminished compared to some 30 years ago. As society becomes ever more diverse and complex, new tasks and responsibilities emerge for governments. Furthermore, the liberalization of certain economic industries has not made governmental interference superfluous. Old methods of intervention (direct provision) have been replaced by new ones (regulation), so that the net impact of these operations on the size of public responsibility has not always and everywhere been as impressive as one might have expected. Admittedly, one can regard APBs as 'governments to a lesser degree', because they function at a certain distance from the political institutions on the one hand and because they are often organized on the basis of models resembling those applied to private businesses on the other hand. The latter is especially true as far as accountability to principals (accountability for results rather than procedures followed or means applied) and the public (a focus on accountability to stakeholders or 'clients') is concerned.[7] In 1995, a British author described the emergence of what he labelled a 'skeletal state'.[8] In 2002, the Organisation for Economic Co-operation and Development (OECD) observed that, in some countries, 'agencies, authorities and other government bodies' accounted for more than half of public expenditure and employed more staff than traditional vertically integrated ministries.[9]

The two waves of APB creation had in common that they were driven by political preference and strategy. In other words: whether or not to introduce APBs in administrative organization was a political choice; a choice of *policy* for national Parliaments and Governments. The political rationalities behind the creation of APBs have been diverse: they range from 'unburdening' central administrations to ensuring specialization or expertise, allowing for civil society to participate in the boards of APBs or simply insulating a certain task from political interference.

This book, however, discusses a new, contemporary source of APB creation: EU law. It demonstrates how some of the most autonomous national APBs in Europe have been established or have seen their

---

[7] ibid 156.

[8] David Wilson, 'Quangos in the Skeletal State' (1995) 48(2) Parliam Aff 181.

[9] OECD, *Distributed Public Governance: Agencies, Authorities and Other Government Bodies*, 2002, 9 (http://www.oecd-ilibrary.org/governance/distributed-public-governance_9789264177420-en). Hereinafter: OECD, *Distributed Public Governance.* See p. 16 for more specific numbers and percentages.

autonomy increased as a direct consequence of EU legislation. At the same time, however, many European states are precisely reconsidering their past enthusiasm for APBs as proper modes of governance. National Parliaments and Governments are increasingly sceptical about APBs as panaceas for organizational challenges. APBs are being abolished, their autonomy is being curtailed, or their creation or abolishment made subject to rationalization efforts. This is the second trend that is central to the analysis developed in this book.

First things first, however: we have still not defined the notion of an 'APB', nor explained the choice of this term, despite the fact that other designations may have been more obvious to describe the phenomenon just sketched.

2. AUTONOMOUS PUBLIC BODIES (APBS): A TERMINOLOGICAL SHIFT AND A WORKING DEFINITION

> [W]hat exactly is the 'idea of agency', which appears, superficially at least, to have gripped so many governments around the world? Is it, in fact, the same idea or are there several versions all masquerading as 'agencification'? Or, are we converging only in the rhetoric, describing the changes, or in reality, or in both?[10]

A. Terminological Chaos

The literature on APBs suffers from terminological chaos, rendering any attempt to clarify the many complex issues that this phenomenon entails more difficult. The chaos is caused by the use of concepts that appear to be well established, but are in fact used in many different meanings and contexts, which are seldom clarified by authors. In its 2002 study on *Distributed Public Governance*, the OECD expressed its belief that 'one important reason for the shortcomings of international comparative research in this area lies in the use of ambiguous terminology and the absence of a coherent classification of the variety of organizational forms'.[11]

---

[10] Colin Talbot, 'The Agency Idea: Sometimes Old, Sometimes New, Sometimes Borrowed, Sometimes Untrue' in Christopher Pollit and Colin Talbot (eds), *Unbundled Government. A Critical Analysis of the Global Trend to Agencies, Quangos and Contractualisation* (Routledge 2004) 3, 4.

[11] OECD, *Distributed Public Governance* 9.

The term 'agencies' is undoubtedly the most notorious example of this problematic use of terms. Recent work in the field of public administration adopts a rather broad definition of the notion of 'government agency', describing it as an organization that (1) is structurally disaggregated from the government and (2) operates under more businesslike conditions than the government bureaucracy.[12]

This broad definition, however, is not always reconcilable with existing national legislation, policy and practice. In many legal systems, the term 'agency' or its (translated) derivatives are reserved for specific types of APBs. More precisely, the notion is often used to refer to APBs that are still part of a government department and subject to the hierarchical authority of a responsible minister, but nevertheless enjoy a certain degree of operational autonomy. This is, for instance, true for the agencies (*agentschappen/agences*) at the Belgian federal level, for the Dutch agencies (*agentschappen*) and for the executive ('Next Steps') agencies operating in the UK. Consequently, 'agency' is a multi-interpretable and therefore confusing term, which makes it unsuitable for studies with European or comparative ambitions.

All the more problematic are references to specific terms or typologies that originate from a particular legal system. An example is 'quango', an acronym that stands for 'quasi-autonomous non-governmental organization', which was introduced in UK literature by Barker. The author himself, however, struggled with its precise meaning within the domestic UK context, describing quangos as 'the many and varied organizations which stand somewhere between the Government Departments, which Ministers control and for which they are formally responsible in every detail to Parliament, and "private society", however that may be defined'.[13] Others have described the concept as 'a piece of catchy jargon

---

[12] Sandra Van Thiel, 'Comparing Agencies across Countries' in Koen Verhoest, Sandra Van Thiel, Geert Bouckaert and Per Lægreid (eds), *Government Agencies Practices and Lessons from 30 Countries* (Palgrave Macmillan 2012) 18, 18 with reference to Colin Talbot, 'The Agency idea. Sometimes old, sometimes new, sometimes borrowed, sometimes untrue' in Christopher Pollit and Colin Talbot (eds), *Unbundled Government. A critical analysis of the global trend to agencies, quangos and contractualisation* (Routledge, 2004).

[13] Anthony Barker, 'Governmental Bodies and the Networks of Mutual Accountability' in Anthony Barker (ed), *Quangos in Britain. Government and the Networks of Public Policy-Making* (Palgrave Macmillan 1982) 3, 3.

to which it is now impossible to attach any meaning'.[14] Currently, 'quango' is often used for the delineation of often comparative studies on APBs subject to minimal supervision (also called 'independent agencies') and its use is no longer confined to the political or legal system of the UK.[15]

The terminological chaos extends to adjectives as well. One example is the use of 'independent' in 'independent agency'. Scholten advises against its use and proposes to use 'autonomous' instead, explaining that 'if autonomy can be measured by various degrees, the term "independent" seems to be an overarching notion of a complete absence of any dependence'.[16] According to the author, the adjective 'independent' has a connotation of excluding any oversight authority.[17] It seems that literature increasingly reserves the term 'independent agency' for those APBs that operate in environments in which neutrality and/or impartiality are highly esteemed values and political interference is regarded as inappropriate. This is typically the case if a government mission relies heavily on (technical) expertise and/or if a task is supervisory in nature and the government itself is subject to that supervision.[18] These rationales indeed tolerate only mild forms of political interference or oversight. Consequently, 'independent' refers to a *species*, instead of the *genus*.

In sum: there is a need for a new umbrella concept to achieve conceptual clarity in the international and European literature on delegation to public bodies that perform their tasks with a certain degree of autonomy. This book suggests that the term 'APB' could fulfil that role of a coordinating concept.

---

[14] Nevil Johnson, 'Accountability, Control and Complexity: Moving Beyond Ministerial Responsibility' in Anthony Barker (ed), *Quangos in Britain. Government and the Networks of Public Policy-Making* (Palgrave Macmillan 1982) 206, 206–207.

[15] See e.g. Christopher Pollit and Colin Talbot (eds), *Unbundled Government. A Critical Analysis of the Global Trend to Agencies, Quangos and Contractualisation* (Routledge 2004); Yseult Marique, 'The Rule-Making Powers of Independent Administrative Agencies ('QUANGOs')' (2007) 11(3) Electronic Journal of Comparative Law.

[16] Miroslava Scholten, 'Independent, Hence Unaccountable? – The Need for a Broader Debate on Accountability of the Executive' [2011] Review of European Administrative Law 5, 7.

[17] ibid 8.

[18] Aalt W Heringa, and Luc F M Verhey, 'Independent Agencies and Political Control' in Tom Zwart and Luc Verhey (eds), *Agencies in European and Comparative Law* (Intersentia 2003) 155, 157 with reference.

B. A Definition of (the Creation of) 'APBs'

For the purpose of this study, creating APBs is defined as 'entrusting entities distinct from the core administration, but with an institutional link with the government apparatus, with government tasks and letting them perform these tasks with a certain degree of autonomy in relation to elected politicians'. This definition deliberately describes the *creation* of APBs. Chapter 3 will demonstrate that the (written or unwritten) Constitutions of the national legal systems that this book studies typically centralize the whole of executive or administrative tasks and powers in the hands of the Government and its ministers and/or an elected President. In this sense, APBs are not 'given', but 'created'. Many aspects of the analysis developed in this book concern the process of 'autonomization' as such, i.e. the process of creating APBs and/or transferring government tasks to them and the choices and options that go hand in hand with that process.

APBs are distinct from the 'core administration'. They are separate organizational units, even when they are embedded within the departmental structure. This 'separateness',[19] however, is hard to define. The notion 'core administration' refers to the entirety of civil servants who prepare or execute decisions in central administrative services, rather than having their own decision-making powers. The term APBs, however, includes services *within* government departments that fit the other constitutive parts of the definition, and especially the requirement of 'autonomy'.[20]

APBs are either established by (central) government (with or without legislative interference) or have another institutional link with it, which can, for instance, take the form of a share or participation in the APB or its board. Institutional constructions that are located on the thin borderline with privatization, such as the accreditation of private companies to perform certain government tasks,[21] lack such an institutional tie. The same is true for delegation via contracts, such as the concession of public services.

---

[19] The feature of APBs is also named in OECD, *Distributed Public Governance*, 12.

[20] See Allen Schick, 'Agencies in Search of Principles' in OECD, *Distributed Public Governance* 33, 35: '[A]gencies are not departments, that is, they are not conglomerations of multiple activities. The typical agency has a single or relatively narrow purpose, and each has substantial operating independence, even if it is still housed within a department.'

[21] In Belgium and the Netherlands, for instance, the periodical quality testing of cars is performed by private actors, authorized or certified by the government.

Creating APBs implies a transfer or delegation of a 'government task'. A 'government task' in this context equals a part of the substantive competence of the government. Advisory bodies are not invested with competences and powers allowing them to take responsibility for the execution of a public task. Their products support the decision-making process, which itself is in the hands of the public body that solicits their advice.[22] Government or public sector enterprises that perform both commercial and industrial tasks in competition with the private sector and provide public services (being government tasks) only qualify as APBs when they act in the latter quality.

In times where the distinction between the private and the public sector has become blurred, it is, however, increasingly difficult to determine which tasks are 'governmental' in nature and which are not. Moreover, the answer to this question is not static, but fluctuates over time.[23] Tasks are 'governmental' as soon as and as long as a political community treats them as such.[24] They are tasks of which the government believes and society accepts that their performance (as well as the conditions under which that performance takes places) can, in principle, not be left to private initiative. EU Member States increasingly undergo the influence of the EU in this regard. Due to the liberalization of the network industries, which will be discussed in Chapter 2, activities such as the management of utilities infrastructure or the operation of transport services are now no longer considered 'government tasks'. They are, however, subject to regulation, which has created the need for a new type of APB: the independent regulator.

The definition of APBs requires 'a degree of autonomy'. What defines APBs and their autonomy is that they have their own decision-making powers. This does not necessarily imply coercive powers vis-à-vis legal subjects, nor the ability to create rights and/or obligations. The question whether or not APBs have coercive powers does, however, play a role in the debate on their accountability, central to Chapter 5 of this book.

---

[22] Some authors do, however, qualify advisory bodies as 'agencies': see e.g. Geert Bouckaert and Guy B Peters, 'What Is Available and What Is Missing in the Study of Quangos?' in Christopher Pollit and Colin Talbot (eds), *Unbundled Government, A Critical Analysis of the Global Trend to Agencies, Quangos and Contractualisation* (Routledge 2004) 22, 40–41.

[23] E.g. J G L van Nus, *Overheidstoezicht op afstand. Verzelfstandiging van toezichthoudende taken naar zelfstandige bestuursorganen verkend* (Maklu 1995) 237.

[24] In that sense: M M den Boer, *Preadvies verzelfstandiging van bestuurstaken op z'n Hollands* (Tjeenk Willink, 1999) 4–9 and 18.

'Autonomy' thus implies investment with a proper, distinctive responsibility for a public mission, irrespective of whether the decisions embedded in the performance of that task are subject to political supervision. Even bodies that are subject to forms of traditional, hierarchical political oversight thus qualify as APBs in the sense of the definition, as long as they hold the (initial) decision-making power. From the viewpoint of constitutional law, APBs that are subject to the hierarchical chain of command provoke fewer questions for lawyers than those that are not. Craig, however, warns not to overestimate the differences between these APBs and others in terms of, for instance, problems of (democratic) accountability.[25]

This book adopts a broad definition of 'autonomy', which is perhaps not an obvious choice, even though some have argued for such a wider perspective in the past as well.[26] One could also opt for a more narrow approach, excluding entities that are still part of the hierarchical chain of command. An important flaw in many assessments on the creation of APBs and their validity, however, is that the choice is often presented as being only twofold. Either one opts for an entity with a substantial degree of autonomy, often implying that hardly any form of oversight is deemed permissible, or one continues to require a ministerial signature for each and every decision taken. *Tertium non datur*. Frequently, however, intermediates offer the suitable solution. As long as they are not incorporated into fundamental analyses on the validity of the creation of APBs, such intermediates will not, however, receive consideration. As a result, the choice between centralization and autonomization will remain a monochrome one and legislatures and governments will not be invited to take into account the full range of options. In many European states, the law on administrative organization indeed presents a rich pallet of possibilities to entrust parts of the administration with a degree of political autonomy.

Literature on APBs has put forward various criteria that help to measure a body's independence or autonomy. Scholten enumerates four

---

[25] Paul Craig, *Administrative Law* (London, Sweet & Maxwell 2012) 82.

[26] A 2005 contribution on agencies and non-departmental public bodies (NDPBs) in the UK speaks of 'an unfortunate schism in relevant public management discourse', because APBs embedded within the departmental structure (typically called 'agencies' in a UK context) and those that operate outside it (NDPBs) are often defined and studied separately: Roger Wettenhall, 'Agencies and Non-Departmental Public Bodies' (2005) 7(4) Public Management Review 615, 629.

criteria: institutional, personnel, financial and functional independence.[27] Verhoest et al. distinguish managerial, policy, financial and legal autonomy, clarifying that there are 'no straightforward relationships between these different kinds of autonomy'.[28] Many of these classifications point to specific areas in which APBs may or may not enjoy a degree of operational freedom that complements or reinforces their (decision-making) autonomy. Such a reinforcement can involve the exclusion of certain types of supervision, the provision of constraints regarding the dismissal of staff members, the enactment of rules regarding incompatibilities etc.

The degree to which APBs can exercise their decision-making powers without external interference is often referred to as their 'functional independence'.[29] Even though a self-contained decision-making power is a necessary but sufficient condition to qualify a body as 'autonomous', there are various gradations of functional autonomy. Verhoest et al. define autonomy as 'the *level* of decision-making competency (discretion) of an organization'.[30] The types of supervision to which APBs are subject influence their degree of (functional) autonomy: APBs that are subject to forms of hierarchical supervision that allow for their decisions to be substituted are less autonomous than APBs in respect of which such powers have been excluded.

This brings us to perhaps the most characteristic element of the definition proposed in this book: the persons or institutions in relation to whom the functional autonomy of APBs is defined, being elected politicians. In parliamentary or semi-presidential systems and at the highest political level, government ministers, appointed and controlled by Parliament, are the primary institutions in relation to whom the autonomy

---

27 Miroslava Scholten, 'Independent, Hence Unaccountable? – The Need for a Broader Debate on Accountability of the Executive' [2011] Review of European Administrative Law 5, 10–29 with references.

28 Sandra Van Thiel, Koen Verhoest, Geert Bouckaert and Per Lægreid, 'Lessons and Recommendations for the Practice of Agencification' in Koen Verhoest, Sandra Van Thiel, Geert Bouckaert and Per Lægreid (eds), *Government Agencies. Practices and Lessons from 30 Countries* (Palgrave Macmillan 2012) 413, 424.

29 See e.g. Miroslava Scholten, 'Independent, Hence Unaccountable? – The Need for a Broader Debate on Accountability of the Executive' [2011] Review of European Administrative Law 5, 22.

30 Koen Verhoest, Sandra Van Thiel, Geert Bouckaert and Per Lægreid, 'Introduction' in Koen Verhoest, Sandra Van Thiel, Geert Bouckaert and Per Lægreid (eds), *Government Agencies Practices and Lessons from 30 Countries* (Palgrave Macmillan 2012) 3, 7 with references to previous work.

of APBs is usually defined. In some cases, however, the autonomy of an APB may also extend to the relationship with Parliament or the assemblies of elected representatives themselves. This book will dedicate much attention to APBs that are set up in order to make the performance of a task immune to political interference as such. In these cases, it is often argued that even Parliament itself cannot or should not interfere in the body's decision-making process in ways that are considered too intrusive. An alternative perspective regards parliaments as more 'neutral' forces, consisting of majorities and oppositions, which would allow for certain control mechanisms to be maintained without compromising a body's political neutrality. This debate is topical for many bodies that are subject to the trend of 'EU impulse' discussed in Chapter 2, such as economic regulators.

Like all definitions, this one has its flaws and does not pretend to be fit for all academic studies. Its general nature nevertheless make it an adequate starting point for future research that wants to adopt a broader view on APBs than most studies – especially legal ones – have done up until now.

3. AUTONOMOUS PUBLIC BODIES IN THE 21ST CENTURY: WHEN LAW TAKES OVER?

Legal scholarship's attention to the subject of APBs has developed quite slowly. Political scientists have outpaced lawyers in making APBs central to their research agendas, more particularly within the research field of public administration. Especially in the course of the last two decades, this discipline has produced and published an impressive amount of research on the subject of APBs, which easily exceeds that of lawyers. Political scientists have indeed been quasi-monopolists in this field for a long time. Since political science is less bound to national traditions than law, it has been able to generate much international and comparative work.[31] The relative absence of legal analysis is, however, perceived as a lacuna by scholars in public administration as well.[32]

---

[31] E.g. Koen Verhoest, Sandra Van Thiel, Geert Bouckaert and Per Lægreid (eds), *Government Agencies Practices and Lessons from 30 Countries* (Palgrave Macmillan 2012).

[32] Geert Bouckaert and Guy B Peters, 'What Is Available and What Is Missing in the Study of Quangos?' in Christopher Pollit and Colin Talbot (eds), *Unbundled Government, A Critical Analysis of the Global Trend to Agencies, Quangos and Contractualisation* (Routledge 2004) 22, 25–26.

Legal research on matters of administrative organization, however, differs from studies in public administration. Whereas most studies in the latter field aim to find out whether a given form of organization is efficient and effective in the light of the goals that it is meant to achieve, lawyers investigate whether it is lawful and legitimate in the light of higher rules and principles.[33] Legal research indeed departs from a set of meta values and fundamental legal principles, which it believes to be guiding precepts for the development of theoretical legal frameworks. These different approaches are nonetheless complementary: only the combination of both perspectives can generate fully fledged frameworks of assessment and evaluation of the APB phenomenon. Many questions with regard to APBs would indeed benefit from a cross-disciplinary view that merges insights. In this book, for instance, considerable attention goes to the reasons why the EU legislature chooses to delegate powers to national APBs (Chapter 2). For that purpose, it strongly relies on literature in the field of political science.

Apart from the desire to contribute to a cross-disciplinary view on APBs, this book also claims scientific relevance from an intra-legal perspective. Since APBs are entrusted with executive tasks, the study of their legal status is usually subsumed under the research field of administrative law. The enormous diversity of entities operating in the administrative landscape nowadays constantly confronts lawyers with the ambiguity of the concepts of 'government', 'executive' and 'administration', which should demarcate the field of administrative law. Legal subjects indeed no longer find themselves in 'a relationship' with 'the government', but in 'various relationships' with 'several governments'. Studying administrative law in any coherent manner becomes increasingly difficult if disorder and randomness dominate administrative organization. However, the topic of APBs raises many questions for which the answer is located in the field of constitutional law as well, since it relates to the way in which state institutions work. Constitutional law uses fundamental principles, which it interprets and puts into new perspectives, as touchstones for evaluation. In the Netherlands, the study of APBs is subsumed under the 'law on administrative organization' (*bestuurlijk organisatierecht*), which is situated on the crossing of constitutional and administrative law.[34] Halberstam regards the study of independent regulatory agencies, a type of APBs, as an illustration of the

[33] In the same sense: John Bell, 'Comparative Administrative Law' in Mathias Reimann and Reinhard Zimmermann (eds), *The Oxford Handbook of Comparative Law* (Oxford University Press 2006) 1259, 1264.

[34] Sjoerd E Zijlstra, *Bestuurlijk Organisatierecht* (Kluwer 2009) 3.

'constitutional perspective of comparative administrative law', since 'it seeks to ground the comparative administrative inquiry in an understanding of comparative constitutional law and, in particular, in an understanding of the constitutional values of public governance'.[35]

The law on administrative organization is often regarded as 'neutral' or value-free, in the sense that it does not have any perceptible, direct impact on citizens. The opposite is true. Chapter 3 will argue, for instance, that the unlimited rise of APBs has contributed to the unrecognizability of the government for legal subjects. The proliferation of APBs has indeed led to administrative opacity, leading to a perception of administrative organization as disordered and chaotic. The greatest threat formed by APBs for the position of citizens in society, however, stems from the fragility of their democratic legitimacy. This is especially so for APBs that enjoy particularly far-reaching degrees of political autonomy, such as independent regulatory authorities (IRAs). As Gilardi and Maggetti point out, the rise of IRAs:

> is not an academic curiosity; its consequences are concrete and wide-ranging. The spread of independent regulators means that more and more aspects of our lives are shaped by decisions made by institutions that are not elected and that are not under the direct control of elected officials, which has important implications for the democratic accountability of policy-making.[36]

There is an increasing consciousness of the fact that administrative organization is not a playground on which governments and political scientists can experiment without worrying about causing damage. Fundamental rules and principles of public law entail certain limits and constraints and do so for compelling reasons. This book aims to raise awareness of these constraints and contribute to the development of a theoretical framework on the legal limits and possibilities that legislatures and governments face when they consider the creation and institutional design of APBs.

The analysis of this book is structured around two distinct trends.

---

[35] Daniel Halberstam, 'The Promise of Comparative Administrative Law: A Constitutional Perspective on Independent Agencies' in Susan Rose-Ackerman and Peter L Lindseth (eds), *Comparative Administrative Law* (Edward Elgar Publishing 2010) 185, 186.

[36] Fabrizio Gilardi and Martino Maggetti, 'The Independence of Regulatory Authorities' in David Levi-Faur (ed), *Handbook on the Politics of Regulation* (Edward Elgar Publishing 2011) 201, 201.

A. A Trend of EU Impulse

Above, it was explained that the emergence of APBs in the European legal sphere has originated from the free will of politicians, inspired, of course, by the popularity of theories such as NPM. Today, however, a new source of APB creation is emerging. In an increasing number of policy domains, European (EU) law relies on national 'independent' administrative bodies to implement and monitor substantive obligations. EU directives increasingly contain legal obligations to establish APBs at the national level. In these cases, national Parliaments and Governments lose their discretion to decide whether or not to create – or abolish – the APBs in question.

The very fact that the creation of APBs has ceased to be voluntary for national elected politicians in all cases is a novelty with important implications. Traditionally, international and supranational law have declined all interference with national administrative organization, which was regarded as a domain pertaining to the core of a state's sovereignty. Almost all national APBs that have up until now originated from this trend of 'EU impulse' have in common that they perform tasks of supervision or regulation. These bodies are commonly referred to as 'independent regulators' or 'independent supervisors'. They are composed of neutral experts instead of (representatives of) elected politicians, hence the name 'non-majoritarian institutions'. The autonomy that they are expected to enjoy is quite far reaching.

B. A Trend of 'National Restraint' in Member States

This trend of EU law obliging or encouraging Member States to create APBs, however, coincides with a trend of restraint and rationalization at the national level. National parliaments are increasingly becoming aware that the uncurbed rise of APBs in previous decades has not been a neutral phenomenon, free from legal and particularly constitutional implications. The quasi-unlimited establishment of APBs in previous decades has been vehemently criticized from a democratic point of view. In some states, constitutional courts have been asked to rule on the extent to which entrusting government tasks to (certain types of) APBs can be reconciled with fundamental constitutional principles governing administrative organization.

This translates itself into a new approach to the use of APBs in administrative organization. National parliaments are taking initiatives to regain their grip on both the creation and functioning of APBs. Attempting to put a brake on the unlimited rise of APBs, some states have developed framework legislation, embedding the creations and status of APBs in conditions that respect the higher framework of their Constitutions. Other states have set up large reform operations. The primacy of politics, the political responsibility of the Government and democratic control are leading values or principles in this evolution. These initiatives are inspired by a revaluation of fundamental constitutional principles that limit the discretion of governments and legislatures when modelling administrative organization. In other words: at the national level, elected politicians are being re-appreciated as central players in public administration.

C. APBs and the Law

In sum, the phenomenon of APBs finds itself on the crossroads of two trends or developments, each representing an evolution in an opposite direction. These trends and the tension between them constitute the central theme of this book. Despite their opposite intentions or effects, both of these trends have something important in common: they have strong foundations in law or legal argument. The impulses stemming from EU law imply that, for some APBs, whether or not to grant political autonomy and to what extent is no longer (exclusively) a case of political choice: it has become one of legal obligation. The trend of 'national restraint', on the other hand, is built upon and around legal rules and principles. Law and legal discourse indeed increasingly dominate the topic of the creation of APBs.

4. AUTONOMOUS PUBLIC BODIES: THE NEED FOR A FOCUS ON EUROPE

This book focuses on APBs in the European legal sphere. APBs and especially regulatory agencies are often thought of as typically American models of administrative organization. As Christensen and Lægreid put it, 'the NPM-inspired regulatory model ... was once seen as an expression of 'American exceptionalism', but this is no longer the case'.[37] The fast creation of APBs that characterized European public sector reforms in the 1980s and 1990s was to an important extent inspired by previous developments in the US. The UK, being the (European) motherland of

[37] Tom Christensen and Per Lægreid, 'The New Regulatory Orthodoxy: A Critical Assessment' in David Levi-Faur (ed), *Handbook on the Politics of Regulation* (Edward Elgar Publishing 2011) 361, 361 with reference.

NPM, has played a significant role in this process of reception. Especially the Thatcher reforms, leading to the development of the British regulatory state, were inspired by US practice. Via the Anglo-Saxon system, the APB fashion[38] later reached the European mainland. The reception of an American model in a European context has, however, not prevented the Old Continent from developing its own problems, insights and solutions. Political scientists have, for instance, argued that 'European polities, partly because they are similarly developed and integrated into international and regional economies, face similar functional pressures for delegations to [non-majoritarian institutions]'.[39]

The constitutional relationship between the different state powers at the central level in the US, moreover, provides an institutional context that is different from the one in which most European legal systems find themselves and entails system-specific problems. From a US perspective, the constitutionality of delegation to APBs in general, and independent regulators in particular, is often questioned from the viewpoint of the separation of powers (checks and balances) doctrine. Delegation of executive power to independent agencies is often perceived as a way for Congress to remove power from the President (especially when the majorities in the Houses pertain to a different party from the President's), who is designated as the head of the executive by the US Constitution.[40] A related question is whether the President, once a rule-making power has been delegated to an agency, has a power of 'decision' (i.e. substitution) or is left with (merely) a power of 'oversight'.[41]

These tensions are absent in, for instance, the UK, where 'a combined operation of the political party system and the principle of [collective ministerial responsibility] means that there is no competition between the

---

[38] Smullen speaks of an 'international fashion': Amanda Jane Smullen, *Translating Agency Reform: Rhetoric and Culture in Comparative Perspective*, PhD thesis, Rotterdam, 2007, see especially 11 ff.

[39] Mark Thatcher and Alec Stone Sweet, 'Theory and Practice of Delegation to Non-Majoritarian Institutions' 25(1) (2002) West European Politics 1, 4.

[40] See e.g. Bruce Ackerman, 'Good-bye, Montesquieu' in Susan Rose-Ackerman and Peter L Lindseth (eds), *Comparative Administrative Law* (Edward Elgar Publishing 2010) 128, 131.

[41] See e.g. Sidney A Shapiro and Richard W Murphy, 'Eight Things Americans Can't Figure Out About Controlling Administrative Power' in Herwig C H Hofmann and Russel L Weaver (eds), *Transatlantic Perspectives on Administrative Law* (Bruylant 2011) 7, 12–14; Peter L Strauss, 'Rule-making and the American Constitution' in Dawn Oliver, Tony Prosser and Richard Rawlings (eds), *The Regulatory State: Constitutional Implications* (Oxford University Press 2010) 50, 60 with references.

executive and Parliament for control of public administration'.[42] Most EU Member States, like the UK, have parliamentary systems. The most notorious exception is the French system, which is semi-presidential. The French Constitution is also characterized by a strong adherence to the separation of powers doctrine. Chapter 3 of this book will demonstrate how this has caused some constitutional questions or concerns regarding APBs to be more pressing in France. However, the French Conseil d'État itself has declared that it has not discerned pressures between the two elected state powers similar to those that have influenced the rise of APBs in the US.[43]

Yet another question embedded in the separation of powers doctrine in the US concerns the extent to which the delegation of rule-making powers to independent regulatory agencies disturbs the balance of powers within the US polity.[44] The President of the US does not have rule-making powers under the Constitution. Nevertheless, the Supreme Court has accepted that Congress delegates such powers to agencies, qualifying these powers as executive and not legislative in nature.[45] In many European systems, the Constitution itself entrusts the executive with rule-making powers. Chapter 3 will demonstrate how the separation of powers doctrine has also raised questions on APBs' rule-making powers in France. The suggestion, however, is not that these APBs encroach on the powers of the legislature, but that such a delegation conflicts with the Prime Minister's (and, thus, the central executive's) rule-making powers. Moreover, upon closer inspection, these concerns appear closely intertwined with democratic arguments.

Chapter 3 will indeed argue that most criticism of APBs in the European legal sphere stems from democratic claims and more precisely from objections about the harm done to the institutions and procedures of representative democracy.[46] Prosser, for instance, ascertains that constitutional concerns about APBs in the UK have been 'centered on the extent

---

[42] Peter Cane, *Administrative Law* (5th edn, Clarendon 2011) 25.

[43] Conseil d'État (FR), *Rapport public 2001 / Jurisprudence et avis de 2000 – Les autorités administratives indépendantes (Études & Documents N° 52)* 370.

[44] Peter L Strauss, 'Rule-making and the American Constitution' in Dawn Oliver, Tony Prosser and Richard Rawlings (eds), *The Regulatory State: Constitutional Implications* (Oxford University Press 2010) 50, 50.

[45] ibid 50.

[46] See also Tom Zwart, 'Independent Regulatory Agencies in the US' in Tom Zwart and Luc Verhey (eds), *Agencies in European and Comparative Law* (Intersentia 2003) 3, 14–16 and 17 (comparing the US with legal systems in which political ministerial responsibility is a central value).

of Parliamentary accountability, rather than any inherent restrictions on delegation', concluding that 'the US constitutional issues about the relationship of agencies with the executive branch have not arisen in explicitly constitutional form in the UK'.[47] Contrasting the US to the UK, Oliver, as well, points out that 'in the UK, lacking any [such] tradition of separation of powers, there are few constitutional or principled objections to independent bodies or ministers being granted rule-making powers in Acts of Parliament, as long as appropriate accountability mechanisms are in place'.[48]

5. OUTLINE AND OVERVIEW

Chapters 2 and 3 of this book discuss the trends of 'EU impulse' and 'national restraint' respectively. Chapters 4 and 5 discuss the relationship between these two contemporary trends. At first sight, the trends seem to be conflicting, since EU law and national law seem to be moving in opposite directions. How and to what degree are the obligations anchored in EU law indeed at odds with the rationales behind the trend of 'Member State restraint'? What are possible avenues for reconciliation? This tension inevitably provokes the somewhat controversial question of whether the EU, which is itself often criticized for lacking democratic legitimacy, is disregarding fundamental democratic principles when imposing these institutional obligations on its Member States. Chapter 6 summarizes the most important findings and draws some general conclusions.

6. METHODOLOGICAL SPECIFICITIES OF THIS BOOK

A. Law as an Evaluative Scientific Discipline

It is often assumed (especially by other academic communities in the humanities or social sciences) that legal scholarship is primarily there to

---

[47] Tony Prosser, 'Models of Economic and Social Regulation' in Dawn Oliver, Tony Prosser and Richard Rawlings (eds), *The Regulatory State: Constitutional Implications* (Oxford University Press 2010) 34, 34–35.

[48] Dawn Oliver, 'Regulation, Democracy and Democratic Oversight in the UK' in Dawn Oliver, Tony Prosser and Richard Rawlings (eds), *The Regulatory State: Constitutional Implications* (Oxford University Press 2010) 243, 249.

study positive law, i.e. the law 'as it is', and is mostly, if not entirely, descriptive in nature. Legal academia is still regarded by many as a discipline that mainly reproduces knowledge. At most, it can shed light on a range of possible interpretations for a given legal norm or concept (i.e. the traditional view of law as a hermeneutic discipline[49]). Certainly, describing the law, in a systematic way, is one aim of legal scholarship. It is, moreover, a valuable one. The law has become so complex and multifaceted that we need legal scholarship to systemize it, which increases the accessibility of the law.

But legal scholarship serves other goals as well. First, it assists in 'finding' or 'identifying' law, an activity that necessarily precedes description. In times in which the law consists of a multiplicity of sources and instruments, this constitutes a particular challenge and requires a thorough understanding of the wider structure and systematics of the law.

Secondly, legal scholarship can have an evaluative purpose. But how does one avoid making unscientific value judgements about positive law? A first possible evaluative purpose of legal scholarship is to assess the law as it is on the basis of higher legal rules or principles or even meta values that underlie the legal system.[50] In this capacity, legal scholarship acts as a guardian of higher laws and consistency.

Anne Ruth Mackor locates the difference between a subjective evaluation on the one hand and a scientific legal assessment on the other hand in the use of extra-legal versus intra-legal criteria. The latter can result in statements on 'which norms should be valid in the positive legal order under investigation or [on] what the content of these norms should be'. These evaluative statements, however, refer 'to the fairly specific and coherent set of intra-legal criteria that allows for a rational reconstruction of the positive legal order as an optimal internally coherent normative system'.[51] They can either assess the formal (declarative and procedural)

---

[49] E.g. Mark Van Hoecke, 'Legal Doctrine: Which Method(s) for What Kind of Discipline?' in Mark Van Hoecke (ed), *Methodologies of Legal Research. Which Kind of Method for What Kind of Discipline?* (Hart Publishing 2011) 1, 4.

[50] The study of principles and fundamentals is becoming increasingly popular in legal scholarship. See J Vranken, 'Exciting Times for Legal Scholarship' [2012] Recht en Methode in Onderzoek en Onderwijs 48.

[51] Anne Ruth Mackor, 'Legal Doctrine As a Non-Normative Discipline' [2012] Recht en Methode in Onderzoek en Onderwijs 22, 27. An earlier record of the author's theory is found in Anne Ruth Mackor, 'Explanatory Non-Normative Legal Doctrine. Taking the Distinction between Theoretical and Practical Reasoning Seriously' in Mark Van Hoecke (ed), *Methodologies of Legal*

validity of legal norms or the extent to which a norm 'is consistent with the *substantive* constraints posed by legal principles and values'. Mackor stresses that 'these principles and values are legal only when they are documented in legal sources like treaties, the constitution and case law and when they are established in accordance with the criteria of legal interpretation and argumentation acknowledged in that specific positive legal order'.[52]

Legal meta values, such as constitutionalism, the rule of law and democracy and the more specific constitutional principles that are derived from these meta values are the intra-legal criteria that are central to the analysis contained in this book.

B. A Practice-oriented Approach to Legal Research

Legal meta values and principles are not the only benchmarks against which positive law can be evaluated. Another important benchmark is practice. Legal research can gauge the societal impact of legal phenomena and mechanisms. Does a statute fulfil the purpose(s) for which it was enacted? Do certain regulations have undesired, unintended or perverse effects? This approach may require the use of social science methods. Van Schaaijk distinguishes between two types of questions that can guide legal scholars in their research and which are both suited to practice-oriented research, which she labels the 'is this allowed?' question and the 'does this work?' question.

The 'is this allowed?' question tests the compatibility of social phenomena with the law. It is related to the activity of a legal practitioner, since it essentially involves solving a 'case'. For a researcher who uses this type of question, the analysis of the 'this' factor in the question, representing the social phenomenon, would imply the use of empirical research. The legal framework against the background of which this phenomenon will be assessed requires the use of traditional legal methods and heuristics.[53] In the 'does this work?' question, the 'this' factor does not refer to a social phenomenon, but to the law itself. This type of question studies the social effects of a legal arrangement or phenomenon. Empirical research would here be used to test whether the

---

Research. Which Kind of Method for What Kind of Discipline? (Hart Publishing 2011) 45.

[52] Anne Ruth Mackor, 'Legal Doctrine As a Non-Normative Discipline' [2012] Recht en Methode in Onderzoek en Onderwijs 22, 37.

[53] Geertje A F M van Schaaijk, 'Praktijkgericht juridisch onderzoek' [2011] Recht en Methode in Onderzoek en Onderwijs 85, 93–95.

law functions in practice as intended by those who enacted it or in accordance with the expectations of society. This type of question is closely related to research in legal sociology.[54] Chapters 2 and 5 of this book contain the results of two sets of in-depth interviews that were carried out in order to test certain hypotheses.

[54] ibid 96–98.

2. EU impulse

1. 'EU IMPULSE' AS AN EMANATION OF THE EUROPEANIZATION OF NATIONAL ADMINISTRATIVE ORGANIZATION

The impact of EU law on national legal traditions, concepts, procedures, rules and principles is omnipresent in legal research. Administrative law in general and the law on administrative organization in particular, however, occupy a peculiar position in this research agenda. Even in this age of globalization, administrative law is still often perceived as a 'national enclave'.[1] For some years now, scholars have nonetheless engaged in a study of the 'Europeanization' of national administrative law. Since administrative law is the instrument through which EU law is generally implemented and enforced, this is hardly surprising.[2]

Literature on the Europeanization of administrative law often focuses on substantive and procedural aspects of law. The influence of the EU on specific branches of administrative law (such as environmental law and the rules on public procurement) is well documented. On a more general level, the dynamics between the development of principles and procedures of good administration in EU law on the one hand and in the distinct national jurisdictions of the Member States on the other hand has attracted the attention of scholars.[3] In 2007, a study on the Europeanization of public law observed that the influence of EU law was 'no

[1] After Giacinto della Cananea, 'Administrative Law in Europe: A Historical and Comparative Perspective' [2010] Online Italian Journal of Public Law 162, 167.

[2] Jan H Jans, Roel de Lange, Sacha Prechal and Rob Widdershoven, *Europeanisation of Public Law* (Europa Law Publishing 2007) 4.

[3] See e.g. Catherine Donnelly, 'Administrative Law and Multi-Level Administration: An EU and US Comparison' in Catherine Barnard and Okeoghene Odudu (eds), *Cambridge Yearbook of European Legal Studies 2008–09* (Hart Publishing 2009) 211.

longer felt only in specific areas of public law but in the whole field of public law, and in particular in administrative law'.[4]

Despite this growing attention, the law on administrative organization remains poorly represented in literature studying the impact of EU law on national public law. Admittedly, the phenomenon is still in its early years. For a long time, EU law has remained silent on issues of national administrative organization, making its impact virtually non-existent. An explanation for this lack of intervention was found in the principle of the institutional autonomy of the Member States, acknowledged in the case law of the European Court of Justice (ECJ).[5] Pursuant to this principle, every Member State individually has the right to decide, following the logic of its own constitutional system, which bodies and which level of authority it entrusts with the execution of EU legislation.[6] Only ten years ago, literature spoke of 'the paradox of institutional autonomy', pointing out that, although EU law depends on national administrative organization for its implementation, the EU had up until then 'taken little note of the constitutional and administrative organisation of the Member States and the division of powers and responsibilities within those Member States.'[7] Linking the principle of institutional autonomy to the better-known principle of procedural autonomy, it is generally believed to imply that:

> unless Community law provides otherwise, national constitutional and procedural rules apply, provided that: (i) the rules that govern a dispute or a case with a community dimension may not be less favourable than those governing similar domestic actions (the principle of equivalence) and (ii) the rules must not render virtually impossible or excessively difficult the exercise of the rights conferred by the Community legal order (the principle of effectiveness).[8]

---

[4] Jan H Jans, Roel de Lange, Sacha Prechal and Rob Widdershoven, *Europeanisation of Public Law* (Europa Law Publishing 2007) 4.

[5] Case C-71/51-54 *International Fruit Company NV et al.* [1971] ECR I-1107, para 4. See e.g. Rostane Mehdi, 'L'autonomie institutionnelle et procédurale et le droit administratif' in Jean-Bernard Auby and Jacqueline Dutheil de la Rochère (eds), *Droit administratif européen* (Bruylant 2007) 685.

[6] Koenraad Lenaerts and Piet Van Nuffel, *Constitutional Law of the European Union* (Sweet & Maxwell 2005) 530.

[7] Jan H Jans, Roel de Lange, Sacha Prechal and Rob Widdershoven, *Europeanisation of Public Law* (Europa Law Publishing 2007) 18 with references to the case law of the ECJ.

[8] Saskia Lavrijssen and Annetje Ottow, 'The Legality of Independent Regulatory Authorities' in Leonard Besselink, Frans Pennings and Sacha Prechal (eds), *The Eclipse of the Legality Principle in the European Union* (Kluwer

The principle of institutional autonomy seems to acknowledge that how national administrations are organized is a matter closely intertwined with the sovereignty of Member States. Recently, however, the EU legislature has begun to depart from its traditional neutrality in this respect and has decided that, in some cases, it should have a say in how national administrations organize themselves if and when they implement EU law. In a 2008 judgment regarding the implementation of the (previous version of the) 2002 Framework Directive for electronic communications, the ECJ ruled that '[a]lthough the Member States enjoy institutional autonomy as regards the organisation and the structuring of their regulatory authorities within the meaning of article 2(g) of the Framework Directive, that autonomy may be exercised only in accordance with the objectives and obligations laid down in that directive'.[9] Since then, however, the EU legislature has laid down specific provisions on the administrative organization of the regulatory state in the area of telecommunications and in other network industries. These provisions, of which the most important examples are discussed in detail in this chapter, imply that adherence to the principles of equivalence and effectiveness no longer suffices, but that further, more specific requirements have to be fulfilled.

Considering that substantive, procedural and institutional aspects of administrative law are often closely interwoven, it is logical that certain objectives pursued by the EU legislature will entail the need for specific requirements of an organizational nature. Indirectly, EU law unavoidably entails transformations in the administrative organization of Member States.[10] The trend studied in the following paragraphs, however, concerns a far more direct method of EU intervention. Increasingly, EU legislation itself imposes an organizational framework, containing clear-cut prescriptions on the status of the bodies that implement the substantive rules enshrined in that very same legislation.[11] Whether the EU

2011) 73, 74 with reference to Jan H Jans, Roel de Lange, Sacha Prechal and Rob Widdershoven, *Europeanisation of Public Law* (Europa Law Publishing 2007) 42 and Case C-82/07 *Comisión del Mercado de las Telecominicaciones* [2008] ECR I-1265.

[9] Case C-82/07 *Comisión del Mercado de las Telecominicaciones* [2008] ECR I-1265, para 24.

[10] See Jan H Jans, Roel de Lange, Sacha Prechal and Rob Widdershoven, *Europeanisation of Public Law* (Europa Law Publishing 2007) 6.

[11] On this issue, see also Jacques Ziller, 'Les autorités administratives indépendantes entre droit interne et droit de l'Union européenne' [2010] RFDA 901.

interfering with Member States' systems of administrative organization is in conformity with the EU treaties and other rules and principles regarding the division of powers between the EU and the Member States (such as the subsidiarity and proportionality principles) are questions that are not as such addressed in this book. An evaluation of this trend will be carried out in Chapters 4 and 5, but it will use meta values and fundamental principles common to the Member States as touchstones, rather than fundamental rules inherent in EU institutional law.

The following sections will demonstrate how EU law increasingly requires Member States to entrust the implementation of EU legislation to APBs. This book studies the influence of EU law on the creation of APBs by national or regional legislatures and governments. It does not study APBs established and operating at the supranational level, i.e. the so-called 'EU agencies'.[12] For the sake of completeness, it should also be noted that the trend of EU impulse coincides with a broader trend of international and regional organizations that increasingly oblige or encourage their member or contracting states to establish APBs.[13] As a supranational legal order, the EU exerts a more far-reaching degree of influence on its Member States than most other international organizations. For one thing, the 'impulse' stemming from EU law usually takes the form of (secondary) legislation, implying that it is strictly binding and enforceable vis-à-vis Member States. Other international fora, on the other hand, unless they succeed in making states agree to conclude a treaty, often have to rely on soft law instruments to exert any influence. Moreover, secondary EU law can bind Member States even if they have voted against and consequently disagreed with (part of) its contents, which is never the case for bi- or multilateral treaties.

This chapter discusses only those requirements of political autonomy or independence for national administrative entities that have more or less explicitly been anchored in EU legislation, including legislation that was declared to contain such an obligation after interpretation by the ECJ. It should be noted, however, that other obligations of independence enshrined in EU law, not specifically targeting the relationship with

---

[12] A lot of work has been dedicated to these agencies already. See e.g. Christoph Ossege, *European Regulatory Agencies in EU Decision-Making – Between Expertise and Influence* (Palgrave MacMillan 2016); Merijn Chamon, *EU agencies: legal and political limits to the transformation of the EU administration* (Oxford University Press 2016).

[13] See Stéphanie De Somer, 'International and European Impulse with Regard to the Creation of Autonomous Public Bodies: An Emerging Trend' [2014] UCL Journal of Law and Jurisprudence 58.

elected politicians or public institutions, may imply a certain degree of political autonomy as well. The 2009 Directive on the safety of nuclear installations, for instance, as adapted in 2014,[14] obliges Member States to 'ensure the effective independence from undue influence of the competent regulatory authority in its regulatory decision-making'. It specifies that the national framework should require that the regulatory authority 'is functionally separate from any other body or organisation concerned with the promotion or utilisation of nuclear energy, and does not seek or take instructions from any such body or organisation when carrying out its regulatory tasks'.[15] The provision does not explicitly require political independence, although the general prohibition of 'undue influence' may be interpreted as including political influence.[16] If the state is the owner of nuclear installations, however, this provision will in any case entail a requirement of independence from central government.[17] Another example is found in the 2009 Regulation on the creation of a single European sky, where the relevant article prescribes that 'the national supervisory authorities shall be independent of air navigation service providers' but at the same time also more generally requires national supervisory authorities to exercise their powers 'independently'.[18] In a case concerning the creation and institutional design of the Belgian federal authority entrusted with the investigation of accidents in the maritime transport sector, the Belgian Constitutional Court read a requirement of political independence in article 8 of Directive 2009/18/EC.[19] Relying on the directive, the court more specifically problematized

---

[14] Council Directive 2014/87/EURATOM of 8 July 2014 amending Directive 2009/71/Euratom establishing a Community framework for the nuclear safety of nuclear installations, OJ L219/42.

[15] Article 5 of Council Directive 2009/71/EURATOM of 25 June 2009 establishing a Community framework for the nuclear safety of nuclear installations, OJ L172/18.

[16] See consideration 6 of the preamble of Directive 2014/87/EURATOM, which refers to 'undue influence associated with changing political, economic or societal conditions'.

[17] See Hubert Delzangles, 'L'indépendance de l'autorité de sûreté nucléaire, des progrès à envisager' [2013] Revue juridique de l'environnement 7, 10 (on the previous version of the Directive, which already required a functional separation).

[18] Article 4 of European Parliament and Council Regulation (EC) 549/2004 of 10 March 2004 laying down the framework for the creation of a single European sky (the framework regulation), OJ L96/1.

[19] European Parliament and Council Directive 2009/18/EC of 23 April 2009 establishing the fundamental principles governing the investigation of accidents

the exercise of hierarchical supervision by the competent minister. The directive, however, does not explicitly require a degree of autonomy vis-à-vis the political executive. According to the court, it could not be precluded that the minister should, in certain circumstances, be regarded as a 'party whose interests could conflict with the task entrusted to [the federal authority]', by which the court referred to the formulation used in the directive. The court annulled the paragraph stipulating that the director of the authority would function under the hierarchical oversight of the minister.[20]

Furthermore, the following sections do not discuss how EU law has inspired states in a less direct, more implicit manner to create APBs. The liberalization directives for network industries, for instance, did not only lead to the creation in EU Member States of independent national regulatory authorities (IRAs), which will be discussed in detail in this chapter. They also led to the conversion of many government enterprises, still operating on the relevant markets, to APBs. Insofar as these government enterprises compete with private market players, they do not qualify as APBs in the sense of the definition introduced in Chapter 1. Many of these government enterprises, however, are still entrusted with tasks that are related to their commercial or industrial activities, but that have not (yet) been liberalized. The performance of these government tasks is often embedded in the same autonomous structure as that of their purely industrial or commercial counterparts, although the decisions made in the context of these public service tasks may be subject to other (more far-reaching) mechanisms of supervision by central government. The combination of these two types of activities within the same organization and the variation in management rules that this dichotomy entails constitute an interesting object of study, which is, however, beyond the scope of this book.

The analysis in this chapter consists of two main sections covering APBs in the fields of economic law and human rights law respectively. Pegram, drawing attention to the diffusion of institutional forms in general, precisely refers to both human rights and regulatory practices to illustrate his point.[21] There are examples of explicit legal obligations in

in the maritime transport sector and amending Council Directive 1999/35/EC and Directive 2002/59/EC of the European Parliament and of the Council [2009] OJ L131/114.

[20] GwH 21 November 2013, no 158/2013.

[21] Thomas Pegram, 'Diffusion Across Political Systems: The Global Spread of National Human Rights Institutions' (2010) 32 Human Rights Quarterly 729, 730.

EU law to grant political autonomy to administrative bodies in other areas of state intervention as well. Often, however, these requirements are not anchored in formal legislation. In the field of education, for instance, the 2015 version of the Standards and Guidelines for Quality Assurance in the European Higher Education Area, issued by the European Association for Quality Assurance in Higher Education (ENQA)[22] contain a provision (standard 3.3.) requiring that external quality assurance agencies 'should be independent and act autonomously. They should have full responsibility for their operations and the outcomes of those operations without third party influence'. The guideline to this standard specifies that this includes organizational independence from governments. The Standards and Guidelines are regarded as a form of 'soft standardization'[23] but are influential. Another example is found in the 2011 European Statistics Code of Practice for the National and Community Statistical Authorities.[24] The first principle found in the Code is that of 'professional independence' and the Code provides that '[t]he independence of the National Statistical Institutes and Eurostat from political and other external interference in developing, producing and disseminating statistics is specified in law and assured for other statistical authorities'.[25]

---

[22] A project funded with the support of the European Commission: http://www.enqa.eu/index.php/home/esg/.

[23] Adrian Curaj, Peter Scott, Lazăr Vlascenau and Lesley Wilson, *European Higher Education at the Crossroads: Between the Bologna Process and National Reforms* (Springer Netherlands 2012) 385.

[24] Adopted by the European Statistical System Committee on 28 September 2011, http://ec.europa.eu/eurostat/web/products-manuals-and-guidelines/-/KS-32-11-955.

[25] See also article 2(1)a) European Parliament and Council Regulation 223/2009 of 11 March 2009 on European statistics and repealing Regulation (EC, Euratom) No 1101/2008 of the European Parliament and of the Council on the transmission of data subject to statistical confidentiality to the Statistical Office of the European Communities, Council Regulation (EC) No 322/97 on Community Statistics, and Council Decision 89/382/EEC, Euratom establishing a Committee on the Statistical Programmes of the European Communities [2009] OJ L87/164. Other, related directives containing rules on statistical information mention similar independence requirements.

2. EU IMPULSE IN THE FIELD OF NETWORK REGULATION

This section studies the way in which EU law currently obliges Member States to establish IRAs in the so-called 'network industries' subject to liberalization. Traditionally, institutional autonomy was regarded as one of the guiding principles for the design of an organizational framework for network regulation in Europe.[26] Recently, however, Member States' discretion with regard to the institutional design of national regulatory authorities (NRAs) has been limited.

A. After Liberalization: The Emergence of the Regulatory State in Europe

Before discussing the contents and scope of the obligations currently imposed by EU law, the following paragraphs sketch the background against which NRAs have emerged, drawing on previous research in the field of political science. The rise of IRAs – and, hence, their *raison d'être* – cannot be seen separately from economic developments and altered opinions on the nature of state intervention in the sectors concerned.

In the course of the 1980s and 1990s, the role of the state as an economic actor in Western Europe became subject to radical changes. The markets of many of the network industries, before largely dominated by state monopolies, were gradually liberalized. From the beginning of the 1980s onwards, European states began to reconsider their role in the economy, adopting the American, more liberal view on state intervention, known as 'regulation'. In the US, the advocates of the New Deal 'saw the state as a corrective, not a substitute to the market' and this was the

---

[26] See e.g. Arjan Geveke, 'Improving Implementation by National Regulatory Authorities' [2003] Eipascope 26, 27; Saskia Lavrijssen and Thomas Nauta, 'De Europeanisering van het toezicht op de energiesector' [2012] Nederlands Tijdschrift voor energierecht 136, 136–137 with reference to Case C-33/76, *Rewe* [1976] ECR I-1989. Directive 2008/6/EC, governing the liberalization of the postal sector, does not contain an obligation to set up politically independent regulators yet, but does contain an obligation of independence of the market players. Recital 47 of its preamble still refers to the principle of institutional autonomy.

model that would henceforth also be adopted in Europe.[27] As a consequence, government-owned companies were privatized and markets were gradually liberalized.[28]

The EU has played an important role in this '"paradigm shift" from the Keynesian to the regulatory state'.[29] EU liberalization legislation was enacted – often spread over different 'generations' or 'packages' – and enforced, with the aim of completing the internal market. The institutional landscape in these sectors was transformed little by little. Henceforth, governments would no longer be intervening in the market through ownership of the market player(s), directly providing the goods or services concerned, but would be 'regulating' the market. As a regulator, the government in a figurative sense positions itself 'above' the market, controlling and monitoring the activities of the market players. Hence, the government has exchanged its ownership or *dominium* for rule-making power or *imperium*, as some authors have strikingly put it.[30] Osborne and Gaebler have famously referred to this shift using the metaphor of a state that would henceforth be 'steering' rather than

---

[27] Paul Magnette, 'The Politics of Regulation in the European Union' in Damien Geradin, Rodolphe Muñoz and Nicolas Petit (eds), *Regulation through Agencies in the EU. A New Paradigm of European Governance* (Edward Elgar Publishing 2005) 3, 4. See also David Levi-Faur, 'Regulation and Regulatory Governance' in David Levi-Faur (ed), *Handbook on the Politics of Regulation* (Edward Elgar Publishing 2011) 3, 12.

[28] See e.g. Phedon Nicolaïdes, 'Regulation of Liberalised Markets: A New Role for the State?' in Damien Geradin, Rodolphe Muñoz and Nicolas Petit (eds), *Regulation through Agencies in the EU. A New Paradigm of European Governance* (Edward Elgar Publishing 2005) 23, 24.

[29] After Paul Magnette, 'The Politics of Regulation in the European Union' in Damien Geradin, Rodolphe Muñoz and Nicolas Petit (eds), *Regulation through Agencies in the EU. A New Paradigm of European Governance* (Edward Elgar Publishing 2005) 3, 4.

[30] Dawn Oliver, 'Regulation, Democracy and Democratic Oversight in the UK' in Dawn Oliver, Tony Prosser and Richard Rawlings (eds), *The Regulatory State: Constitutional Implications* (Oxford University Press 2010) 243 with references. See also David Levi-Faur, 'The Regulatory State and Regulatory Capitalism: An Institutional Perspective' in David Levi-Faur (ed), *Handbook on the Politics of Regulation* (Edward Elgar Publishing 2011) 662, 666; Jørgen Grønnegård Christensen, 'Competing Theories of Regulatory Governance: Reconsidering Public Interest Theory of Regulation' in David Levi-Faur (ed), *Handbook on the Politics of Regulation* (Edward Elgar Publishing 2011) 96, 96; Matthias Finger, 'Towards a European Model of Regulatory Governance?' in David Levi-Faur (ed), *Handbook on the Politics of Regulation* (Edward Elgar Publishing 2011) 525, 526.

'rowing'.[31] Even though most European countries still have government-owned enterprises that operate in these markets, their monopolies have disappeared.

For a good understanding of the missions of IRAs, the question *why* regulation, being a weakened form of government intervention, remains necessary after liberalization, should briefly be addressed. This is necessary to make informed statements on the necessity of NRAs being as independent as EU law currently wants them to be (Chapters 4 and 5). It is widely accepted that liberalization 'does not remove all reasons for intervention'.[32] The basic idea behind regulation is that markets that are subject to competition are imperfect.[33] They suffer from market failures.[34] So called public interest theory regards regulation as necessary in order to secure the public interest, which is threatened by the possibility of the liberalized market not generating the desired results.[35] 'Regulation almost by definition is introduced where the unconstrained market cannot by itself guarantee goals that society wishes.'[36] In the area of economic regulation, the first concern of governments is to ensure fair competition between market players, which benefits consumers. Even after the abolition of monopolies, 'many incumbents continue to enjoy significant market power, not least because they own essential infrastructure, which

---

[31] David Osborne and Ted Gaebler, *Reinventing Government: How the Entrepreneurial Spirit Is Transforming the Public Sector* (Addison-Wesley 1992) 25 ff.

[32] Phedon Nicolaïdes, 'Regulation of Liberalised Markets: A New Role for the State?' in Damien Geradin, Rodolphe Muñoz and Nicolas Petit (eds), *Regulation through Agencies in the EU. A New Paradigm of European Governance* (Edward Elgar Publishing 2005) 23, 24.

[33] Matthias Finger, 'Towards a European Model of Regulatory Governance?' in David Levi-Faur (ed), *Handbook on the Politics of Regulation* (Edward Elgar Publishing 2011) 525, 529.

[34] Marc Allen Eisner, 'Beyond the Logic of the Market: Toward an Institutional Analysis of Regulatory Reforms' in David Levi-Faur (ed), *Handbook on the Politics of Regulation* (Edward Elgar Publishing 2011) 129, 130.

[35] E.g. Fabrizio Gilardi, *Delegation in the Regulatory State. Independent Regulatory Agencies in Western Europe* (Edward Elgar Publishing 2008) 16 with references, pointing out that market failures arise when a competitive market does not lead to a Pareto-efficient allocation of resources, and are caused by several factors. See also Gérard Marcou, 'La notion juridique de régulation' [2006] AJDA 347, 349.

[36] Richard Macrory, 'Reforming Regulatory Sanctions – Designing a Systematic Approach' in Dawn Oliver, Tony Prosser and Richard Rawlings (eds), *The Regulatory State: Constitutional Implications* (Oxford University Press 2010) 229, 229.

cannot be easily duplicated. This in turn requires regulatory solutions to ensure competition in the market.'[37]

Because sufficient competition is regarded as necessary to ensure fair prices for consumers, it is of special importance in the network industries. These industries produce so-called 'merit goods', to which most members of society agree that everyone should have access, regardless of their income and thus of whether they can afford to pay the price that the market would generate should competition be unrestricted or 'unregulated'.[38] The goal that is pursued is often referred to as 'universal service'.[39] Here, regulation typically takes the form of tariff or price limits. In the welfare state, it is expected that 'merit goods' are accessible to all and that the state assumes responsibility for this. Market players may provide less than necessary to supply the good or service concerned to the entire population or may raise prices, so that the product or the service in question is not affordable for people in all layers of society. Precisely to avoid these negative side-effects of liberalization, governments do not retreat from the markets of the network industries entirely. On the one hand, liberalization implies quite a strong confidence in market efficiency, presuming that it is sufficiently interesting for private players to invest. On the other hand, the need to ensure that goods or services are accessible to everyone makes supervision indispensable. In sum, 'governments may still have to intervene in liberalized markets because liberalization removes only one of the causes of market imperfection – that of statutory monopoly. Other causes of imperfection remain and, therefore, regulation may in principle be required.'[40]

---

[37] Saskia Lavrijssen and Annetje Ottow, 'The Legality of Independent Regulatory Authorities' in Leonard Besselink, Frans Pennings and Sacha Prechal (eds), *The Eclipse of the Legality Principle in the European Union* (Kluwer 2011) 73, 77.

[38] Fabrizio Gilardi, *Delegation in the Regulatory State. Independent Regulatory Agencies in Western Europe* (Edward Elgar Publishing 2008) 16.

[39] Christina Spyrelli, 'Regulating the Regulators? An Assessment of Institutional Structures and Procedural Rules of National Regulatory Authorities' [2003–04] International Journal of Communications Law and Policy 1.

[40] Phedon Nicolaïdes, 'Regulation of Liberalised Markets: A New Role for the State?' in Damien Geradin, Rodolphe Muñoz and Nicolas Petit (eds), *Regulation through Agencies in the EU. A New Paradigm of European Governance* (Edward Elgar Publishing 2005) 23, 28.

B. The Role of the EU and the Member States in Matters of Network Regulation

Network regulation, as sector-specific regulation, exists alongside general competition law. The relationship between both systems is a delicate one. It is assumed that general competition law, as enforced by the EU and its Member States jointly, will not suffice to neutralize the risk of market failures as sketched above. In the early stages of liberalization, sector-specific rules that take the form of specific *ex ante* obligations of a preventive nature, such as price caps, are necessary to obtain satisfying results.[41] If competition in the liberalized network industries should fail, the public interest is at stake, which justifies a more thorough form of market supervision. Whereas regulators mainly operate through powers of rule making and adjudication (e.g. licensing), general competition authorities' remit tends to focus more on *ex post* control and penalizing measures, implying that their decisions are often quasi-judicial in nature.[42]

Sector-specific regulation also differs from general competition law in the extent to which its enforcement is entrusted to the EU institutions on the one hand and to the Member States on the other hand. Whereas the European Commission is the 'principal enforcer'[43] in the field of competition law, the EU does not hold similar autonomous administrative powers as far as sector-specific regulation is concerned, where the 'first line enforcers'[44] are NRAs.

Craig points out that the mode of administration used for the regulation of telecommunications and energy utilities is that of shared administration.[45] He refers to the definition proposed by the Committee of Independent Experts, which describes 'shared administration' as 'management of those Community programmes where the Commission and the Member States have distinct administrative tasks which are

---

41 ibid 28.

42 This does not mean that regulatory bodies do not hold such powers.

43 E.g. Damian Chalmers, Gareth Davies and Giorgio Monti, *European Union Law* (Cambridge University Press 2010) 924.

44 Pierre Larouche, 'Coordination of European and Member State Regulatory Policy: Horizontal, Vertical and Transversal Aspects' in Damien Geradin, Rodolphe Muñoz and Nicolas Petit (eds), *Regulation through Agencies in the EU. A New Paradigm of European Governance* (Edward Elgar Publishing 2005) 164, 166.

45 Also referred to as 'mixed administration': Jan H Jans, Roel de Lange, Sacha Prechal and Rob Widdershoven, *Europeanisation of Public Law* (Europa Law Publishing 2007) 29–32.

inter-dependent and set down in legislation and where both the Commission and the national administrations need to discharge their respective tasks for the Community policy to be implemented successfully'.[46] There are sound reasons why the EU opts for a system of shared administration. The fact that the Commission does not have sufficient personnel or resources to organize the administration of the various EU regulatory regimes in a centralized way is most often mentioned as the primary *raison d'être* of shared administration.[47] Furthermore, Member States' preferences can be taken into account more effectively and the EU can benefit from their expertise to a greater extent in a system of shared administration. Shared administration may, moreover, be required because Member State-specific applications of EU legislation are necessary or desirable. 'This is exemplified by the universal service obligations applicable to network industries, which require, inter alia, that certain services should be available to consumers at "affordable" prices. The determination of affordable price is left to the national regulatory authority, and this may be different as between Member States.'[48]

C. The Rise of NRAs and IRAs and the Influence of EU Law

The administration of network regulation in the EU is primarily in the hands of national administrations. The EU administration does not have powers to act as a regulator for the national network industries. At the same time, however, the EU has found another, more indirect way to exert influence on national regulatory administrations: it now issues legislation on the administrative organization of the regulatory state at Member State level.

---

[46] Paul Craig, 'Shared Administration, Disbursement of Community Funds and the Regulatory State' in Herwig C H Hofmann and Alexander H Türk (eds), *Legal Challenges in EU Administrative Law. Towards an Integrated Administration* (Edward Elgar Publishing 2009) 34, 34 with reference to Committee of Independent Experts, *Second Report on Reform of the Commission, Analysis of Current Practice and Proposals for Tackling Mismanagement, Irregularities and Fraud* (10 September 1999), Vol. I, para 3.2.2.

[47] Shared administration is a typical characteristic of the EU's system of 'executive federalism', as explained in Philipp Dann, 'The Political Institutions' in Armin von Bogdandy and Jürgen Bast (eds), *Principles of European Constitutional Law* (Hart 2009) 237, 243–244.

[48] Paul Craig, 'Shared Administration, Disbursement of Community Funds and the Regulatory State' in Herwig C H Hofmann and Alexander H Türk (eds), *Legal Challenges in EU Administrative Law. Towards an Integrated Administration* (Edward Elgar Publishing 2009) 34, 35.

According to regulatory theory, the liberalization of network sectors implies a clear distinction between three different sets of tasks or missions: policy making, regulation and operationalization or provision of services.[49] Before liberalization, national providers often took the form of government-owned enterprises or even ministerial services, meaning that they 'incorporated the roles of policymaker, service provider and market regulator at the same time'.[50] Today, state institutions are no longer responsible for supplying the goods and services generated in the network sectors ('operationalization'), since this activity is transferred to the various market players operating in the liberalized market, among which are primarily[51] private enterprises. The state, however, remains responsible for the regulation of the market. Whereas parliaments and the political executive are responsible for the development of general regulatory policy, its enforcement has typically been entrusted to separate authorities, established and designed especially for this purpose. National regulators are and remain an emanation of the state. That state, however, has evolved from an active, providing actor in the economy to a regulating actor.

The specific tasks that NRAs perform are quite diverse in nature and their definition depends on the sector in which they operate. Increasingly, EU legislation itself contains vast and detailed lists of NRAs' responsibilities.[52] Broadly speaking, NRAs' tasks are twofold: they have regulatory missions on the one hand and an important advisory function on the other hand.

Before EU legislation even mentioned NRAs, such sector-specific entities had already been set up in many Member States, often inspired by the British example.[53] Many of these bodies had, moreover, been granted a certain degree of political autonomy. Those were then referred

---

[49] Christina Spyrelli, 'Regulating the Regulators? An Assessment of Institutional Structures and Procedural Rules of National Regulatory Authorities' [2003–04] International Journal of Communications Law and Policy 1, 12.

[50] Arjan Geveke, 'Improving Implementation by National Regulatory Authorities' [2003] Eipascope 26, 27.

[51] Apart from the government-owned enterprises that still operate in the market.

[52] See e.g. article 37 of European Parliament and Council Directive 2009/72/EC of 13 July 2009 concerning common rules for the internal market in electricity and repealing Directive 2003/54/EC, [2009] OJ L211/55, containing a list of 21 different tasks entrusted to the national energy regulators.

[53] Tony Prosser, 'Models of Economic and Social Regulation' in Dawn Oliver, Tony Prosser and Richard Rawlings (eds), *The Regulatory State: Constitutional Implications* (Oxford University Press 2010) 34, 34; Richard Rawlings,

to as independent regulatory authorities. Neither NRAs, nor IRAs are thus a product or invention of EU legislation.[54] However, EU legislation has embraced this model of organization for the regulatory state by formulating institutional requirements for the design and functioning of NRAs. Regulatory independence and political autonomy in particular have been considered key values in this regard. Moreover, the standards imposed by EU law with regard to regulators' political autonomy are now often substantially stricter than those implemented by the Member States prior to EU interference.

D. Institutional Obligations Imposed by EU Law

a. General characteristics

The EU's concern with NRAs has its own history and characteristics. To begin with, comparing the various liberalized network industries, the development of EU law has been asymmetric: the requirements regarding NRA design anchored in EU directives differ from sector to sector. The EU has furthermore opted for a gradual introduction of ever more sophisticated and far-reaching requirements into the directives, adding further and stricter specifications with every new change in legislation. Currently, not all liberalization directives have yet reached the same degree of harmonization when it comes to the rules governing the design of NRAs.

The provisions on NRA design in the liberalization directives do, however, all have one common feature: they have treated regulatory independence as two-dimensional. Chronologically, requirements on political independence were preceded by provisions on the independence of the market players themselves. The rationale behind this was the creation of 'a level playing field':[55] by equalizing their starting positions,

---

'Introduction: Testing Times' in Dawn Oliver, Tony Prosser and Richard Rawlings (eds), *The Regulatory State: Constitutional Implications* (Oxford University Press 2010) 1, 5 with references.

[54] The EU legislature has thus definitely sought inspiration at Member State level. The spread of NRAs or IRAs at Member State level has in turn been the result of a process of horizontal influence. See Stéphanie De Somer, 'The Europeanisation of the Law on National Independent Regulatory Authorities from a Vertical and Horizontal Perspective' [2012] Review of European Administrative Law 93.

[55] Saskia Lavrijssen and Annetje Ottow, 'The Legality of Independent Regulatory Authorities' in Leonard Besselink, Frans Pennings and Sacha Prechal (eds), *The Eclipse of the Legality Principle in the European Union* (Kluwer 2011), 73 and 79.

all enterprises operating in the market are given a fair chance. Market supervision can only achieve its goals if the regulator is entirely unbiased. If a market player does succeed in making the regulator inclined to decide in its favour by means of lobbying, the industry suffers from 'regulatory capture',[56] which is detrimental to a well-functioning competitive market.

Political independence, on the other hand, refers to NRAs' relationship with the institutions of central government. The definition of 'APBs' adopted in Chapter 1 defined autonomy as the possession of distinct decision-making powers. This is true for all NRAs. The concept of an 'IRA', however, is usually reserved for NRAs subject to additional requirements of institutional and/or functional autonomy vis-à-vis elected politicians. EU legislation has over time extended the scope of these requirements.

It should be noted, however, that the requirements regarding independence of NRAs vis-à-vis market players on the one hand, and elected politicians on the other, are sometimes closely intertwined. Lavrijssen and Ottow, for instance, refer to a 2008 judgment of the ECJ[57] in which the court ruled that the requirement of independence of the market parties would make it unacceptable for a directorate of a ministry to be invested with regulatory tasks if another directorate of that same ministry is one of the market players under supervision.[58] The analysis of the various network industries undertaken in the following paragraphs will reveal that the general requirements of independence vis-à-vis all external actors, both private and public, was typically preceded, in every industry, by a requirement of separation of the state's roles as service provider on the one hand, and as a regulator on the other. This was important for those states who still had (the whole or partial) ownership of certain market players. At the basis of these provisions was a concern that conflicts of interest would hamper fair and proper regulation. In practice,

---

[56] See e.g. Barry M Mitnick, 'Capturing "Capture": Definition and Mechanisms' in David Levi-Faur (ed), *Handbook on the Politics of Regulation* (Edward Elgar Publishing 2011) 34.

[57] Case C-69/91 *Decoster* [1993] ECR I-5335.

[58] Saskia Lavrijssen and Annetje Ottow, 'The Legality of Independent Regulatory Authorities' in Leonard Besselink, Frans Pennings and Sacha Prechal (eds), *The Eclipse of the Legality Principle in the European Union* (Kluwer 2011) 73, 82.

this requirement thus resulted in the creation of IRAs, being NRAs that enjoyed specific guarantees of independence vis-à-vis the political executive.[59]

b. Overview by sector

Energy and electronic communications: pioneer-fields for obligations regarding NRAs' political independence The sectors of energy and telecommunications have known quite a comparable development when it comes to EU requirements on the institutional design of the regulatory state.[60] At the same time, it is unclear whether and to what extent the current prevailing legislation for both sectors differs as to the actual level of regulatory independence that is expected.

In telecommunications or – since the 2002 Framework Directive – electronic communications, article 7 of Directive 90/388 has already contained an obligation for Member States to ensure that the grant of operating licences, the control of type approval and mandatory specifications, the allocation of frequencies and surveillance of usage conditions was carried out by a body independent from the telecommunications organizations.[61] In 1997, an article 5a was inserted into Directive 90/387, henceforth requiring that NRAs would be legally distinct from and functionally independent of all organizations providing telecommunications networks, equipment or services. It also obliged Member States that retained ownership or a significant degree of control of organizations providing telecommunications networks and/or services to ensure an effective structural separation of the regulatory function from activities associated with ownership or control.[62] This provision aimed to avoid

---

[59] See e.g. Arjan Geveke, 'Improving Implementation by National Regulatory Authorities' [2003] Eipascope 26, 26.

[60] Leigh Hancher and Pierre Larouche, 'The Coming of Age of EU Regulation of Network Industries and Services of General Economic Interest' in Paul Craig and Grainne de Búrca (eds), *The Evolution of EU Law* (Oxford University Press 2011) 743, 767.

[61] Commission Directive 90/388/EEC of 28 June 1990 on competition in the markets for telecommunications services [1990] OJ L192/10.

[62] Article 5a of Council Directive 90/387/EEC of 28 June 1990 on the establishment of the internal market for telecommunications services through the implementation of open network provision [1990] OJ L192/1, inserted by European Parliament and Council Directive 97/51/EC of 6 October 1997 amending Council Directives 90/387/EEC and 92/44/EEC for the purpose of adaptation to a competitive environment in telecommunications [1997] OJ L295/23.

conflicts of interest and in practice had already resulted in those Member States granting a degree of political autonomy to their NRAs.

The 2002 Framework Directive[63] added to these obligations specific provisions with regard to, for instance, transparency in the work of the regulatory body. In its current version, article 3 of the Framework Directive provides that Member States shall ensure that each of the tasks assigned to NRAs in the directive itself and the specific directives is undertaken by a competent body (para 1). Member States have to guarantee the independence of NRAs by ensuring that they are legally distinct from, and functionally independent of, all organizations providing electronic communications networks, equipment or services. Member States that retain ownership or control of undertakings providing electronic communications networks and/or services are under the obligation to ensure effective structural separation of the regulatory function from activities associated with ownership or control (para 2). Member States furthermore have to ensure that NRAs exercise their powers impartially and transparently and that they have adequate financial and human resources to carry out the tasks assigned to them (para 3).

Since its revision in 2009,[64] article 3 of the Framework Directive contains a new paragraph 3a. It stipulates that, without prejudice to the provisions of paragraphs 4 and 5, NRAs responsible for *ex ante* market regulation or for the resolution of disputes between undertakings in accordance with articles 20 or 21 of the directive shall act independently and shall not seek or take instructions from any other body in relation to the exercise of these tasks assigned to them under national law implementing Community law. This does not, however, prevent supervision in accordance with national constitutional law. Furthermore, only appeal bodies set up in accordance with article 4 shall have the power to suspend or overturn decisions by the NRAs. Specific guarantees were introduced regarding the dismissal of the head of an NRA or, where applicable, members of the collegiate body fulfilling that function within the NRAs or their replacements. These persons may be dismissed only if

---

[63] European Parliament and Council Directive 2002/21/EC of 7 March 2002 on a common regulatory framework for electronic communications networks and services (Framework Directive) [2002] OJ L108/33.

[64] European Parliament and Council Directive 2009/140/EC 25 November 2009 amending Directives 2002/21/EC on a common regulatory framework for electronic communications networks and services, 2002/19/EC on access to, and interconnection of, electronic communications networks and associated facilities, and 2002/20/EC on the authorisation of electronic communications networks and services [2009] OJ L337/37.

they no longer fulfil the conditions required for the performance of their duties which are laid down in advance in national law.[65] Member States are furthermore obliged to ensure that NRAs have separate annual budgets. These budgets shall be made public. Member States also have to ensure that NRAs have adequate financial and human resources to enable them to actively participate in and contribute to the Body of European Regulators for Electronic Communications (BEREC).

Even though the energy liberalization directives, discussed in the following paragraphs, anchor independence vis-à-vis the government more explicitly and specifically than the Framework Directive, the prohibition on receiving instructions in the Framework Directive is formulated in such general wording that it is likely to apply to the relationship with public institutions as well. The preamble of Directive 2009/140 (the most recent directive to revise the Framework Directive) states, moreover, that:

> express provision should be made in national law to ensure that, in the exercise of its tasks, a national regulatory authority responsible for *ex-ante* market regulation or for resolution of disputes between undertakings is protected against external intervention *or political pressure* liable to jeopardise its independent assessment of matters coming before it.[66]

---

[65] The decision to dismiss the head of the national regulatory authority concerned, or where applicable members of the collegiate body fulfilling that function, shall be made public at the time of dismissal. The dismissed head of the national regulatory authority, or where applicable, members of the collegiate body fulfilling that function shall receive a statement of reasons and shall have the right to request its publication, where this would not otherwise take place, in which case it shall be published.

[66] Recital 13 (emphasis added). See also European Commission, Information Society and Media Directorate-General, Communications Committee, *Working Document on the Implementation of the Revised Framework Directive – Independence of National Regulatory Authorities*, Brussels, 15 April 2010, DG INFSO/B2, COCOM10-16, p. 5. In the eyes of the Communications Committee, an assistant body of the European Commission, '[t]he amended Framework Directive contains explicit provisions with regard to the political independence of NRAs from other state bodies' and the prohibition on seeking or taking instructions 'acknowledge[s] that the NRAs have to carry out their task without external intervention or political pressure from other State bodies'. The document has no binding value and does not necessarily reflect the official position of the Commission.

For the energy sector, the liberalization directives of the first generation – Directives 96/92/EC (on electricity) and 98/30/EC (on gas)[67] – did not contain any specific provisions on the establishment of NRAs. 'The energy directives merely stipulated that the Member States shall create appropriate and efficient mechanisms for regulation, control and transparency so as to avoid any abuse of dominant position.'[68] Even though it could be argued that various provisions[69] in the directives 'presumed' the existence of a separate administrative authority in charge of regulatory matters, the NRA did not explicitly appear in EU energy legislation until the second liberalization package. The obligation to establish a national regulator was incorporated into secondary European law by Directives 2003/54/EG (electricity) and 2003/55/EG (gas).[70] Moreover, by virtue of articles 23 and 25 respectively of these directives, the NRA had to be independent from the players operating in the relevant market.

At present, article 35 of Directive 2009/72[71] provides that each Member State shall designate a single national regulatory authority at national level and shall guarantee the independence of the regulatory authority, as well as ensuring that it exercises its powers impartially and transparently (paras 1 and 4). For that purpose, Member States have to

---

67 European Parliament and Council Directive 96/92/EC of 19 December 1996 concerning common rules for the internal market in electricity [1997] OJ L27/20; Directive 98/30/EC of the European Parliament and of the Council of 22 June 1998 concerning common rules for the internal market in natural gas [1998] OJ L204/1.

68 Saskia Lavrijssen and Annetje Ottow, 'The Legality of Independent Regulatory Authorities' in Leonard Besselink, Frans Pennings and Sacha Prechal (eds), *The Eclipse of the Legality Principle in the European Union* (Kluwer 2011) 73, 77 with reference to article 22 of Directive 96/92 and article 22 of Directive 98/30.

69 See e.g. article 20 of Directive 96/92 and article 21 of Directive 98/30, obliging Member States to designate a competent body, independent from the market parties, to settle disputes concerning network access; Saskia Lavrijssen and Annetje Ottow, 'The Legality of Independent Regulatory Authorities' in Leonard Besselink, Frans Pennings and Sacha Prechal (eds), *The Eclipse of the Legality Principle in the European Union* (Kluwer 2011) 73, 77.

70 European Parliament and Council Directive 2003/54/EC of 26 June 2003 concerning common rules for the internal market in electricity and repealing Directive 96/92/EC [2003] OJ L176/37; European Parliament and Council Directive 2003/55/EC of 26 June 2003 concerning common rules for the internal market in natural gas and repealing Directive 98/30/EC [2003] OJ L176/57.

71 See article 35 of European Parliament and Council Directive 2009/72/EC of 13 July 2009 concerning common rules for the internal market in electricity and repealing Directive 2003/54/EC [2009] OJ L211/55.

ensure that the regulatory authority is legally distinct and functionally independent from any other public or private entity and that it ensures that its staff and the persons responsible for its management act independently from any market interest and do not seek or take direct instructions from any government or other public or private entity when carrying out the regulatory tasks (para 4). In order to protect the independence of the regulatory authority, Member States in particular have to ensure that the regulatory authority can take autonomous decisions, independently from any political body, and has separate annual budget allocations, with autonomy in the implementation of the allocated budget, and adequate human and financial resources to carry out its duties. The members of the board of the regulatory authority or, in the absence of a board, the regulatory authority's senior management have to be appointed for a fixed term of between five and seven years, renewable once. Member States have to ensure an appropriate rotation scheme for the board or senior management. The members of the board or, in the absence of a board, members of senior management, may be relieved of office during their term only if they no longer fulfil the conditions set out in the article or have been guilty of misconduct under national law (para 5). Article 39 of Directive 2009/73[72] contains identical obligations for the gas sector.

The conclusion is that, for both electronic communications and energy, only the most recent directives contain real requirements on the independence of NRAs vis-à-vis other state or public institutions. Via the enactment of Directives 2009/72, 2009/73 and 2009/140, the EU has clearly intensified its grip on the concept of the NRA. In 2009, Craig observed that the proposed amendments to the liberalization legislation for both telecommunications and energy showed very similar tendencies at the institutional level, referring precisely to the growing independence of NRAs. 'There is a continuing concern to ensure that national regulators have the requisite independence, autonomy and power to perform the tasks required of them by the Community regulatory regime, and this concern has become more pronounced with the expansion of the EU from 15 to 27 Member States', the author concluded.[73]

[72] European Parliament and Council Directive 2009/73/EC of 13 July 2009 concerning common rules for the internal market in natural gas and repealing Directive 2003/55/EC [2009] OJ L211/94.

[73] Paul Craig, 'Shared Administration, Disbursement of Community Funds and the Regulatory State' in Herwig C H Hofmann and Alexander H Türk (eds), *Legal Challenges in EU Administrative Law. Towards an Integrated Administration* (Edward Elgar Publishing 2009), 34, 62.

Railway transport As far as the railway sector is concerned, until recently, article 30(1) of Directive 2001/14/EC[74] provided that the regulatory body, which Member States are obliged to establish, could be the ministry responsible for transport matters or any other body, but would have to be independent in its organization, funding decisions, legal structure and decision making from any infrastructure manager, charging body, allocation body or applicant. Recently, however, Directive 2012/34/EU[75] introduced an enhanced independence requirement, also targeting the regulator's relationship with political or public bodies.[76] Pursuant to article 55(1), the national regulatory body for the railway sector:

> shall be a stand-alone authority which is, in organisational, functional, hierarchical and decision-making terms, legally distinct and independent from any other public or private entity. It shall also be independent in its organisation, funding decisions, legal structure and decision making from any infrastructure manager, charging body, allocation body or applicant. It shall furthermore be functionally independent from any competent authority involved in the award of a public service contract.

It follows from article 55(3) that Member States have to ensure that the regulatory body is staffed and managed in a way that guarantees its independence. Persons in charge of decisions to be taken by the regulatory body in accordance with article 56, such as members of its executive board, where relevant, have to be appointed under clear and transparent rules which guarantee their independence by the national cabinet or council of ministers or by any other public authority which does not directly exert ownership rights over regulated undertakings. Member States shall decide whether these persons are appointed for a fixed and renewable term, or on a permanent basis which only allows dismissal for disciplinary reasons not related to their decision making. They have to be selected in a transparent procedure on the basis of their

[74] European Parliament and Council Directive 2001/14/EC of 26 February 2001 on the allocation of railway infrastructure capacity and the levying of charges for the use of railway infrastructure and safety certification [2001] OJ L75/29.

[75] European Parliament and Council Directive 2012/34/EU of 21 November 2012 establishing a single European railway area [2012] OJ L343/32.

[76] There are traces in the case law of the ECJ, however, that even under the regime of Directive 2001/14, the railway regulators had to enjoy a certain degree of political independence, more specifically in case of a risk of conflicts of interest arising. Case C-369/11 *Commission/Italy* (ECJ, 3 October 2013) paras 49–70 and Case C-545/10 *Commission/Czech Republic* (ECJ, 11 July 2013) paras 89–105.

merit, including appropriate competence and relevant experience, preferably in the field of railways or other network industries. A separate paragraph is dedicated to ensuring that these persons act independently from any market interest related to the railway sector. Finally, the staff is prohibited from seeking or taking instructions from any government or other public or private entity when carrying out the functions of the regulatory body. Recital 77 of the preamble adds that the financing of the regulatory body should guarantee its independence and should come either from the state budget or from contributions of the sector levied in a compulsory way, while respecting the principles of fairness, transparency, non-discrimination and proportionality.

Audiovisual media: to be or not to be independent? Regulation of audiovisual media is not always regarded as 'network regulation', since the rationales behind it to some extent differ from those in the network industries just discussed. Obviously, the regulation of economic activities regarding electronic communications on the one hand and the regulation of audiovisual media on the other hand are to a large extent intertwined. The media, moreover, has in common with the more traditional network industries that, in many European countries, parts of it were subject to state monopolies until fairly recently.

Up to now it has remained unclear to what extent the Audiovisual Media Services (AVMS) Directive[77] requires regulatory independence. The directive does not as such contain a separate provision requiring that Member States should set up an (independent) national media regulator.[78] However, the existence of an IRA seems to be 'presumed' by article 30 of the directive, requiring that Member States take appropriate measures to provide each other and the Commission with the information necessary for the application of the provisions of the directive, in particular articles 2, 3 and 4, *in particular through their competent independent regulatory bodies*. The preamble, moreover, stipulates that Member States are free to choose the form of their competent independent

---

[77] European Parliament and Council Directive 2010/13/EU of 10 March 2010 on the coordination of certain provisions laid down by law, regulation or administrative action in Member States concerning the provision of audiovisual media services (Audiovisual Media Services Directive) [2010] OJ L 95/1.

[78] E.g. Annetje Ottow, 'The Different Levels of Protection of National Supervisors' Independence in the European Landscape' in Suzanne Comtois and Kars J de Graaf (eds), *On Judicial and Quasi-judicial Independence* (Boom Juridische Uitgevers 2013) 139, 154.

regulatory bodies and that close cooperation between competent regulatory bodies of the Member States and the Commission is necessary to ensure the correct application of the directive.[79] According to the INDIREG study,[80] the AVMS Directive does not contain a strict formal obligation for the Member States to create an independent regulatory body if one does not already exist.[81] However, it does not seem improbable that recital 94 does indeed imply the creation of an IRA, leaving only its specific form subject to the discretion of the Member States. Consequently, the EU legislature assumes or at least strongly suggests that Member States should have an independent media regulator and that its independence should also include the relationship with the government.[82]

For the sake of completeness, it should be noted that the need for media regulators to be politically independent has been recognized by international and regional institutions that promote human rights, such as the Council of Europe.[83]

---

79 Recitals 94 and 95.

80 Full title: 'Indicators for independence and efficient functioning of audiovisual media services regulatory bodies for the purpose of enforcing the rules in the AVMS Directive', http://www.indireg.eu. The INDIREG study was ordered by the European Commission. In February 2011, the final report became available.

81 See page 7 of the final report. The report does, however, suggest that the basic requirement of independence of AVMS-regulatory bodies could find a broader legal basis in article 10 ECHR and article 288, para 3 TFEU, especially when read in connection with the objectives of the AVMS Directive. See also Saskia Lavrijssen and Annetje Ottow, 'Independent Supervisory Authorities: A Fragile Concept' (2012) 39(4) Legal Issues of Economic Integration 419, 434 with reference to INDIREG.

82 See the original Commission proposal COM (2005) 646. From recital 47 of the explanatory memorandum of the proposal, one can derive that the notion of independence concerns both audiovisual media providers and national governments. See also COM (2016) 287, the Commission's proposal of 25 May 2016 to amend the AVMS Directive, which contains provisions on the independence of the regulatory authority, also *vis-à-vis* public bodies.

83 See, for instance, Recommendation No. R (2000) 23 of the Committee of Ministers to Member States on the independence and functions of regulatory authorities for the broadcasting sector, adopted on 20 December 2000.

Postal services: no obligation of political independence (yet) The EU legislature does not (yet) require political independence for post regulators. Directive 2008/6/EC[84] did, however, insert a new article 22 in Directive 97/67/EC[85] requiring Member States to 'designate one or more national regulatory authorities for the postal sector that are legally separate from and operationally independent of the postal operators. Member States that retain ownership or control of postal service providers shall ensure effective structural separation of the regulatory functions from activities associated with ownership or control.' This obligation aims to create a level playing field and to avoid bias in favour of incumbents,[86] it does not require general and overall political independence. Given the previous evolutions in the other sectors, it nonetheless seems likely that a next stage of the liberalization process in this sector (a third-generation liberalization directive) will entail such a requirement.

c. The European Commission's interpretative note (energy)

In January 2010, the European Commission issued an interpretative note on the provisions regarding NRAs in Directives 2009/72 and 2009/73.[87] This note is not legally binding. As the Commission indicates, it 'aims to enhance legal certainty but does not create any new legislative rules'. In two recent ECJ judgments, a similar interpretative document issued by the Commission's services, which concerned the independence of the infrastructure manager in the railway sector, was declared to have no

[84] Directive 2008/6/EC of the European Parliament and of the Council of 20 February 2008 amending Directive 97/67/EC with regard to the full accomplishment of the internal market of Community postal services [2008] OJ L52, 3–20.

[85] European Parliament and Council Directive 97/67/EC of 15 December 1997 on common rules for the development of the internal market of Community postal services and the improvement of quality of service [1998] OJ L15/14.

[86] See recital 47 of the preamble of Directive 2008/6/EC: 'In accordance with the principle of separation of regulatory and operational functions, Member States should guarantee the independence of the national regulatory authorities, thereby ensuring the impartiality of their decisions.'

[87] Commission Staff Working Paper 22 January 2010, Interpretative Note on Directive 2009/72/EC concerning common rules for the internal market in electricity and Directive 2009/73/EC concerning common rules for the internal market in natural gas – The Regulatory Authorities, http://ec.europa.eu/energy/en/content/interpretive-note-regulatory-authorities-electricity-directive-and-natural-gas-directive (hereinafter: Commission, interpretative note regulatory authorities).

legal value.[88] The court took into consideration that it had not been published in the Official Journal, that it had been issued after the expiry of the transposition date for the relevant directives and that the criteria that it anchored did not appear in these directives, nor in any other legislative document. Since the first and third arguments (the latter being regarded as the conclusive one) also apply to the interpretative note on energy NRAs, it is likely that the court will come to a similar conclusion with regard to its legal effect.

Nevertheless, the note has been regarded (both by lawyers and national parliaments which had to implement the directives) as an important and authoritative source in determining the scope and precise meaning of the current obligations regarding NRAs. Possible infringement procedures initiated by the Commission will, moreover, undoubtedly be based on arguments relying on this interpretation.[89]

The note categorizes the requirements regarding NRA independence in sub-requirements, which are more or less separable but at the same time intertwined. First, the directives make a distinction between the requirements regarding the independence of the NRA as an organization on the one hand, and those regarding the independence of its staff and management on the other.[90] Secondly, at the level of the organization, a distinction is made between requirements regarding NRAs' decision-making autonomy, requirements regarding their financial autonomy and requirements regarding their autonomy to take decisions concerning their staff. Given the definition of APBs adopted in Chapter 1, the decision-making autonomy that the entity enjoys is of central importance.

In this regard, the Commission's interpretative note contains the following clarifications.

- The regulatory authority is legally distinct and functionally independent from any other public or private entity (art. 35(4)(a) Directive 2009/72 and art. 39(4)(a) Directive 2009/73).

The Commission believes that 'legally distinct' 'means that the NRA must be created as a separate and distinct legal entity from any Ministry or government body'. It emphasizes that this provision is closely linked to the requirement that the NRA should be able to take autonomous decisions. According to the Commission, the NRA will obviously have to

---

[88] See Case C-555/10 *Commission v Austria* (ECJ, 28 February 2013) para 58; Case C-556/10 *Commission v Germany* (ECJ, 28 February 2013) para 62.
[89] Commission, interpretative note regulatory authorities, 3.
[90] ibid 5.

be created in accordance with the constitutional and administrative rules of each Member State, but only 'insofar as they are consistent with European Union law'. Notwithstanding national administrative rules, it is the sole responsibility of the NRA to determine how it operates and is managed, including staffing-related matters.

Any hierarchical link between the NRA and any other body or institution is ruled out and the NRA can no longer be part of a ministry.[91]

- The staff and persons responsible for the management of the NRA should act independently from any market interest and do not seek or take direct instructions from any government or other public or private entity when carrying out the regulatory tasks (art. 35(4)(b) Directive 2009/72 and art. 39(4)(b) Directive 2009/73).

The Commission submits that, when taking a decision, the NRA's staff and management must not be inclined to take account of considerations other than the general interest.[92] Moreover, staff and management cannot seek or take any direct instructions from any government body or other public or private entity. 'An instruction in this context is any action calling for compliance and/or trying to improperly influence an NRA decision and thus includes the use of pressure of any kind on NRA's staff or on the persons responsible for its management.'[93]

However, the Commission also adds that the Electricity and Gas Directives do not deprive the government of the possibility of establishing and issuing its national energy policy. 'This means that, depending on the national constitution, it could be the government's competency to determine the policy framework within which the NRA must operate, e.g. concerning security of supply, renewables or energy efficiency targets. However, general energy policy guidelines issued by the government must not encroach on the NRA's independence and autonomy.'[94]

- The regulatory authority can take autonomous decisions, independently from any political body (art. 35(5) Directive 2009/72 and art. 39(5) Directive 2009/73).

The Commission claims that the requirement of autonomous decision making has consequences both *ex ante* (before a decision is taken) and *ex post* (after a decision has been taken).

---

[91] ibid 6.
[92] ibid 6.
[93] ibid 7.
[94] ibid 7.

> From an *ex ante* perspective, this requirement excludes any interference from the government or any other public or private entity prior to an NRA decision. It also implies that if the NRA is to draft a work programme for the coming year(s), it should be able do so autonomously, i.e. without the need for the approval or consent of public authorities or any other third parties.

Again, the Commission emphasizes that this requirement does not discharge the NRA from complying with the Member State's energy policy insofar as it is in accordance with European Union law.

> The *ex post* aspect of the requirement of having an NRA being able to take independent decisions means that the decisions of the NRA are immediately binding and directly applicable without the need for any formal or other approval or consent of another public authority or any other third parties. Moreover, the decisions by the NRA cannot be subject to review, suspension or veto by the government or the Ministry. This, of course, precludes neither judicial review nor appeal mechanisms before any other bodies independent of the parties involved and of any government.[95]

It is clear that the European Commission's interpretation does not leave any room for oversight of regulators' decisions by Governments or ministers, i.e. by the political executive. As far as parliamentary supervision is concerned, both the directives and the interpretative note remain remarkably vague. According to the Commission, the directives do not preclude parliamentary supervision in accordance with the constitutional laws of the Member States.[96] It is not clear what exactly this 'concession' comprises. Only the right of Parliament to approve the regulator's budget and the right to appoint its board members seem explicitly recognized, as well as the right to organize a hearing on these occasions.[97] Referring to recitals 34 and 30 of Directives 2009/72 and 2009/73 respectively, the Commission even *promotes* accountability of this kind to national parliaments.[98] However, the Commission hastens to add that 'the power

---

[95] ibid 9.

[96] ibid 11.

[97] ibid 20; recital 34 Directive 2009/72 and recital 30 Directive 2009/73. It is explicitly recognized that approval of the NRA's budget by the national legislator does not violate the regulator's budgetary autonomy: ibid 10 with reference to the preambles of the Directives.

[98] 'Although the Electricity and Gas Directives do not require Member States to organise accountability before national parliaments, the Commission's services are of the opinion that this could be an appropriate means of ensuring increased NRA accountability. Especially when discussing the NRA budget, national parliaments may ask to organise a hearing with the NRA. Similarly, the

of Member States to appoint members of the board of the NRA, the power to approve the budget and any measure of accountability set up by a Member State should not result in any instruction being given concerning the regulatory powers and duties of the NRA'.[99] 'While accountability is very important under the new legislative framework, it cannot be used as an excuse to infringe the requirements on independence of the NRA.'[100]

As explained, the actual legal value of the interpretative note is limited. Whether the directives indeed exclude every form of oversight by Governments and/or parliaments may eventually become an issue for the European Courts to assess. At present, (interpretative) case law is not yet available. It is furthermore unclear to what extent this interpretative note also gives an indication on how to implement the equivalent provisions in Directive 2009/140 for electronic communications, as well as the more recent provisions anchored in Directive 2012/34 for railway transport, for which no comparable interpretative documents exist.

3. EU IMPULSE IN THE FIELD OF HUMAN RIGHTS MONITORING AND SUPERVISION

A. Background: The Emergence of General and Right-specific Human Rights Institutions

In the past few decades, states all over the world have established dedicated human rights institutions. These entities supervise the implementation of, or monitor compliance with, human rights. Where some of them have a general competence, others have a remit that is right-specific (overseeing, for instance, only adherence to equality rights or the right to privacy). Some of these entities primarily perform advisory tasks, others assume quasi-judicial roles and have coercive powers. Often, the creation and empowerment of 'National Human Rights Institutions' (NHRIs) has been inspired by international, regional or supranational law. Smith speaks of 'international bodies who encourage and

---

accountability of the NRA board could be enhanced by organising a parliamentary hearing prior to the appointment of the board members. The accountability of the NRA can also be enhanced if Member States require the NRA, while submitting its draft budget for approval by the national parliament, to present a draft work programme as well.'

99 ibid 11.

100 ibid 20.

assist in the creation of independent NHRIs'.[101] Via the enactment of legislation, treaties or soft law instruments and through case law, pressure is exercised on (contracting) states to 'autonomize' their human rights institutions. According to Cardenas, 'international actors are directly engaged in creating and strengthening these institutions'.[102] The United Nations,[103] the Council of Europe[104] and the EU have played an important role in the diffusion of these APBs in the European legal sphere.

B. Institutional Obligations Imposed by EU Law

Parallel to the trend of ever stricter obligations regarding the political independence of NRAs, there is a similar trend in EU legislation with regard to bodies responsible for the implementation or monitoring of legislation in the field of human rights law, operating at Member State level. The most important example is found in the field of data protection, where data protection authorities (DPAs) assume that responsibility.

Until recently, Directive 95/46/EC[105] contained the general legislative framework on data protection in the EU. Pursuant to article 28 of this directive, each Member State was under an obligation to provide that one or more public authorities were responsible for monitoring the application within its territory of the provisions adopted by the Member States pursuant to the directive. These authorities had to act with 'complete independence' in exercising the functions entrusted to them.[106]

---

[101] Anne Smith, 'The Unique Position of National Human Rights Institutions: A Mixed Blessing?' [2006] Human Rights Quarterly 904, 907.

[102] Sonia Cardenas, 'Emerging Global Actors: The United Nations and National Human Rights Institutions' (2003) 9 Global Governance 23, 23.

[103] See in particular General Assembly resolution 48/134 of 20 December 1993 encouraging states to establish independent national human rights institutions.

[104] See e.g. Recommendation No. R (1997) 14 of the Committee of Ministers to Member States on the establishment of independent national institutions for the promotion and protection of human rights, adopted on 30 September 1997.

[105] European Parliament and Council Directive 95/46/EC of 24 October 1995 on the protection of individuals with regard to the processing of personal data and on the free movement of such data [1995] OJ L281/31.

[106] See also article 8(3) of the Charter of Fundamental Rights of the European Union [2012] OJ C326/391, on the right to protection of personal data: 'Compliance with these rules shall be subject to control by an independent authority.'

Contrary to the liberalization directives discussed in Section 2, this directive did not provide any further explanation as to the scope of the concept of ('complete') independence. In its judgment in *Commission/Germany*,[107] however, the ECJ put forward its own interpretation of this requirement. The case involved the status of the German DPAs responsible for monitoring the processing of data in the private sector (i.e. by non-state bodies). In Germany, the court observed, data processing by public bodies was supervised by the federal representative responsible for the protection of personal data and freedom of information and by the representatives responsible for the protection of regional data, all of whom are responsible vis-à-vis their respective parliaments. These representatives were 'not normally subject to any scrutiny, instruction or other influence from the public bodies which are the subjects of their supervision'. The supervision of data processing by non-public bodies, on the other hand, was organized differently in every *Land*, but all the laws of the *Länder* had in common that they explicitly organized some kind of state scrutiny of the acts of the supervisory authorities.[108] According to the European Commission, these provisions violated the directive.

Consequently, the court was asked to interpret the notion of 'complete independence' and to test the German systems against this interpretation. The Grand Chamber of the court argued that the notion of 'complete independence' precluded not only any influence exercised by the supervised bodies, contrary to what Germany had argued,[109] but also any directions or any other external influence, whether direct or indirect, which could call into question the performance by those authorities of their task of establishing a fair balance between the protection of the right to private life and the free movement of personal data.[110] This broad interpretation of the concept of 'complete independence' was inspired by the rationales that the court discerned behind the independence requirement:

---

[107] Case C-518/07 *Commission/Germany* [2010] ECR I-1885; see the case note by Annetje Ottow and Margot Aelen, 'Commission v. Federal Republic of Germany' [2010] European Human Rights Cases 679; Saskia Lavrijssen and Thomas Nauta, 'De Europeanisering van het toezicht op de energiesector' [2012] Nederlands Tijdschrift voor energierecht 136, 140; Fabienne Kauff-Gazin, 'Vers une conception européenne de l'indépendance des autorités de regulation? – À propos de l'affaire C-518/07, Commission c/ Allemagne' [2010] Europe, étude 9.

[108] Paras 7–10.

[109] Para 19.

[110] Para 30.

> The guarantee of the independence of national supervisory authorities is intended to ensure the effectiveness and reliability of the supervision of compliance with the provisions on protection of individuals with regard to the processing of personal data and must be interpreted in the light of that aim. It was established not to grant a special status to those authorities themselves as well as their agents, but in order to strengthen the protection of individuals and bodies affected by their decisions. It follows that, when carrying out their duties, the supervisory authorities must act objectively and impartially. For that purpose, they must remain free from any external influence, including the direct or indirect influence of the State or the *Länder*, and not of the influence only of the supervised bodies.[111]

The court furthermore referred to the EDPS,[112] the DPA operating at the EU level, which is also subject to a requirement of 'complete independence' pursuant to article 44(1) of Regulation 45/2001. This regulation clarifies in article 44(2) that the notion of complete independence entails that the EDPS may neither seek nor take instructions from anybody.[113]

> In view of the fact that Article 44 of Regulation No 45/2001 and article 28 of Directive 95/46 are based on the same general concept, those two provisions should be interpreted homogeneously, so that not only the independence of the EDPS, but also that of the national authorities, involve the lack of any instructions relating to the performance of their duties.[114]

According to the court, the German system of state scrutiny with regard to the body supervising data protection in the private sector was irreconcilable with this broad concept of independence.

In 2012, the ECJ was once again invited to rule on a Member State's implementation of the 'complete independence' requirement. This time, the European Commission had launched infringement proceedings against Austria (*Commission/Austria*).[115] Three allegations were made. First, the Commission criticized the fact that the managing member of the Austrian DPA (*Datenschutzkommission* or DSK) was a federal official subject to supervision. Secondly, the integration of the authority's office

---

[111] Para 25 (emphasis added).

[112] European Data Protection Supervisor.

[113] Para 27.

[114] Para 28.

[115] Case C-614/10 *Commission/Austria* (ECJ, 16 October 2012). See Alexander Balthasar, '"Complete Independence" of National Data Protection Supervisory Authorities – Second Try: Comments on the Judgment of the CJEU of 16 October 2012, C-614/10 (*European Commission v. Austria*), with Due Regard to its Previous Judgment of 9 March 2010, C-518/07 (*European Commission v. Germany*)' (2013) 9(3) Utrecht Law Review 26.

with the departments of the Federal Chancellery was deemed harmful to the authority's independence. Finally, the unconditional right to information given to the Federal Chancellor as to the work of the authority was thought to violate the directive. Once again, the court gave a broad interpretation of the notion of 'complete independence' and agreed with all three of the Commission's allegations. Referring to its precedent in *Commission/Germany*, the court ruled that functional independence, meaning in Austria's case that the law guarantees that the authority's members are not bound by instructions of any kind in the performance of their duties, is essential, but 'is not by itself sufficient to protect that supervisory authority from all external influence'.[116] According to the court, the notion of 'complete independence' 'is intended to preclude not only direct influence, in the form of instructions, but also, ... any indirect influence which is liable to have an effect on the supervisory authority's decision'.[117] The court ascertained that the managing member of the Austrian DPA was a federal official and was in charge of managing the supervisor's day-to-day business.[118] Furthermore, the 'service-related link' between the managing member and the federal authority to which he belonged allowed the activities of the managing member to be supervised by his hierarchical superior. This hierarchical superior, the ECJ continued, had an extensive power of supervision over the officials in his department. This situation was deemed contrary to article 28 of the Data Protection Directive.[119] As to the second violation identified by the Commission, the court found that 'the integration of the DSK office with the departments of the Federal Chancellery also does not allow the inference to be drawn that the DSK can exercise the functions entrusted to it free from all influence from the Federal Chancellery'.[120] It referred to the composition of the office by officials of the Federal Chancellery, which is itself subject to supervision by the DSK, a configuration which was deemed to carry a risk of influence over its decisions. According to the court, this 'organisational overlap' could give rise to a suspicion of partiality and was therefore incompatible with the requirement of 'complete independence'.[121] Lastly, the court also concurred with the final objection formulated by the Commission, regarding the right of information granted to the Federal Chancellor by the legislation. According to

116 Para 42.
117 Para 43.
118 Paras 45–46.
119 Paras 48–49.
120 Para 57.
121 Para 61.

the ECJ, this duty was 'also liable to subject the DSK to indirect influence'. The fact that the right to information was far reaching since it concerned all aspects of the work of the supervisor as well as its unconditional character inspired the court's assessment.[122]

In April 2016, a new Data Protection Regulation was issued. It replaces the 1995 Data Protection Directive.[123] The regulation dedicates a separate section to the independence of the national supervisory authorities. Pursuant to article 52 of the regulation, each supervisory authority shall act with complete independence in performing its tasks and exercising its powers in accordance with the regulation (para 1). The member or members of each supervisory authority shall, in the performance of their tasks and exercise of their powers in accordance with the regulation, remain free from external influence, whether direct or indirect, and shall neither seek nor take instructions from anybody (para 2). A member or members of each supervisory authority shall refrain from any action incompatible with their duties and shall not, during their term of office, engage in any incompatible occupation, whether gainful or not (para 3). Each Member State shall ensure that each supervisory authority is provided with the human, technical and financial resources, premises and infrastructure necessary for the effective performance of its tasks and exercise of its powers, including those to be carried out in the context of mutual assistance, cooperation and participation on the board (para 4). Each Member State shall ensure that each supervisory authority chooses and has its own staff, which shall be subject to the exclusive direction of the member or members of the supervisory authority concerned (para 5). Finally, Member States are under an obligation to ensure that the supervisory authority is subject to financial control which does not affect its independence and that it has separate, public annual budgets, which may be part of the overall state or national budget (para 6).[124]

---

[122] Para 63.

[123] European Parliament and Council Regulation 2016/679/EU of 27 April 2016 on the protection of natural persons with regard to the processing of personal data and on the free movement of such data, and repealing Directive 95/46/EC (General Data Protection Regulation) [2016] OJ L119/1.

[124] Article 53 furthermore anchors some general conditions with regard to the members of the supervisory authority. Member States have to provide that each member of their supervisory authorities is appointed by means of a transparent procedure by their parliament, their government, their head of State or an independent body entrusted with the appointment under Member State law (para 1). Each member shall have the qualifications, experience and skills, in particular in the area of the protection of personal data, required to perform its duties and exercise its powers (para 2). The duties of a member shall end in the event of the

In 2012, the European Commission had initially launched a proposal for a new Data Protection Directive.[125] Eventually, a regulation was issued instead of a new directive, but important parts of the proposed amendments with regard to the independence of the DPAs in the Commission's initial proposal were transposed to the regulation. In the explanatory memorandum to its proposal, the Commission confirmed that these proposed amendments intended to implement the case law of the ECJ.[126]

The preamble to the new regulation clarifies that '[t]he independence of supervisory authorities should not mean that the supervisory authorities cannot be subject to control or monitoring mechanisms regarding their financial expenditure or to judicial review'.[127]

Another domain within the field of human rights law in which EU provisions on the creation of APBs are emerging is that of discrimination law.[128] Compared to DPAs, the APBs created on the basis of these provisions have less far-reaching decision-making powers, which makes their independence less contestable.

4. WHAT THESE INSTANCES OF 'EU IMPULSE' HAVE IN COMMON

The requirements on the functional independence of NRAs and DPAs just discussed share two characteristics. They concern APBs with broad

---

expiry of the term of office, resignation or compulsory retirement, in accordance with the law of the Member State concerned (para 3). A member shall be dismissed only in cases of serious misconduct or if the member no longer fulfils the conditions required for the performance of the duties (para 4). Article 54 names the elements mentioned in articles 52 and 53 concerning the creation and status of the supervisory authorities that the Member States have to provide by law.

125 Proposal for a Directive of the European Parliament and of the Council on the protection of individuals with regard to the processing of personal data by competent authorities for the purposes of prevention, investigation, detection or prosecution of criminal offences or the execution of criminal penalties, and the free movement of such data, 24 January 2012, COM/2012/010 final – 2012/0010 (COD).

126 See p. 11 of the proposal.

127 Recital 118.

128 E.g. article 13 of Council Directive 2000/43/EC of 29 June 2000 implementing the principle of equal treatment between persons irrespective of racial or ethnic origin [2002] OJ L180/22.

discretionary powers whose decisions have to be insulated from all forms of political interference.

A. Broad Discretionary Powers

The NRAs and DPAs that are subject to requirements of political autonomy pursuant to EU legislation have in common that this same legislation confers broad, discretionary powers on them. Discretion can be described as the power to decide whether a given option is more expedient than another option and to choose accordingly. In a public law context, 'expedient' equals 'in the public interest'. A discretionary judgment is required as soon as it does not immediately follow from the applicable norm which of many possible solutions or decisions should be adopted. Choosing between different options and deciding which one serves the public interest best is the core business of politics. Therefore, exercising discretion in administrative matters in fact equals making policy, albeit on a micro level.

An often implicit presumption behind many initiatives to create APBs in general, and IRAs in particular, is that their tasks are purely technical in nature and do not involve the exercise of discretion. Lindseth, writing about the administrative nature of EU governance, however, argues that:

> The administrative realm is not merely technical or limited, as some may take the term to suggest. Rather, it is deeply political and discretionary, often beyond hierarchical control, if not de jure than at least de facto, given the diffusion and fragmentation of modern governance more generally. And yet, despite its effective degree of autonomy, administrative governance also remains deeply dependent on the centrally *constituted* bodies of representative government on the national level (legislative, executive, and judicial) for both legal authority and ultimate democratic and constitutional legitimacy.[129]

Apart from the fact that it is highly debatable whether many APBs indeed comply with the 'ideal scheme' of separation of policy and (technical) execution, it is now quite generally recognized that it does not apply to the species of regulatory bodies. However technical the decisions of NRAs and however 'objective' the criteria that they use,[130] these bodies

---

[129] Peter L Lindseth, *Power and Legitimacy: Reconciling Europe and the Nation State* (Oxford University Press 2010) xiii and xiv.

[130] See Gerard C Rowe, 'Administrative Supervision of Administrative Action in the European Union' in Herwig C H Hofmann and Alexander H Türk (eds), *Legal Challenges in EU Administrative Law: Towards an Integrated Administration* (Edward Elgar Publishing 2009) 179, 187: 'Even where it might

indeed often exercise a substantial degree of discretion.[131] Griller and Orator point out that 'it remains doubtful whether a useful definition of "technical" as opposed to "political" issues can be developed, and how "efficiency issues" could at the same time include "important policy-making powers" without crossing the border from "technical" to "political".'[132] Others agree that 'the range of tasks performed by an NRA does not lend itself easily to formalistic categories such as "policy making" and "implementation". Rather, regulatory decisions essentially involve policy trade-offs.'[133] Policy and implementation or execution may be perfectly separable in theory: they are not in practice.[134] In fact, regulators have been established precisely in order to deny politicians the possibility of defining policies and to entrust that mission to expert regulators, bodies that are free from a constant focus on re-election.[135] Majone, a leading scholar in the literature that has promoted regulatory independence, also recognizes that '[b]ecause regulation consists in applying general rules to particular situations, regulatory discretion is unavoidable'.[136]

---

be claimed that decision-making has no discretionary component, every assessment of supposedly objective legal criteria and their fulfilment involves a certain range of judgment.'

[131] Jørgen Grønnegård Christensen, 'Competing Theories of Regulatory Governance: Reconsidering Public Interest Theory of Regulation' in David Levi-Faur (ed), *Handbook on the Politics of Regulation* (Edward Elgar Publishing 2011) 96, 101; Tony Prosser, 'Regulation and Legitimacy' in Jeffrey Jowell and Dawn Oliver (eds), *The Changing Constitution* (7th edn, Oxford University Press 2011) 312, 321.

[132] Stefan Griller and Andreas Orator, 'Everything Under Control? The "Way Forward" for European Agencies in the Footsteps of the Meroni Doctrine' (2010) 35(1) European Law Review 3, 22.

[133] Leigh Hancher and Pierre Larouche, 'The Coming of Age of EU Regulation of Network Industries and Services of General Economic Interest' in Paul Craig and Grainne de Búrca (eds), *The Evolution of EU Law* (Oxford University Press 2011) 743, 773.

[134] E.g. Colin Talbot, 'The Agency Idea: Sometimes Old, Sometimes New, Sometimes Borrowed, Sometimes Untrue' in Christopher Pollit and Colin Talbot (eds), *Unbundled Government. A Critical Analysis of the Global Trend to Agencies, Quangos and Contractualisation* (Routledge 2004) 3, 10.

[135] *Infra*, section 5.

[136] Giandomenico Majone, *Temporal Consistency and Policy Credibility: Why Democracies Need Non-Majoritarian Institutions*, EUI Working Paper RSC No. 96/57 (European University Institute, Robert Schuman Centre 1996) 3. In another contribution, the author speaks of 'a highly technical and discretionary

Some authors point out that, in fields such as economic regulation, the role of the (central) government is to define general policy objectives,[137] which are implemented by regulators at the micro level. Within an EU context, moreover, the EU liberalization directives themselves contain vast provisions on the general policy objectives of regulation.[138] These objectives require further implementation at the national level. In theory, thus, the definition of policy regarding the regulation of the market in the network sectors is left to the European and national legislature and executive power[139] whereas (national) regulators exclusively engage in supervision of market players as such and the market itself generates the products and services concerned.[140] However, both the implementation of the EU directives in national legislation and day-to-day regulatory practice demonstrate that reality differs from this 'ideal'.[141] Some authors have observed that the goal of limiting the role of politicians to 'frame-steering' as 'general regulators' suffers from a lack of realism, especially when politically salient issues are at stake.[142] Black points out that the outcomes or objectives that regulators pursue are typically formulated in general terms and may compete with each other. Their

---

activity': Giandomenico Majone, *Independence vs. Accountability? Non-Majoritarian Institutions and Democratic Government in Europe, EUI Working Paper SPS No. 94/3* (European University Institute, Department of Political and Social Sciences and Robert Schuman Centre 1994) 22.

[137] E.g. Phedon Nicolaïdes, 'Regulation of Liberalised Markets: A New Role for the State?' in Damien Geradin, Rodolphe Muñoz and Nicolas Petit (eds), *Regulation through Agencies in the EU. A New Paradigm of European Governance* (Edward Elgar Publishing 2005) 23, 31.

[138] See, for instance, article 36 of Directive 2009/72/EC on electricity regulation, enumerating eight 'general objectives of the regulatory authority'. See also article 8 of the Framework Directive (2002/21/EC) on policy objectives and regulatory principles.

[139] The European Commission also emphasizes that the third generation of directives regarding the markets of electricity and gas do not deprive the government of the possibility to issue its own energy policy. See Commission, interpretative note regulatory authorities, 7.

[140] Christina Spyrelli, 'Regulating the Regulators? An Assessment of Institutional Structures and Procedural Rules of National Regulatory Authorities' [2003–04] International Journal of Communications Law and Policy 1, 17.

[141] See also Jacques Ziller, 'Les autorités administratives indépendantes entre droit interne et droit de l'Union européenne' [2010] RFDA 901–906.

[142] Tom Christensen and Per Lægreid, 'Regulatory Agencies – The Challenges of Balancing Agency Autonomy and Political Control' (2007) 20(3) Governance: An International Journal of Policy, Administration, and Institutions 499, 500 and 517.

legal mandates, moreover, 'rarely give any indication of how trade-offs between objectives are to be made'.[143]

> Regulators in the area of telecommunications, water and energy, for example, have been required to consider a wide range of social objectives in addition to their economic objectives, and which in some cases may conflict with them. For example, there is an economic case for charging those in rural areas more for receiving some services than those in urban areas, but the social objectives require universal service at uniform prices, and cross-subsidy of one set of consumers by the other.[144]

Similarly, some 15 years ago, Graham had already established that:

> [t]he legislation does not offer a coherent vision of the regulator's job, nor does it provide guidance on prioritizing the various interests and issues which may be of concern to particular industries. What the legislation really does is to set out a series of factors which pull in different directions. The job of the regulator, unaided by any open guidance from government, is to decide on priorities and how to balance competing interests.[145]

For Marcou, an essential element of the definition of 'regulation' is that regulators have to find a compromise between economic and non-economic values, such as consumer protection, sustainable development etc. Regulation therefore always includes 'une composante politique'.[146]

The discretion exercised by APBs in the field of economic regulation is most obvious in the case of rule-making powers, which are normative in nature. The directives indeed entrust IRAs with important powers to make regulations (i.e. quasi-legislative powers).[147] An example is the power of energy regulators to fix or approve the appropriate tariff methodology for transmission or distribution tariffs (anchored in article

---

[143] Julia Black, 'Calling Regulators to Account: Challenges, Capacities and Prospects' in Nicholas Bamforth and Peter Leyland (eds), *Accountability in the Contemporary Constitution* (Oxford University Press 2013) 354, 361. See also Robert Baldwin, Martin Cave and Martin Lodge, *Understanding Regulation* (Oxford University Press 2012) 28.

[144] Julia Black, 'Calling Regulators to Account: Challenges, Capacities and Prospects' in Nicholas Bamforth and Peter Leyland (eds), *Accountability in the Contemporary Constitution* (Oxford University Press 2013) 354, 362.

[145] Cosmo Graham, *Regulating Public Utilities: A Constitutional Approach* (Hart Publishing 2000) 32.

[146] Gérard Marcou, 'La notion juridique de régulation' [2006] AJDA 347, 351.

[147] See, for instance, article 37.6 of Directive 2009/72 for the electricity regulators.

37(1)(a) of Directive 2009/72). According to some, this is the 'core task of the regulatory authorities' in the energy sector.[148] Even though it is widely acknowledged that such decisions are based on scientific, economic models that require a high degree of technical insight, the preference for a specific methodology over another is also grounded in a political assessment. Therefore, tariff regulation may entail 'difficult socio-economic choices'.[149] The literature acknowledges that NRAs enjoy 'broad discretion' in order to achieve cost-oriented prices.[150] Some tariff models, more than others, encourage market players to invest in infrastructure, which may be a much desired outcome from a political viewpoint for various reasons. The British energy regulator Ofgem, for instance, in 2010 decided to replace its 'price-cap model' with an alternative methodology. In doing so, it aimed to foster investments, which were deemed necessary for reasons of security of supply as well as for reasons related to environmental and climate goals, such as the 'decarbonization' of the electricity grid.[151] The so-called 'RIIO model' that was adopted makes tariff calculations dependent on the results that networks operators have achieved in terms of policy goals such as consumer satisfaction, safety and environmental impact. McHarg speaks of:

> a decisive break with the notion that the regulator is no more than a 'competition-substitute' engaged in a limited and technical task. Rather, the new system clearly acknowledges that the regulator's role is to drive forward a positive policy agenda, and that this inevitably involves balancing a range of sometimes conflicting goals and values.[152]

In its interpretative note on energy NRAs, the European Commission acknowledges that '[t]he core duties of the NRA as regards network tariffs do not deprive the Member State of the possibility to issue general

148 Emmanuel Cabeau, 'National Regulatory Authorities' in Christopher Jones (ed), *EU Energy Law, Vol. I, The Internal Energy Market, The Third Liberalisation Package* (Claeys & Casteels 2010) 217, 236.

149 Saskia Lavrijssen and Annetje Ottow, 'Independent Supervisory Authorities: A Fragile Concept' (2012) 39(4) Legal Issues of Economic Integration 419, 431–432.

150 Tom Maes, 'The Energy Regulators' Competence: Network Tariff Setting' in Bram Delvaux, Michael Hunt and Kim Talus (eds), *EU Energy Law and Policy Issues* (Intersentia 2012) 123, 129.

151 See Aileen McHarg, 'Evolution and Revolution in the British Energy Network Regulation: from RPI-X to RIIO' in Martha Roggenkamp et al. (eds), *Energy Networks and the Law* (Oxford University Press 2012) 314.

152 ibid 326.

policy guidelines which ultimately will have to be translated by the NRA into the tariff structure and methodology'. It adds, however, that 'these guidelines should not encroach on the NRA's competences or infringe any of the requirements of the Electricity and Gas Directives and Regulations'. 'Although a Member State could e.g. issue a general policy guideline with regard to attracting investments in renewables, the Commission's services would consider a rule setting the profit margin in the cost-plus tariff as a prohibited direct instruction to the NRA.'[153] Such general guidelines can be helpful in order to inform the regulator about the policy objectives that it should take into account. The problem, however, is that energy regulation has to serve multiple goals nowadays, all anchored in legislation and/or general policy guidelines. These goals can conflict and regulators may have to choose, when they take the actual decisions regarding, for instance, tariff methodology, which one(s) will prevail or how to strike a proper balance between them. Such assessments have to be made *in concreto*, on the level of specific decisions.

At the same time, individual decisions made by NRAs may also encompass discretionary assessments and, therefore, may have political implications.[154] Pursuant to article 56(9) of Directive 2012/34 (railway transport), concerning the NRA's power of dispute resolution, the regulatory body shall, where appropriate, decide on its own initiative on appropriate measures to correct discrimination against applicants, market distortion and *any other undesirable developments* in these markets. This is an example of a provision concerning administrative decisions with an individual scope that aims to invest the NRA with a large discretionary power.

Moreover, studies point out that the ECJ is inclined to give a broad interpretation to NRAs' tasks and powers. In recent contributions on the extent to which the European independence requirements for NRAs allow for a full application of the Dutch principle of legality, the Dutch literature has established that the ECJ adopts a 'flexible and teleological interpretation when interpreting the competences of the national telecom authorities'. The authors suggest that this tendency may also prove to be relevant for the interpretation of the powers of the national energy regulators. They more specifically draw attention to the fact that the court

[153] Commission, interpretative note regulatory authorities, 14.

[154] E.g. Salo Covlosky, Roberto Pires and Susan S Silbey, 'The Pragmatic Politics of Regulatory Enforcement' in David Levi Faur (ed), *Handbook on the Politics of Regulation* (Edward Elgar Publishing 2011) 322, 322–323.

endorses the NRAs' discretionary powers.[155] Their conclusion is that a Dutch definition of the principle of legality, implying that NRAs' powers should be interpreted restrictively and that NRAs cannot be invested with far-reaching discretionary powers[156] can no longer apply in regulatory matters. 'This means,' the authors point out, 'that the procedural and institutional autonomy for shaping powers and the room for the applicability of national interpretations of constitutional principles, such as the principle of legality, has been seriously limited.'[157]

A frequently used image to portray regulatory bodies is that of quasi-judicial entities. Because of the way in which they work, with proceedings that sometimes resemble those applied by the judiciary, regulators are indeed often compared to courts and this resemblance is used as an argument to substantiate their political independence[158] and/or the lack of political accountability that characterizes them.[159] In terms of remit or mission, regulators, just like courts, often apply general rules or legislation to specific cases (using a French expression: 'ils disent le droit'), are increasingly involved in dispute resolution and are entrusted with powers to impose penalties.[160] Insofar as regulators, when they perform such tasks, do indeed only interpret and apply the law without

---

[155] Saskia Lavrijssen and Annetje Ottow, 'The Legality of Independent Regulatory Authorities' in Leonard Besselink, Frans Pennings and Sacha Prechal (eds), *The eclipse of the legality principle in the European Union* (Kluwer 2011) 73, 95. In the same sense: Jacques Ziller, 'Les autorités administratives indépendantes entre droit interne et droit de l'Union européenne' [2010] RFDA 901–906. See also European Commission, Information Society and Media Directorate-General, Communications Committee, *Working Document on the Implementation of the revised Framework Directive – Independence of National Regulatory Authorities*, Brussels, 15 April 2010, DG INFSO/B2, COCOM10-16, p. 7 with reference to ECJ judgments. See for instance Case C-424/07, *Commission/Germany* (ECJ, 3 December 2009).

[156] Saskia Lavrijssen and Annetje Ottow, 'The Legality of Independent Regulatory Authorities' in Leonard Besselink, Frans Pennings and Sacha Prechal (eds), *The Eclipse of the Legality Principle in the European Union* (Kluwer 2011) 73, 76.

[157] Saskia Lavrijssen and Thomas Nauta, 'De Europeanisering van het toezicht op de energiesector' [2012] Nederlands Tijdschrift voor energierecht 136, 143.

[158] E.g. Giandomenico Majone, *Temporal Consistency and Policy Credibility: Why Democracies Need Non-Majoritarian Institutions*, EUI Working Paper RSC No. 96/57 (European University Institute, Robert Schuman Centre 1996) 3.

[159] Jean-Bernard Auby, 'Remarques terminales' [2010] RFDA 931, 934.

[160] Aude Rouyère, 'La constitutionnalisation des autorités administratives indépendantes: quelle signification?' [2010] RFDA 887, 895.

any (intended) discretionary powers, their political independence seems justified and even preferable. This is the reason why, in some countries, such as Belgium, the general competition authority was originally established and qualified as an administrative court and not, as for instance in France, as an APB.[161] However, economic regulators increasingly assume tasks that are atypical for judicial bodies. As pointed out above, regulatory bodies often have rule-making powers as well as powers to make decisions in individual cases. When they exercise these powers, moreover, they make policy trade-offs, which distinguishes them from judges.[162] One could argue that, today, courts are increasingly entrusted with powers to weigh different considerations, particularly when they impose penalties. In those cases, their task comprises more than a mere interpretation of legislation. However, often, these assessments relate to factual rather than political or societal considerations: judges are invited by the legislature to take into account the particularities of a case and/or of the people involved. These assessments are, moreover, often embedded in the application of general legal principles, such as the proportionality principle.

The line between applying and interpreting the law on the one hand and making discretionary assessments on the other, is, however, a thin one.[163] For instance, one should be careful not to qualify the power of regulators to impose sanctions as 'apolitical' too easily.[164] Penalties imposed by regulators differ from criminal penalties: they are administrative in nature. Like criminal penalties, they are meant to be punitive

---

161 See, however: René Poésy, 'La nature juridique de l'Autorité de la concurrence' [2009] AJDA 347.

162 See Jeannette Bougrab, 'Independent Administrative Authorities in France' in Roberto Caranta, Mads Adenas and Duncan Fairgrieve (eds), *Independent Administrative Authorities* (British Institute of International and Comparative Law 2004) 47, 58; Chris Hanretty, Pierre Larouche and Andreas Reindl, 'Independence, Accountability and Perceived Quality of Regulators – A CERRE Study', Brussels, 6 March 2012, http://www.cerre.eu/publications/independence-accountability-and-perceived-quality-regulators, 10.

163 This is very well illustrated by the debate sketched in René Poésy, 'La nature juridique de l'Autorité de la concurrence' [2009] AJDA 347. See also Paule Quilichini, 'Réguler n'est pas juger: Réflexions sur la nature du pouvoir de sanction des autorités de régulation économique' [2004] AJDA 1060; Sonia Ben Hadj Yahia, 'Controverses autour des autorités de régulation' (2010) 18 La Semaine Juridique Entreprise et Affaires 17.

164 In that sense: L F M Verhey and N Verheij, 'De macht van marktmeesters, markttoezicht in constitutioneel perspectief' [2005] Toezicht, Handelingen Nederlandse Juristenvereniging 135, 206–209.

and to correct the behaviour of market players. However, when taking a decision on the type and level of the penalty, regulators will take into account a variety of policy objectives that will often imply a room for manoeuvre that is much broader than that entrusted to judicial bodies. In young or fragile markets, where competition is only slowly achieved, regulators may, for instance, feel inclined to keep their penalties low in order not to discourage potential investors. Such choices are based on discretionary assessments in which trade-offs are made.[165] Moreover, regulators, unlike many courts, typically have a certain discretion to define and rank priorities in this regard. The Belgian Council of State, Legislation Section, has on multiple occasions criticized the conferral of powers to impose penalties on APBs when this does not go hand in hand with any possibility of political control or input. The Council does not exclude that such powers may involve discretionary assessments.[166] To sum up: in the case of administrative penalties, discretionary appreciation is not incidental, unintended or unexpressed, it is indispensable and takes place in a conscious and explicit manner. The proportionality of an administrative fine is not judged in relation to the facts only, but also in relation to the policy motives underlying it.

One may be inclined to qualify the decisions made by NHRIs as considerably less inspired by political assessments than those of NRAs. Many NHRIs indeed only have powers to exert informal pressure on both governments and private parties to respect and/or implement human rights obligations. They draft reports, keep the media informed, act as claimants or intervening parties before the courts and so on. They mainly monitor and report facts with regard to human rights compliance. However, there are instances in which NHRIs take decisions or make assessments that do involve political assessments.[167] The European Court of Human Rights (ECtHR), interpreting the European Convention on Human Rights (ECHR), arguably the most important human rights catalogue within Europe, has acknowledged that, sometimes, states enjoy a (large) margin of appreciation when they balance the full protection of

[165] On the administrative penalty as an instrument of policy, see Martin Collet, 'Autorités de régulation économique: l'émergence d'une catégorie nouvelle?' [2008] Revue juridique de l'économie publique comm. 11.

[166] See the references and analysis in Denis Delvax, 'Les contrôles administratives pesant sur les autorités administratives indépendantes' (2008) 37 Revue de droit de l'ULB 107, 119–126.

[167] E.g. Martin Collet, 'La création des autorités administratives indépendantes: symptôme ou remède d'un Etat en crise?' (2007) 330 Regards sur l'actualité 5, 11.

(qualified) human rights against other goals of public interest. These interests often correspond to political preferences that prevail at the national level. As far as the EU is concerned, DPAs rule on what is permissible under the right to privacy: in doing so, they necessarily take into account the national context and, hence, make assessments in which they balance various interests that may relate to political choices.

Pursuant to the Data Protection Regulation, moreover, DPAs should henceforth be invested with the power to impose administrative fines.[168] The regulation defines some limits, but leaves a large discretionary power to the DPAs.

B. Insulation from All Forms of Political Supervision or Interference on the Level of Decision Making

Secondly, the EU requirements on NRA and DPA independence have in common that they seem to exclude all forms of political supervision or interference on the level of day-to-day decision making by these APBs. This prohibition is particularly explicit in the field of energy regulation, where the European Commission's interpretative note rules out all possible forms of government intervention on the level of individual decision making, *ex ante or ex post* (see the detailed discussion *supra*, Section 2 of this chapter).

For electronic communications, for which no similar interpretative note was issued, the situation at first sight seemed less clear. Pursuant to article 3, paragraph 3a of the Framework Directive, the prohibition on seeking or taking instructions anchored in that same paragraph does not prevent supervision in accordance with national constitutional law. One interpretation of this clause could be that traditional forms of supervision rooted in the constitutional traditions of the Member States could remain in effect. However, article 3, paragraph 3 of the Framework Directive also provides that only appeal bodies set up in accordance with article 4 shall have the power to suspend or overturn decisions by the NRAs. This article 4 anchors the right of users or undertakings providing electronic communications networks and/or services who are affected by a decision of a national regulatory authority to an effective mechanism at national

[168] Unless the legal system of the Member State does not provide for administrative fines. See article 83 of European Parliament and Council Regulation 2016/679/EU of 27 April 2016 on the protection of natural persons with regard to the processing of personal data and on the free movement of such data, and repealing Directive 95/46/EC (General Data Protection Regulation) [2016] OJ L119/1.

level under which they have the right to appeal against the decision to an appeal body that is independent of the parties involved. This body, *which may be a court*, shall have the appropriate expertise to enable it to carry out its functions effectively, the article clarifies.[169] Paragraph 2, moreover, adds that, where the appeal body referred to in paragraph 1 is not judicial in nature, written reasons for its decision shall always be given. Furthermore, in such a case, its decision shall be subject to review by a court or tribunal within the meaning of Article 234 of the Treaty. This provision does not seem to exclude regulated parties, for instance, filing an administrative appeal with a political body that has the power to annul the decision, as long as the annulment decision can subsequently be challenged before a judicial body.[170] In the meantime it has become clear that, as far as the European Commission is concerned, the directive excludes powers of suspension or annulment by members of the political executive. Chapter 4 will discuss how a Belgian attempt to retain a limited possibility of political supervision via a power of suspension provoked an infringement procedure, since the Commission deemed this irreconcilable with the independence requirements in the Framework Directive.

With regard to the railway sector, article 55(3) of Directive 2012/34 only mentions a prohibition on receiving or accepting instructions from public entities. This at least seems to exclude forms of hierarchical supervision. It is less clear whether and to what extent other (milder) forms of supervision are admissible. The formulation of the independence requirement(s), however, is to that extent similar to the one anchored in the energy directives, that it is likely that a similar interpretation should be given to both.

As far as the field of data protection is concerned, the ECJ's rulings in *Commission/Germany* and *Commission/Austria*[171] have made it clear that all forms of supervision that may result in any directions being given to the supervisory authority or any other form of external influence, whether

---

[169] Member States furthermore have to ensure that the merits of the case are duly taken into account and that there is an effective appeal mechanism. Pending the outcome of the appeal, the decision of the national regulatory authority shall stand, unless interim measures are granted in accordance with national law.

[170] For Member States where government enterprises are still active as players on the liberalized market, such an administrative procedure may, however, raise questions in the light of the independence requirement vis-à-vis the market parties, anchored in article 4.

[171] Discussed *supra*, Section 3.

direct or indirect, are irreconcilable with the notion of 'complete independence'. This includes mechanisms of supervision that solely target the legality of a decision. This prohibition is now anchored in article 52, para 2 of the 2016 Data Protection Regulation, discussed earlier. According to the ECJ, moreover, the prohibition is not limited to powers that result in a replacement of the decision, but also extends to powers of cancellation or annulment.

In sum, the EU independence requirements on energy, electronic communications, railway transport and data protection supervisors no longer seem to allow for the political executive to assume the role of 'democratic legitimizer'. Admittedly, both the EU legislative regime for energy and electronic communications and the case law of the ECJ regarding the notion of 'complete independence' in the Data Protection Directive seem to leave some room for direct parliamentary supervision. It seems rather unlikely, however, that national parliaments would be allowed, under the EU directives, to scrutinize NRAs' day-to-day decisions in the same way that a minister would be able to do, should he be invested with powers of supervision. The 2016 Data Protection Regulation, for instance, clarifies that the financial control to which supervisory authorities are subject may not affect their independence. As pointed out earlier, the Commission's interpretative note on the energy regulators emphasizes that the powers of appointment and approval of the budget, being measures of accountability that are often applied by parliaments, 'should not result in any instruction being given concerning the regulatory powers and duties of the NRA'.[172] As far as the right to approve the budget is concerned, the Commission states, moreover, that this process 'cannot in any way be used as a means of influencing the NRA's priorities or to jeopardise its ability to carry out its duties and exercise its powers in an efficient and effective manner'.[173] This indicates that national parliaments are all but free in deciding whether, to what extent and under which conditions, they will approve the regulator's budget, as is traditionally the case in representative democracies, where it is the privilege of the representatives of the people to allocate budgets to the administration. For that reason, it is doubtful whether parliaments could rely on individual decisions or dossiers as reasons to, for instance, reduce the budget of the energy regulator. Such a power would imply that Parliament could use the leverage offered by its budgetary power vis-à-vis NRAs that make decisions that are undesirable from a political

---

[172] Commission, interpretative note regulatory authorities, 11.
[173] ibid 10.

viewpoint. In that way, Parliament's power of approval could be applied to put pressure on the regulator to comply with the majority's policy preferences in day-to-day decision making,[174] which qualifies as an indirect instruction and is likely to conflict with the independence requirements in the directives. Whereas budgetary control at first sight seems a powerful control instrument,[175] it seems unlikely that parliaments are still allowed to use their power of approval as a genuine instrument to hold the regulator accountable and to sanction him, when necessary, for political reasons.

The most traditional instrument available to parliaments that want to sanction the executive for maladministration in the framework of political ministerial responsibility – although applied with providence and even reluctance – is arguably their power of dismissal. This power, however, is also limited by the EU legislation on NRAs and DPAs discussed in Sections 2 and 3. As far as energy regulation is concerned, the national Parliament has the right to appoint the head of the NRA or the board and its individual members, but it is limited in its possibilities to dismiss them. The latter is only possible if they no longer fulfil the conditions set out in the EU directives or have been guilty of misconduct under national law. In other words: EU law makes dismissal for purely political reasons (i.e. discontent with the policy conducted) impossible. In conclusion, on the level of their specific, day-to-day regulatory decisions, energy regulators seem immune to all parliamentary supervision, even indirectly. At most, Parliament can express its discontent with certain policies followed by the regulator when it hears its members on the periodical occasion of the nomination of the board or the debate on the budget, but any formal right of intervention is or should be absent pursuant to EU law.

As to regulation in the field of electronic communications, the abovementioned clause in article 3, paragraph 3a, explicitly stating that supervision in accordance with national constitutional law is not prevented, begs the question whether full parliamentary control of the executive, via political ministerial responsibility as organized by the national Constitutions, can indeed remain in place. This includes traditional privileges regarding budget allocation and the ultimate sanction of dismissal for political dissatisfaction. As far as the latter possibility is concerned, the Framework Directive, as opposed to the directives for the energy sector, does not contain a limited list of grounds that can lead to

---

[174] It is, on the contrary, explicitly recognized that the general energy policy is still defined by national politics. See ibid 7 and 9.

[175] ibid 20: 'Especially when discussing the NRA budget, national parliaments may ask to organise a hearing with the NRA.'

dismissal, but mentions that dismissal of the regulator's members is only possible if they no longer fulfil the conditions required for the performance of their duties which are laid down in advance in national law. The preamble of Directive 2009/140 clarifies that 'rules should be laid down at the outset regarding the grounds for the dismissal of the head of the national regulatory authority in order to remove any reasonable doubt as to the neutrality of that body and its imperviousness to external factors'.[176] Consequently, for the NRAs in electronic communication as well, national parliaments are constrained in their freedom to use their power of dismissal as they think expedient.

Article 55(3) of Directive 2012/34 for railway transport stipulates that the members of the board can only be dismissed for disciplinary reasons not related to their decision making.

Article 53 of the 2016 Data Protection Regulation provides that the duties of the members of the DPA shall end in the event of the expiry of the term of office, resignation or compulsory retirement, in accordance with the law of the Member State concerned. A member shall be dismissed only in cases of serious misconduct or if the member no longer fulfils the conditions required for the performance of the duties. Under the regime of the (former) Data Protection Directive, the ECJ has ruled that Member States cannot prematurely bring to an end the term served by a DPA for reasons of institutional reform. According to the court, the threat of such premature termination could lead to behaviour of 'prior compliance' by the authority, which is incompatible with its functional independence.[177]

It is safe to conclude that the EU independence requirements seem to rule out most parliamentary scrutiny on the micro level, i.e. on the level of day-to-day decision making. Certainly, the national parliaments typically appoint the management of the NRAs and DPAs, receive annual reports and have the formal power to grant the authorities their annual budgets. On top of that, national parliaments remain entitled to define general policy objectives in the legislation that they enact, but cannot interfere at the level of the actual decision-making process.

The question may arise whether the lack or limitation of political control at Member State level is not compensated by supervision at the EU political level. To some extent, IRAs are indeed subject to supranational control mechanisms. Hancher and Larouche point to the possibilities for the European Commission to put pressure on the regulators

---

176 Recital 13.
177 Case C-288/12 *Commission/Hungary* (ECJ 8 April 2014).

and to the fact that the NRAs are obliged to answer to the other national regulators with whom they form networks.[178] According to Nicolaïdes, oversight of national regulatory decisions is the task of the European Commission. The powers of the Commission are threefold. First, the Commission can initiate procedures against a Member State when EU rules are not applied or misapplied. However, this is not 'full' control, covering all aspects of NRAs decisions, the author points out, as this possibility only exists when there is a legal infraction (and not, for instance, when the Commission is of the opinion that the NRA might have taken a more efficient decision). Secondly, the Commission can review the decisions of the NRAs that, according to the directives, have to be notified. Again, this only covers a certain number of decisions. Lastly, the Commission manages the networks of European regulators, as far as they have been set up by the Commission itself.[179] Lavrijssen and Ottow refer to specific possibilities for interference in the NRA decision-making process by the Commission, anchored in the Framework Directive, such as binding veto decisions against NRA drafts.[180] These instruments and mechanisms, however, are specific in nature and purpose: they typically aim to protect the single market and do not form a permanent and comprehensive system of supervision.[181] Moreover, they do not allow for input that takes into account valid national political considerations.

---

[178] Leigh Hancher and Pierre Larouche, 'The Coming of Age of EU Regulation of Network Industries and Services of General Economic Interest' in Paul Craig and Grainne de Búrca (eds), *The Evolution of EU Law* (Oxford University Press 2011) 743, 775.

[179] Phedon Nicolaïdes, 'Regulation of Liberalised Markets: A New Role for the State?' in Damien Geradin, Rodolphe Muñoz and Nicolas Petit (eds), *Regulation through Agencies in the EU. A New Paradigm of European Governance* (Edward Elgar Publishing 2005) 23, 35.

[180] Article 7(4)–(5) of the directive. Another example may be found in article 39(5)–(6) of Directive 2009/72 and article 43(5)–(6) of Directive 2009/73 (energy).

[181] Saskia Lavrijssen and Annetje Ottow, 'The Legality of Independent Regulatory Authorities' in Leonard Besselink, Frans Pennings and Sacha Prechal (eds), *The Eclipse of the Legality Principle in the European Union* (Kluwer 2011) 73, 88–89.

5. THE RATIONALES BEHIND 'EU IMPULSE'

A. Discussion

EU law increasingly obliges Member States to create APBs that assist in the implementation of, or ensure compliance with, its substantive rules. The question arises whether there is any meaningful link between these obligations in terms of the reasons or justifications that inspire them. Are all of these demands expressions of a similar concern?

As far as network regulation is concerned, there is an impressive body of literature on the reasons behind the need for regulatory independence. It should be noted that IRAs constitute just one type of NRA or – phrased differently – represent just one manner in which the institutional design of NRAs can be conceived. Nicolaïdes rightly distinguishes two key questions regarding regulatory governance. Preceding the question why regulatory authorities ought to be independent is the question why regulatory tasks should be entrusted to a separate authority in the first place. The author answers this first question referring to reasons of efficiency, being the main and omnipresent goal for almost every initiative to establish an APB. 'Assignment of regulatory tasks to a separate authority enables that authority to develop technical, economic and legal expertise and to benefit from economies of scale in dealing with many similar cases.'[182] Entrusting the authority with a narrow mandate can ensure that it is able to avoid so-called policy trade-offs, the author argues.[183] These objectives, however, do not require the NRA to be 'independent'. Separate regulatory authorities may be functioning within existing ministries or departments, just as they may be independent agencies.[184]

But what, then, are the specific rationales behind the independence requirements applicable to NRAs, anchored in EU law? As Gilardi points out, emulation has been an important driver in the diffusion of NRAs across Europe, prior to the adoption of the independence requirements

---

[182] Phedon Nicolaïdes, 'Regulation of Liberalised Markets: A New Role for the State?' in Damien Geradin, Rodolphe Muñoz and Nicolas Petit (eds), *Regulation through Agencies in the EU. A New Paradigm of European Governance* (Edward Elgar Publishing 2005) 23, 29.

[183] This chapter has argued, however, that this is unavoidable in practice.

[184] Phedon Nicolaïdes, 'Regulation of Liberalised Markets: A New Role for the State?' in Damien Geradin, Rodolphe Muñoz and Nicolas Petit (eds), *Regulation through Agencies in the EU. A New Paradigm of European Governance* (Edward Elgar Publishing 2005) 23, 29.

currently anchored in EU law. This process has more to do with the symbolic value of independence[185] than with rational and well-advised options. Even though these types of dynamics have to be taken seriously (admittedly, the popularity of APBs has to a large extent been the result of a 'fashion trend'), more substantive, inherent values or goals are associated with regulatory independence as well.

Like many other APBs, NRAs find their origins in neoliberalism and NPM, which led to (respectively) the liberalization of markets and the modernization of government services. To some extent, however, IRAs also constitute a distinctive case, signifying that other, more specific rationales underlie delegation to these bodies. Even though most theories on the need for or desirability of regulatory independence stem from the field of political science or law and economics, a good understanding of these rationales is key for this book, which adopts a legal approach to the phenomenon, as well. A substantiated evaluation of the current EU requirements, which will be the subject of Chapters 4 and 5, requires that all relevant considerations, including the results of research on the benefits of regulatory independence, are taken into account. Is the 'IRA' trend indeed substantiated by sufficient and compelling reasons or motives? And how to balance these motives against the (mostly democratic) objections invoked by critics?

The first and primary reason for delegation of IRAs distinguished in the literature revolves around the value of safeguarding the credibility of regulation. Delegating regulatory tasks to an autonomous agent should increase the market's belief in the consistency of regulatory policy. Elected politicians may be tempted to change their policies in election periods in order to secure their re-election, whereas IRAs are not affected or driven by similar concerns. Majone, a rational choice theorist,[186] was among the first to point out that IRAs promote stability and continuity.[187] Independent experts are able to make judgements free from short-term political considerations: they are immune to the so-called 'pro tempore

---

[185] Fabrizio Gilardi, *Delegation in the Regulatory State. Independent Regulatory Agencies in Western Europe* (Edward Elgar Publishing 2008) 5–6, 7–8 and 72.

[186] Mark Bevir, *Democratic Governance* (Princeton University Press 2010) 105.

[187] E.g. Giandomenico Majone, *Temporal Consistency and Policy Credibility: Why Democracies Need Non-Majoritarian Institutions*, EUI Working Paper RSC No. 96/57 (European University Institute, Robert Schuman Centre 1996); Giandomenico Majone, 'The Agency Model: The Growth of Regulation and Regulatory Institutions in the European Union' (1997) 3 Eipascope 1, 2.

nature of democratic governance'[188] and, unlike politicians, are able 'to credibly commit themselves to a long-term strategy'.[189] Politically legitimized institutions are represented as being most likely to adopt short-term visions on the economy and society and lacking the ability to transcend this attitude and to change their behaviour accordingly. Majone's thesis was followed and further developed by others and is currently still widely promulgated.[190] It is also known as the argument of 'time consistency'. Investors who are active in sectors that are particularly infrastructure-reliant, such as the network industries, need guarantees that regulatory policy will not be subject to sudden changes. Consequently, '[t]he creation of independent regulators who apply stable and predictable rules is a way of encouraging investment'.[191] Therefore, it is argued that independent regulators staffed with experts and acting without any political pressure whatsoever are more legitimate supervisory bodies than authorities that are politically steered. Pursuant to the preamble of Directive 2009/140, the most recent directive amending the Framework Directive, '[t]he independence of the national regulatory authorities should be strengthened in order to ensure a more effective application of the regulatory framework and to increase their *authority* and the *predictability* of their decisions'.[192]

The references to 'experts' hint at another, related reason underlying the creation of IRAs, i.e. that of ensuring an independent assessment by specialists in the field. Regulation requires highly technical judgements to be made, which often fall outside the knowledge and skills of elected politicians. Economic choices in these industries are indeed often inextricably linked to scientific judgement. As Rose-Ackerman points out, '[i]ndependence is defended as a way to assure that decisions are

---

188 Giandomenico Majone, *Temporal Consistency and Policy Credibility: Why Democracies Need Non-Majoritarian Institutions*, EUI Working Paper RSC No. 96/57 (European University Institute, Robert Schuman Centre 1996) 18.

189 Giandomenico Majone, 'The Agency Model: The Growth of Regulation and Regulatory Institutions in the European Union' (1997) 3 Eipascope 1, 2.

190 E.g. Fabrizio Gilardi, 'Policy Credibility and Delegation to Independent Regulatory Agencies: A Comparative Empirical Analysis' [2002] Journal of European Public Policy 873; Matthias Finger, 'Towards a European Model of Regulatory Governance?' in David Levi-Faur (ed), *Handbook on the Politics of Regulation* (Edward Elgar Publishing 2011) 525, 527.

191 Phedon Nicolaïdes, 'Regulation of Liberalised Markets: A New Role for the State?' in Damien Geradin, Rodolphe Muñoz and Nicolas Petit (eds), *Regulation through Agencies in the EU. A New Paradigm of European Governance* (Edward Elgar Publishing 2005) 23, 30.

192 Recital 13 (emphasis added).

made by neutral professionals with the time and technical knowledge to make competent, apolitical choices'.[193] The core idea seems to be that regulation by elected politicians is at the same time inefficient due to reasons of lack of expertise, and undesirable, inappropriate or even 'suspicious' because, unlike experts, elected politicians are regarded as unpredictable. Consequently, credibility is not just about time consistency, but also about experts being in charge of highly technical fields of policy and making decisions on the basis of objective criteria.[194]

For the proponents of the 'credible commitment' argument, however, removing the influence of elected politicians from regulatory decision making is a goal as such, not a mere side-effect of the desire to entrust experts with these missions. This is also the reason why some have pointed out that principal-agent theory cannot serve as an explanatory model for delegation to IRAs, as a type of APBs:

> Principal-agent models argue that principals tend to choose agents that are as similar to them as possible in terms of preferences, and tend to control the behavior of the agent in sophisticated ways. By contrast, delegation to IRAs is characterized by the fact that these do not necessarily share the views of their political principals, and second that they are deliberately made independent from political influence.[195]

The independence of regulators should first and foremost be regarded as a means to achieve 'apolitical decision making'.[196] This does not, however, imply that the decisions made by IRAs are not political in nature or have no political implications. Grønnegård Christensen contrasts credible commitment theory to public interest theory (closely connected to the concept of a classic Weberian administration), in which

---

[193] Susan Rose-Ackerman, 'The Regulatory State' in Michel Rosenfeld and András Sajó (eds), *The Oxford Handbook of Comparative Constitutional Law* (Oxford University Press 2012) 671, 676.

[194] E.g. Dawn Oliver, 'Regulation, Democracy and Democratic Oversight in the UK' in Dawn Oliver, Tony Prosser and Richard Rawlings (eds), *The Regulatory State: Constitutional Implications* (Oxford University Press 2010) 243, 251.

[195] Fabrizio Gilardi, *Delegation in the Regulatory State. Independent Regulatory Agencies in Western Europe* (Edward Elgar Publishing 2008) 28–30. See also Dawn Oliver, 'Regulation, Democracy and Democratic Oversight in the UK' in Dawn Oliver, Tony Prosser and Richard Rawlings (eds), *The Regulatory State: Constitutional Implications* (Oxford University Press 2010) 243, 248.

[196] David Levi-Faur, 'The Regulatory State and Regulatory Capitalism: An Institutional Perspective' in David Levi-Faur (ed), *Handbook on the Politics of Regulation* (Edward Elgar Publishing 2011) 662, 666.

bureaucrats could be compared to robots, since the administration neither 'adds to nor subtracts from the policy decided by law makers'. The author considers the latter approach to be a naive one.[197] Credible commitment theory, on the other hand, recognizes the role that NRAs, as administrative bodies, play in creating regulatory policy and points at the benefits of such a system:

> The regulatory bureaucrat of credible commitment theory is a technocrat, ideally an economist, who applies her analytic insights to the device of solutions furthering the public interest in terms of economic efficiency. The idea is that these analytical skills are applicable both in decisions on individual cases and in the making of general policy. Thus credible commitment theory does not see the motivation of bureaucrats as a potential problem for regulation in the public interest.[198]

The European Commission has recognized that credible commitment has been the main rationale behind the obligations regarding NRAs' independence in the liberalization directives for the energy sector.[199]

Apart from time consistency and expertise, other motives occur in the discourse on the desirability of regulatory independence as well, but these are often seen as derivatives of those two main motives. One such motive that is often mentioned is that of shifting blame:[200] regulatory decisions may be unpopular or may entail a high risk of failure, implying that the government prefers to renounce any direct responsibility for them.

To this list of motives distinguished in political science literature, at least one other rationale should be added that is specific to the EU. Within an EU context, 'the potential conflict of interest arising when the

---

[197] Jørgen Grønnegård Christensen, 'Competing Theories of Regulatory Governance: Reconsidering Public Interest Theory of Regulation' in David Levi-Faur (ed), *Handbook on the Politics of Regulation* (Edward Elgar Publishing 2011) 96, 97.

[198] ibid 98.

[199] Commission, interpretative note regulatory authorities, 6: 'These provisions on the independence of the NRA's staff and persons responsible for their management are key requirements because they are aimed at ensuring that regulatory decisions are not affected by political and specific economic interests, thereby creating a stable and predictable investment climate.'

[200] Tom Christensen and Per Lægreid, 'Agencification and Regulatory Reforms' in Tom Christensen and Per Lægreid (eds), *Autonomy and Regulation, Coping with Agencies in the Modern State* (Edward Elgar Publishing 2006) 8, 35; Christopher Hood, *The Blame Game. Spin, Bureaucracy, and Self-Preservation in Government* (Princeton University Press 2011) 122.

state is both responsible for the regulation of the sector and holds a significant interest in one of the players (the incumbent)'[201] also constitutes an important motivation behind the independence requirements enshrined in the directives.[202] This rationale is related to the historical configuration of the network industries and more precisely to the role that many governments in Europe assumed with regard to their functioning prior to liberalization: that of operator or service provider, typically in a monopolist's position. Currently, some of these enterprises or their successors still operate in these markets, but now in a competitive environment. These companies can either be partly or entirely government-owned. Moreover, sometimes governments hold golden shares in companies that they do not necessarily have a historical tie with and that are currently active as market players as well. If the minister who is ultimately responsible for the success and well-being of such a government enterprise is at the same time able to influence the decisions of the regulatory body, there is a real chance of a conflict of interest arising. Cutting all the ties between the regulator and the government in terms of possibilities of steering and supervision is often considered the best way of preventing such conflicts and their harmful consequences from occurring. Thus, regulatory independence from the government aims 'to prevent any temptation to protect or artificially support the "national champion"'.[203] 'In that sense, the independence of the NRA from the legislature and the executive was an extension of the separation of regulatory and operational functions', Hancher and Larouche point out, referring to telecoms legislation, where the independence requirement has for a long time been exclusively linked to ownership of, or control on, the market players.[204] Nonetheless, even if Member States have no direct interest in any of the market players, 'regulatory decisions

[201] Leigh Hancher and Pierre Larouche, 'The Coming of Age of EU Regulation of Network Industries and Services of General Economic Interest' in Paul Craig and Grainne de Búrca (eds), *The Evolution of EU Law* (Oxford University Press 2011) 743, 773.

[202] Susan Rose-Ackerman, 'The Regulatory State' in Michel Rosenfeld and András Sajó (eds), *The Oxford Handbook of Comparative Constitutional Law* (Oxford University Press 2012) 671, 676–677.

[203] Emmanuel Cabeau, 'National Regulatory Authorities' in Christopher Jones (ed), *EU Energy Law, Vol. I, The Internal Energy Market, The Third Liberalisation Package* (Claeys & Casteels 2010) 217, 222–223.

[204] Leigh Hancher and Pierre Larouche, 'The Coming of Age of EU Regulation of Network Industries and Services of General Economic Interest' in Paul Craig and Grainne de Búrca (eds), *The Evolution of EU Law* (Oxford University Press 2011) 743, 773–774.

still have to be made in an environment which is shielded from undue influence as much as possible'.[205] The goals of making regulation consistent over time and ensuring that regulatory decisions are based on expert judgements explain why, currently, the independence requirements that are imposed by the most recent directives are not exclusively directed towards Member States that are still – in the quality of (partial) owner of a government-owned enterprise – operating as a market player in the relevant sectors themselves.[206]

One could argue that the three main rationales or values behind the creation of IRAs, i.e. time consistency, expertise and avoiding conflicts of interest,[207] all contribute to a single, overall goal, i.e. making market supervision sufficiently *credible*.

Are any of these rationales that apply for network regulators also relevant for NHRIs such as DPAs? The logical justification for NHRI independence is that they are still primarily supposed to monitor and control the acts and behaviour of state actors, which makes political interference inappropriate. Despite evolutions towards direct and indirect horizontal effects of human rights, these rights are still primarily enforced in the citizen–state relationship. Consequently, government actors are the direct subjects of most human rights obligations. If central government and mainly the political executive becomes too involved in the supervisory tasks of NHRIs, a conflict of interest is likely to emerge.[208] In *Commission/Germany*, the ECJ substantiated the need to screen national DPAs from 'any external influence' with a concern for ensuring 'the effectiveness and reliability of the supervision'.[209] This reliability argument can be linked to the credibility motive mentioned above. In its assessment of the compatibility of the German system of government supervision at the level of the *Länder*, the court more

---

[205] ibid 773–774.

[206] About this (partial) shift in rationale behind the independence requirements, see also Gabriel Eckert, 'L'indépendance des autorités de régulation économique à l'égard du pouvoir politique' [2012] RFAP 629, 630–634.

[207] See Fabrizio Gilardi and Martino Maggetti, 'The Independence of Regulatory Authorities' in David Levi-Faur (ed), *Handbook on the Politics of Regulation* (Edward Elgar Publishing 2011) 201, 205, where a lack of bias vis-à-vis the incumbent via delegation to IRAs is regarded as an aspect of 'credibility' as well.

[208] Anne Smith, 'The Unique Position of National Human Rights Institutions: A Mixed Blessing?' [2006] Human Rights Quarterly 904, 909: '[S]tates are creating institutions that will or should act as a watchdog of the very body that created them.'

[209] Para 25.

specifically referred to the possible conflicts of interest that could arise. Remarkably, the conflict-of-interest argument was here applied to a situation in which the monitoring body was not supervising the government itself, since the DPAs at stake only supervised non-public bodies. The validity of this line of reasoning is further addressed in Chapter 4.

The clue for another important rationale is found in the requirements on the composition of the APBs in question. As far as the DPAs are concerned, the 2016 regulation provides that each member of the supervisory authority 'shall have the qualifications, experience and skills, in particular in the area of the protection of personal data, required to perform its duties and exercise its powers'.[210] Hence, the need for independence is at least partly located in the wish to secure expert decision making.

Just as in the case of IRAs, both of these values – avoiding conflicts of interest and enabling expert decision making – can be seen as conditions for credible decision making. Literature on NHRIs also explicitly refers to the notion of 'credibility' in order to explain the expedience of political autonomy.[211] The political neutrality of NHRIs and their commitment to human rights inspire public confidence.[212] NHRIs are, moreover, considered 'more likely to be able to guarantee a certain expertise which is free from any politically partisan approach'.[213] The EU still relies on the administration of its member or contracting states to implement the law that it creates and to make sure it is effectively applied at the national level. For reasons of credibility, the EU increasingly regards apolitical implementation as an important guarantee of the success of its projects. This applies to both IRAs and DPAs or the supervisory bodies responsible for the monitoring of the legislation on

---

[210] Article 53, para 2.

[211] Anne Smith, 'The Unique Position of National Human Rights Institutions: A Mixed Blessing?' [2006] Human Rights Quarterly 904, 904, 906 and 909; Rachel Murray, 'National Human Rights Institutions. Criteria and Factors for Assessing Their Effectiveness' (2007) 25(2) Netherlands Quarterly of Human Rights 189, 211; Sonia Cardenas, 'Emerging Global Actors: The United Nations and National Human Rights Institutions' (2003) 9 Global Governance 23, 38.

[212] Anne Smith, 'The Unique Position of National Human Rights Institutions: A Mixed Blessing?' [2006] Human Rights Quarterly 904, 925.

[213] Brice Dickson, 'The Contribution of Human Rights Commissions to the Protection of Human Rights' [2003] Public Law 272, 278; Rachel Murray, 'National Human Rights Institutions. Criteria and Factors for Assessing Their Effectiveness' (2007) 25(2) Netherlands Quarterly of Human Rights 189, 212.

combating discrimination. The status of independent supervisor is associated with integrity, quality and freedom from bias, characteristics that the political executive is not always and under all circumstances able to guarantee.

A side-effect of granting political autonomy to national administrative bodies that implement EU law is that these entities become more dependent on another public authority: that of the supranational organization. Paradoxically, research has revealed that EU law often has a 'centralizing effect' on Member States. The EU usually has a strong preference for centralization, since this facilitates communication between EU institutions and national governments and makes it easier to identify those responsible for the implementation of EU law.[214] The adoption of independence requirements for NRAs has been the result of a compromise. Whereas the European Commission would ultimately have preferred European agencies to regulate the market (with the help of NRAs), the Member States did not share that preference and in return agreed to reinforce the position of NRAs. Consequently, their independence from national governments was explicitly anchored in the directives and their competences and powers were extended. NRAs' independence from the government at the national level, combined with the existence of European networks in which the Commission assumes an active role, nevertheless reinforce the Commission's grip on national regulation.[215] Whereas NRAs can no longer be subject to supervision by national political actors, they are increasingly made subject to supervision by the Commission, via network participation, reporting obligations and sometimes even veto rights. Some literature argues that agencies at the national level that operate at arm's length from ministries are 'stable partners' for the European Commission when it comes to the implementation of EU directives: 'In order to enhance the degree of consistency and harmonization across the Union the Commission would benefit from being able to interact directly with parts of national administrations that

---

[214] Jan H Jans, Roel de Lange, Sacha Prechal and Rob Widdershoven, *Europeanisation of Public Law* (Europa Law Publishing 2007) 22.

[215] See e.g. Tom Christensen and Per Lægreid, 'Agencification and Regulatory Reforms' in Tom Christensen and Per Lægreid (eds), *Autonomy and Regulation, Coping with Agencies in the Modern State* (Edward Elgar Publishing 2006) 8, 39 with references.

enjoy a certain leeway for independent action.'[216] This is an important unofficial reason behind the rise of national APBs in the administration of EU law.

B. Evaluation from a Theoretical and Tentative Empirical Viewpoint

a. The validity of the motives behind political independence for supervisors from a theoretical viewpoint

The previous section distinguished three distinct, but intertwined dimensions of credibility. First, the EU requirements on political autonomy discussed in this chapter have in common that they concern entities that are at least partly in charge of the supervision of other state actors. Delegation of these supervisory tasks to APBs neutralizes the risk of conflicting interests, which is one reason why IRAs can enhance the credibility of decision making. Secondly, the expertise that is bundled in the APBs, on their boards and in their staff plays a crucial role for credible decision making. This expertise can relate to specific technical knowledge or to academic or practical experience. Thirdly, and especially in the field of economic regulation, there is yet another dimension to credibility: long-term commitment or consistency.

To justify (the scope of) the current independence requirements in the field of economic regulation, the EU seems to rely on a combination of the three main arguments behind NRA independence sketched above. The preamble to Directive 2009/140, amending the Framework Directive, states that '[t]he independence of the national regulatory authorities should be strengthened in order to ensure a more effective application of the regulatory framework and to increase their *authority* and the *predictability* of their decisions'.[217] This statement seems to refer to both the expertise argument and that of time consistency. According to Hancher and Larouche, the latest generation of EU liberalization directives, however, also points:

> towards a generalization of the conflict-of-interest rationale: in short, even if Member States have no direct interest in any of the market players, regulatory matters are high-stake games where market players will deploy considerable resources to try to influence the outcome (rent-seeking behavior). Regulatory

---

[216] Morten Egeberg, 'Europe's Executive Branch of Government in the Melting Pot: an Overview' in Morten Egeberg (ed), *Multilevel Union Administration. The Transformation of Executive Politics in Europe* (Palgrave Macmillan 2006) 9–11.

[217] Recital 13 (emphasis added by the author).

> decisions must therefore be made in an environment which is shielded from undue influence as much as possible ...[218]

Reference is made to the preamble of the 2009 directives in both electronic communications and energy, which invoke the avoidance of undue influence as a reason why the independence of NRAs should be strengthened.[219]

There is little doubt about the validity of the conflict-of-interest argument as such: bias is unacceptable in regulatory matters and supervision without an independent relationship between the supervisor and the one who is supervised is no supervision at all.

The same is true for the argument of involving sufficient expertise in the supervisory process. The most obvious way to make sure that all relevant technical and experience-based considerations are taken into account in government decision making is to consult public or private advisory bodies. Sometimes, however, a profound knowledge of the relevant sector or subject is so conclusive to ensuring a desirable outcome that it seems only reasonable to entrust the actual decision-making power to an APB. In those cases, the degree of expertise required to make a justified decision exceeds the degree to which a decision requires thorough political debate. This argument applies to economic regulation in the network sectors and can also be defended for human rights adjudication or monitoring, especially in the area of data protection, which requires sufficient knowledge of e.g. computer science. If public decision making has to be well informed and take place on rational grounds, it is only fair to accept that elected politicians are sometimes not sufficiently knowledgeable or trained to take the lead in certain decision-making processes. Consequently, in some cases, experts have a bigger

---

[218] Leigh Hancher and Pierre Larouche, 'The Coming of Age of EU Regulation of Network Industries and Services of General Economic Interest' in Paul Craig and Grainne de Búrca (eds), *The Evolution of EU Law* (Oxford University Press 2011) 743, 773, 774.

[219] Recital 13 of Directive 2009/140/EC of the European Parliament and of the Council of 25 November 2009 amending Directives 2002/21/EC on a common regulatory framework for electronic communications networks and services, 2002/19/EC on access to, and interconnection of, electronic communications networks and associated facilities, and 2002/20/EC on the authorisation of electronic communications networks and services [2009] OJ L337, 37–69; recitals 33–34 of Directive 2009/72/EC of the European Parliament and of the Council of 13 July 2009 concerning common rules for the internal market in electricity and repealing Directive 2003/54/EC [2009] OJ L211, 55–93.

role to play in administrative decision making, even when coercive measures are involved, than elected politicians.

A motive that is quite specific to economic regulation and that has not or to a far lesser extent played a role in the traditional discourse on APBs in general is that of time consistency. The idea behind this argument is that politicians, because of periodical elections, cannot make commitments for sufficiently long periods to give investors a satisfactory degree of certainty that the government's policy will not be subject to sudden changes. Since the network industries are highly reliant on large-scale infrastructure, they require substantial investments. These need time to become profitable and the possibility of sudden policy shifts is detrimental to that goal.[220] Therefore, attracting investors requires guarantees that regulatory policy will remain reasonably constant over a sufficiently long period of time. According to Majone and the scholarship developed in his footsteps, politicians are likely to change their policies whenever they believe that this will be beneficial to them in an electoral sense, which makes their policies capricious and unpredictable. A non-political body is believed to create more stable policies, to foster investments and to attract new market players, which is crucial for reasons of (sufficient) competition.

Majone's time consistency argument is based on rational choice theory. 'In his view, majority rule is a rational strategy of decision making because unanimity is simply impossible to reach. Yet, if the costs become too high, the rationality of majoritarianism ceases to apply, and non-majoritarian institutions become rational.'[221]

The effect of time consistency on market players' confidence and willingness to invest is considered such a cost of political decision making, which makes governance via non-majoritarian institutions 'a rational response'.[222] It can hardly be denied that consistency and predictability in policy are desirable from a legal viewpoint, since they contribute to legal certainty. However, there is something perverse about the consistency argument as well. It aims to insulate particular sectors from the possibility of politicians changing their minds about the policies to be followed, even when the public interest would require them to do so. One of the basic premises of public law in European democracies is

---

[220] Giandomenico Majone, *Temporal Consistency and Policy Credibility: Why Democracies Need Non-Majoritarian Institutions*, EUI Working Paper RSC No. 96/57 (European University Institute, Robert Schuman Centre 1996).

[221] Mark Bevir, *Democratic Governance* (Princeton University Press 2010) 106–107.

[222] ibid 107.

precisely that the government's duty to promote the public interest may require that government to change its policies. In French-inspired systems, this rule is enshrined in the legal principle (one of the so-called 'lois du service public') of *adaptabilité or mutabilité*. Creating an APB in order to avoid policy fluctuations is consequently at odds with an essential characteristic of administrative decision making. All legal subjects have to endure changes in policy, precisely because the government should constantly evaluate its policies and assess whether these still serve the public interest in the best way possible. Adapting policies to contemporary needs is the core business or duty of politics and politicians. Therefore, it hardly seems justifiable to give a guarantee to a specific group of economic actors that the prevailing policies will be consistent for a certain period. This would create unjustifiable inequalities and disturb the basis of the relationship between government and citizen in public law. Hence, the institutions of representative democracy should not a priori renounce their influence in a given public sector for the benefit of any group of legal subjects.

Inequality, however, is not the only legal objection to political insulation with the aim of achieving consistency. The legitimacy of government decisions cannot be assessed on the basis of the opinions of those directly affected by them (investors) only. These decisions yield wider consequences and may affect other areas of public intervention and other stakeholders. This is especially problematic in light of the fact that, today more than ever, policy domains are strongly intertwined. Consequently, the need to adapt policies adopted in one domain can originate from concerns or needs arising in other domains for which the government accepts responsibility. Public decision making therefore requires caution to avoid mutual frustration of policy domains. In order to ensure that all government decisions, including those of APBs, fit the general policy conducted by central government and that none of them are contradictory or impede each other's realization, some kind of (central) political oversight is necessary.

b. The validity of the time consistency claim: Towards more empirical evidence on the preferences of economic actors

The need for empirical evidence Even though time consistency may be based on an invalid claim from a theoretical perspective, it remains a very tempting argument from a practical point of view, considering the concern of attracting investments. Moreover, it seems reasonable and it is to some extent empirically verifiable[223] that time consistency can indeed foster investments and competition. But is there really a direct link between the political independence of regulators and the consistency of their policies? A direct causal link between both is difficult to prove. What can to a certain extent be verified, however, is whether regulatory independence of the type advocated by the current EU requirements is indeed an indispensable and decisive factor in market players' *decisions* whether or not to invest. Are independent regulators indeed 'taken for granted'[224] by regulated parties in this sense? Legal scholarship increasingly takes into account the economic implications of the law, a trend that is reflected in the emergence of the field of 'law and economics', which essentially studies how legal norms affect human (economic) behaviour.[225] This, however, does not mean that lawyers have to take economic theories for granted, even if they are well established. Such theories are falsifiable. Seeking inspiration in van Schaaijk's approach to 'practice-oriented' research[226] and applying this to the topic of regulatory independence, the question arises: *do* the requirements for political independence *work*? Do they more precisely achieve the goal of inspiring confidence in the eyes and minds of market players about the consistency and predictability of regulatory policies? This question probes the *perception* of regulated parties. What is significant about the credible commitment argument is that it does not so much rely on the belief that elected politicians are indeed less likely to produce consistent policies – it would be very hard to test whether the average politician indeed changes his or her mind more often than the average expert – but rather relies on the presumption that this is *what market players assume or expect*. Perception matters in economics: the *presumptions* on which possible candidates for investments base their decision to enter the market or not are relevant. What needs to be tested, consequently, is not whether or not politicians cannot be trusted to transcend their own electoral interests (it would indeed be difficult to falsify this statement), but whether this is what market players *believe*. Empirical research has demonstrated that limitations on policy change in political systems

223 E.g. Witold J. Henisz, 'The Institutional Environment for Infrastructure Investment' [2002] *Industrial and Corporate Change* 355–389.

224 David Levi-Faur, 'Regulation and Regulatory Governance' in David Levi-Faur (ed), *Handbook on the Politics of Regulation* (Edward Elgar Publishing 2011) 11–12.

225 Wolfgang Weigel, *Economics of the Law: A Primer* (Routledge 2008) 3.

226 *Supra*, Chapter 1.

foster investments in infrastructure, without, however, proving that such an outcome requires the establishment of politically independent regulators.[227]

Examples of previous empirical studies Some research on the preferences of market players in this regard has already been performed. The conclusion of a survey of which the results were published in a study of the UK House of Lords on the accountability of the regulatory state, which will be discussed in Chapter 3, was that:

> independence of regulators from Ministers is welcomed by Ministers and is seen as a vital ingredient for maintaining consistency, for ensuring that regulatory decisions are taken by 'competent authorities' (which accords well with current and prospective developments in the governance of the European Union), and for promoting confidence about regulation among the regulated, those investing in regulated enterprises, and the customers and citizens on whose behalf regulation is carried out.[228]

A survey among investors confirmed that 96 per cent of them regarded the independence of the water regulator as particularly important. Similar results were reported for the railway sector.[229] Note that this survey was carried out more than 10 years ago, when liberalization was in an earlier stage, and that it did not reveal much about the precise *degree* of independence that market players expect regulatory bodies to be invested with. A 2010 parliamentary study of the French Assemblée Nationale, also discussed in Chapter 3, ascertained that regulated parties welcomed the political independence enjoyed by the autorités administratives indépendantes (AAIs) in question, but criticized the way in which these bodies interpreted their powers ever more broadly.[230]

A 2012 academic study by the Centre on Regulation in Europe or CERRE, written by Hanretty, Larouche and Reindl, investigated the

---

[227] See Witold J. Henisz, 'The Institutional Environment for Infrastructure Investment' [2002] *Industrial and Corporate Change* 355–389

[228] Select Committee on the Constitution, *The Regulatory State: Ensuring its Accountability* (HL 2003-01, 68-I) 41.

[229] ibid 43.

[230] See Assemblée Nationale No 2925 – Comité d'Évaluation et de Contrôle des Politiques Publiques – *Rapport d'Information sur les Autorités Administratives Indépendantes* par MM. René Dosière et Christian Vanneste, Députés, Tome I: Rapport (2010) 50.

independence, accountability and perceived quality of regulators.[231] The study aimed to 'provide empirical support for the EU approach to the design of regulatory agencies, which combines independence and accountability and seeks to find the optimal balance between them'.[232] The report contained the results of a peer benchmarking exercise, of which the object was 'to elicit attendees' perceptions of the quality of regulators in four sectors – competition, energy, rail and telecoms – in five countries – Belgium, France, Germany, the Netherlands and the United Kingdom. Three groups of experts were involved in the survey: regulators, regulatees and academics.[233] The study found a positive relationship between resources, independence, accountability and perceived quality.[234] Its first broad recommendation was therefore to increase both the independence and accountability of regulators. It argued that the results demonstrated 'that legal literature that emphasizes hard mechanisms (sanctions, annulment, *etc.*) as against softer accountability criteria such as transparency or disclosure, might be misguided'. It emphasized that its results were based on 'judgments of quality provided by informed experts in regulation in selected sectors'.[235] Although the study demonstrated that 'the link between quality and accountability is stronger than the link between quality and independence', it did not want to conclude that:

> regulators should devote all their effort to becoming more accountable, rather than more independent, since more accountability will deliver greater increases in perceived quality. This would be the wrong conclusion to draw, and does not take account of the relationship between independence and accountability. The most natural interpretation of the positive link between independence and accountability is that politicians grant independence if they are satisfied that mechanisms of accountability exist.[236]

---

[231] Chris Hanretty, Pierre Larouche and Andreas Reindl, 'Independence, Accountability and Perceived Quality of Regulators – A CERRE Study', Brussels, 6 March 2012, http://www.cerre.eu/sites/cerre/files/120306_IndependenceAccountabilityPerceivedQualityofNRAs.pdf.

[232] ibid 10.

[233] Each of the experts had to compare the regulators operating in their own country with respect to the quality of their work. Subsequently, they had to compare the regulators operating in the sector in which they were involved for all five countries studied. The leading question was: 'Which regulator does better work?' The complete design of the survey is described at pp. 51ff.

[234] ibid 78.

[235] ibid 83–84.

[236] ibid 83–84.

Although this study contains interesting and valid results, the instrument used by the authors, i.e. a survey, did not allow for an in-depth study of preferences and arguments. For instance, it was not able to assess questions such as *why* precisely regulated parties or other 'informed experts' have a preference for regulatory independence and what role – if any – they still see for elected politicians. On top of that, studies that gauge the quality of regulation do not necessarily reveal anything about its overall (perceived) legitimacy.

Design of and justification for eight in-depth interviews with Belgian market players One can reasonably predict that market players will prefer at least *a* degree of political independence for NRAs. The question arises, however, whether the degree of independence currently required by the EU liberalization directives is necessary to satisfy regulated parties' preferences for regulatory independence. Hardly any evidence has been produced to substantiate the claim that ensuring confidence and credibility in the minds of market players indeed requires precluding political influence on regulatory decisions to such a far-reaching extent. The rest of this chapter presents the results of eight in-depth interviews carried out with market players operating in Belgian network industries, set up in order to gain more insight in their preferences, beliefs, fears and expectations with regard to regulatory independence. Admittedly, it is impossible to get a full perspective on this issue from only eight interviews carried out within just a single legal system. In order to obtain meaningful and reliable results for the EU legal sphere as a whole, an EU-wide empirical test should be set up and all relevant sectors should be involved. The results discussed in the following paragraphs, however, first and foremost want to raise awareness about the danger of taking for granted too easily what seem to be compelling economic arguments for political independence. Moreover, they may give some idea about the possible design of future, more ambitious qualitative empirical work. Thus, their only intention is to deliver a first, exploratory contribution to the development of a more nuanced theory on regulatory credibility.

The interviews departed from Majone's time consistency theory and aimed to verify whether this fits market players' true perceptions. At the same time, they probe the possibility of developing a new, nuanced theory on regulatory independence. This type of qualitative research is not so much concerned with the representativeness of its sample, but more with ensuring a sufficient degree of diversity.[237] Methodological literature suggests that a well-designed qualitative study:

> will usually also provide findings that capture a broad range of experiences rather than those from only a few people or situations. The findings will be representative in the sense of capturing the range or variation in a phenomenon, but not in the sense of allowing for the estimation of the distribution of the phenomenon in the population as a whole.[238]

The sample was limited to players operating in the sectors of energy and electronic communications because of the advanced stage of the liberalization process and the corresponding stage of the provisions on NRA independence for these sectors.

Five of the interviewed market players were active in the energy sector. Diversity was ensured by selecting two grid managers and three producers and/or suppliers. The latter group, moreover, consisted of companies with varied market shares and a different track record on the Belgian market. For the market of electronic communications, the criteria of market share and track record were also used to select and contact potential interviewees. However, despite repeated attempts via different media to contact relatively new and/or small players currently operating on the market, no response was obtained and no interviews could be planned within the relevant time frame. Another criterion was sufficient diversification as to the submarkets on which these companies (primarily) operated: internet, television, fixed or mobile telephony etc. This criterion of diversification was sufficiently achieved.

The position of the interviewees within their company was either manager, director or head of regulatory affairs, director corporate affairs, general counsel or member of the management board in another capacity. All interviewees were promised anonymity in the stage of the publication of the results, both as to the name of their firm and as to their person.

---

[237] Lisa Webley, 'Qualitative Approaches to Empirical Legal Research' in Peter Cane and Herbert M Kritzer (eds), *The Oxford Handbook of Empirical Legal Research* (Oxford University Press 2010) 926, 934: 'Qualitative researchers are not (usually) concerned that these people or situations should be statistically representative because they do not seek to reach findings that are generalizable to an entire population. Instead, focused, in-depth studies are designed to go beyond description, to find meaning, even if that meaning is related to an individual's experiences of the justice system (for instance), or the perceptions of a small number of people on access to justice (for instance).'

[238] ibid 934.

The incumbent Belgian operator in the area of telecommunications was not interviewed because of its quality of government-owned enterprise. Such companies could be biased vis-à-vis the question of the political independence of NRAs, since more political influence on regulatory bodies is likely to benefit them. In other words: there is an element here that applies only to the government-owned company and that may distort the study's result. Since anonymity would have been promised here as well, the study would not have been able to handle the government-owned company's answers to the questions in a different way from the other results. Consequently, it would not have been able to be open about a possible link between the incumbent's (possibly divergent) replies and its position as the government-owned player. In the Belgian energy sector, there is a structural embedment of (holdings of) local communities as shareholders in the grid managers. Since this is the case for all of them, there was no need and no possibility for exclusions here.

The interviews were semi-structured and started out from a list of statements. The interviewees were then asked to what extent they did or did not agree with these statements. The most important results of the interviews are summarized in the following paragraphs.

Results All interviewees agreed that at least a certain degree of political independence for regulatory bodies was desirable. Some, however, did point out that this was not one of their main concerns or not something that they frequently monitored. Two of the interviewees, before even addressing the topic of the regulator's political independence, stressed the importance of regulatory independence vis-à-vis the other market players. One of them explicitly labelled the aspect of political independence as being of 'subordinate' importance in comparison with independence vis-à-vis the regulated parties. Two of the interviewees operating in the sector of electronic communications, however, pointed out that, as long as the incumbent was still operating on the market, political independence constituted a requirement to ensure equal treatment of all market players. The political appointment or affiliation of members on the regulator's board was not as such deemed problematic by these interviewees, as long as all market players were treated equally and as long as the regulator's decisions were sound.

All interviewees regarded the technical expertise of regulators as a valuable characteristic. Most of them agreed that there was a link between political independence and expertise as well as a relationship between expertise and credibility. This was more explicitly stressed (sometimes even multiple times) by the interviewees operating in the energy sector than by those in the sector of electronic communications.

Most interviewees agreed that political independence was likely to be conducive to more stability in the long term, compared with political or politically steered regulation, since regulators are not subject to concerns about being re-elected. Two interviewees, however, put this assumption in perspective. One of them explicitly expressed their belief that there was no relationship whatsoever between the two, referring to the limited tenure of the members of the regulator's board. According to these interviewees, the priorities or accents and the way of working shifted along with the rotation of the personalities on the board of directors. In that sense, consistency would always be relative. Another interviewee was also rather reluctant to associate political independence with consistency too strongly, but did think it likely that the lack of a possibility of constant political interference would indeed make it easier for the regulator to develop a long-term vision. One of the interviewees, moreover, believed that the characteristic feature of regulators that ensures consistency in regulatory policy is the fact that regulators have to act within a theoretical framework that uses objective criteria. Another interviewee regarded the objective nature of the criteria used by the regulator as crucial for its credibility as well. Two other interviewees linked the fact that regulatory decisions had a technical substantiation to the consistency of regulatory policy.

Two of the interviewees expressed their doubts as to the importance of an independent regulator for attracting new investors. Other factors, such as the tax climate and (most importantly) business opportunities are substantially more crucial, both of them observed. Whereas stability was regarded as important, one of these interviewees pointed out that, in the free, Western world, a stable investment climate was taken for granted. The same interviewee, moreover, added that, if stability was a factor, the main problems were located in the lack of legislative stability. The other interviewee explained that regulatory independence was *a* factor, but definitely not a decisive one. They admitted that this had been the case in the 1990s, when the market was just about to abandon its monopoly structure, but was no longer the case today. Moreover, they also regarded the lack of a long-term vision for the legislative framework owing to electoral reasons as problematic in the light of giving confidence to market players, as investors, in the long term. Three other interviewees also stressed the importance of legislative and regulatory stability for investments, but added that the regulator could only do so much: in the end, he can only implement and not amend legislation. In its advisory capacity, however, two of them pointed out, the regulator is able to warn the legislature of the possible harmful effects of legislation in the light of fostering investments. One of the interviewees, who also regarded the policy adopted by the legislature as crucial in terms of return on investment, indicated that they welcomed this division of competences from a democratic viewpoint. The role and duty of the regulator is (only) to advise the legislature on the basis of its expertise, this person pointed out. Yet another interviewee agreed that the stability of the legislative framework was more important than regulatory independence if the aim was to attract investors. A market player that had only recently started their activities, moreover, confirmed that the political independence of the regulator had not played a decisive role in their decision to enter the market, whereas concerns about unclear legislation had indeed caused some hesitation.

A few statements related to the proper division of competences between politicians and regulators in the eyes of the market players. One interviewee believed that it was not for the regulator to decide on policy matters, using the striking metaphor: '[a] police officer should not make the traffic rules'. The same interviewee, however, regarded the advisory capacity of the regulator as especially important, also when it comes to the development of policy. When the Government exercises its own competences and prepares decisions or measures that it deems politically desirable, it is up to the regulator, as an expert, to inform the Government about the technical feasibility as well as the reconcilability of its plans with the economic structure of the market and about possible risks of distortion of competition. This is especially true when the regulator is also appointed as the body responsible for implementing these measures, the interviewee pointed out.

Another interviewee expressed largely similar concerns: they pointed out that the regulator sometimes acts as a 'pure administrative extension' of the minister when it implements policy, which hampers its independence. This interviewee regarded the fact that regulators are increasingly entrusted with tasks of implementation in sensitive political domains such as consumer protection as compromising for their credibility. That the regulator had to take a variety of considerations, such as consumer protection, into account in a broader assessment process was not as such regarded as problematic, but it was felt that the main focus or mission had to be competition-oriented. The same interviewee pointed out that the idea behind a sector regulator is that, after a while, the necessity for it is supposed to be lost, enabling it to disappear. Instead, however, at present, the interviewee pointed out, the Government entrusts the regulator with additional missions that do not fit its original remit. According to the interviewee, it was clear that these new missions had to rest with the Government, since somebody had to assume political responsibility for them.

Yet another interviewee, a supplier in electricity and gas, had the impression that the regulator profiled itself on social policy, whereas they thought it had to concentrate more on the actual regulation of the market. They declared that the choices in the area of social policy had to be made by politicians, not regulators and/or that a stronger political influence in this area was desirable. When asked to explain how regulatory decisions touched upon social policy, this player referred to the regulator's power to decide on tariffs. When asked whether they would prefer a totally independent regulator, or one that was partly or entirely politically steered, they replied that limited political steering would be preferable. This was not deemed harmful for the (development of the) market, even though they did think it likely that a change of government or minister would also result in shifting policies and would therefore have an effect on regulatory stability. The same interviewee declared that the vague nature of the legislative framework had constituted a serious hurdle in the attempt of their company to enter the market. In the phase of preparing its application to obtain a permit to enter the market, this player had noticed, along the way, that the legislative framework left a lot of doubt as to the precise content of the applicable criteria. They added that the regulator had been given too much room for interpretation or discretion by the legislation, which made too much use of open terminology and norms. Moreover, they had the impression that the regulator used its discretion in individual cases without keeping a clear line. The same interviewee declared that regulation could never be free of a political vision, since the sector generated primary needs for people. The possibility of control and rectifying measures by politicians was therefore deemed important.

Another interviewee agreed that decisions such as those on tariffs or tariff methodology in the energy sector had to be taken by the regulator and not by politicians. At the same time, however, they acknowledged that tariff decisions are highly complex and closely intertwined with certain policy objectives. Because these decisions have an impact on investments, they, for instance, indirectly influence the extent to which a policy promoted by the Government on renewable energy, decentralized production or security of supply will succeed. In that regard, they acknowledged that the question of who should have which powers (the regulator or politicians) was not an easy one to answer. Another interviewee referred to a declaration made by one of the Belgian regulators that it would only assume tasks of implementation, as defined by the European directives, and did not wish to be burdened with political assessments. According to the interviewee, this was a sane decision, but many of the regulator's decision-making powers were located on the edge or borderline of politics or strategy and implementation and this could give rise to difficulties. This interviewee regarded it as crucial that the Government keep the power to decide on strategies in their sector, because that same Government had to be able to take responsibility for these decisions.

One interviewee observed that, from a democratic viewpoint, some decisions that were currently taken by regulatory bodies did not belong there and should be the subject of debates in Parliament. The interviewee, for instance, expressed their concerns about the possibility that the energy regulator would in the future deem itself competent to decide on the possible introduction of a 'single tariff' at the regional level. Such a tariff would imply that people living in rural, non-urban areas would henceforth pay an equal amount of money for the distribution of electricity as people living in cities. According to the interviewee, social considerations were involved, which required political decision making. 'Too many competences go to the regulator, of which I think that they require societal choices, which do not belong with a regulator,' they indicated. Even though the interviewee indicated that their company was not overly concerned, either with the political independence of the regulator, or with the division of competences between regulators and politicians, they indicated that the company did feel more comfortable if certain political choices were made via the process of parliamentary debate. This interviewee, however, made a clear distinction between policy, which belonged to the area of parliamentary democracy, and technical execution, which in their opinion, was an undisputed task of the regulator. Tariff methodology was therefore a matter for the regulator to decide on, but Parliament had to be able to ensure that the policy guidelines that it issued were indeed complied with. The interviewee also referred to the regulatory decisions of whether or not to introduce injection tariffs, an issue closely intertwined with policy objectives of stimulating renewable energy. Since this is a political choice, the input of Parliament has to remain possible. According to the same interviewee, it was a good thing that EU legislation left room for policy guidelines, but it was unclear how far these could reach. Still according to this market player, input on matters of policy 'had nothing to do with a regulator being a puppet on the string of politicians'. Another interviewee had a similar viewpoint, pointing out that it is not because the regulator and politicians talk to each other, that the former are not independent and that such conversation could not lead to a better understanding of each other's positions.

Two interviewees acknowledged that tariff decisions also involved the allocation of costs between families, small and large companies and so on. They observed that such decisions were dependent on political preferences. For the first interviewee, this was a reason to increase the influence of elected politicians. For the second, who added that the regulator had deliberately been entrusted with such discretionary powers (which were not merely technical), it was not. The latter interviewee, however, added that they were definitely not in favour of a regulator that would take severe political decisions for which it could not assume political accountability. They believed, however, that the legislative framework offered a good delineation of the regulator's tasks. This interviewee referred to situations in the past where the regulator had made attempts to substitute political decisions with its own judgement. In such cases, the regulator loses credibility, in the eyes of both politicians and market players. Another interviewee was also of the opinion that the regulator itself should have the room to make trade-offs between the different policy guidelines that it has to comply with, albeit on the basis of the input of stakeholders. Interest groups such as consumer organizations were mentioned, but especially consultation of the sector itself was deemed important in order to ensure that the regulator would make well-informed decisions. Political input was deemed unnecessary in this regard: the regulator was considered able to take the decision itself, relying on the input of stakeholders.

One interviewee pointed out that they regarded the continued existence of certain types of political supervision at the level of the decisions taken by the regulator as detrimental to its independence. Even though the Government had never before used this power, its mere existence was, according to the interviewee, problematic, because there was a risk that the regulator would feel obliged to comply with the Government's desires when taking 'strategic' decisions in order to prevent the latter feeling obliged to use its power. In this way, the Government's supervisory powers would to a certain extent create an atmosphere of 'preconditioning'. According to this interviewee, the legislative framework within which the regulator has to operate offered sufficient democratic legitimacy. Supervisory powers for the Government would consequently create 'a double democratic layer', which was, according to the interviewee, redundant.

Discussion The results of the interviews contain a diversity of opinions and statements. Each interviewee had their own points that they wished to stress and formulated their own nuances. It was not possible to identify any meaningful overall differences between opinions expressed by representatives of the energy sector on the one hand and those of the sector of electronic communications on the other. In both sectors, there were proponents of regulators with an extensive mandate and a substantial degree of political independence as well as critics or market players who adopted a more nuanced position. Within the energy sector, moreover, differences did not run along the lines of the size of the suppliers that were interviewed, nor did the suppliers adopt a radically different view compared with the grid managers.

Although the sample of this series of interviews was small and limited to just one country, the following tentative conclusions could be drawn.

- Market players agree that network regulators should enjoy at least some degree of political autonomy.
- Most interviewees believe that the goal of achieving regulatory stability will not primarily be achieved by making regulators politically independent, although it can play a (subordinate) role. Many indeed declare that the main problem in terms of stability is located in the frequent changes in legislation. However, none of the interviewees who deemed this lack of continuity to be problematic regarded this legislative intervention as illegitimate or contended that further delegations to the regulator were necessary. On the contrary: they acknowledged that the legislature was entitled to make legislation in the policy areas concerned, which has to be implemented by the regulator. In other words: stability is most needed in those areas where the decision-making power is not in the hands of the regulator. At the same time, there is a general acknowledgement that these powers should not be part of the remit of an independent regulator, although some believe that the regulator should be more (pro)active as an independent, expert advisory body to the Government and legislature.
- As a consequence, the importance of a politically independent regulator in the light of the goal of attracting investors, because such a body would foster regulatory stability, seems at least overrated. There was a general feeling that other factors play a much more crucial role in such decision-making processes. Most of these are not related to the regulatory environment as such, but some are. Again, legislative uncertainty was identified as a key concern.
- None of the interviewees was in favour of entrusting regulatory bodies with tasks of (broad) policy definition. On the contrary, sometimes off-loading policy responsibility to regulators was deemed detrimental to their credibility. Some of the interviewees

explicitly linked this concern to the notion of political responsibility, which can be hollowed when regulators assume too many policy-making powers.

- The opinions as to where to draw the line precisely do, however, differ. Most of the interviewees explicitly acknowledged (and the others did not deny) that apparently technical decisions sometimes require important policy trade-offs. Especially in the energy sector, the interpretative or discretionary powers enjoyed by the regulators (and delegated to them by European or domestic legislation) were deemed problematic by the majority of the interviewees. All of these interviewees, however, thought it particularly challenging to offer a clear-cut solution to this problem. All of them recognized that the primary decision-making power had to rest with the regulator, but that politicians had to make sure that their influence over policy matters remained intact. Most of the interviewees did not have an immediate answer to the question of how to achieve that outcome. Two interviewees (one in energy, one in electronic communications), however, were of the opinion that these trade-offs should be the full responsibility of the regulator and that, on this level, no political input was required, since the legislative framework already provided for a sufficient democratic basis. Input by interested parties was, however, regarded as crucial in this phase.
- A general tendency in the majority of the interviews was that market parties seem more concerned about, and attach more importance to, the technical expertise embodied by (independent) regulatory bodies than to consistency as such. Some, however, link the two: the use of objective criteria and/or the ability to substantiate decisions in a way that is technically sound adds to consistency in regulatory decision making and to the credibility of NRAs.
- Apart from expertise, equal treatment of all market players, including the incumbent, was labelled as a key concern.

Conclusion With the interviews an attempt was made to offer an account of what it is that the economic actors operating in the network industries expect in terms of regulatory independence or governance more broadly. The interviews offer an indication that the time consistency theory that is often invoked to justify the extensive mandate given to NRAs, combined with a far-reaching degree of political independence, should at least be nuanced. Considering that the market players themselves see only a limited correlation between the political independence of regulators on the one hand and continuity or stability in regulatory matters on the other, time consistency does not seem a sufficient reason to substantiate the particularly far-reaching standards of political autonomy imposed by the EU legislature. Whereas the importance of regulatory stability remains intact, the solution, according to most interviewees, should not or not primarily be found in the political independence of the NRA, nor in an increase of its political power. On the contrary, all interviewees agree that policy should be developed by the legislature, even if that legislature is at the basis of much regulatory uncertainty. A majority of the interviewees nevertheless observed that regulators are increasingly involved in policy making. Whereas some players regard the current division of decision-making competences between those who are politically responsible and the regulator as sound, many, especially in the energy sector, worry about the thin line between policy definition and implementation, especially when trade-offs have to be made. This also puts the assertion that market players are in demand of regulators with broad mandates, often proclaimed by proponents of politically independent regulators and currently also assumed by EU legislation, in perspective.

The results of these interviews do not present a strong case for the time consistency argument. They do, however, demonstrate that two other central reasons behind regulatory independence identified above are of considerable importance to market players. Technical expertise and the objectivity of the criteria for assessment used by these experts are regarded as crucial assets of a politically independent regulator. Moreover, political independence is regarded as necessary to ensure that market players are treated without discrimination, especially vis-à-vis the incumbent.

c. Conclusion: Expertise and avoiding bias as the two main rationales behind the independence of NRAs

In order to decide how to mediate between autonomy and political input in regulatory matters, it is important to give the correct weight to each of the possible motives behind political autonomy. It has been argued that the time consistency or credible commitment argument leads to more far-reaching forms of political autonomy than other motives for creating APBs. Thatcher and Stone Sweet point out that commitment problems lead to a decrease of *ex post* controls by principals on agents and that this is to a lesser extent the case when the non-majoritarian institution has been established for reasons of lack of expertise:

> Where delegation takes place in order to secure credible commitment, principals cannot impose many ex post controls over the agent without undermining the very purpose of delegation. The more acute the commitment

> problem that principals face (or believe they face), the more discretion they will delegate – for example, in enforcing EU law or in monetary policy. Where officials delegate to increase technical efficiency, reduce their workload, or improve their information, extensive ex post controls are often more compatible with objectives.[239]

Consequently, if one accepts that expertise and avoiding bias rather than time consistency should be regarded as the primary motives behind regulatory independence, then this has implications for the degree of political autonomy that one can reasonably expect to be granted to regulatory authorities. This argument will be central to the analysis in Chapter 4.

---

[239] Mark Thatcher and Alec Stone Sweet, 'Theory and Practice of Delegation to Non-Majoritarian Institutions' 25(1) (2002) West European Politics 1, 14–15.

3. National restraint

1. SETTING THE SCENE

A. A Retrospective, Yet Visionary Approach to APBs

> Il faut maintenant cesser cette 'course à l'échalote' où l'on crée toujours plus d'AAI: il est tout aussi important de savoir finir que de savoir commencer ce mouvement.[1]

In most European legal systems, the rise of APBs has long remained devoid of a proper legal theory on the creation, institutional design and functioning of these bodies. As pointed out earlier, legal academia has been relatively late in developing any real and sustained interest in the subject. More recently, however, a legal movement has started to deploy in many European states, which is characterized by a reticent stance towards APBs. The criticism often adopts a retrospective view, reconsidering past initiatives, but it also results in reflections about future desirable attitudes vis-à-vis APBs. Gradually, governments and legislatures are becoming more reluctant to create APBs and/or more inclined to give their establishment or preservation more consideration. This legal movement is closely related to subjects of scholarly research in political science known under terms such as 'whole of government'[2] or 'post-NPM'[3] movements. In this context, it has been acknowledged that 'there is now a search for reform concept[s] and models that recognize the embeddedness of public management in the larger context of democratic

---

[1] Assemblée Nationale N° 2925 – Comité d'Évaluation et de Contrôle des Politiques Publiques – *Rapport d'Information sur les Autorités Administratives Indépendantes* par MM. René Dosière et Christian Vanneste, Députés, Tome I: Rapport (2010) 69. Hereinafter: Assemblée Nationale, *Rapport sur les AAIs*, I (2010).

[2] See e.g. Koen Verhoest, Sandra Van Thiel, Geert Bouckaert and Per Lægreid, 'Introduction' in Koen Verhoest, Sandra Van Thiel, Geert Bouckaert and Per Lægreid (eds), *Government Agencies Practices and Lessons from 30 Countries* (Palgrave Macmillan 2012) 3, 10 with references.

[3] ibid 4.

government that, indeed, sees public management as an instrument for strengthening democratic governance'.[4] As early as 2002, the OECD established that:

> in most countries, priorities have moved away from the need to create new separate bodies to the challenge of finding the right balance between accountability and autonomy, openness, performance management, as well as strengthening the steering capacity of central ministries … In some countries, 'whole-of-government' issues such as how to ensure policy coherence or a coherent public service, or how to maintain the clarity of the administrative organisational system, have also arisen as crucial issues.[5]

Both movements question the same phenomena, but use different criteria of assessment. This recent restraint towards APBs has indeed generated new research questions for political scientists[6] as well as legal scholars. As Olsen ascertains, '[a] new generation of post-NPM studies is concerned with central political capacity and coordination and how public administration can be made more responsive to elected leaders'.[7] It is, however, the translation of these concerns to *legal discourse* and scholarship that forms the object of the analysis in this chapter.

The criteria used by lawyers to criticize uncurbed APB creation are those fundamental constitutional principles that govern administrative organization and that have to some extent been threatened by the proliferation of APBs in the past. This chapter will identify a common denominator of such principles in four European legal systems and will examine how the creation of APBs interferes with them. This type of

---

4 J Jean-Michel Eymeri-Douzans and Jon Pierre, 'Conclusion' in Jean-Michel Eymeri-Douzans and Jon Pierre (eds), *Administrative Reforms and Democratic Governance* (Routledge 2011) 202, 205.

5 OECD, *Distributed Public Governance*, 21–22.

6 See the questions raised in e.g. Tom Christensen and Per Lægreid, 'Rebalancing the State: Reregulation and the Reassertion of the Centre' in Tom Christensen and Per Lægreid (eds), *Autonomy and Regulation, Coping with Agencies in the Modern State* (Edward Elgar Publishing 2006) 359, 362.

7 Johan P Olsen, 'Democratic Government, Institutional Autonomy and the Dynamics of Change' (2009) 32(3) West European Politics 439, 453 with reference to Tom Christensen and Per Lægreid (eds), *Autonomy and Regulation, Coping with Agencies in the Modern State* (Edward Elgar Publishing 2006); Tom Christensen and Per Lægreid (eds), *Transcending New Public Management. The Transformation of Public Sector Reforms* (Ashgate 2011).

analysis corresponds to what Mackor calls a non-empirical law description.[8] It uses rules and principles of constitutional value as intra-legal criteria.

Subsequently, this chapter will demonstrate how APBs are being 'reinvented' to better fit these principles. Any process of 'rethinking' something is naturally contemplative or reflective in nature. There is a risk that this type of exercise mainly takes place in the heads of legal scholars, with no guarantee of it having any real impact on the status of APBs in positive law. This is, however, not the case for the legal movement studied in this chapter, which will explain how legislatures and governments, as recipients of these ideas, have considered them appealing starting points for reform initiatives and have started to adapt their policies on the establishment of APBs accordingly.

A remarkable way in which states have been doing precisely this is via the enactment of framework legislation aiming to rationalize decisions on the creation and the institutional design of APBs. Another conclusion of the 2002 OECD study mentioned earlier was that governments were 'striving to improve institutional clarity' on two levels: first, '[a]t the systemic level, by clarifying the types of agencies, authorities, and other government bodies and their accountability mechanisms; establishing some general principles for their good governance; improving the legal basis of autonomous bodies; and setting government-wide criteria for their establishment'; secondly, '[a]t the level of agencies, authorities and other bodies, by justifying the choice of organisational form and accountability mechanisms, and by improving transparency on agency tasks and performance'.[9] These very issues are at the core of the rationale behind framework legislation, being an innovative legal instrument in the attempts of national legislatures to rationalize the APB landscape.

B. Selection of European Legal Systems: Justification

This chapter studies four national legal systems within the European legal sphere, all EU Member States. It attempts to identify a common core of principles and to investigate whether recent reforms have indeed been inspired by common concerns. Comparative legal analysis is often focused on identifying, explaining and appreciating differences between legal systems. This study, on the contrary, uses the comparative method

8 *Supra*, Chapter 1.

9 OECD, *Distributed Public Governance*, 28.

in order to bring to the surface similarities and more precisely common core principles from which a European theory on APBs can be deduced.[10]

The legal systems selected for this study are Belgium, France, the Netherlands and the UK. The question may arise whether this selection is reconcilable with the aim of this comparative analysis. In order to identify common European principles, the selection of systems should be sufficiently significant for the European legal sphere. The representativeness of the results is likely to increase with the number of legal systems studied. Within the scope of this monograph, however, only a limited number of systems can be studied thoroughly. European public or administrative law, however, can more or less be divided into three main spheres of influence or three distinct traditions: those of France, Germany and the UK.

Of these three systems, only Germany does not figure in the selection. The reason for this exclusion is that Germany is generally regarded as 'the odd man out' when it comes to the proliferation of APBs within Europe. It is often emphasized in the literature that the German system has indeed managed to remain relatively immune to the 'APB madness' that came over Europe some 30 years ago.[11] Döhler describes Germany an 'agency laggard'.[12] Rose-Ackermann ascertains that 'in Germany faith in the capacity of the legislature and executive to define and pursue

---

[10] On this use of comparative administrative law, see Giacinto della Cananea, 'Administrative Law in Europe: A Historical and Comparative Perspective' [2010] Online Italian Journal of Public Law 162 and in particular 209. The approach also fits von Bogdandy's '*Ius Publicum Europaeum*': Armin von Bogdandy, 'Comparative Constitutional Law: A Contested Domain – A. Comparative Constitutional Law: A Continental Perspective' in Michel Rosenfeld and András Sajó (eds), *The Oxford Handbook of Comparative Constitutional Law* (Oxford University Press 2012) 25, 34–36.

[11] E.g. Jacques Ziller, 'Les autorités administratives indépendantes entre droit interne et droit de l'Union européenne' [2010] RFDA 901, 906.

[12] Marian Döhler, 'Institutional Choice and Bureaucratic Autonomy in Germany' (2002) 25(1) West European Politics 101, 101–102. See also Daniel Halberstam, 'The Promise of Comparative Administrative Law: A Constitutional Perspective on Independent Agencies' in Susan Rose-Ackerman and Peter L Lindseth (eds), *Comparative Administrative Law* (Edward Elgar Publishing 2010) 185, 185.

rational policy remains reasonably strong. Outside certain narrow, functionally specific domains, there are few calls for independent administrative agencies.'[13]

Since Germany has never experienced proliferation of APBs comparable to that in most other European systems,[14] there is no trend of 'national restraint'. What Germany shares with European systems in which a legal movement of restraint is currently observed is, however, the rationale behind this maintained (Germany) respectively sudden (many other European states) reserve towards APBs. Arguably, the very same concerns that now dominate the trend of 'national restraint' have been at the basis of Germany's sustained reluctance to allow APBs to become a dominant model of administrative organization in the first place. If Germany has never truly participated in the 'agency-fashion' adopted by its neighbouring countries, this is so because the German system – to a greater extent than most other European systems – has acknowledged that these reforms derogated from fundamental constitutional principles, from which it was unwilling to depart. If Germany does not figure in the list of states that are currently in the process of revaluing the principles identified in this chapter, it is because it has never left them to the same extent. The principles and guarantees offered by representative democracy have been particularly central to German objections to APBs.[15]

Unsurprisingly, delegation to APBs in Germany is embedded in a set of legal rules and precepts, which precisely aim to uphold more fundamental principles such as political ministerial responsibility. Döhler refers to the theory of *ministerialfreie Räume* or 'areas free from ministerial oversight', a 'legal doctrine based on the idea of a continuous chain of democratic legitimacy and control, [which] provides that an exemption from ministerial oversight should be limited to very special and well-founded cases'.[16] Pursuant to the *Ressortprinzip* ('departmental principle'), anchored in article 65 of the German Constitution, APBs 'retain a

[13] Susan Rose-Ackerman, 'The Regulatory State' in Michel Rosenfeld and András Sajó (eds), *The Oxford Handbook of Comparative Constitutional Law* (Oxford University Press 2012) 671, 677.

[14] Marian Döhler and Werner Jann, 'Germany' in OECD, *Distributed Public Governance* 97, 108.

[15] Marian Döhler, 'Institutional Choice and Bureaucratic Autonomy in Germany' (2002) 25(1) West European Politics 101, 102.

[16] ibid 104–105.

subordinate status and are not given the chance to become "non-majoritarian" in terms of escaping ministerial control'.[17]

More than most other European systems, Germany has qualified and upheld political ministerial responsibility as a principle imposing limits on the administrative design of government authorities. The German system is thus characterized by a strong adherence to the Constitution in general and to the provisions ensuring democratic control of the executive in particular. It therefore did not come as a surprise that Germany was the first Member State to clash with the ECJ over the political independence currently required by EU law for DPAs (see Chapters 2 and 4: *Commission/Germany*). In an attempt to make the court see reason and dismiss the European Commission's broad interpretation of the independence requirement, Germany precisely relied on the commonality of democratic principles and conceptions in the EU Member States, as Chapter 4 will further explain. Consequently, readers may find it interesting to combine this book with work on APBs in Germany and the way in which German law has received and implemented the EU legislation discussed in Chapter 2.

The selection of both Belgium and the Netherlands is primarily dictated by the existence, in these systems, of a legal novelty: framework legislation regarding APBs. For that reason, much of the focus for Belgium will be on the Flemish regional level, where such legislation was enacted as early as 2003.

2. A BRIEF INTRODUCTION TO THE TYPOLOGIES AND CHARACTERISTICS OF AUTONOMOUS PUBLIC BODIES IN BELGIUM (AND FLANDERS), THE NETHERLANDS, THE UK AND FRANCE

The four selected legal systems each have their own specific terminology and taxonomies for APBs. These cover the most important types of APBs. Every system, however, knows ad hoc or *sui generis* bodies as well.

---

[17] ibid 105. See also Johan P Olsen, 'Democratic Government, Institutional Autonomy and the Dynamics of Change' (2009) 32(3) West European Politics 439, 453 explaining that, in Germany, 'ministerial influence is seen as a legitimate expression of the political supremacy over administrative affairs and not as subverting administrative expertise and neutrality'.

A classic distinction, found in many international and comparative studies, is that between APBs embedded within a ministerial department and those that are not.[18] This dichotomy, however, largely corresponds to another distinction, which relies on a more legal criterion: that of the presence or lack of 'hierarchical authority' of ministers vis-à-vis APBs. Although the definition of hierarchical authority may differ from legal system to legal system, it usually comprises the power of ministers to give instructions in individual cases and/or to replace the entity's individual decisions with their own.

A. Belgium/Flanders

Flemish literature refers to the phenomenon of APBs using the umbrella term *verzelfstandiging* (autonomization).[19] The notion was borrowed from the Dutch system. Traditionally, two types of *verzelfstandiging* have been distinguished in Belgium: deconcentration and decentralization.[20] Both concepts were introduced in the aftermath of World War II and were borrowed from the French system. The precise definition of 'deconcentration' and 'decentralization' has, however, been the subject of debate.[21]

Traditionally, deconcentrated entities have been distinguished from their decentralized counterparts by a lack of legal personality. Deconcentration, moreover, implies hierarchical supervision, whereas decentralization excludes this form of control and replaces it with alternative

---

[18] See e.g. Colin Talbot, 'The Agency Idea: Sometimes Old, Sometimes New, Sometimes Borrowed, Sometimes Untrue' in Christopher Pollit and Colin Talbot (eds), *Unbundled Government. A Critical Analysis of the Global Trend to Agencies, Quangos and Contractualisation* (Routledge 2004) 3, 5. The OECD distinguishes between departmental agencies and public law administrations (PLAs): OECD, *Distributed Public Governance*, 17–19.

[19] French-speaking scholarship prefers *paraétatisme*: see e.g. Pierre Jadoul, Bruno Lombaert and François Tulkens (eds), *Le paraétatisme. Nouveaux régards sur la décentralisation fonctionnelle en Belgique et dans les institutions européennes* (la Charte 2010).

[20] Kaat Leus, 'Een klassiek bestuursrechtelijke benadering van het verschijnsel "verzelfstandiging" van openbare diensten: naar een nieuw evenwicht tussen autonomie en centrale sturing' in J. E. Krings (ed), *Liber Amicorum Prof. Dr. G. Baeteman*, (Kluwer Rechtswetenschappen België 1997) 585, 585–624 and particularly 585–587.

[21] See e.g. André Alen, *Poging tot een juridische begripsomschrijving van unitarisme, centralisatie, deconcentratie, decentralisatie, regionalisme, federalisme en confederatie* (U.G.A. 1975) 23–24.

forms of supervision (in most cases with a form of so-called 'administrative oversight', typically consisting of powers of approval, authorization, advice, suspension or annulment).

Creative legislatures, looking for intermediates, have opted for variations on this dichotomy and have created entities that mix features of both categories. A type of APB that is still quite popular is that of bodies with legal personality (a feature of 'decentralization') that nonetheless function under the hierarchical authority of a minister (a feature of 'deconcentration'). Consequently, the distinction has become blurred.

Furthermore, legislatures increasingly rely on private law for the institutional design of APBs with legal personality. Because many of these entities are not subject to traditional forms of administrative oversight, the question arises whether these entities qualify as forms of 'decentralization'.[22] Many government enterprises are subject to a double regime of supervision, since they are both public service providers and companies entrusted with purely commercial or industrial missions. They do not fit the traditional definition of 'decentralization' either.

Another distinction frequently made in the literature on APBs and closely related to the deconcentration/decentralization dichotomy is that of internal autonomization versus external autonomization. The difference is situated in the presence or absence of hierarchical authority, i.e. the possibility for political principals to give orders and/or to substitute the entity's decision with their own.[23] This distinction, which does not attach any relevance to the criterion of legal personality, is more straightforward than that between deconcentration and decentralization. More recently, some (mainly French-speaking) Belgian literature has moreover adopted the notion of *autorités administratives indépendantes* to refer to (following the example of the French system) APBs that are neither subject to hierarchical supervision, nor to any form of administrative oversight.[24]

---

[22] Kaat Leus and Sven Baeten, 'Nieuwe vormen van overheidsrechtspersonen' in Willy Van Eeckhoutte (ed), *Het Rechtspersonenrecht, XVe postuniversitaire cyclus Willy Delva 1998–1999* (Mys & Breesch 1999) 149, 151.

[23] Kaat Leus, 'Een klassiek bestuursrechtelijke benadering van het verschijnsel "verzelfstandiging" van openbare diensten: naar een nieuw evenwicht tussen autonomie en centrale sturing' in J E Krings (ed), *Liber Amicorum Prof. Dr. G. Baeteman*, (Kluwer Rechtswetenschappen België 1997) 585, 591–592 and 597–598.

[24] E.g. Denis Delvax, 'Les contrôles administratives pesant sur les autorités administratives indépendantes' (2008) 37 Revue de droit de l'ULB 107; Robert Andersen, 'Les autorités administratives indépendantes en droit belge' [2008]

The classifications just discussed use abstract legal concepts. Both the federal government and the Flemish level have, however, developed further, more refined typologies. At the federal level, two main types of APBs exist.

The first are the so-called 'public institutions', which all have in common that they possess legal personality. Most of these institutions are subject to traditional administrative oversight, which makes them forms of decentralization and external autonomization. However, a considerable number of them are subject to the hierarchical authority of a government minister as well: they qualify as forms of internal autonomization. For the purpose of regulating the administrative as well as financial supervision of these 'public institutions', a statutory act was passed in 1954, dividing them into four types of institutions (A, B, C and D), each subject to their own regime of control.

The second type of federal APBs are called 'federal agencies'. They are part of the departmental structure, have not been endowed with legal personality and are subject to hierarchical control by a minister.

Apart from these two types of institutions, autonomous government-owned enterprises exist at the federal level as well. Most of these function in liberalized markets now, performing many of their activities in competition with private actors, but have nevertheless remained responsible for the performance of public services as well. Their legal status is regulated by a statute of 1991, which takes due account of this dichotomy of responsibilities. These entities are actually 'half' APBs: only when they act in the quality of public service providers and thus perform government tasks can they be labelled as such. They enjoy considerable autonomy as APBs, but are subject to a form of administrative oversight.

At the Flemish level, most APBs qualify as one of the four types of agencies discerned by the *Kaderdecreet Bestuurlijk Beleid*. This typology and the broader rationale in which it is embedded, will be discussed further on in this chapter. The other administrative legal orders in Belgium (the Walloon Region, the Brussels Region, the French Community and the German community) have not introduced a similar, specific typology for their deconcentrated and decentralized entities. Many of their APBs are still labelled 'public institutions' and function under the regime of the 1954 federal statute.

Annuaire Européen d'administration publique 25; Francis Delpérée, 'Synthèse. Les autorités administratives indépendantes' [2008] Annuaire Européen d'administration publique 317.

For the sake of completeness, it should be mentioned that APBs function at the level of the provinces and municipalities as well. Since the Regions are competent to make legislation on the administrative organization of local government, they also determine whether and under what conditions provinces and municipalities can create APBs. In Flanders, for instance, the *Provinciedecreet* or *Gemeentedecreet* contain provisions on APBs, which make use of very much the same typology as the one developed in the Flemish framework legislation.

B. The Netherlands

The Dutch concept *verzelfstandiging* is not as such a legal concept: 'it only structures the debate about the size of the government task and organization itself'.[25]

Like Belgium, the Netherlands makes a distinction between APBs that are subject to hierarchical authority and those that are not. *Agentschappen* (agencies) or *baten-lastendiensten* (benefits-expenses services)[26] constitute the first category. They enjoy autonomy in operational matters.[27] *Zelfstandige Bestuursorganen* (ZBOs) constitute the second category. Their defining characteristic is that they lack a hierarchical relationship with a minister, implying that the political principal (a government minister) does not have powers to issue directions in individual cases.[28] In order to qualify as a ZBO, a body does not have to be invested with legal personality.[29]

The Netherlands is familiar with the distinction between internal and external autonomization, although only a few authors actually use this

---

[25] Sjoerd E Zijlstra, *Bestuurlijk Organisatierecht* (Kluwer 2009) 100.

[26] This is their statutory denomination: see article 10 of the Dutch *Comptabiliteitswet* 2001. They enjoy financial autonomy, since their system of financial accountability is based on a benefit/cost system.

[27] Thomas Schillemans, 'Verantwoording na verzelfstandiging – Continuïteit, verwarring en vernieuwing' in Wieger Bakker and Kutsal Yesilkagit (eds), *Publieke verantwoording* (Boom 2005) 71, 75.

[28] Henk R B M Kummeling and Antonius P W Duijkersloot, 'Agencies and the Netherlands' in Tom Zwart and Luc Verhey (eds), *Agencies in European and Comparative Law* (Intersentia 2003) 79, 81–82: the power to give directions in individual cases is constitutive of hierarchical authority.

[29] H J de Ru, 'Publiekrechtelijke of privaatrechtelijke rechtspersonen' [2002] NJB 1099, 1101.

terminology.[30] Moreover, not all Dutch legal literature agrees on the qualification of entities that are subject to hierarchical supervision as forms of *verzelfstandiging*.[31]

It should be noted that the term 'functional decentralization' exists in Dutch administrative law as well, but there is a debate about whether ZBOs should be regarded as functionally decentralized bodies in the Dutch sense.[32] Instead, the term 'functional administration' is sometimes used to refer to ZBOs, as an alternative.[33] Another 'false friend' is the concept of 'deconcentration', which has a more limited meaning than it does within the Belgian legal system. Deconcentration (also labelled 'attribution to subordinates'[34]) is not a synonym for APBs subject to hierarchical authority, but constitutes one specific way[35] in which a Dutch 'agency' can be invested with government tasks, i.e. directly via legislation.[36]

The Netherlands also knows government enterprises that still (partly) fulfil public services. APBs function at the local level as well. Some authors reserve the term ZBO for entities operating at the central (state) level,[37] others use it to refer to certain local APBs as well.[38]

---

[30] See e.g. Henk R B M Kummeling and Antonius P W Duijkersloot, 'Agencies and the Netherlands' in Tom Zwart and Luc Verhey (eds), *Agencies in European and Comparative Law* (Intersentia 2003) 79, 80.

[31] E.g. M M den Boer, *Preadvies verzelfstandiging van bestuurstaken op z'n Hollands* (Tjeenk Willink, 1999) 21.

[32] See e.g. J L Boxum, J de Ridder and M Scheltema, *Zelfstandige bestuursorganen in soorten: verslag van een onderzoek naar de praktijk van zelfstandige bestuursorganen* (Kluwer 1989) 17–50 and in particular 12–16.

[33] M M den Boer, *Preadvies verzelfstandiging van bestuurstaken op z'n Hollands* (Tjeenk Willink, 1999) 4; Sjoerd E Zijlstra, *Bestuurlijk Organisatierecht* (Kluwer 2009) 82.

[34] *Attributie aan ondergeschikten.*

[35] See Sjoerd E Zijlstra, *Bestuurlijk Organisatierecht* (Kluwer 2009) 186–187.

[36] Van Nus, however, contrasts 'decentralisation' with 'deconcentration' in much the same way as Belgian authors do. See J G L van Nus, *Overheidstoezicht op afstand. Verzelfstandiging van toezichthoudende taken naar zelfstandige bestuursorganen verkend* (Maklu 1995) 136.

[37] See the definition in J L Boxum, J de Ridder and M Scheltema, *Zelfstandige bestuursorganen in soorten: verslag van een onderzoek naar de praktijk van zelfstandige bestuursorganen* (Kluwer 1989) 7–16, in particular 8.

[38] Sjoerd E Zijlstra, *Bestuurlijk Organisatierecht* (Kluwer 2009) 80–81.

C. The UK

In 2008, Matthew Flinders wrote that in the UK 'the most exhausting challenge confronting those interested in delegated governance is simply finding out exactly what bodies exist, why they have been designated as a certain organizational form, and the principles on which delegation is based'.[39]

It is largely accepted in the literature that the UK knows two main types of APBs: executive agencies on the one hand and non-departmental public bodies (NDPBs) on the other hand. Whereas the former are part of the departmental structure of a ministry, the latter are detached from the departments. The majority of NDPBs are created by statute, whereas executive agencies are set up via framework documents, i.e. agreements between ministers and the agency heads. Executive agencies are also referred to as 'Next Steps Agencies', since they originate from the UK Government's 'Next Steps Programme', launched in 1988 under the premiership of Margaret Thatcher. The goal behind these reforms was to create a fundamental division between service delivery (policy implementation) and policy making. The former, representing the bulk of public service activity, would henceforth be entrusted to agencies, which would enjoy operational autonomy, whereas the departments would remain in charge of the latter.[40] The 'Next Steps' programme has been a major inspiration for other countries worldwide to establish similar agencies.[41]

In principle, ministers should not intervene in the day-to-day operations of the agencies.[42] The literature, however, observes that the policy/

---

[39] Matthew Flinders, *Delegated Governance and the British State: Walking without Order* (Oxford University Press 2008) 128.

[40] Gavin Drewry, 'Revolution in Whitehall: The Next Steps and Beyond' in Jeffrey Jowell and Dawn Oliver (eds), *The Changing Constitution* (3rd edn, Oxford University Press 1994) 155, 157. For more on the philosophy behind and the process towards Next Steps see Kate Jenkins, *Politicians and Public Services. Implementing Change in a Clash of Cultures* (Edward Elgar Publishing 2008).

[41] Colin Talbot, 'The Agency Idea: Sometimes Old, Sometimes New, Sometimes Borrowed, Sometimes Untrue' in Christopher Pollit and Colin Talbot (eds), *Unbundled Government. A Critical Analysis of the Global Trend to Agencies, Quangos and Contractualisation* (Routledge 2004) 3, 3.

[42] Colin Turpin, 'Ministerial Responsibility' in Jeffrey Jowell and Dawn Oliver (eds), *The Changing Constitution* (Clarendon Press 1994) 109, 125.

operations divide has proven artificial or 'in practice elusive'[43] since ministers have in the past often felt obliged to intervene in agencies' day-to-day operations, precisely because they touched upon matters of policy. The *Next Steps Report*, moreover, did not exclude the possibility of ministerial interference for reasons of public or parliamentary concern.[44]

Because executive agencies function under the authority of the minister and/or department, they are often labelled 'semi-autonomous' or 'semi-independent'. They do not have their own legal identity or personality.

One step higher on the ladder of (formal) autonomy are the so-called NDPBs or quangos.[45] NDPB is the more official term to designate these bodies, whereas quango is often considered a word of abuse, used by critics.[46] Quango stands for Quasi Autonomous Non-Governmental Organization.

Describing NDPBs as 'non-governmental' is, however, incorrect, as well as misleading: 'non-departmental' is more accurate.[47] The term 'quango' has, moreover, been criticized for having 'been applied to just about everything and anything'.[48] In most literature, quangos are considered the counterparts of executive (Next Steps) agencies. NDPBs'

---

43 Gavin Drewry, 'Revolution in Whitehall: The Next Steps and Beyond' in Jeffrey Jowell and Dawn Oliver (eds), *The Changing Constitution* (3rd edn, Oxford University Press 1994) 155, 165.

44 Colin Turpin and Adam Tomkins, *British Government and the Constitution* (7th edn, Cambridge University Press 2011) 432–433 with reference to *Next Steps Report 1997*, Cm 3889/1998, p. v and Memorandum by Lord Armstrong, Select Committee on the Public Service, *Special Report*, HL 68 of 1996–97, p. 1.

45 'Quango' can be defined in either a wide or a narrow sense, but in its narrow definition, 'quango' is regarded as a synonym for 'NDPB'. See e.g. Institute for Government, 'Read before Burning', http://www.institutefor government.org.uk/publications/read-burning, 17.

46 See Anthony Barker, 'Governmental Bodies and the Networks of Mutual Accountability' in Anthony Barker (ed), *Quangos in Britain. Government and the Networks of Public Policy-Making* (Palgrave Macmillan 1982) 3, 3: according to Barker, 'the word "quango" has helped to give [these] quasi-official or quasi-unofficial organisations some popular (or, rather, unpopular) image in the public's mind. As a means of describing anything, however, the word is useless.'

47 Luc F M Verhey, 'British Agencies: Surveying the Quango State' in Tom Zwart and Luc Verhey (eds), *Agencies in European and Comparative Law* (Intersentia 2003) 19, 19–20.

48 Carsten Grave, Matthew Flinders and Sandra Van Thiel, 'Quangos – What's in a Name? Defining Quangos from a Comparative Perspective' 12(2) (1999) Governance 129, 136.

'arm's-length' distance from the Government expresses itself via 'substantial operational autonomy, but within limits set by any relevant statute and by government policy'.[49]

The Cabinet Office has defined an NDPB as 'a body which has a role in the processes of national government, but [is] not a government department or part of one, and operate[s] to a greater or lesser extent at arm's length from Ministers'.[50] It distinguishes four types of NDPBs.[51] The first are labelled 'executive NDPBs': they carry out 'executive, administrative, regulatory and/or commercial functions'. The second category are the 'advisory NDPBs', which 'provide independent, expert advice to ministers on a wide range of issues'. A third type are the 'tribunal NDPBs', which 'have jurisdiction in a specialised field of law'. Finally, 'Independent Monitoring Boards (IMBs)' 'are independent watchdogs attached to each prison establishment, immigration removal centre and holding room in England and Wales'.[52] The Cabinet Office emphasizes, however, that this NDPB classification is not a legal, but an administrative one. Unlike the three other legal systems studied, the UK system does not have legal concepts to categorize APBs, such as 'decentralization' or 'deconcentration'. This ties in with the relative lack of any real legal theory or doctrine on APBs more generally.[53] Advisory and tribunal NDPBs are not APBs in the sense of the definition introduced in Chapter 1. Since political autonomy is regarded as a

---

[49] Colin Turpin and Adam Tomkins, *British Government and the Constitution* (7th edn, Cambridge University Press 2011) 435.

[50] Cabinet Office, 'Public Bodies 2014', https://www.gov.uk/government/publications/public-bodies-2014, 16.

[51] The devolved countries adopt similar classifications. See e.g. Scottish Executive, *Public Bodies: Proposals for Change*, June 2001, 17.

[52] Cabinet Office, 'Public Bodies 2014', https://www.gov.uk/government/publications/public-bodies-2014, 6.

[53] See Anthony Barker, 'Governmental Bodies and the Networks of Mutual Accountability' in Anthony Barker (ed), *Quangos in Britain. Government and the Networks of Public Policy-Making* (Palgrave Macmillan 1982) 3, 7; Geert Bouckaert and Guy B Peters, 'What Is Available and What Is Missing in the Study of Quangos?' in Christopher Pollit and Colin Talbot (eds), *Unbundled Government. A Critical Analysis of the Global Trend to Agencies, Quangos and Contractualisation* (Routledge 2004) 22, 26; Mark Thatcher, 'Delegation to Independent Regulatory Agencies: Pressures, Functions and Contextual Mediation' (2002) 25(1) West European Politics 125, 127 and Mark Thatcher, 'The Third Force? Independent Regulatory Agencies and Elected Politicians in Europe' (2005) 18(3) Governance 347, 352.

desirable or even indispensable characteristic of these bodies, they nevertheless often face the same criticisms as executive NDPBs in the UK.

Apart from executive agencies and NDPBs, the UK also knows so-called 'Non-Ministerial Government Departments'. These are – as the term suggests – government departments that do not have a minister and are usually set up by statute. They are governed by a statutory board. 'The precise nature of their relationship with ministers varies according to their individual policy and statutory framework, but the general rationale is to distance the day-to-day administration of the particular activity from *direct* ministerial control, while retaining some governmental input to the wider policy context.'[54] Many regulatory bodies are or have in the past been qualified as Non-Ministerial Government Departments.

Another category not yet mentioned is that of public corporations, which have an industrial or commercial remit.[55] Whether (any of) these can be qualified as APBs has to be assessed on a case-by-case basis.

D. France

The French system is traditionally known as one with a strongly centralized administration that has never ceased to adhere to the principles of a Weberian, hierarchical bureaucracy in any way worth mentioning.[56] Even though one could indeed argue that, in quantitative terms, APBs have perhaps never been as numerous in France as they have been, for instance, in the UK, the country has not remained immune to the trend. On the contrary, French administrative organization currently contains a number of entities that enjoy a substantial degree of political autonomy: the so-called *autorités administratives indépendantes* (AAIs).

The delineation of the notion of 'AAIs' has been the subject of a major debate in French doctrine. Currently, there seems to be general agreement that what defines AAIs and distinguishes them from other French APBs is the fact that they are not subject to either hierarchical control or

---

[54] Matthew Flinders, *Delegated Governance and the British State: Walking without Order* (Oxford University Press 2008) 111–112.

[55] See *Classification Of Public Bodies: Guidance For Departments* (https://www.gov.uk/government/publications/classification-of-public-bodies-information-and-guidance) 29.

[56] See e.g. Gavin Drewry, 'The Executive: Towards Accountable Government and Effective Governance?' in Jeffrey Jowell and Dawn Oliver (eds), *The Changing Constitution* (Oxford University Press 2011) 187, 196.

administrative oversight (*tutelle*).[57] Some authors use the notion 'AAI' in a restrictive sense, as referring to independent regulatory authorities only.[58] Another ongoing discussion in France concerns the extent to which the power to take (binding) decisions is a characteristic feature of AAIs. A broad conception of the notion includes authorities that issue authoritative advices or recommendations to the government.[59] The notion 'AAI' is mostly reserved for entities without legal personality. APBs that are not subject to *tutelle* and that have not been invested with legal personality have been labelled *autorités publiques indépendantes* (APIs).[60] APIs in both public and private law forms exist.

Another category of French APBs is that of the so-called *agences*. In a 2012 study on *les agences*, the French Council of State ascertained that, in everyday political and legal discourse, the concept was often used as an umbrella term[61] to designate an otherwise undetermined group of APBs. In an attempt to create some conceptual clarity, the Council suggested that the *agences* could henceforth best be regarded as the counterpart of AAIs, treating these two types of APBs as mutually exclusive categories.[62] Whereas AAIs are 'independent',[63] *agences* were characterized as 'autonomous', signifying that the executive does not intervene in their day-to-day functioning, but has the power to define the policy that the agencies are supposed to implement.[64] AAIs, on the other

---

[57] Conseil d'État – Rapport public 2001/Jurisprudence et avis de 2000 – Les autorités administratives indépendantes (Études & Documents No 52) 291. Hereinafter: Conseil d'État – Rapport public 2001.

[58] See e.g. Aalt W Heringa, 'Agencies in France. Autorités Administratives Centrales Indépendantes/National Independent Administrative Authorities' in Tom Zwart and Luc Verhey (eds), *Agencies in European and Comparative Law* (Intersentia 2003) 37, 49 and 56.

[59] See e.g. Jacques Chevallier, 'Réflexions sur l'institution des autorités administratives indépendantes' [1986] JCP-G I-3254; Jeannette Bougrab, 'Independent Administrative Authorities in France' in Roberto Caranta, Mads Adenas and Duncan Fairgrieve (eds), *Independent Administrative Authorities* (British Institute of International and Comparative Law 2004) 47, 51.

[60] Michel Degoffe, 'Les autorités publiques indépendantes' [2008] AJDA 622, 622–623.

[61] Conseil d'État, *Les agences: une nouvelle gestion publique? Étude annuelle adoptée par l'assemblée générale du Conseil d'État le 5 juillet 2012*, Paris, 2012, 56–57. Hereinafter: Conseil d'État, *Les agences*, 2012.

[62] Some AAIs are nevertheless named *agence*, which can cause confusion: ibid 50.

[63] Which also translates itself into the irrevocability of the (mandate of the) members of their boards: ibid 48.

[64] ibid 12.

hand, define their own policies.[65] *Agences* are not subject to hierarchical supervision (they cannot receive instructions), but, unlike AAIs, they do know a system of *tutelle* or administrative oversight.[66] The most notorious types of *agences* are the so-called *établissements publics*. These can take two forms: that of *établissement public administratif* (EPA) or that of *établissement public industriel et commercial* (EPIC). Both are characterized by their legal personality[67] but differ from APIs because they are subject to forms of *tutelle*. These two characteristics make EPAs forms of *décentralisation par service*, comparable to the Belgian decentralized APBs.[68] EPICs, on the other hand, are public enterprises, signifying that their activities are industrial or commercial in nature, but at the same time constitute public services.[69]

The *tutelle* or administrative oversight applicable to French *agences* can take several forms. Traditionally, it expresses itself through one or more of the following powers entrusted to ministers: annulment, approval, authorization and – exceptionally – substitution (*d'office*: only in the case of neglect of duties).[70] These powers can be exercised for reasons related to both the legality and expediency (*opportunité*) of decisions.[71] Powers of instruction and reformation are, on the other hand, excluded.[72]

Both the regional and local level in France know APBs, which can take several forms.[73] These should not be confused with forms of *déconcentration*. The latter concept is used to designate services of central (national) government ministries that operate at the level of regions,

---

[65] ibid 51.

[66] ibid 49. On their autonomy, see also p. 57.

[67] Conseil d'État, *Les établissements publics – Etude adoptée par l'assemblée générale plénière*, 15 Octobre 2009, 28. See also p. 40: *agences* that have not been invested with legal personality are the so-called *services à competence nationale* (SCN).

[68] Philippe Georges and Guy Siat, *Droit Public* (Dalloz 2006) 165 and 218.

[69] ibid 222; Claude Rochet, Marc Cabane and Simon Formery, 'France' in OECD, *Distributed Public Governance* 71, 75.

[70] Sébastien Martin, 'Les autorités publiques indépendantes: réflexions autour d'une nouvelle personne publique' [2013] RDP 53, 59.

[71] Philippe Georges and Guy Siat, *Droit Public* (Dalloz 2006) 167.

[72] Conseil d'État, *Les établissements publics – Etude adoptée par l'assemblée générale plénière*, 15 Octobre 2009, 56 with reference to case law.

[73] See Conseil d'État, *Les agences*, 2012, 58–60; Philippe Georges and Guy Siat, *Droit Public* (Dalloz 2006) 218. For the overseas areas, see e.g. Jean-Jacques Menuret, 'Bientôt des autorités administratives indépendantes (AAI) territoriales' [2013] La Semaine Juridique Edition Générale 2231.

departments or local entities. These local representatives, such as *préfets*, remain subject to the hierarchical authority of their superiors at the central level. This authority expresses itself via powers of instruction (orders of general or specific nature), approval, annulment, reformation or suspension. Only in exceptional circumstances does the law also provide a possibility for substitution. Table 3.1 provides a schematic comparative overview of the typology of APBs in Belgium/Flanders, the Netherlands, the UK and France.

Table 3.1 Simplified schematic overview

	Hierarchical authority	***Lack of hierarchical authority***
Belgium/Flanders	– Federal agencies – Flemish IVAs	– Federal 'public institutions' – Flemish EVAs
The Netherlands	Agencies	ZBOs
UK	Executive agencies (Next Steps agencies)	– NDPBs (quangos) – Non-ministerial government departments
France	Déconcentration*	Agencies/AAIs

Note: *These forms of *déconcentration* differ from APBs subject to hierarchical power in the other three systems studied in that they have a territorial definition of competence, which is usually not the case for those other APBs.

3. COMMON CONSTITUTIONAL PRINCIPLES AND CONCERNS

> Fallacies do not cease to be fallacies because they become fashions.
>
> G K Chesterton

In many European states, legal academia has, for the last two decades, engaged in an enterprise of developing a legal framework in which to locate the phenomenon of APBs. It has done so by revisiting and revaluing those fundamental principles – often constitutional in nature – that underlie systems of administrative organization. These principles serve as touchstones against the background of which existing law and practices can be assessed.

The law on administrative organization is still often perceived as largely formal, neutral or value-free in nature. The way in which the Government and the administration are organized does not at first sight seem to affect citizens' rights or interests. The administration being organized in way X rather than in way Y can obviously have consequences in terms of efficiency, but there seems to be no higher legal rule or principle that obliges the government to prefer Y over X or to opt for a different solution altogether. This formalistic view on administrative organization is obsolete. Governmental organization being instrumental does not mean that it is designed in a vacuum, free from meta values imposing certain boundaries. In European legal traditions, administrative organization is, on the contrary, governed by fundamental principles, which underlie the specific and often rather formal or technical rules that give form to the administration. These meta principles impose restrictions on the legislature's or Government's discretion.

The following section will demonstrate that the four legal traditions selected for the comparative analysis, despite varying accents and priorities, share a common core of principles against which decisions on administrative organization, among which the decision to create APBs, should be weighed. The common core identified can then serve as a touchstone against which the current obligations anchored in EU law and described in Chapter 2 can be tested, as will be done in Chapter 4.

From a functional viewpoint, APBs are part of the state apparatus. This has led the Dutch scholar Zijlstra to conclude that their creation and functioning should comply with the so-called 'principles of the democratic *Rechtsstaat*'.[74] Zijlstra himself has used these principles to develop a legal, normative framework for Dutch governmental organization in general and for APBs more specifically. He labels these principles as 'pre-positive' in nature, since they work as normative principles in relation to the development of law by the government.[75] For the Netherlands, he discerned three central (clusters of) principles: the principle of democracy; the intertwined principles of liberty, legal certainty and equality; and the principle of social justice. These central principles were subsequently concretized in 'further principles'.[76] The following section is indebted to Zijlstra's work in that it will adopt a similar approach, the main difference being that it aims to identify common European principles, applying the comparative method.

---

74 Sjoerd E Zijlstra, *Zelfstandige bestuursorganen in een democratische rechtsstaat – een onderzoek naar democratisch-rechtsstatelijke en positiefrechtelijke aspecten van het gebruik van zelfstandige bestuursorganen, meer in het bijzonder op gemeentelijk niveau* (VUGA 1997).

75 ibid 38.

76 Sjoerd E Zijlstra, *Bestuurlijk Organisatierecht* (Kluwer 2009) 6–7.

A. Approach: A Triangle of Meta Values

In the following sections, six key principles will be identified and their relation to the subject of APBs will be studied from a comparative viewpoint: separation of powers (1), transparency, publicity and legal certainty (2), legality (3), political ministerial responsibility (4), democratic control of the administration by elected representatives (5) and centrality (6). Modern constitutional law theory classifies these principles under three main denominators, representing fundamental meta values that are generally regarded as the defining foundations of state power in contemporary constitutional scholarship: constitutionalism, the rule of law and democracy. These meta values are not usually expressed as such in written Constitutions or mentioned as constitutional principles in textbooks. They represent assumptions that underlie an entire constitutional system and that are reflected by rules and principles that are explicitly named in the Constitution(s).[77]

Even though both the rule of law and democracy are anything but clear-cut and uncontested values as far as their definition and scope are concerned, most constitutionalists share a general understanding of the complex of sub-principles and values that they embody. *In abstracto*, the rule of law is a particularly difficult notion or concept to capture. According to Krygier, 'the feature that makes the rule of law distinctive and precious' is the 'constraint by law on the ways in which power can be exercised'.[78] The rule of law intends to 'institutionaliz[e] ways of reducing arbitrary power'.[79] An important principle derived from the rule of law is that of legal certainty. Closely related values are those of transparency and publicity, understood as requirements for a proper ordering of the administrative landscape.

Democracy, a concept serving as an umbrella for multiple theories, is here understood as a denominator for the principles of legality, political ministerial responsibility, democratic control of the administration by elected representatives and centrality. These principles all relate to the concept of representative democracy. There are other conceptions of

---

[77] For this understanding of constitutional principles, see e.g. Gary Jeffrey Jacobsohn, 'Constitutional Values and Principles' in Michel Rosenfeld and András Sajó (eds), *The Oxford Handbook of Comparative Constitutional Law* (Oxford University Press 2012) 777, 780 and the references there.

[78] Martin Krygier, 'Rule of Law' in Michel Rosenfeld and András Sajó (eds), *The Oxford Handbook of Comparative Constitutional Law* (Oxford University Press 2012) 233, 235.

[79] ibid 241.

democracy, however, such as participatory and deliberative democracy. Their relationship to the 'problem' of APBs is briefly examined in Chapter 5.[80]

Constitutionalism is an altogether more difficult concept to capture. There is no generally accepted definition or circumscription of constitutionalism in legal academia. Besson nevertheless describes the idea behind the concept by stating that 'its main and common claim is that political and legal power should be exercised only within the limits of a constitution, such as the separation of powers, checks and balances, the rule of law, democracy and fundamental rights'.[81] According to Fellman, 'the touchstone of constitutionalism is the concept of limited government under a higher law'.[82] In a narrow sense, constitutionalism does no more nor less than refer to the requirement that a state should have a Constitution, constraining the organization and functioning of the state and the government. This conception indeed does not formulate any further claims as to the values that should underlie the Constitution, such as democratic aspirations.[83] According to Besson, the relationship

---

[80] For an overview of the different concepts of democracy, see Günter Frankenberg, 'Democracy' in Michel Rosenfeld and András Sajó (eds), *The Oxford Handbook of Comparative Constitutional Law* (Oxford University Press 2012) 250, 252–256.

[81] Samantha Besson, 'Whose Constitution(s)? International Law, Constitutionalism and Democracy' in Jeffrey L Dunoff and Joel P Trachtman, (eds), *Ruling the World? Constitutionalism, International Law and Global Governance* (Cambridge University Press 2008) 381, 387.

[82] David Fellman, 'Constitutionalism' in Philip P Wiener (ed), *Dictionary of the History of Ideas: Studies of Selected Pivotal Ideas, vol. 1* (Charles Scribner's Sons 1974) 485, 485.

[83] There are other conceptions of constitutionalism as well, in which the concept serves as an umbrella principle under which substantive claims such as the rule of law and democracy are subsumed. See e.g. Mark Tushnet, 'Comparative Constitutional Law' in Mathias Reimann and Reinhard Zimmermann (eds), *The Oxford Handbook of Comparative Law* (Oxford University Press 2006) 1225, 1230. See also, on a more normative concept of constitutionalism, David Fellman, 'Constitutionalism' in Philip P Wiener (ed), *Dictionary of the History of Ideas: Studies of Selected Pivotal Ideas, vol. 1* (Charles Scribner's Sons 1974) 485; Andrew Harding and Peter Leyland, 'Comparative Law in Constitutional Contexts' in Esin Örücü and David Nelken (eds), *Comparative Law. A Handbook* (Hart Publishing 2007) 313, 323 ff; Andreas L Paulus, 'The International Legal System as a Constitution' in Jeffrey L Dunoff and Joel P Trachtman (eds), *Ruling the World? Constitutionalism, International Law and Global Governance* (Cambridge University Press 2008) 69, 107–108.

between constitutionalism and democratic sovereignty is indeed ambiguous, since 'a constitution constrains a legal order, thus making it (materially) legitimate in a constitutional democracy', but 'it can do so democratically only if those constitutional constraints also constitute that democratic order'.[84] Consequently, constitutionalism seems to require the existence of constraints, without, however, suggesting that they should be characterized by any particular qualitative conditions. Nevertheless, the principle of separation of powers, which does of course have its own inherent value, is usually regarded as an emanation of constitutionalism,[85] as it will be in this book. The idea that there is no Constitution, and hence no constitutionalism, without adherence to some kind of principle of separated powers is acknowledged in the formulation of article 16 of the French *Déclaration des Droits de l'Homme et du Citoyen*, pursuant to which '[t]oute société dans laquelle la garantie des droits n'est pas assurée, ni la séparation des pouvoirs déterminée, n'a point de Constitution'. Table 3.2 provides a schematic overview of the meta values that are central to the analysis in this chapter and the more specific principles that are derived from these values.

Table 3.2 Overview of meta values and derived principles

Constitutionalism	**Rule of law**	**Democracy**
Separation of powers	Legal certainty Transparency/ publicity	Legality Political ministerial responsibility Democratic control by elected representatives Centrality

B. Claims Derived from Constitutionalism

Montesquieu's traditional account of separation of powers is still the starting point for most analyses of this principle. Equally recognized,

[84] Samantha Besson, 'Whose Constitution(s)? International Law, Constitutionalism and Democracy' in Jeffrey L Dunoff and Joel P Trachtman, (eds), *Ruling the World? Constitutionalism, International Law and Global Governance* (Cambridge University Press 2008) 381, 389.

[85] E.g. Daniel Halberstam, 'The Promise of Comparative Administrative Law: A Constitutional Perspective on Independent Agencies' in Susan Rose-Ackerman and Peter L Lindseth (eds), *Comparative Administrative Law* (Edward Elgar Publishing 2010) 185, 192–193.

however, is its inability to be applied in any rigorous manner in political reality.[86] Rather than requiring a strict separation between the legislature, executive and judiciary power, a more pragmatic and functional approach to the theory promotes a system of checks and balances via mutual controls.[87]

As pointed out in Chapter 1, separation of powers plays a less dominant role in debates on the legitimacy of APBs in Europe than it does in the US. This is especially so for the parliamentary systems discussed in this chapter, namely those of Belgium, the Netherlands and the UK. In France, with a semi-presidential system that is therefore closer to the US, a very vivid debate has indeed developed on the effect of APBs, and more precisely AAIs, on the preservation of the principle of separation of powers. However, as we will see, many issues that are framed as problems of separation of powers often appear upon consideration to link up with concerns of democratic control.[88]

The debates revolve around a limited number of APBs only. Their defining characteristic is that they not only implement rules or policies by means of individual decisions, but combine these powers with rule-making powers and/or assume a quasi-judicial role, possessing powers of dispute resolution and/or powers to impose administrative penalties.[89] Among these bodies are precisely the regulators or supervisors discussed in Chapter 2 of this book, whose institutional design is now subject to

---

[86] See e.g. Koen Lenaerts and Amaryllis Verhoeven, 'Institutional Balance as a Guarantee for Democracy in EU Governance' in Cristian Joerges and Renaud Dehousse (eds), *Good Governance in Europe's Integrated Market* (Oxford University Press 2002) 35, 39ff.

[87] See e.g. Andrew Harding and Peter Leyland, 'Comparative Law in Constitutional Contexts' in Esin Örücü and David Nelken (eds), *Comparative Law. A Handbook* (Hart Publishing 2007) 313, 317.

[88] For instance: the issue of entrusting APBs with rule-making powers. The same, moreover, seems true for the US: see e.g. David Levi-Faur, 'Regulation and Regulatory Governance' in David Levi-Faur (ed), *Handbook on the Politics of Regulation* (Edward Elgar Publishing 2011) 3, 15, where the criticism that regulatory agencies attract with regard to separation of powers is regarded as an aspect of their democratic deficit.

[89] See e.g. Conseil d'État Rapport public 2001, 285; Martin Collet, 'La création des autorités administratives indépendantes : symptôme ou remède d'un Etat en crise?' in (2007) 330 Regards sur l'actualité 5, 12; Jean-Philippe Feldman, 'Les "autorités administratives indépendantes" sont-elles légitimes? Sur les AAI en général et le Conseil supérieur de l'audiovisuel en particulier' [2010] Receuil Dalloz 2852, 2855; Arnaud Hacquet, 'Le pouvoir réglementaire des autorités administratives indépendantes. Réflexions sur son objet et sa légitimité' [2008] RDP 393, 394.

EU legislation. It has been alleged that such a combination of powers violates article 16 of the *Déclaration des Droits de l'Homme et du Citoyen*, enshrining the principle of separation of powers.[90] Economic regulators increasingly find themselves in this situation.[91] In its capacity of administrative court, the French Conseil d'État has ruled that article 6 of the ECHR is not violated if a regulatory body possesses the power to make rules as well as to enforce these rules via powers of control and sanctioning, if this sanctioning power is designed in such a way that the right of defence and the contradictory nature of the procedure, as well as the principle of impartiality, are respected.[92] Even though the Council did not assess this combination of rule-making and enforcement powers on the basis of the principle of separation of powers as such, this case law on article 6 ECHR does suggest that the highest French administrative court does not regard a concentration of powers as such as too problematic. Nonetheless, in the judgment just cited, the Council did assess carefully whether the procedural guarantees that it distinguished as necessary conditions for accepting such a concentration of powers had indeed been respected. Because this was not the case, the Council annulled the challenged decision.

A vast body of case law and doctrine has developed on the delineation of AAIs' competences vis-à-vis those of the three traditional state powers. One of the very first issues that the French Conseil Constitutionnel (CC) had to examine with respect to the constitutionality of AAIs concerned the conferral of rule-making powers on these entities. Whereas part of the criticism regarding this type of delegation stems from democratic concerns,[93] part of the complaints are formulated in terms of violations of separation of powers. Pursuant to article 21 of the French Constitution, the *pouvoir réglementaire* at the national level is exclusively entrusted to the French Prime Minister, notwithstanding the powers conferred on the President. When the legislature confers rule-making powers on AAIs, it detracts from the powers of the Prime Minister, which is difficult to justify from the viewpoint of separation of

---

[90] E.g. Martine Lombard, 'Institutions de régulation économique et démocratie politique' [2005] AJDA 530, 539–540.

[91] E.g. Jean-Louis Autin, 'Le devenir des autorités administratives indépendantes' [2010] RFDA 875, 880; Jacques Chevallier, 'Le statut des autorités administratives indépendantes: harmonisation ou diversification?' [2010] RFDA 896, 896.

[92] Conseil d'État, No 238169 du 30 juillet 2003.

[93] E.g. Michel Degoffe, 'Les autorités publiques indépendantes' [2008] AJDA 622, 629.

powers. In two decisions of 1986 and 1989 respectively, the CC ruled that the provisions of article 21 of the Constitution do not prevent the legislature from entrusting an authority, other than the Prime Minister, with the task of fixing norms to execute statutory law in a predefined matter and within the framework defined by statutory and secondary law.[94] This principle was later confirmed in other decisions.[95] Whereas the 1986 decision emphasized the need for the AAI to respect the statutory framework in the application of which it was invited to assist,[96] an obligation that flows from the principle of legality, the 1989 judgment added an important constraint for the legislature itself, clarifying that the rule-making powers could only involve measures of a limited reach, with respect to both their scope and contents.[97] In other words: AAIs can be entrusted with a power to make rules, but it is up to the national, political competent body (the Prime Minister) to define the essential elements of the norm.[98] This case law has entailed many doctrinal attempts to develop theories that aim to delineate the rule-making powers of AAIs on the one hand and those of the Prime Minister (and the President) on the other.[99] The recent literature contests that all AAIs respect these limits to

---

[94] CC, déc. 86-217 DC du 18 Septembre 1986, para 58; CC, déc. 88-248 DC du 17 Janvier 1989, para 15.

[95] See e.g. CC, déc. 2004-497 DC du 1 Juillet 2004, para 6.

[96] Catherine Teitgen-Colly, 'Les instances de régulation et la constitution' [1990] RDP 153, 173.

[97] Michel Gentot, *Les autorités administratives indépendantes* (Montchrestien 1994) 75–76; Jeannette Bougrab, 'Independent Administrative Authorities in France' in Roberto Caranta, Mads Adenas and Duncan Fairgrieve (eds), *Independent Administrative Authorities* (British Institute of International and Comparative Law 2004) 47, 58–59. This case law was confirmed in e.g. CC, déc. 89-260-DC du 28 Juillet 1989, para 30; CC, déc. 91-304 DC du 15 Janvier 1992, para 12; CC, déc. 96-378 DC du 23 Juillet 1996, para 11; CC, déc. 2004-504 DC du 12 Aôut 2004, para 40.

[98] Louis Favoreu, Patrick Gaïa, Richard Ghevontian, Jean-Louis Mestre, Otto Piersmann, André Roux and Guy Scoffoni, *Droit Constitutionnel* (Dalloz 2009) 623.

[99] One popular theory relies on the distinction between *exécution* and *application* of statutory law. See Jean-Marie Auby, 'Le pouvoir réglementaire des autorités des collectivités locales' [1984] AJDA 468. See also Daniel Halberstam, 'The Promise of Comparative Administrative Law: A Constitutional Perspective on Independent Agencies' in Susan Rose-Ackerman and Peter L Lindseth (eds), *Comparative Administrative Law* (Edward Elgar Publishing 2010) 185, 197–198.

their rule-making powers in practice.[100] In order to pass the constitutional test, AAIs' rule-making powers both have to be of a subordinate nature and their contents have to be sufficiently specific or specialized.[101] The CC deems it inadmissible in the light of article 21 of the Constitution that the legislature would make the Prime Minister's rule-making powers subordinate to those of an AAI.[102] The literature suggests that this protection of the constitutional role of the Prime Minister is inspired by democratic arguments, since the Constitution has entrusted the development of national politics to the Prime Minister, who is politically responsible vis-à-vis Parliament.[103] The CC has, for instance, ruled that the legislature cannot make regulations issued by the Prime Minister subject to a binding advice of an AAI.[104]

A more recent debate related to separation of powers involves the extent to which AAIs can be invested with powers to impose sanctions. AAIs' political independence at first sight makes them eligible as neutral dispute settlers or law enforcers. However, dispute settlement or law enforcement is not traditionally regarded as an administrative or executive task, which makes it an atypical mission for APBs to perform. The state power that is best suited and equipped to deal with legal disputes is of course the judiciary. The functioning of the judicial apparatus is embedded in fundamental guarantees legitimizing its sanctioning capacity. These guarantees are enshrined in national Constitutions, but also in international and regional treaties. Of particular significance for European legal systems is article 6 ECHR, anchoring the right to a fair trial. The question whether and to what extent the legislature or AAIs themselves should ensure that the latter comply with these principles has

---

[100] Jean-Philippe Feldman, 'Les "autorités administratives indépendantes" sont-elles légitimes? Sur les AAI en général et le Conseil supérieur de l'audiovisuel en particulier' [2010] Receuil Dalloz 2852, 2857.

[101] Conseil d'État – Rapport public 2001, 295; Arnaud Hacquet, 'Le pouvoir réglementaire des autorités administratives indépendantes. Réflexions sur son objet et sa légitimité' [2008] RDP 393, 406ff.

[102] CC, déc. 86-217 DC du 18 Septembre 1986, para 60; Michel Gentot, *Les autorités administratives indépendantes* (Montchrestien 1994) 74–75.

[103] Catherine Teitgen-Colly, 'Les instances de régulation et la constitution' [1990] RDP 153, 175.

[104] CC, déc. 2006-544 DC du 14 Décembre 2006, para 37; Philippe Luppi, 'L'unité du pouvoir réglementaire du Premier ministre et son caractère *ab initio*' [2007] AJDA 1643, 1643–1645; Aude Rouyère, 'La constitutionnalisation des autorités administratives indépendantes: quelle signification?' [2010] RFDA 887, 894.

been debated on multiple occasions before the highest courts in France. The CC has played a pivotal role in this regard.

The first cases that were brought before the CC on this matter revolved around the very principle of whether entrusting AAIs with punitive powers could be reconciled with the Constitution. Claimants discerned possible violations of the separation of powers doctrine in both the fact that such a delegation would detract from the competences of the judiciary, being one of the three traditional state powers, as well as in the fact that the AAIs under scrutiny were invested with rule-making powers and sanctioning powers simultaneously.[105] For the first time in 1989[106] the CC ruled that the principle of separation of powers did not preclude that AAIs would be invested with sanctioning powers, if and to the extent that this were necessary to perform their mission.[107] Some doubt that the condition of necessity for the accomplishment of an AAI's mission is being respected in practice.[108]

In the 1989 decision, the CC added that it would be up to the legislature to ensure that the exercise of an AAI's sanctioning power went hand in hand with respect for the rights and liberties that are guaranteed by the Constitution.[109] Gradually, however, the CC itself began to add further qualifications and requirements to this condition.[110] Consequently, the constitutionality of entrusting AAIs with sanctioning powers is conditional and depends on a number of guarantees being respected.[111] In its most recent case law, the CC refers to the principles of legality of penalties, the rights of defence and the principles of independence and

---

105 Michel Gentot, *Les autorités administratives indépendantes* (Montchrestien 1994) 85–86.

106 This principle was reaffirmed in later judgments. See the references in Sébastien Renaud, 'Les autorités de régulation et le démembrement du pouvoir central' (2001) 16 Revue de la recherche juridique. Droit prospectif 2203, 2214.

107 CC, déc. 88-248 DC du 17 janvier 1989, para 27.

108 Jean-Philippe Feldman, 'Les "autorités administratives indépendantes" sont-elles légitimes? Sur les AAI en général et le Conseil supérieur de l'audiovisuel en particulier' [2010] Receuil Dalloz 2852, 2855.

109 Para 28.

110 Emmanuel Piwnica, 'La dévolution d'un pouvoir de sanction aux autorités administratives indépendantes' [2010] RFDA 915, 916.

111 Marie-José Guédon, *Les autorités administratives indépendantes* (Librairie générale de droit et de jurisprudence 1991) 121.

impartiality as conditions to be respected by the legislature when entrusting AAIs with such powers.[112]

Another question that has received considerable attention in French doctrine is whether, within an AAI that has been invested with sanctioning powers, a functional separation should be guaranteed between the stages of investigation, prosecution and adjudication.[113] The CC subsumes this question under respect for the principles of independence and impartiality and scrutinizes the procedure before the AAI in order to determine whether there is a danger of a mix-up between the various stages (*poursuite* and *instruction* versus *sanction*). Sometimes it finds no violation,[114] sometimes it does.[115,116] In the procedure leading to one of the CC's decisions, the claimants had also argued that the very fact that the AAI under scrutiny combined administrative or regulatory tasks with sanctioning powers violated the principle of separation of powers or functions. The CC, however, omitted to address this part of the claim, leaving doctrine to conclude that the court did not regard this combination of functions as problematic, an attitude that was labelled 'paradoxical'.[117]

---

[112] See e.g. CC, déc. 2012-280 QPC du 12 Octobre 2012, para 16; A R.-T., 'Une juridictionnalisation rampante, mais incomplète, des autorités administratives indépendantes' [2013] RFDA 144, 146–147.

[113] See e.g. Dominique Custos, 'Independent Administrative Authorities in France: Structural and Procedural Change at the Intersection of Americanization, Europeanization and Gallicization' in Susan Rose-Ackerman and Peter L Lindseth (eds), *Comparative Administrative Law* (Edward Elgar Publishing 2010) 277, 287–288; Fabien Zivy, 'La séparation des fonctions d'instruction et de décision au sein de l'Autorité de la concurrence' [2012] La Semaine Juridique Entreprise et Affaires 1142.

[114] CC, déc. 2012-280 QPC du 12 Octobre 2012, paras 20–21 (with regard to *l'Autorité de la Concurrence*); CC, déc. 2013-359 QPC du 13 Décembre 2013, para 6 (concerning the *Conseil supérieur de l'audiovisuel*); CC, déc. 2015-489 QPC du 14 Octobre 2015, para 7 (with regard to the *Conseil de la concurrence*).

[115] CC, déc. 2013-331 QPC du 5 Juillet 2013, para 12, a decision regarding *l'Autorité de régulation des communications électronique et des postes*.

[116] A. R.-T., 'Les exigences constitutionnelles d'indépendance et d'impartialité appliquées à l'Autorité de régulation des communications électroniques et des postes', [2013] RFDA 1262, 1262–1263; David Bosco, 'La séparation des fonctions d'instruction et de jugement constitutionnalisée!' [2013/10] *Contrats Concurrence Consommation* 20; Pascal Wilhelm, '3 QUESTIONS Le Pouvoir de sanction de l'ARCEP annulé par le Conseil constitutionnel sur QPC', [2013] La Semaine Juridique Entreprise et Affaires 608.

[117] A R-T, 'Une juridictionnalisation rampante, mais incomplète, des autorités administratives indépendantes' [2013] RFDA 144, 148.

Furthermore, the CC has also added a more substantive limitation to the possibility of entrusting AAIs with sanctioning powers. In a decision of 2009, it ruled that the legislature could not entrust an AAI with a power of imposing penalties that was not limited to a specific category of persons but extended to the entire population, regardless of the guarantees in which the legislature embedded the exercise of this power.[118] The fundamental nature of the right that would be restricted by the sanction imposed by the AAI (in this case the freedom of communication) arguably played a crucial role in the CC's judgment.

To what extent do we find similar concerns rooted in the separation of powers doctrine in the other legal systems studied?

In Belgium and the Netherlands, APBs seem to raise fewer questions in this respect. The delegation of rule-making powers to APBs is a delicate matter in both legal systems, but one that is more often linked to the issue of democratic legitimacy than to considerations of separation of powers. Initially, these legal systems did not have a real tradition of entrusting APBs with powers of dispute resolution or sanctioning powers (at least not to the same extent as France). The most notorious exceptions have been regulatory bodies.[119] A 1995 study on Dutch ZBOs with supervisory tasks, such as regulators, recommended that these bodies should clearly separate the different functions that they exercise (such as licensing, supervising adherence to licence conditions, imposing sanctions etc.) by entrusting them to different branches within the organization.[120] A 2005 study on market regulators assessed their constitutionality from the angle of separation of powers as well.[121] A recent contribution on AAIs operating in Belgium observes that these bodies combine various functions and powers and claims that this raises

---

[118] CC, déc. 2009-580 DC du 10 Juin 2009, para 16.

[119] For the Netherlands, see e.g. R A J van Gestel, Ph Eijlander and J A F Peters, 'The Regulatory Powers of Quangos in the Netherlands: Are Trojan Horses Invading Our Democracy?' (Paper for the Nederlandse Vereniging voor Rechtsvergelijking/Netherlands Comparative Law Association), http://www.ejcl.org/111/abs111-9.html, p. 17.

[120] See J G L van Nus, *Overheidstoezicht op afstand. Verzelfstandiging van toezichthoudende taken naar zelfstandige bestuursorganen verkend* (Maklu 1995) 702–703, 745 and 754. Similar concerns were raised in H J de Ru, 'Toezicht moet geen nieuwe staatsmacht worden. Commentaar op de preadviezen voor de VAR 2003 over: Toezicht op markten' [2003] M&M 178.

[121] L F M Verhey and N Verheij, 'De macht van marktmeesters, markttoezicht in constitutioneel perspectief' [2005] Toezicht, Handelingen Nederlandse Juristenvereniging 135, 179–180.

questions from the viewpoint of separation of powers, without dedicating any further attention to the matter.[122]

In the UK, some have raised concerns about the combination of the three traditional state powers by regulators[123] but the debate is not as present and fierce as it has been in France. Scott suggests that the creation of tribunals in the UK made the extension of the powers of UK regulators (and more specifically the power to apply sanctions) 'relatively unproblematic from the perspective of constitutionalism'.[124]

Finally, when it comes to the influence of APBs and mainly regulators on separation of powers, the sword cuts both ways. Referring to the US example, where independent agencies are often regarded as a counterweight for the President's executive power, Heringa and Verhey point out that delegation of powers to APBs may have to be classified 'under the heading of a new separation of powers, that is limiting an ever-growing executive and cutting its powers in separate pieces in order to prevent further accumulation of powers from taking place'.[125] From this viewpoint, APBs can indeed reinforce, rather than endanger, separation of powers.

C. Claims Derived from the Rule of Law

The creation of APBs is increasingly criticized because it is believed to have led to an opaque and impenetrable administrative landscape. A 2002 OECD study ascertained that '[a] consequence of the *ad hoc* creation of government bodies, and of the centrifugal tendencies of the 1980s and the 1990s, has been the dispersion of government entities and a resulting lack of "readability" of the institutional system'.[126]

---

[122] Robert Andersen, 'Les autorités administratives indépendantes en droit belge' [2008] Annuaire Européen d'administration Publique 25, 26.

[123] See A W Bradley and K D Ewing, *Constitutional & Administrative Law* (Longman Pearson 2011) 299; Tony Prosser, 'Regulation and Legitimacy' in Jeffrey Jowell and Dawn Oliver (eds), *The Changing Constitution* (Oxford University Press 2011) 312, 317; Carol Harlow and Richard Rawlings, *Law and Administration* (7th edn, Cambridge University Press 2009) 284.

[124] Colin Scott, 'Regulatory Governance and the Challenge of Constitutionalism' in Dawn Oliver, Tony Prosser and Richard Rawlings (eds), *The Regulatory State: Constitutional Implications* (Oxford University Press 2010) 15, 25–26.

[125] Aalt W Heringa and Luc F M Verhey, 'Independent Agencies and Political Control' in Tom Zwart and Luc Verhey (eds), *Agencies in European and Comparative Law* (Intersentia 2003) 155, 168.

[126] OECD, *Distributed Public Governance*, 24.

Bevir claims that '[a] lack of coordination is one of the most widely invoked consequences of the first wave of public sector reform. Services are delivered by a complex combination of government, special-purpose bodies, and the voluntary and private sectors. ... It is no wonder the critics complain that marketization led to excessive fragmentation.'[127] The concluding section of a recent, comparative study on agencification in 30 countries links their proliferation and the variation in their appearance to a decrease in transparency and advocates a more systematic approach to (types of) agencies. The authors also claim that a lack of transparency hampers accountability 'as it is less clear who is responsible for what'.[128] Consequently, complaints about a lack of transparency are often closely connected to concerns regarding democratic control and legitimacy, discussed in the next section.

In the Netherlands, Zijlstra has warned of the harmful effect of the increase of APBs, especially ZBOs in private law form, on the recognizability of the public landscape.[129] Other authors endorse this concern.[130] In Belgium, the semi-public, semi-private nature of some APBs has been denounced because it raises confusion as to their nature.[131] Flinders has characterized the UK's landscape of 'delegated governance' as one that is 'walking without order'. The author argues that:

> the British state is evolving in an ad hoc, arbitrary, and unprincipled manner which is evident in three ways: (1) in the existence of widespread and fundamental confusion about the administrative structure of the state; (2) in confusion about the existence and utility of the control and accountability mechanisms surrounding delegated organizational forms; and (3) in the

---

[127] Mark Bevir, *Democratic Governance* (Princeton University Press 2010) 211.

[128] Sandra Van Thiel, Koen Verhoest, Geert Bouckaert and Per Lægreid, 'Lessons and Recommendations for the Practice of Agencification' in Koen Verhoest, Sandra Van Thiel, Geert Bouckaert and Per Lægreid (eds), *Government Agencies. Practices and Lessons from 30 Countries* (Palgrave Macmillan 2012) 413, 417.

[129] Sjoerd E Zijlstra, *Bestuurlijk Organisatierecht* (Kluwer 2009) 10.

[130] E.g. J L W Broeksteeg, 'Ministeriële verantwoordelijkheid voor zelfstandige bestuursorganen' in J L W Broeksteeg, J Th J van den Berg and L F M Verhey (eds), *Ministeriële verantwoordelijkheid opnieuw gewogen* (Kluwer 2006) 87, 89–90; L F M Verhey and N Verheij, 'De macht van marktmeesters, markttoezicht in constitutioneel perspectief' [2005] Toezicht, Handelingen Nederlandse Juristenvereniging 135, 179 and 324–325.

[131] See e.g. Council of State, Legislation Section in *Parl.St.* Vl.Parl. 2012–13, nr. 1867/1, 175.

> absence of any explicit logic or rationale that can explain the ambitions, consequences, or trajectory of this process.[132]

According to Drewry, '[t]he biggest obstacle to effective public accountability is lack of transparency'.[133] Referring to NPM reforms, the author points out that there is much that is confusing about the delineation of the executive and its functions and, hence, about whom to hold accountable for what.[134]

Verhey points at the interrelatedness between issues of fragmentation, leading to a lack of coordination in government policy, and accountability, which he labels the 'two major objections to quangos' in the UK.[135] Proponents of more transparency with regard to ZBO policies in the Netherlands have argued that this would lead to a clarification of responsibilities as well.[136] In France, AAIs are sometimes considered to jeopardize the coherence of the public landscape.[137] A report on AAIs adopted by the Assemblée Nationale in 2010 (and discussed in more detail later in this chapter) observed that citizens were confronted with a problem of 'readability' of the institutional system, going hand in hand with a risk that the system would become uncontrollable.[138] The same report acknowledged that the multiplication of AAIs could be a source of complexity and legal uncertainty.[139] In Flanders, the Netherlands and the UK, arguments about improving transparency were interwoven with democratic claims in order to substantiate the case for the framework

---

[132] Matthew Flinders, *Delegated Governance and the British State: Walking without Order* (Oxford University Press 2008) 1.

[133] Gavin Drewry, 'The Executive: Towards Accountable Government and Effective Governance?' in Jeffrey Jowell and Dawn Oliver (eds), *The Changing Constitution* (Oxford University Press 2011) 187, 211.

[134] ibid 188.

[135] Luc F M Verhey, 'British Agencies: Surveying the Quango State' in Tom Zwart and Luc Verhey (eds), *Agencies in European and Comparative Law* (Intersentia 2003) 19, 30.

[136] M M den Boer, 'Zelfstandige bestuursorganen uit de zelfkant van de democratie?' in C P J Goorlen, M M Den Boer and F K Buijn (eds), *Zbo's, verzelfstandiging en privatisering* (Tjeenk Willink 1997) 124, 129.

[137] Sébastien Martin, 'Les autorités publiques indépendantes: réflexions autour d'une nouvelle personne publique' [2013] RDP 53, 73.

[138] Assemblée Nationale, *Rapport sur les AAIs*, I (2010) 66–67.

[139] Les autorités administratives indépendantes – Audition par MM. Christian Vanneste et René Dosière, Députés, rapporteurs de la mission mise en place par le Comité d'évaluation et de contrôle des politiques publiques (CEC) sur les autorités administratives indépendantes – Jeudi 11 février 2010, 10h00 – Intervention de Jean-Marc SAUVÉ Vice-président du Conseil d'État, 5.

legislation discussed later in this chapter. The OECD study cited earlier also ascertained that '[t]he lack of "readability" of the institutional system can also potentially undermine citizens' trust if responsibilities and systems of accountability are unclear'.[140]

D. Claims Derived from Democracy

The 'meta value' of democracy is undoubtedly central to normative assessments on the validity of APBs in a European context. Even in France, where the principle of separation of powers has for a long time dominated the case law of the CC as well as doctrinal contributions on AAIs, democracy and democratic accountability slowly but surely start to become the central values against which to assess initiatives to create new AAIs or to retain, abolish or reform existing ones.

The four principles that this section subsumes under the meta value of 'democracy' are closely related to each other and cooperate to ensure that the primacy of politics in administration is upheld to the best extent possible. Together, they secure the involvement of elected representatives in the way in which executive powers are defined, constrained, supervised and revised. They protect the continued influence of representative democracy in the entire cycle of executive power.

The following subsections will discuss the content and scope of these principles, with a focus on their relationship with (the creation of) APBs. Given their interrelatedness, it is not possible to make a sharp distinction between the concerns flowing from these distinct constitutional principles. The analysis will therefore pay attention to how these principles complement and reinforce each other.

a. Legality

The cycle of executive power has its starting point in the requirements that flow from the principle of legality. In the context of the law on administrative organization, this principle implies that the executive only has binding or coercive powers if and insofar as it has explicitly been invested with them, either by virtue of the Constitution itself or by statutory law. Only the Constitution or the elected representatives of the people can entrust coercive powers to executive office holders, who are not or not necessarily elected. These powers interfere with citizens' personal freedoms, the protection of which is guaranteed in democratic societies. Since freedom is the rule and limitations to freedom constitute

---

140 OECD, *Distributed Public Governance*, 25.

the exception, a statutory basis for executive power should not be too broadly defined or interpreted. This is where a possible conflict with the rationales behind the creation of many APBs emerges. APBs are often established to deal with quite specific problems of a complex nature and it is no easy task for the legislature to determine with sufficient precision how much and what type of power they require to fulfil their missions in a proper way. If the body's mandate is defined too narrowly, the legislature risks defeating the purpose. Too broad a remit, however, may give rise to bodies becoming over-confident and assuming a greater role than the one that was envisaged. Since there is a trend, especially when it comes to regulatory bodies, to invest APBs with broad powers, many contemporary initiatives to establish APBs put pressure on the principle of legality.

Dutch scholarship in particular has been raising concerns over the risk that creating APBs entails an erosion of the 'institutional principle of legality'.[141] The principle is defined as the requirement 'that unilateral administrative action impinging on the rights and freedoms[142] of the citizens should be exercised on the basis of, and in accordance with, a legal basis'.[143] The legal basis required for an act of government that imposes unilateral obligations on citizens is typically understood to be a statutory basis:[144] the power to bind citizens unilaterally has to originate from a representative institution.[145] As a minimum requirement, the legislature should decide on the most essential contents of a power.[146] It

---

141 Term used in Saskia Lavrijssen and Annetje Ottow, 'The Legality of Independent Regulatory Authorities' in Leonard Besselink, Frans Pennings and Sacha Prechal (eds), *The Eclipse of the Legality Principle in the European Union* (Kluwer 2011) 73, 74.

142 Other authors speak of 'breaches of freedom and encumberment of property': Henk R B M Kummeling and Antonius P W Duijkersloot, 'Agencies and the Netherlands' in Tom Zwart and Luc Verhey (eds), *Agencies in European and Comparative Law* (Intersentia 2003) 79, 88.

143 Saskia Lavrijssen and Annetje Ottow, 'The Legality of Independent Regulatory Authorities' in Leonard Besselink, Frans Pennings and Sacha Prechal (eds), *The Eclipse of the Legality Principle in the European Union* (Kluwer 2011) 73, 74.

144 Jan H Jans, Roel de Lange, Sacha Prechal and Rob Widdershoven, *Europeanisation of Public Law* (Europa Law Publishing 2007) 23.

145 M C Burkens, Henk R B M Kummeling, Ben P Vermeulen and Rob J G M Widdershoven, *Beginselen van de democratische rechtsstaat. Inleiding tot de grondslagen van het Nederlandse staats- en bestuursrecht* (Kluwer 2006) 42.

146 Saskia Lavrijssen and Annetje Ottow, 'The Legality of Independent Regulatory Authorities' in Leonard Besselink, Frans Pennings and Sacha Prechal

has to provide a sufficient normative framework for its exercise.[147] Moreover, the legal basis has to be sufficiently specific.[148] A minority disagrees and argues that the principle of legality does not preclude the legislature from entrusting public bodies with 'powers with vague criteria of application or powers that involve considerable discretionary power'.[149]

After delegation, the powers of executive bodies have to be interpreted as restrictively as possible.[150] This is especially the case for APBs, since most of them constitute, so to speak, exceptions to the rule that the administration functions under the full hierarchical supervision and responsibility of a minister, who has a political mandate. From that perspective, legality is closely linked to political ministerial responsibility.[151] The principle of legality aims to give effect to the principle of democracy 'in the phase of the allotment of a competence' and ensures that 'the legal subjects themselves in the end, via legislation, determine by which law they will be bound'.[152]

As explained in the previous section, the CC insists on a firm statutory basis for AAIs' rule-making powers, referring to article 34 of the French Constitution. This is especially the case when fundamental rights are at

---

(eds), *The Eclipse of the Legality Principle in the European Union* (Kluwer 2011) 73, 74.

[147] Saskia Lavrijssen and Thomas Nauta, 'De Europeanisering van het toezicht op de energiesector' [2012] Nederlands Tijdschrift voor energierecht 136, 137.

[148] Frank Julius van Ommeren, *De verplichting verankerd. De reikwijdte van het legaliteitsbeginsel en het materiële wetsbegrip* (W.E.J. Tjeenk Willink 1996) 107.

[149] See e.g. Wim Voermans, *Toebedeling van bevoegdheid. Rede uitgesproken bij de aanvaarding van het ambt van hoogleraar op het gebied van het staats- en bestuursrecht op de universiteit Leiden op 12 september 2003* (Boom Juridische uitgevers 2004) 25–26.

[150] Saskia Lavrijssen and Thomas Nauta, 'De Europeanisering van het toezicht op de energiesector' [2012] Nederlands Tijdschrift voor energierecht 136, 137 and 140.

[151] Henk R B M Kummeling and Antonius P W Duijkersloot, 'Agencies and the Netherlands' in Tom Zwart and Luc Verhey (eds), *Agencies in European and Comparative Law* (Intersentia 2003) 79, 95; S Saskia Lavrijssen and Annetje Ottow, 'The Legality of Independent Regulatory Authorities' in Leonard Besselink, Frans Pennings and Sacha Prechal (eds), *The Eclipse of the Legality Principle in the European Union* (Kluwer 2011) 73, 79.

[152] Saskia Lavrijssen, *Onafhankelijke mededingingstoezichthouders, regulerende bevoegdheden en de waarborgen voor good governance* (Boom Juridische uitgevers 2006) 72.

stake.[153] Furthermore, the CC expects AAIs to remain strictly within the scope of the mandate entrusted to them by the legislature.[154] Similar conditions apply to powers of AAIs to take administrative decisions with an individual scope. If the legislature invests AAIs with a power of delivering licences or permits, the CC expects a sufficiently elaborate legislative framework within which the exercise of this power is embedded.[155] The CC scrutinizes whether the powers entrusted to AAIs are 'strictly limited and precisely defined', facilitating judicial control.[156] A 2010 parliamentary report on AAIs based itself on interviews with parties that were regulated by AAIs to conclude that, often, once these bodies have been invested with a mission, they surpass their responsibilities.[157]

In the UK, the principle of legality requires that public officials act within the powers that have been conferred on them, implying that all decisions and acts of public officials must be legally authorized. 'Parliamentary legislation is the ultimate source of what those duties and powers are.'[158] The principle of legality does not exclude delegation of discretionary powers, but demands that these are exercised 'in accordance with the purpose and objects of the power conferred on the decision-maker, fairly and not in a way that is capricious or arbitrary'.[159]

In Belgium, it follows from article 105 of the Constitution that the King has no other powers than those entrusted to him by the Constitution or by statute. Article 108 of the Constitution anchors the King's power to make regulations and issue decisions that are necessary to execute

---

[153] Pursuant to article 34(2) of the French Constitution, the French Parliament has an exclusive competence to determine 'les règles concernant les garanties fondamentales accordées aux citoyens pour l'exercice des libertés publiques'.

[154] Catherine Teitgen-Colly, 'Les instances de régulation et la constitution' [1990] RDP 153, 168–169.

[155] See e.g. CC, déc. 84-173 DC du 26 Juillet 1984, para 4; CC, déc. 86-217 DC du 18 Septembre 1986, para 35; Sébastien Renaud, 'Les autorités de régulation et le démembrement du pouvoir central' (2001) 16 Revue de la recherche juridique. Droit prospectif 2203, 2218.

[156] See the references in Aalt W Heringa, 'Agencies in France. Autorités Administratives Centrales Indépendantes/National Independent Administrative Authorities' in Tom Zwart and Luc Verhey (eds), *Agencies in European and Comparative Law* (Intersentia 2003) 37, 42.

[157] Assemblée Nationale, *Rapport sur les AAIs*, I (2010) 50.

[158] Peter Cane, *Administrative Law* (5th edn, Clarendon Press 2011) 35–36.

[159] Jeffrey Jowell, 'The Rule of Law and Its Underlying Values' in Jeffrey Jowell and Dawn Oliver (eds), *The Changing Constitution* (7th edn, Oxford University Press 2011) 11, 18.

statutory law. Together with article 105, it is believed to enshrine the principle of legality for all acts of the (federal[160]) executive. The executive's scope for action can only be extended insofar as Parliament has given its consent.[161] Compared with French and Dutch constitutional law, the Belgian tradition does not adhere to a strict interpretation of legality in the sense that tasks and powers entrusted to the executive have to be interpreted in a narrow sense. In the 1924 *Mertz* case, the Belgian Court of Cassation ruled that the government 'can derive from the principle behind the statute and the general purpose that it serves the consequences that naturally follow from it pursuant to the spirit of the statute and the goals that it pursues'.[162] This precept has been confirmed by the Belgian Constitutional Court and by the Council of State.[163] As we will see later in this chapter, this lenience towards broad executive powers is compensated by a strong emphasis on *ex post* political (and ultimately parliamentary) control, especially with regard to the tasks performed by APBs.

As an organizational principle, legality is not exclusively derived from the meta value of democracy, but can also be regarded as an attribute of the rule of law, discussed under the previous title.[164] In the UK, it is indeed the rule of law that is often regarded as the normative basis for the principle that '[all] decisions and acts of public officials must be legally authorized'.[165] 'However, in reviewing the exercise of such powers, courts will have a further constitutional fundamental in mind, in addition

---

[160] Analogous provisions for the regions and communities can be found in articles 78 and 20 respectively of the *Bijzondere Wet Hervorming Instellingen* (BWHI).

[161] Karel Rimanque, *De grondwet toegelicht, gewikt en gewogen* (Intersentia 2005) 239.

[162] Cass. 18 November 1924, *Pas.* 1925, 25. E.g. Anne Ooms, 'De uitvoerende bevoegdheid van de Koning: van conforme proclamatie tot eerste staatsmacht. Een historische analyse van artikel 108 Grondwet' [2009] CDPK 195, 197–199.

[163] See the discussion in Patricia Popelier, *Democratisch Regelgeven* (Intersentia 2001) 156; Anne Ooms, 'De uitvoerende bevoegdheid van de Koning: van conforme proclamatie tot eerste staatsmacht. Een historische analyse van artikel 108 Grondwet' [2009] CDPK 195, 209–211.

[164] See e.g. Bernardo Sordi, '*Révolution*, *Rechtsstaat*, and the Rule of Law: Historical Reflections on the Emergence of Administrative Law in Europe' in Susan Rose-Ackerman and Peter L Lindseth (eds), *Comparative Administrative Law* (Edward Elgar Publishing 2010) 23, 29–31.

[165] Jeffrey Jowell, 'The Rule of Law and Its Underlying Values' in Jeffrey Jowell and Dawn Oliver (eds), *The Changing Constitution* (7th edn, Oxford University Press 2011) 11, 18.

to the doctrine of the rule of law. They will also have in mind the sovereignty of Parliament', Tomkins points out, thereby linking the precept of a statutory basis to the meta value of democracy.[166] In Belgium, Popelier grounds legality in the 'democratic state'.[167] Some Dutch scholars regard legality as an aspect of the rule of law[168] but it is largely accepted that the political interpretation of the principle of legality lies in the 'primacy of the legislator'[169] or in the principle of democracy.[170] Most Dutch scholars refer to the 'democratic Rechtsstaat' as the normative basis for its requirements, accepting that both democracy and the rule of law inspire the principle.[171]

b. Political ministerial responsibility

Executive and administrative power to an important extent equals non-elected power. Government ministers are appointed, but have not necessarily – although this is sometimes the case, for instance in the UK – participated in the elections. They in turn appoint the members and services of the (core) administration who have to assist them in performing their tasks. Therefore, the legitimacy that the executive derives from

---

166 Adam Tomkins, 'The Struggle to Delimit Executive Power in Britain' in Paul Craig and Adam Tomkins (eds), *The Executive and Public Law. Power and Accountability in Comparative Perspective* (Oxford University Press 2006) 16, 41–42.

167 Patricia Popelier, *Democratisch Regelgeven* (Intersentia 2001) 105 ff.

168 E.g. Frank Julius van Ommeren, *De verplichting verankerd. De reikwijdte van het legaliteitsbeginsel en het materiële wetsbegrip* (W.E.J. Tjeenk Willink 1996) see e.g. 61 and 199; M C Burkens, Henk R B M Kummeling, Ben P Vermeulen and Rob J G M Widdershoven, *Beginselen van de democratische rechtsstaat. Inleiding tot de grondslagen van het Nederlandse staats- en bestuursrecht* (Kluwer 2006) 17.

169 Saskia Lavrijssen and Annetje Ottow, 'The Legality of Independent Regulatory Authorities' in Leonard Besselink, Frans Pennings and Sacha Prechal (eds), *The Eclipse of the Legality Principle in the European Union* (Kluwer 2011) 73, 74–75.

170 Annetje Ottow, *Telecommunicatietoezicht. De invloed van het Europese en Nederlandse bestuurs(proces)recht*, doctoral thesis in law, University of Amsterdam, 2006, http://dare.uva.nl/document/2/41206, 86.

171 E.g. Wim Voermans, *Toebedeling van bevoegdheid. Rede uitgesproken bij de aanvaarding van het ambt van hoogleraar op het gebied van het staats- en bestuursrecht op de universiteit Leiden op 12 September 2003* (Boom Juridische uitgevers 2004) 4 with reference to Popelier; M C Burkens, Henk R B M Kummeling, Ben P Vermeulen and Rob J G M Widdershoven, *Beginselen van de democratische rechtsstaat. Inleiding tot de grondslagen van het Nederlandse staats- en bestuursrecht* (Kluwer 2006) 16–17 and 41.

the system of representative democracy is primarily constituted via an indirect, rather than a direct mechanism. It revolves around a single constitutional principle: that of political ministerial responsibility before Parliament. Pursuant to this principle, Parliament holds a right to hold ministers responsible for their political decisions and actions. It applies to both parliamentary and semi-presidential systems. It is flanked by attributes such as a right to ask ministers for information and to question them on their behaviour and that of their administration etc. Ultimately, it offers Parliament the opportunity to impose upon ministers or the Government as a whole the severe penalty of dismissal. Consequently, ministers are dependent on Parliament for the continuation of their appointment. They hold their office by the grace of the elected representatives by whom they have been appointed, to whom they answer and by whom they can be dismissed.

In Belgium, France and the Netherlands, the principle of the responsibility of ministers vis-à-vis Parliament is anchored in the written, codified Constitution. Article 101(1) of the Belgian Constitution stipulates that (federal) ministers are responsible vis-à-vis the Chamber of Representatives of the Belgian Parliament. The precise scope of the principle, however, finds its source in customary law and is still subject to (political) evolution.[172] For the Belgian regions and communities, i.e. the federalized entities, article 70 of the Special Act on the Reform of Institutions (*Bijzondere Wet Hervorming Instellingen* or BWHI) anchors the principle of political ministerial responsibility. It specifies that not only the Government as a whole, but also each individual member, is responsible vis-à-vis Parliament.

The Constitution of the Netherlands anchors the responsibility of ministers to Parliament in article 42. It does not provide any further qualifications or conditions.

Pursuant to articles 20, 49 and 50 of the French Constitution, the French Government is responsible to Parliament. The *Assemblée Nationale* is, however, not the only elected body that gives its confidence to the Government. Because France is a semi-presidential system, 'Parliament has lost the monopoly of political representation in the regime'.[173] However, Parliament's role in holding the Government to account is not of lesser significance in France's semi-presidential system than it is in

---

[172] Yves Sacreas, 'De politieke ministeriële verantwoordelijkheid' [2001] TBP 624, 626.

[173] Denis Baranger, 'Executive Power in France' in Paul Craig and Adam Tomkins (eds), *The Executive and Public Law. Power and Accountability in Comparative Perspective* (Oxford University Press, 2006) 217, 241.

parliamentary systems. On the contrary, it has been labelled 'l'élément clé du regime parlementaire'.[174]

Since the middle of the 19th century, the UK's administrative system has been characterized by its departmental structure, consisting of civil servants, with each department headed by a minister, responsible to Parliament.[175] Ministerial responsibility has traditionally been qualified as a constitutional convention. It has long been characterized by the absence of any written constitutional basis.[176] In 1997, however, both the House of Commons and the House of Lords issued resolutions on the principle,[177] meaning that Parliament 'took ownership of the rules of ministerial responsibility for itself, removing them from the government of the day'.[178] The House of Lords Select Committee on the Constitution argues that these resolutions 'translated the formerly unwritten convention of ministerial responsibility into a clear parliamentary rule, which was no longer unilaterally alterable by government'.[179] The parliamentary resolutions of 1997 have been adopted by the UK Government via the so-called Ministerial Code,[180] a document containing rules and guidance for UK Government ministers, which is regularly revised.

There are only a few statutory references to the principle of political ministerial responsibility. Article 1(3) of the UK's Health and Social Care

---

[174] Louis Favoreu, Patrick Gaïa, Richard Ghevontian, Jean-Louis Mestre, Otto Piersmann, André Roux and Guy Scoffoni, *Droit Constitutionnel* (Dalloz 2009) 755.

[175] Paul Craig, *Administrative Law* (Sweet & Maxwell 2012) 76.

[176] See Colin Turpin, 'Ministerial Responsibility' in Jeffrey Jowell and Dawn Oliver (eds), *The Changing Constitution* (Oxford University Press 1994) 109, 150–151.

[177] HL Deb 20 March 1997, cols 1055–62; HC Deb 19 March 1997, cols 1046–47; Gavin Drewry, 'The Executive: Towards Accountable Government and Effective Governance?' in Jeffrey Jowell and Dawn Oliver (eds), *The Changing Constitution* (Oxford University Press 2011) 187, 204–205.

[178] Adam Tomkins, 'The Struggle to Delimit Executive Power in Britain' in Paul Craig and Adam Tomkins (eds), *The Executive and Public Law. Power and Accountability in Comparative Perspective* (Oxford University Press 2006) 16, 39.

[179] Select Committee on the Constitution, *The Accountability of Civil Servants* (HL 2012-13, 61) para 5; Colin Turpin and Adam Tomkins, *British Government and the Constitution* (7th edn, Cambridge University Press 2011) 574 with references.

[180] Nicholas Bamforth, 'Accountability of and to the Legislature' in Nicholas Bamforth and Peter Leyland (eds), *Accountability in the Contemporary Constitution* (Oxford University Press 2013) 259, 269.

Act, for instance, confirms that '[t]he Secretary of State retains ministerial responsibility to Parliament for the provision of the health service in England', as an aspect of his duty to promote a comprehensive health service. The constitutional documents of the UK's devolved countries also contain written references to political ministerial responsibility.[181]

Some debate exists on the question whether political ministerial responsibility is a legal or rather a political principle. According to Sacreas (Belgium), a distinction has to be made between two separate questions. On the one hand, there is the question whether a minister is responsible, which is legal in nature. On the other hand, there is the question whether that minister is liable to resign, which – according to the author – clearly constitutes a political issue.[182] Similarly, van Nus argues that, in the Netherlands, the so-called 'rule of confidence', on the basis of which Parliament can dismiss a minister if he no longer enjoys Parliament's confidence, is entirely based on political criteria,[183] whereas the scope of political responsibility depends on legal criteria and primarily on the extent to which the minister has powers of influence.[184] The question of whether a minister has to resign, depends on the extent to which he is culpable for his behaviour in the eyes of Parliament. Culpability, however, does not play a role in determining whether ministerial responsibility is at stake in the first place.[185]

A similar reasoning seems to apply in the UK, where the political nature of the principle is often reiterated, but mostly with regard to its enforceability (which takes place in Parliament and not before the

---

[181] See e.g. section 45(2) of the (revised) Scotland Act.

[182] Yves Sacreas, 'De politieke ministeriële verantwoordelijkheid' [2001] TBP 624, 626–627 and 633.

[183] J G L van Nus, *Overheidstoezicht op afstand. Verzelfstandiging van toezichthoudende taken naar zelfstandige bestuursorganen verkend* (Maklu 1995) 53.

[184] See also D J Elzinga, 'De doctrine van de politieke ministeriële verantwoordelijkheid. Over de verhouding tussen staatsrechtelijke normen en de politieke praktijk' in Interuniversitair Centrum voor Staatsrecht v.z.w. (ed), *De ministeriële verantwoordelijkheid / La responsabilité ministérielle* (Kluwer 1991) 17, 23; H G Warmelink, 'Ministeriële verantwoordelijkheid voor ambtelijk handelen' in D J Elzinga (ed), *Ministeriële verantwoordelijkheid in Nederland* (W.E.J. Tjeenk Willink 1994) 103, 104–105.

[185] J G L van Nus, *Overheidstoezicht op afstand. Verzelfstandiging van toezichthoudende taken naar zelfstandige bestuursorganen verkend* (Maklu 1995) 53; J L W Broeksteeg, *Verantwoordelijkheid en aansprakelijkheid in het staatsrecht* (Kluwer 2004) 26 and 56–62.

courts).[186] Whereas the duty to answer to parliamentary questions as well as, according to Turpin, an 'obligation to make redress for defects of policy or administration' are constitutive elements of political ministerial responsibility, this is not the case for the duty to resign, which 'may be induced or avoided according to political circumstances'.[187]

Political ministerial responsibility is deeply rooted in many European Constitutions, since it has up until the present day been regarded by many as an indispensable guarantee to assure genuine parliamentary and thus democratic control of all government activity. Within the European legal sphere, the principle of ministerial responsibility originated from and was first developed in the UK, where its scope gradually crystallized. In the 21st century it remains especially central to government accountability in the Anglo-Saxon tradition.[188] The reconcilability of APBs' status with political ministerial responsibility is indeed regarded as key in many debates on their legitimacy in the UK. This has not only been the case for NDPB-type bodies, but even for executive agencies, which enjoy only a limited degree of political autonomy.

Political ministerial responsibility serves as a 'catch-all principle'. As a device, it allows Parliament to hold the entire administration accountable via just a small group of responsible actors, i.e. ministers. For that reason, ministers are responsible not only for their own actions, but also for those of their civil servants, services and other institutions functioning under their authority or supervision. Political ministerial responsibility for the acts of civil servants, government services and other executive bodies is, however, a qualified and variable mechanism in all four legal systems discussed. The extent to which a minister can be held responsible by Parliament for the acts of an APB is directly proportional to the extent to which he can influence the body's decisions.

Because political ministerial responsibility depends on the statutory powers of steering, oversight, control or supervision that ministers have

---

186 See e.g. Adam Tomkins, 'The Struggle to Delimit Executive Power in Britain' in Paul Craig and Adam Tomkins (eds), *The Executive and Public Law. Power and Accountability in Comparative Perspective* (Oxford University Press 2006) 16, 37; Nicholas Bamforth, 'Accountability of and to the Legislature' in Nicholas Bamforth and Peter Leyland (eds), *Accountability in the Contemporary Constitution* (Oxford University Press 2013) 259, 269.

187 Colin Turpin, 'Ministerial Responsibility' in Jeffrey Jowell and Dawn Oliver (eds), *The Changing Constitution* (Clarendon Press 1994) 109, 109–110.

188 Adam Tomkins, 'The Struggle to Delimit Executive Power in Britain' in Paul Craig and Adam Tomkins (eds), *The Executive and Public Law. Power and Accountability in Comparative Perspective* (Oxford University Press 2006) 16, 37.

been invested with, the creation of most APBs will affect the extent to which the principle applies. As soon as a body is no longer hierarchically subordinate to a ministry or department, ministerial influence necessarily decreases and becomes limited to those powers that are explicitly mentioned in the establishing act. Consequently, ministers are no longer fully accountable.

The Dutch Parliament as well as Dutch scholarly literature[189] increasingly acknowledge that ministers are not fully responsible for ZBOs, but only retain responsibility for the use of their statutory powers, as well as a so-called 'systematic responsibility'. The latter 'entails the care for the general functioning of the ZBO as well as the obligation to evaluate, after a certain period of time, whether the choice for a ZBO for the execution of the government task in question is still justified'.[190] As early as 1982, Lubberdink dedicated an entire book to the significance of political ministerial responsibility for administrative organization, which he called the 'keystone' of Dutch democracy.[191] He approached political ministerial responsibility as an elastic liability: it increases with the powers that ministers have.[192] Zijlstra has argued that political responsibility is a 'normative starting point' of the law on administrative organization: administrative tasks and powers should be entrusted to representative bodies or to those who are responsible to such bodies (such as ministers).[193] 'Delegation to other (autonomous) administrative bodies is only permissible in exceptional circumstances and provided that this is properly motivated.'[194]

In Belgium as well, it is recognized that ministers are not responsible (only) insofar that they are incompetent, meaning that they lack powers of influence, supervision etc.[195] Velaers argues that neither 'the legislature, nor the executive can organize the administration in such a way that

---

189 E.g. Saskia Lavrijssen, *Onafhankelijke mededingingstoezichthouders, regulerende bevoegdheden en de waarborgen voor good governance* (Boom Juridische uitgevers 2006) 97.

190 Eerste Kamer 2012–2013, 23 186, D, 21.

191 H G Lubberdink, *De betekenis van de ministeriële verantwoordelijkheid voor de organisatie van het openbaar bestuur* (Kluwer 1982) 4.

192 ibid 11–13. The author emphasizes that it is not the actual exercise of influence, but the legal possibility to do so, that matters.

193 Sjoerd E Zijlstra, *Bestuurlijk Organisatierecht* (Kluwer 2009) 71–72.

194 ibid 72.

195 See Jan Velaers, 'Over de politieke verantwoordelijkheid van ministers' in Maurice Adams, Renate Barbaix, Herman Braeckmans et al. (eds), *Verantwoordelijkheid en recht: eerste facultair congres Faculteit Rechten Universiteit*

the Government no longer has any say about it and can hence no longer be called to account by Parliament'.[196] Therefore, the author submits that there is no room for complete political autonomy of government institutions in the Belgian system, but only for a qualified and limited form, with sufficient powers of supervision for ministers, allowing them to be held responsible by Parliament.[197] The situation becomes problematic from a constitutional viewpoint 'when the legislature entrusts government tasks to bodies vis-à-vis which the minister has no say at all, so that he can also no longer be held accountable'.[198] Observing that APBs have become 'inevitable' in administrative organization, Velaers argues that they nevertheless have to be embedded in the framework that is designed for the conduct of government in the Constitution. Political ministerial responsibility is an essential element in this configuration. The author is particularly worried about bodies invested with unilateral decision-making powers. '[I]t does not suffice that they are subject to administrative, financial, budget-technical or legal supervision. There also has to be a form of political supervision, which ensures that ministerial responsibility remains intact.'[199]

In France, the CC's case law on the effect of AAIs on political ministerial responsibility has, perhaps deliberately, remained vague. The Council of State has ascertained that the CC has definitely not declared the mere nature of AAIs to be incompatible with the principle of political ministerial responsibility.[200] At the same time, however, the CC has acknowledged that ministerial responsibility also applies to the missions of AAIs, because the Government has the power to challenge the legality of AAIs' actions before the courts.[201] This form of 'oversight', however, has obvious limits. In its 2006 report, the *Assemblée Nationale* acknowledged that, because AAIs do not function under the Government's

Antwerpen, 14 November 2008 (Kluwer 2008) 361, 367 with reference to the advisory practice of the Council of State, Legislation Section.

196 ibid 369ff.

197 ibid 370.

198 ibid 371.

199 ibid 373.

200 Conseil d'État – Rapport public 2001, 294.

201 CC, déc. 86-217 DC du 18 Septembre 1986, para 23; Catherine Teitgen-Colly, 'Les instances de régulation et la constitution' [1990] RDP 153, 249ff.

authority, democratic control on their performance cannot be accomplished via the mechanism of political ministerial responsibility before Parliament.[202]

Even though 'ministerial responsibility is not enforced by the judiciary' in the UK, it has been observed that 'in the case law, there are examples of *dicta* which clearly recognise the principle'.[203] In one of these judgments, *Carltona Ltd v Commissioner of Works*,[204] it was recognized by the court that '[w]here the power to make a discretionary decision affecting an individual is vested in a minister, an official within the department may in general take that decision on behalf of the minister (the *Carltona* principle), unless there are express or implied limitations in the statute conferring the power'.[205] This case law consequently 'recognised that ministerial powers could, in appropriate cases, be exercised on their behalf by civil servants in their department without infringing the legal principle that delegated powers cannot normally be further delegated: *delegatus non potest delegare*'.[206] However, a decision taken by officials in the name of the minister after delegation was to be regarded as 'the act of the minister, in the sense that the minister was responsible to Parliament for its consequences'.[207] The reverse of ministers' (individual) responsibility for their own decisions or actions and those of the officials working in their departments is the lack of responsibility and anonymity of the civil service. Indeed, it is generally assumed that 'civil servants bear no responsibility to Parliament distinct from that of their minister'.[208]

---

[202] Assemblée Nationale No 3166 / Sénat No 404 – Office Parlementaire d'Évaluation de la Législation – *Rapport sur les Autorités Administratives Indépendantes* par M. Patrice Gélard, Sénateur, Tome I: Rapport (2006) 115. Hereinafter: Assemblée Nationale, *Rapport sur les AAIs*, I (2006).

[203] Peter Leyland and Gordon Anthony, *Textbook on Administrative Law* (Oxford University Press 2009) 110 with reference to *Carltona Ltd v Commissioner of Works* [1943] 2 All ER 560 and *R v Secretary of State for the Home Department, ex p Oladehinde* [1991] 1 AC 254.

[204] *Carltona Ltd v Commissioner of Works* [1943] 2 All ER 560.

[205] A W Bradley and K D Ewing, *Constitutional & Administrative Law* (Longman Pearson 2011) 275.

[206] O Hood Phillips, Paul Jackson and Patricia Leopold, *Constitutional and Administrative Law* (Sweet & Maxwell 2001) 379.

[207] Peter Leyland and Gordon Anthony, *Textbook on Administrative Law* (Oxford University Press 2009) 105 with references.

[208] Colin Turpin, 'Ministerial Responsibility' in Jeffrey Jowell and Dawn Oliver (eds), *The Changing Constitution* (Clarendon Press 1994) 109, 120–121.

The rise of APBs in the UK's administrative organization has caused doubts about both the scope of the *Carltona* doctrine and its sustainability, especially when it comes to its consequences for ministerial responsibility. The success of the 'Next Steps programme' in particular, resulting in the delegation of various administrative responsibilities to executive agencies, has encouraged these debates. It has more precisely reinforced ideas about a possible doctrinal distinction between responsibility on the one hand and accountability on the other.[209] Adherents of the theory argue that, whereas ministers are always accountable for the acts or omissions of the administration, they cannot always be held responsible. The notion of responsibility is here linked to that of imputability and hence to the question of whether the minister could be blamed or reproached for the erroneous behaviour of the person or body under scrutiny.[210] Since executive agencies possess so-called 'operational autonomy', under this theory, ministers would not be responsible for their operational decisions. 'Where an error occurs at the level of operations as opposed to policy the minister may, for example, discharge his accountability by reporting to Parliament that he has dismissed or disciplined the head of the agency.'[211] For (broad) policy matters, on the other hand, responsibility would remain intact.[212]

Some have warned that '[t]he distinction between accountability and responsibility requires close scrutiny, since it provides a means by which a minister may avoid liability for unpopular or mistaken decisions; and it opens up potential areas of government for which no one is "responsible"

---

[209] O Hood Phillips, Paul Jackson and Patricia Leopold, *Constitutional and Administrative Law* (Sweet & Maxwell 2001) 379.

[210] Select Committee on the Constitution, *The Accountability of Civil Servants* (HL 2012–13, 61) paras 13–14. See also A W Bradley and K D Ewing, *Constitutional & Administrative Law* (Longman Pearson 2011) 113; Margaret L Liu, 'Ministerial Responsibility and Constitutional Law' (2002) 7(2) Coventry Law Journal 25, 29.

[211] O Hood Phillips, Paul Jackson and Patricia Leopold, *Constitutional and Administrative Law* (Sweet & Maxwell 2001) 379.

[212] Margaret L Liu, 'Ministerial Responsibility and Constitutional Law' (2002) 7(2) Coventry Law Journal 25, 29; Gavin Drewry, 'The Executive: Towards Accountable Government and Effective Governance?' in Jeffrey Jowell and Dawn Oliver (eds), *The Changing Constitution* (7th edn, Oxford University Press 2011) 187, 203 with reference to the paper *The Civil Service – Taking Forward Continuity and Change*, Cm. 2748 (1995) 28, http://www.official-documents.gov.uk/document/cm27/2748/2748.pdf.

to Parliament, even though a minister remains "accountable"'.[213] A further problem with the theory 'is that highly contentious political issues often arise out of individual operational decisions. There is no neat line to be drawn between policy and operation.'[214] The House of Lords Select Committee on the Constitution has firmly rejected the existence of a constitutional dichotomy between accountability and responsibility in its 2012 report *The Accountability of Civil Servants*.[215]

Finally, it should be noted that the relationship between APBs as a model for administrative organization on the one hand and political ministerial responsibility on the other is not one-sidedly negative. In the Netherlands one of the main arguments developed for establishing APBs in the 1980s and 1990s was precisely that they would contribute to the proper functioning of political ministerial responsibility. APBs were more precisely regarded as useful instruments in the battle against 'incidentalism'. Political ministerial responsibility for each and every individual decision was deemed to hold a risk of ministers having to focus too much on the details, rather than on long-term policies.[216]

APBs can indeed contribute to the preservation of the primacy of politics. If tasks of policy execution are entrusted to APBs, central government is partly discharged, meaning that the political executive has more time to engage in its task of policy development. This was explicitly recognized by the drafters of the Flemish framework legislation.[217] Flinders argues that APBs can free ministers from day-to-day political concerns and thus help them to focus on strategic matters.[218] It

---

213 A W Bradley and K D Ewing, *Constitutional & Administrative Law* (Longman Pearson 2011) 113–114. Similarly: Margaret L Liu, 'Ministerial Responsibility and Constitutional Law' (2002) 7(2) Coventry Law Journal 25, 37.

214 R Baldwin, '"The Next Steps": Ministerial Responsibility and Government by Agency' (1988) 51(5) MLR 622, 625.

215 Select Committee on the Constitution, *The Accountability of Civil Servants* (HL 2012–13, 61) para 17.

216 Sjoerd E Zijlstra, 'Weg met de zelfstandige bestuursorganen?' (2004) 38 NJB 1980, 1981 with reference to the report of the Scheltema Commission ('Rapport Steekhoudend Ministerschap', Kamerstukken II 1992/93, 21 427, nrs. 40 and 41). See also J L Boxum, 'Ministeriële verantwoordelijkheid en zelfstandige bestuursorganen' in D J Elzinga (ed), *Ministeriële verantwoordelijkheid in Nederland* (W.E.J. Tjeenk Willink 1994) 257, 274–276.

217 *Parl.St.* Vl.Parl. 2002–03, nr. 1612/1, 7.

218 Matthew Flinders, *Delegated Governance and the British State: Walking without Order* (Oxford University Press 2008) 145.

was believed that the Next Steps programme would enable ministers to 'concentrate their minds on policy'.[219]

c. Democratic control of the administration by elected representatives

Political ministerial responsibility ensures that all government power orbits around the elected democratic centre, constituted by Parliament. The mechanism of political ministerial responsibility facilitates the process of control by the elected representatives of the people on the political executive and the administration. Mulgan observes that legislatures in parliamentary systems with large bureaucracies are largely left 'in the role of legitimators and scrutinisers of government activity', pointing out that '[o]verall, however, holding the executive accountable through public inquiry and debate has become the dominant function of all modern legislatures'.[220] In France, a constitutional revision of 2008 explicitly enshrined the controlling role of the French Parliament vis-à-vis governmental action. Pursuant to article 24 of the Constitution, Parliament controls the action of the Government and evaluates public policies.

Political ministerial responsibility and democratic control by elected representatives 'act like mirrors', so to speak, with political ministerial responsibility fulfilling the role of an 'umbrella instrument' for parliamentary control.[221] Consequently, 'ministerial accountability and parliamentary (democratic) control have become communicating vessels'.[222] Since parliamentary supervision of the administration is still to an important degree dependent upon political ministerial responsibility, the harm done to the latter principle by creating APBs naturally affects the

---

[219] Gavin Drewry, 'Revolution in Whitehall: The Next Steps and Beyond' in Jeffrey Jowell and Dawn Oliver (eds), *The Changing Constitution* (3rd edn, Oxford University Press 1994) 155, 159.

[220] Richard Mulgan, *Holding Power to Account: Accountability in Modern Democracies* (Palgrave Macmillan 2003) 45.

[221] D J Elzinga, 'De politieke ministeriële verantwoordelijkheid' in D J Elzinga (ed), *Ministeriële verantwoordelijkheid in Nederland* (W.E.J. Tjeenk Willink 1994) 31, 31 and 35.

[222] Henk R B M Kummeling and Antonius P W Duijkersloot, 'Agencies and the Netherlands' in Tom Zwart and Luc Verhey (eds), *Agencies in European and Comparative Law* (Intersentia 2003) 79, 83.

former.[223] In France, the loss of democratic scrutiny by elected representatives as a consequence of the loss of ministerial supervision is considered a particular challenge for (the controlling capacity of) Parliament.[224]

Political ministerial responsibility enables parliaments to control the administration, but it is not the only instrument conceivable to achieve this goal. The further development of forms of direct parliamentary supervision is increasingly advocated.[225] One of the debates surrounding such direct parliamentary supervision of APBs revolves around the constitutionality of lineal relationships of authority between Parliament and civil servants, including those that work for APBs. In Belgium, it is generally believed that, as a rule, civil servants cannot be held accountable by the Chamber of Representatives in any direct manner. It is the competent minister who is held responsible for their actions.[226] This is also true for (the staff of) APBs.[227]

In the Netherlands, it is assumed that civil servants are not obliged to appear before Parliament directly to give evidence, unless ministers instruct them to do so.[228] It has been argued that this principle (*a fortiori*) applies to directors within ZBOs.[229] Some, conversely, argue that such objections are invalid, because there is no hierarchical relationship between ministers and civil servants working for ZBOs. Consequently, Parliament does not encroach on the constitutionally protected powers of

---

[223] Sjoerd E Zijlstra, 'Weg met de zelfstandige bestuursorganen?' (2004) 38 NJB 1980, 1981.

[224] See Assemblée Nationale, *Rapport sur les AAIs*, I (2006) 20.

[225] E.g. Aalt W Heringa and Luc F M Verhey, 'Independent Agencies and Political Control' in Tom Zwart and Luc Verhey (eds), *Agencies in European and Comparative Law* (Intersentia 2003) 155, 164.

[226] Jan Velaers, 'Over de politieke verantwoordelijkheid van ministers' in Maurice Adams, Renate Barbaix, Herman Braeckmans et al. (eds), *Verantwoordelijkheid en recht: eerste facultair congres Faculteit Rechten Universiteit Antwerpen, 14 November 2008* (Kluwer 2008) 361, 365.

[227] ibid 365–366; Yves Sacreas, 'De politieke ministeriële verantwoordelijkheid' [2001] TBP 624, 629.

[228] E.g. E Geurink, 'Ministeriële verantwoordelijkheid voor ambtenaren' in J L W Broeksteeg, J Th J van den Berg and L F M Verhey (eds), *Ministeriële verantwoordelijkheid opnieuw gewogen* (Kluwer 2006) 4, 46.

[229] M M den Boer, 'Zelfstandige bestuursorganen uit de zelfkant van de democratie?' in C P J Goorden, M M Den Boer and F K Buijn (eds), *Zbo's, verzelfstandiging en privatisering* (Tjeenk Willink 1997) 124, 151 and 160.

the Government vis-à-vis the administration when it interrogates these civil servants.[230]

In France, the objections against direct parliamentary control seem less fierce. The literature on AAIs admits that it is a constitutional tradition that Parliament does not itself control the administration directly, but that it is difficult to respect that principle with regard to AAIs.[231]

Because of the sheer size of ministries in the UK today, as well as increasing decentralization, the assumption that ministerial responsibility extends to all the acts of the administration has been labelled 'largely a mythical aspiration'.[232] Some believe that the current reforms with regard to the APB landscape 'overplay the importance of democracy to the maintenance of accountability within the modern constitution and implicitly over-emphasise the continuing effectiveness of the doctrine of ministerial responsibility'.[233] A popular suggestion has been the reinforcement (in terms of people and means) of select committees in both Houses of Parliament.[234] Turpin, for instance, rather than emphasizing the importance of political ministerial responsibility as such, was one of the first to focus on its purpose or effect in a democratic society, i.e. ensuring responsibility vis-à-vis representative institutions. The author

---

[230] E.g. J G L van Nus, *Overheidstoezicht op afstand. Verzelfstandiging van toezichthoudende taken naar zelfstandige bestuursorganen verkend* (Maklu 1995) 47–48; L F M Verhey and N Verheij, 'De macht van marktmeesters, markttoezicht in constitutioneel perspectief' [2005] *Toezicht, Handelingen Nederlandse Juristenvereniging* 135, 239–240.

[231] Jean-Louis Autin, 'Le devenir des autorités administratives indépendantes' [2010] RFDA 875, 883.

[232] Gavin Drewry, 'The Executive: Towards Accountable Government and Effective Governance?' in Jeffrey Jowell and Dawn Oliver (eds), *The Changing Constitution* (7th edn, Oxford University Press 2011) 187, 188.

[233] Richard Kirkham, 'Quangos, Coalition Government and the Ombudsmen' (2010) 32(4) Journal of Social Welfare & Family Law 411, 412. See also (as an early example) Nevil Johnson, 'Accountability, Control and Complexity: Moving Beyond Ministerial Responsibility' in Anthony Barker (ed), *Quangos in Britain. Government and the Networks of Public Policy-Making* (Palgrave Macmillan 1982) 206, 218.

[234] E.g. Peter Leyland and Gordon Anthony, *Textbook on Administrative Law* (Oxford University Press 2009) 115; Public Administration Select Committee, *Smaller Government: Shrinking the Quango State* (HC 2010–11, 537) 35. Select committees can also reinforce political ministerial responsibility instead of serving as a substitute for its controlling function. This is the case when select committees question ministers and/or encourage them to take action against deficiencies in the administration.

acknowledged, however, that if Parliament itself was to hold the administration accountable, it needed new instruments.

> Parliament must be able to get answers from those who are responsible to it about their actions and reasons for acting (or for not acting) and must have power to exact what seems necessary, in the light of the information so obtained, by way of redress, change of behaviour or acknowledgment of default on the part of those answering to it.[235]

As early as 1994, it was acknowledged that civil servants increasingly played a role in policy matters. The lack of a theory on procedures and mechanisms to ensure (direct) responsibility to Parliament for these civil servants was deemed problematic.[236]

There is, however, a long-standing debate in the UK on the extent to which civil servants are under an obligation to appear before select committees and to answer their questions when they are summoned to do so. In 1980, the Cabinet Office formulated an answer to these questions in the so-called Osmotherly rules, which have been updated on various occasions since, and which were meant to serve as guidelines for civil servants. It is questionable, however, whether the select committees should feel at all restricted by these rules, which have no legal, let alone constitutional value.[237] The 2014 version of the Osmotherly rules[238] strongly emphasizes that civil servants who give evidence to select committees do so as representatives of their ministers and act under their directions when giving evidence. Consequently, it is the minister and not the civil servant who is accountable to Parliament for the evidence given to the committee.[239] Even though the staff of NDPBs and other arm's-length bodies (ALBs) usually do not qualify as civil servants, the Cabinet Office has declared the Osmotherly rules applicable to them as well. Members of NDPBs are allowed to give evidence to select committees directly[240] but it is unclear whether and to what extent they do so in their

---

[235] Colin Turpin, 'Ministerial Responsibility' in Jeffrey Jowell and Dawn Oliver (eds), *The Changing Constitution* (Clarendon Press 1994) 109, 112 with references.

[236] ibid 123.

[237] Select Committee on the Constitution, *The Accountability of Civil Servants* (HL 2012–13, 61) para 70 in particular.

[238] Hereinafter: Osmotherly rules 2014, https://www.gov.uk/government/uploads/system/uploads/attachment_data/file/364600/Osmotherly_Rules_October_2014.pdf.

[239] Osmotherly rules 2014 paras 4, 9 and 10.

[240] Osmotherly rules 2014, paras 16 and 17.

own name or on behalf of the minister. It is an established practice that chief executives of executive agencies answer written questions of MPs.[241] As far as NDPBs are concerned, questions regarding their day-to-day operations will, in practice, be answered by the chief executive officer. In the case of complex or sensitive issues, the minister himself will usually reply.[242] When questions concern policies and the frameworks within which the bodies operate, ministers themselves will answer.[243] The House of Lords Select Committee on the Constitution has adopted the view that '[t]aking evidence from civil servants is complementary to, not a replacement for, the accountability of ministers'[244] and has consequently not acknowledged or endorsed a division of responsibilities in this regard.

This recent statement of the House of Lords Select Committee on the Constitution, combined with its firm rejection of the accountability/responsibility dichotomy (*supra*) indicate that political ministerial responsibility is still considered the ultimate and preferred mechanism for ensuring the democratic legitimacy of the administrative state in the UK. Whereas the committee in its above-mentioned 2012 report acknowledged that APBs perform essential functions and are often established for valid reasons, it also argued that their insulation from ministerial responsibility was neither obvious nor feasible. The committee, for instance, referred to the fact that 'matters which are, on a technical level, purely concerned with implementation are nonetheless extremely politically sensitive, such that ministers will on occasion wish to retain control over them'. It therefore concluded that '[t]he accountability mechanisms of ALBs are a supplement to ministers' constitutional responsibility to

---

[241] Margaret L Liu, 'Ministerial Responsibility and Constitutional Law' (2002) 7(2) Coventry Law Journal 25, 33; Cabinet Office, 'Executive Agencies: A Guide for Departments', https://www.gov.uk/government/uploads/system/uploads/attachment_data/file/80076/exec_agencies_guidance_oct06_0.pdf, 16.

[242] Paul Craig, *Administrative Law* (Sweet & Maxwell 2012) 94, referring to Cabinet Office, 'Public Bodies: A Guide for Departments. Chapter 8: Policy – Openness and Accountability', https://www.gov.uk/government/uploads/system/uploads/attachment_data/file/80085/PublicBodiesGuide2006_8_policy_openness_0.pdf, para 5.1.

[243] Cabinet Office, 'Public Bodies: A Guide for Departments. Chapter 8: Policy – Openness and Accountability', https://www.gov.uk/government/uploads/system/uploads/attachment_data/file/80085/PublicBodiesGuide2006_8_policy_openness_0.pdf, para 5.2.

[244] Select Committee on the Constitution, *The Accountability of Civil Servants* (HL 2012–13, 61) para 79. On this issue, see also A W Bradley and K D Ewing, *Constitutional & Administrative Law* (Longman Pearson 2011) 277–279.

Parliament, not a replacement for it. The primary means by which civil servants in ALBs are held to account is via the convention of individual ministerial responsibility'.[245]

In 'Public Bodies: A Guide for Departments', the Cabinet Office deems ministers accountable to Parliament for the degree of independence given to NDPBs, for their usefulness as instruments of government policy and for their overall effectiveness and efficiency.[246] The House of Lords Select Committee on the Constitution in turn seems to decline the 'policy-implementation divide' as a reason to attenuate ministerial responsibility, pointing out that 'even where a split between policy and implementation is possible and desirable, the accountability for implementation remains intact'.[247] At the same time, however, the committee acknowledges that 'the nature of the decisions taken makes it inappropriate for ministers to be directly involved in the oversight of those decisions'.[248] These statements seem difficult to reconcile: if ministers cannot exercise oversight on day-to-day decisions, implementing policy, how can they nonetheless be expected to assume responsibility for that implementation? Such contradictions are illustrative for the ambiguous attitude that the UK Parliament has been adopting towards APBs in general and NDPBs in particular for some years now and that was also present in the debates on the Public Bodies Bill, discussed later in this Chapter. On the one hand, it is felt that a substantial number of these entities are performing well and should genuinely enjoy a certain degree of autonomy vis-à-vis elected politicians. On the other hand, genuine concerns exist that many of these bodies are perceived by the public as undemocratic and Parliament feels that it should be able to hold central government, i.e. the competent minister, accountable for their actions and decisions.

---

[245] Select Committee on the Constitution, *The Accountability of Civil Servants* (HL 2012–13, 61) para 132.

[246] Cabinet Office, 'Public Bodies: A Guide for Departments. Chapter 2: Policy and Characteristics of a Public Body', https://www.gov.uk/government/uploads/system/uploads/attachment_data/file/80079/PublicBodiesGuide2006_2_policy_Characteristics_0.pdf, para 6.1.

[247] Select Committee on the Constitution, *The Accountability of Civil Servants* (HL 2012–13, 61) paras 112–113.

[248] ibid para 107.

d. Centrality

Legality, political ministerial responsibility and control by elected representatives have a 'centralizing impact'[249] since they ensure that administrative power originates from and is at all times (re)traceable to Parliament. Centrality is a derivative of the three fundamental principles that were just discussed. Therefore, unlike these principles, centrality as such is not a constitutional principle with any intrinsic value. It describes a starting position: an alpha point of administrative organization.

In a centralized system, ministers are assisted by civil servants, organized in departments or government services. Characteristic of these civil servants is at the same time (and somewhat paradoxically) their independence of the political system and the hierarchical position that they are in vis-à-vis their political principal, i.e. the competent minister. In this Weberian model, '[b]ureaucrats are expected to be loyal to elected leaders, but not a tool for executing arbitrary commands'.[250] The hierarchical relationship between civil servants and ministers typically implies that the latter can give orders to civil servants and/or have the power to substitute their decisions with their own, subject to the limitation of non-arbitrariness. If ministers control the administration and elected representatives control ministers, this closes the circle and the administration is ultimately under democratic control. Consequently, a centralized system of administration founds all state power on political decision making. The Constitutions of the four systems discussed present a system in which no administrative decision can a priori escape the influence of elected politicians. This is the result of, and the rationale behind, the interplay of the three principles discussed above.

Administrative organization through APBs often detracts from the principle of centrality, since it places administrative power at a certain distance from Parliament and, hence, from the elected representatives of the people. In many cases, though not always, the creation of APBs goes hand in hand with the loss of powers of hierarchical steering and supervision, breaking the metaphorical circle at least to a certain extent.

---

[249] Nevil Johnson, 'Accountability, Control and Complexity: Moving Beyond Ministerial Responsibility' in Anthony Barker (ed), *Quangos in Britain. Government and the Networks of Public Policy-Making* (Palgrave Macmillan 1982) 206, 213.

[250] Johan P Olsen, 'Democratic Government, Institutional Autonomy and the Dynamics of Change' (2009) 32(3) West European Politics 439, 449. See also Linda Deleon, 'Public Management, Democracy, and Politics' in Ewan Ferlie, Laurence E Lynn and Christopher Pollit (eds), *The Oxford Handbook of Public Management* (Oxford University Press 2008) 102, 107.

Since centrality is the outcome of the combined action of three fundamental principles, it can be considered a normative principle as such. From a constitutional viewpoint, APBs are always an exception, never the rule. For that reason, the principle of centrality is the basis for requiring a sound justification whenever APBs are entrusted with government tasks. This line of reasoning plays a central role for the phenomenon of framework legislation with respect to APBs, discussed further on in this chapter.

Even though centrality as such is first and foremost a derivative of the three other principles discussed under this title, rather than an autonomous precept, there are traces of an idea of centrality as such in the (codified) Constitutions of Belgium, France and the Netherlands. Pursuant to article 33 of the Belgian Constitution, all powers are derived from the Nation and are exercised as prescribed by the Constitution. Article 37 of the Constitution stipulates that the federal executive power, as conceived by the Constitution, rests with the King (i.e. the federal government). According to the Council of State, Legislation Section, executive power cannot be transferred unless the central executive retains some power of supervision.[251] Since all forms of decentralization are deviations from the constitutional setting, they can only be justified if due compensation is provided in the form of control mechanisms. In other words: administrative tasks have to be performed *by* or at least under the control of the Government, which is itself under the democratic control of Parliament.[252] The Council consequently adopts a teleological interpretation of articles 33 and 37 of the Constitution, allowing for deviations of the centralized scheme, but expecting compensations in order to ensure that the goal behind centralization, i.e. preserving the democratic legitimacy of the administration, is achieved.

Similarly to the Belgian Constitution, article 56 of the Constitution of the Netherlands used to provide that the executive power rested with the King. This provision implied a presumption of hierarchical subordination of the administration to the King (or the Government).[253] Pursuant to article 44 of the current Dutch Constitution, ministries are led by a minister. Today, this provision is accepted as the basis for the rule that civil servants in ministerial departments find themselves in a hierarchical

---

251 *Parl.St.* Kamer 2001–02, nr. 1937/1, 60.

252 See Jan Velaers, *De Grondwet en de Raad van State, Afdeling wetgeving* (Maklu 1999) 266 on article 37 of the Constitution with reference to the advisory practice of the Council of State, Legislation Section.

253 H G Lubberdink, *De betekenis van de ministeriele verantwoordelijkheid voor de organisatie van het openbaar bestuur* (Kluwer 1982) 77–78.

relationship with their competent minister.[254] Dutch scholarship argues that exceptions to this rule require a thorough motivation, deriving this requirement from the principle of democracy and the principle that government tasks are performed under political responsibility, both of which are considered 'starting points' for the design of administrative organization.[255]

As far as France is concerned, article 20, §2 of the Constitution, which occupies a central position in French public law,[256] provides that the government shall have the public service and the armed forces at its disposal. Consequently, 'the 1958 Constitution is premised on the idea that the administration of the state is subordinate hierarchically to a minister (or the Prime Minister)'.[257] France's strong 'scheme of centralized hierarchy',[258] anchored in its written Constitution, provokes the expectation that the integration of APBs in the administrative system has met with difficulties or objections. A 2002 OECD study labelled APBs as 'unusual' in the French system 'insofar as they constitute an exception to the traditional French approach to administration, whereby the administrative apparatus of the state culminates in the minister and is subject to the guidance, or at least the supervision, of the government'.[259] A 2003

---

[254] A D Belinfante and J L de Reede, *Beginselen van het Nederlandse staatsrecht* (Kluwer 2012); J L W Broeksteeg, *Verantwoordelijkheid en aansprakelijkheid in het staatsrecht* (Kluwer 2004) 55.

[255] E.g. Sjoerd E Zijlstra and Kirsten Wilkeshuis, 'Verantwoordelijkheid: bevoegdheid en publieke taak' in J L W Broeksteeg, J Th J van den Berg and L F M Verhey (eds), *Ministeriële verantwoordelijkheid opnieuw gewogen* (Kluwer 2006) 9, 13.

[256] Catherine Teitgen-Colly, 'Les instances de régulation et la constitution' [1990] RDP 153, 214.

[257] E.g. Aalt W Heringa, 'Agencies in France. Autorités Administratives Centrales Indépendantes / National Independent Administrative Authorities' in Tom Zwart and Luc Verhey (eds), *Agencies in European and Comparative Law* (Intersentia 2003) 37, 37. See also Jean-Philippe Feldman, 'Les "autorités administratives indépendantes" sont-elles légitimes? Sur les AAI en général et le Conseil supérieur de l'audiovisuel en particulier' [2010] Receuil Dalloz 2852, 2854.

[258] Aalt W Heringa, 'Agencies in France. Autorités Administratives Centrales Indépendantes / National Independent Administrative Authorities' in Tom Zwart and Luc Verhey (eds), *Agencies in European and Comparative Law* (Intersentia 2003) 37, 38.

[259] Claude Rochet, Marc Cabane and Simon Formery, 'France' in OECD, *Distributed Public Governance* 71, 76. See also Jacques Chevallier, 'Réflexions sur l'institution des autorités administratives indépendantes' [1986] JCP-G I-3254.

Dutch study on French AAIs concludes that they could be considered an infringement of the central hierarchy laid down in article 20 of the Constitution.[260] In 2006, the French *Assemblée Nationale*, referring to article 20 of the Constitution, labelled AAIs 'a major innovation in administrative organisation'.[261]

Up until now and perhaps surprisingly, the question of the compatibility of AAIs with article 20 of the Constitution has never been brought before the French CC, nor has the CC ever put it forward *ex officio*. According to some literature, the CC has endorsed the existence of AAIs by not declaring them unconstitutional, even though it has had the opportunity to do so.[262] Other literature shares this conclusion, pointing out, however, that this endorsement has not been unqualified, since certain limits have been imposed on the possibility of delegation to AAIs,[263] most of which were discussed in greater or lesser detail earlier in this chapter.

Apart from article 20 of the Constitution, France's article 3 of the *Déclaration des Droits de l'Homme et du Citoyen* enshrines a provision similar to the one anchored in article 33 of the Belgian Constitution (*supra*), stipulating that 'le principe de toute souveraineté réside dans la Nation. Nul corps, nul individu ne peut exercer d'autorité qui n'en émane expressément'. This provision reinforces the centrality claim.[264]

E. Common Concerns

The previous titles of this section have demonstrated how APBs raise questions from the viewpoint of three constitutional meta values that all four legal systems studied have in common: constitutionalism, the rule of law and democracy. As regards constitutionalism, the threat that some

---

260 Aalt W Heringa and Luc F M Verhey, 'Independent Agencies and Political Control' in Tom Zwart and Luc Verhey (eds), *Agencies in European and Comparative Law* (Intersentia 2003) 155, 159.

261 Assemblée Nationale, *Rapport sur les AAIs*, I (2006) 29.

262 E.g. Jeannette Bougrab, 'Independent Administrative Authorities in France' in Roberto Caranta, Mads Adenas and Duncan Fairgrieve (eds), *Independent Administrative Authorities* (British Institute of International and Comparative Law 2004) 53.

263 Catherine Teitgen Colly, 'Les instances de régulation et la constitution' [1990] RDP 153, 211; Aalt W Heringa and Luc F M Verhey, 'Independent Agencies and Political Control' in Tom Zwart and Luc Verhey (eds), *Agencies in European and Comparative Law* (Intersentia 2003) 155, 159.

264 Catherine Teitgen-Colly, 'Les instances de régulation et la constitution' [1990] RDP 153, 215.

APBs pose to the principle of separation of powers was discussed and identified as especially problematic within the French legal system. The reason for that is that France has a particular tradition of AAIs combining rule-making, adjudicatory and quasi-judicial powers. The fact that debates on APBs and separation of powers are fewer or less intense in Belgium, the Netherlands and the UK does not mean that reflection on such issues will remain largely inexpedient for these legal systems in the future. This is especially so because the obligations and requirements that flow from the trend of 'EU impulse' described in Chapter 2 increasingly involve bodies that, like many French AAIs today, indeed combine the functions originally entrusted to the three traditional state powers separately.

The relationship between the creation of APBs and the rule of law was examined exclusively from the angles of transparency and legal certainty. This is not to say that APBs are entirely unproblematic from the viewpoint of other aspects of the rule of law, such as legal protection by the courts and/or due process. The reinforcement of both of these values has, however, from the very outset, been promoted as going hand in hand with the proliferation of APBs rather than being hollowed out by that very phenomenon.[265] Of course, debates exist on the proper way in which to organize judicial accountability for APBs. Moreover, APBs are sometimes accused of being established to avoid the application of binding and protective rules of administrative law. However, in many cases, the protection that citizens enjoy vis-à-vis the acts of APBs from a judicial and procedural viewpoint is of a more sophisticated nature than the mechanisms and guarantees available vis-à-vis the actions of the more traditional state institutions. Therefore, this chapter has focused on legal certainty and transparency as derivatives of the rule of law. Observations on the particular problem of a lack of insight in the organizational chart of the administration because of the rise of APBs increasingly feature in critical reports and contributions issued by parliaments and academic communities.

Even though the detriment posed by APBs to the principles of separation of powers and legal certainty should not be discounted as immaterial or of inferior importance, it cannot be denied that, today, most legal questions surrounding APBs stem from the meta value of democracy.[266] The central concern is that of how to ensure that administrative

---

[265] See the discussion on procedural and legal accountability in Chapter 5.

[266] And, as the preceding analysis confirms, both objections formulated on the basis of separation of powers and those that flow from the principle of legal

decisions that involve discretion and thus decisions on policy are made under the ultimate responsibility of elected government.

Throughout the four systems studied, different actors (parliaments, advisory bodies, courts, scholars etc.) tend to place their emphasis differently, in the sense that they choose a different principle as the primary lens through which they analyse and evaluate the democratic nature of administrative organization. Sometimes, differences run largely along country lines: compared with political ministerial responsibility, legality seems less central in the British and Belgian tradition, whereas the opposite seems true for the French system, especially when it comes to the delegation of rule-making powers. The Dutch system, in turn, seems to value both equally.

An example makes this claim about different presentations, angles of incidence or solutions for the same democratic claim more tangible. It was explained that entrusting AAIs with rule-making powers in France was originally regarded as a problem of separation of powers. However, the same issue recurred as an aspect of the principle of legality, which was qualified as a dimension of the meta value of democracy.

The CC's flexible approach towards entrusting bodies that are devoid of political supervision with rule-making powers may seem to jeopardize the political legitimation of the administration via elected representation. The CC indeed does not regard the lack of hierarchical supervision or a system of *tutelle*, traditionally applied to government services or bodies, as unconstitutional. Although it acknowledges the right of the Government to take legal action before the courts against the acts of AAIs, it omits to demand of the legislature that it provides means through which the Government can control the discretionary powers exercised by AAIs.

When we compare this position to the tradition of interpretation and application of the Constitution with regard to APBs in Belgium, the French CC may look like a rather poor protector of democracy. Pursuant to the Belgian Council of State, Legislation Section, APBs that have been invested with coercive powers that involve discretion, should be subject to some form of political control, so that their decisions can subsequently, via political ministerial responsibility, be controlled by Parliament.[267] Consequently, the Belgian Council of State does require a form of political supervision *sensu stricto*, whereas the French CC has fully recognized the legitimacy of AAIs lacking any such form of control. This

certainty or transparency are often reformulated as derivatives of democratic concerns.

267 E.g. *Parl.St.* Kamer 2001 02, nr. 1937/1, 54 73 and especially 60–62 with reference to some of its former opinions and to legal doctrine.

laxity on behalf of the CC on the dimension of political control is, however, compensated by a more rigid attitude when it comes to requirements of legality, whereas the opposite is true for the Belgian Council of State.

Indeed, the Belgian Council of State's advisory practice has no real tradition of formulating restrictions with regard to the possibility of delegating rule-making powers in the first place. As long as political supervision is ensured, even large discretionary powers have often turned out to be delegable. The case law of the French CC, on the other hand, suggests that AAIs' rule-making powers have to be embedded in a solid legislative framework, implying that the legislature makes the political decisions and that AAIs do not hold broad discretionary powers. As Rose-Ackerman and Perroud have observed, in France, 'the concern for democratic legitimacy is answered by limiting the power of agencies to make binding rules and by requiring them to enforce rules promulgated by a cabinet ministry'.[268] This, rather than a requirement of *ex post* controls on APBs with political power, is the way in which the aspiration of keeping elected politicians in charge of political decisions is expressed in France.[269] Comparing France with the UK, Perroud explains how the UK legislature has often reserved powers for ministers or secretaries of state to give directions to regulatory authorities. In France, on the other hand, regulatory bodies are not subject to such forms of political interference. Compared to their UK counterparts, the powers that the French AAIs enjoy, however, are much more restricted and do not involve that much discretionary power.[270] In the Netherlands, Direction 124c of the Directions for Legislation provides that ZBOs can only be entrusted with rule-making powers for subjects that are organizational or technical in nature (this limits the legislative freedom to invest them with broad discretionary powers and, consequently, relates to the principle of legality) *or*, in special cases, under the condition that a ministerial right of approval is provided.

Certainly, the picture is not all black and white for Belgium and France either. In Belgium, both the Council of State, Legislation Section and the Constitutional Court have formulated restrictions as to the delegation of

---

[268] Susan Rose-Ackerman and Thomas Perroud, 'Policymaking and Public Law in France: Public Participation, Agency Independence, and Impact Assessment' [2013] Colum. J. Eur. L. 225, 311.

[269] Catherine Teitgen-Colly, 'Les instances de régulation et la constitution' [1990] RDP 153, 256.

[270] Thomas Perroud, 'L'indépendance des autorités de régulation au Royaume-Uni' [2012] RFAP 735, 745–746.

rule-making powers as such.[271] Popelier and Van Nieuwenhove conclude that the Belgian Council of State has been reluctant to allow for the delegation of such powers to APBs. Only delegations with a limited, technical scope that do not involve choices regarding policy seem permissible.[272] In some of its opinions, the Council has explicitly taken the technical nature of the delegated task into consideration, arguing that this characteristic made the APB more eligible to perform the task than the King or the Government.[273] However, the question of whether any form of political supervision is provided remains crucial for the Council to accept such transfers of power, since it seems more likely to endorse such a delegation if ministers retain powers of political supervision, such as, for instance, a possibility of evocation and substitution in case of negligence.[274] The Council has indeed sometimes required both a limited scope of delegation and the provision of some form of political control, confining the admissibility of entrusting APBs with rule-making powers to 'technical matters', while at the same time formulating a requirement of prior approval by the Government or competent minister in order to allow for political ministerial responsibility to be assumed.[275] In its older case law, the Constitutional Court would accept the delegation of rule-making powers to APBs by the legislature, but only for specific matters, the general power to make subordinate legislation being

[271] See e.g. (the references in) Pascal Boucquey and Pierre-Olivier de Broux, 'Les recours juridictionnels contre les décisions des autorités de régulation' in Hugues Dumont, Pierre Jadoul and Sébastien van Drooghenbroeck (eds), *La protection juridictionnelle du citoyen face à l'administration* (la Charte 2007) 209, 227–229.

[272] Patricia Popelier and Jeroen Van Nieuwenhove, 'Decentralisering en privatisering van wetgeving' in Jef De Mot (ed), *Liber Amicorum Boudewijn Bouckaert* (die Keure 2012) 261, 277 with reference to two unpublished opinions and to *Parl.St.* Kamer 2008–09, nr. 1967/1, 57.

[273] See the references in Pierre Nihoul, Marc Joassart and Vinciane Franck, 'Le Conseil d'Etat, Chronique de jurisprudence 2007' [2008] RBDC 237, 278; Marc Joassart, Elisabeth Willemart, Florence Piret and Raphaël Born, 'Le Conseil d'Etat, Chronique de jurisprudence 2009' [2010] RBDC 93, 121.

[274] Patricia Popelier and Jeroen Van Nieuwenhove, 'Decentralisering en privatisering van wetgeving' in Jef De Mot (ed), *Liber Amicorum Boudewijn Bouckaert* (die Keure 2012) 261, 277 with reference to *Parl.St.* Kamer 2006–07, nr. 51 2844/1, 13. See also *Parl.St.* Kamer 2008–09, nr. 1967/1, 57.

[275] E.g. Pascal Boucquey and Pierre-Olivier de Broux, 'Les recours juridictionnels contre les décisions des autorités de régulation' in Hugues Dumont, Pierre Jadoul and Sébastien van Drooghenbroeck (eds), *La protection juridictionnelle du citoyen face à l'administration* (la Charte 2007) 209, 229 with reference to *Parl.St.* Fr.Parl. 2002–03, nr. 357/1, 140–155.

entrusted by the Constitution to the King and the Government.[276] More recently, the court has affirmed that the legislature can delegate tasks to administrative authorities (or even private parties) whose decisions are not subject to administrative oversight or any other form of political control if that task concerns a 'modality of execution' and has a limited and technical scope, which does not involve political choices.[277] Consequently, the court protects the role of the central executive power by confining the legislature's delegatory power, ensuring that the scope of rule-making powers entrusted to APBs remains limited.

In France, on the other hand, AAIs' rule-making powers are also sometimes criticized because of lack of political or democratic legitimation through political supervision.[278] Consequently, the differences in approach are not absolute: the emphasis is different, but both legal systems worry about the legality of APBs' powers as well as about the lack of political supervision of their decisions and acts. The conclusion, though, is that both positions or perspectives revolve around the same aspiration: ensuring that administrative decisions with a political dimension remain sufficiently embedded in the system of representative democracy.

4. AVENUES AND TOOLS FOR REFORM

The uncontrolled manner in which APBs were created in the course of the last decades of the 20th century was often characterized by a disregard for the broader constitutional framework. This framework, the leading principles of which were outlined above, sets the borders within which legislatures and Governments are free to design the administrative landscape as they see fit. They are broad and sometimes flexible principles, open to (re)interpretation should the circumstances so require. However, since they are and remain part of the systems' prevailing

[276] See Patricia Popelier and Jeroen Van Nieuwenhove, 'Decentralisering en privatisering van wetgeving' in Jef De Mot (ed), *Liber Amicorum Boudewijn Bouckaert* (die Keure 2012) 261, 268 with reference to Arbitragehof 10 maart 1998, nr. 24/98.

[277] GwH 10 November 2011, no 166/2011, para B.58.3; Emmanuel Slautsky, 'Droit européen, constitution et autorités administratives indépendantes' [2012] APT 104, 112–113. See also GwH 18 November 2010, no 130/2010, para B.5; GwH 21 November 2013, no 158/2013, para B.14.4.

[278] Arnaud Hacquet, 'Le pouvoir réglementaire des autorités administratives indépendantes. Réflexions sur son objet et sa légitimité' [2008] RDP 393, 394.

Constitutions, there is a concern that their core significance and the purpose that they serve should be upheld.

Administrative organization has long served as a testing ground, a laboratory or even a playground with no rules and few attendants to make sure that the law (and especially constitutional law) is adhered to. This very critique is now inspiring parliaments and their Governments to revalue the above-mentioned principles, rethinking, adapting and rationalizing their approach to APBs. This trend expresses itself in a number of ways. The first one is a clear change in discourse of the central state institutions when it comes to addressing and debating the subject of APBs. Increasingly, parliamentary debates contain references to concerns grounded in or prompted by the meta values outlined above. A second way of reinstating these values is by initiating programmes with the aim of streamlining the landscape of APBs, often resulting in cuts in their numbers. A third phenomenon related to this trend of revaluation is that of soft law instruments (policy documents) being issued with the aim of encouraging government departments to carefully consider initiatives regarding the creation and institutional design of APBs. A fourth and final way is that of framework legislation on APBs.

This section will discuss the first three routes towards revaluation. A separate title, containing a more substantial study and appreciation, will be dedicated to the instrument of framework legislation, which is particularly interesting from a legal viewpoint. The four phenomena outlined above are of course related and, especially for the Dutch system, where all four of them have constituted specific phases in the ongoing process of 'national restraint', it may seem somewhat artificial to divide them. When appropriate, the following analysis will therefore also address the links between the distinct phenomena.

A. Studies, Plans and Dreams: A Change in Discourse of Constitutional Bodies on Autonomous Public Bodies

Changes in discourse are not necessarily predictors for actual reforms. They can, however, give vent to evolutions in governmental or parliamentary awareness and sometimes constitute a phase in which ideas about how to address particular legal problems ripen or mature.

a. The Netherlands

The Netherlands knows a long tradition of political and parliamentary debates on the constitutional embedment of APBs and especially ZBOs in administrative organization. The enactment of the Dutch framework legislation was preceded by a series of public reports, resolutions, motions and debates, eventually triggering a desire to take legislative action.[279] Early examples were an advice of the Council for Internal Affairs (*Raad voor binnenlands bestuur)* on functional decentralization (1988) and the Cabinet's note 'Functional administration, why and how?' ('Functioneel bestuur, waarom en hoe?') (1990).[280] These initiatives were triggered by the so-called 'Lauxtermann motion', in which a group of MPs demanded a clarification on the notions of 'functional decentralization' and 'ZBOs'.[281] Most sources, however, refer to the middle of the 1990s as a genuine turning point for the attitude towards the use of ZBOs, making the Netherlands one of the first legal systems to become responsive to growing concerns about their spread.[282]

A first parliamentary document that has played a crucial role in every debate on ZBOs since the middle of the 1990s is the report issued by the so-called 'Scheltema Commission' with the title 'Steekhoudend ministerschap', which is best translated as 'Valid ministry'.[283] It was issued in June 1993. The report favoured the creation of ZBOs because it believed that they would revalue the principle of political ministerial responsibility by preventing so-called 'incidentalism'.[284] However, the Commission was also one of the first to suggest that the main rules and principles on ZBOs would have to be anchored in framework legislation.[285]

A further influential report was issued at the level of the civil service by the so-called (interdepartmental) Sint Commission and was titled 'Responsible Autonomization'.[286] It was delivered in 1994 and focused on the decision to create ZBOs. It recommended that ZBOs should only be established if one of three valid arguments were fulfilled (independent judgment, direct participation by civil society or execution with regard to

---

[279] See e.g. the overview in Algemene Bestuursdienst Ministerie van Binnenlandse Zaken en Koninkrijksrelaties, 'Onderzoek naar de herpositionering van zbo's', http://www.rijksoverheid.nl/documenten-en-publicaties/rapporten/2014/01/22/rapport-herpositionering-zbo-s.html, 11–15.

[280] Kamerstukken II 1990/91, 21042, nrs. 3 and 4.

[281] Kamerstukken II 1987/88, 20 200, nr. 43. See the reaction of the Minister of Internal Affairs in Brief van de Minister van Binnenlandse Zaken, Kamerstukken II 1988/89, 21 042, nr. 1 and Notitie, Kamerstukken II 1988/89, 21 042, nr. 2.

[282] Tweede Kamer 2000–2001, 27 426, nr. 5, 26.

[283] Kamerstukken II 1992/93, 21 427, nr. 40; Kamerstukken II 1992/93, 21 427, nr. 41.

[284] See pp. 40, 49 and 52.

[285] See pp. 51–52 of the report.

[286] 'Verantwoord verzelfstandigen', Rapportage van de commissie-Sint, 14 September 1994.

individual cases[287]). It furthermore argued that the performance of a government task under complete ministerial responsibility had to remain the rule.[288]

Immediately following this report, the Dutch General Chamber of Auditors launched a report on 'Zelfstandige bestuursorganen en ministeriële verantwoordelijkheid' ('*Zelfstandige bestuursorganen* and ministerial responsibility').[289] The Chamber among other things criticized the lack of clarity about the qualification of public bodies as 'ZBOs'. It also recommended that the Government take action against the uncoordinated proliferation of ZBOs and bring more uniformity to the landscape. It furthermore ascertained that ministers had not been invested with sufficient instruments and powers of supervision in the light of their political ministerial responsibility and advised that this situation be remedied. A more recent study on autonomization and privatization retrospectively ascertained that this report has had a considerable impact on the government's approach to ZBO creation in subsequent years. It also led to an increased focus on internal autonomization (via *agentschappen*), which would from then on be regarded as a valid alternative for ZBOs.[290] In 1995, such a change in attitude was, moreover, announced when the Dutch Cabinet responded to the Chamber's report with a statement on 'Restoring the primacy of politics in the steering of *zelfstandige bestuursorganen*' ('Herstel van het primaat van de politiek bij de aansturing van zelfstandige bestuursorganen').[291] The statement announced among other things the draft of the so-called 'Aanwijzingen voor de regelgeving inzake zbo's' ('Directions for legislation on ZBOs'). This soft law instrument, of which the first version appeared in 1996, has in the meantime been adjusted following the enactment of statutory framework legislation in 2006. It is discussed (in its current version) under heading C of this section.

The millennium change saw the first proposal on framework legislation for ZBOs. In 2002, the laborious parliamentary debates on this legislative initiative were, however, interrupted by the Government, which wished to take some time to further contemplate the question whether it would be sensible to continue with the use of ZBOs. In 2004, yet another report

---

287 These very motives are currently enshrined in the Dutch framework legislation, discussed in the next section.

288 See pp. 13 and 21 (recommendation 6.2).

289 Kamerstukken II 1994/95, 24 130, nr. 3.

290 Parlementair Onderzoek Privatisering/Verzelfstandiging Overheidsdiensten, Kamerstukken I 2012/13, C, A-B, 33–34

291 Kamerstukken II 1994/95, 24 130, nr. 5, 8.

was issued, this time by an interdepartmental working group. The report was named 'Een herkenbare staat: investeren in de overheid' ('A recognizable state: investing in the government').[292] It criticized the autonomization policy of the 1980s and the 1990s because it had led to much indistinctness, mainly in the relationships between ZBOs, competent ministers and Parliament. It adopted a particularly restrictive view towards the use of ZBOs, making some of the literature wonder whether the report was announcing the end of the ZBO concept altogether.[293] According to the report '(as good as) all ZBOs [could] be abolished, since, both substantively and legally, there [was] no need for them'.[294] The working group only discerned a single valid argument for the creation of ZBOs, being the situation in which the nature of the government task would be irreconcilable with political influence. The report nevertheless clarified that even this motive did not automatically require or justify the establishment of a ZBO. The working group formulated a proposal consisting of three variants of administrative organization that could serve the independence motive, of which the ZBO (which would henceforth be called *zelfstandige overheidsrechtspersoon* or ZOR) would constitute only one. In its subsequent statement, the Cabinet did not adopt the rigid view developed by the Kohnstamm working group. It did, however, among other things, commit to a stricter dealing with the motives or justifications for the creation of ZBOs.[295]

In 2006, the Dutch Parliament enacted the *Kaderwet Zelfstandige Bestuursorganen* (KWZBO), i.e. the current statutory framework on ZBOs, which is discussed in detail in Section 5. More recently, however, it decided to dedicate another study to the phenomenon of APBs, this time in combination with that of privatization. On 4 October 2011, the First Chamber of the Dutch Parliament appointed a Parliamentary Inquiry

---

[292] See also J L W Broeksteeg, 'Ministeriële verantwoordelijkheid voor zelfstandige bestuursorganen' in J L W Broeksteeg, J Th J van den Berg and L F M Verhey (eds), *Ministeriële verantwoordelijkheid opnieuw gewogen* (Kluwer 2006) 87, containing a comparison of the Kohnstamm Report and the Scheltema Report.

[293] Sjoerd E Zijlstra, 'Weg met de zelfstandige bestuursorganen?' (2004) 38 NJB 1980.

[294] Page 8 of the report.

[295] Kabinetsstandpunt 'Een herkenbare staat: investeren in de overheid', Kamerstukken II 2004/05, 25 268, nr. 20. See also the discussion of the report and the Cabinet's subsequent Statement in Sjoerd E Zijlstra, *Bestuurlijk Organisatierecht* (Kluwer 2009) 207–208.

Commission Privatization/Autonomization (of) Government Services.[296] The Commission looked into the Dutch policy regarding both privatization and APBs of the last 20 years. The investigation aimed to improve the quality of future parliamentary decision making and to map the effects of these processes on citizens, government and society. It focused on the scrutiny of parliamentary debates and preparatory documents preceding statutory acts anchoring initiatives of privatization or autonomous government. A report of the Commission's proceedings, with the title 'Verbinding Verbroken'[297] was submitted to the President of the First Chamber in October 2012. It contained recommendations for future legislation and was followed by a parliamentary debate.

In the main report, the Commission concluded that 'the Netherlands has entered the path of privatization and autonomization without well-defined frameworks or an overall vision'.[298] A desire to bring order, structure and reason to the policy as well as to parliamentary initiatives was central to the Commission's mission. It was felt that Parliament had lost its grip and was in need of a handhold for the future. 'Contemplation' was the key word and, according to the Commission, three (clusters of) leading principles had to be taken into account in that process: those of democratic legitimacy, transparent public accountability and the normative role of the legislature.[299] The Commission recommended a restrictive attitude with regard to the creation of new ZBOs.[300] It also recommended that new and appropriate instruments for supervision, accountability and steering of ZBOs be developed in order to facilitate communication over political issues.[301]

A separate part of the report ('besliskader') offers a framework that is meant to ensure that decisions regarding privatization and autonomization are taken with care and consideration. It is explicitly intended to serve as guidance for Parliament in the phase of the discussion of Bills. The report indicates what elements and considerations should be taken into account during the different steps of the decision-making process, starting from the initial intention to privatize or autonomize and ending with the evaluation of the initiative after implementation.

---

[296] *Parlementaire Onderzoekscommissie Privatisering/Verzelfstandiging Overheidsdiensten.*

[297] Translation: 'Disconnected'. Parlementair Onderzoek Privatisering/Verzelfstandiging Overheidsdiensten, Kamerstukken I 2012/13, C, A–B.

[298] Page 5.

[299] Page 9.

[300] Page 10.

[301] Page 12.

b. France

Within the French legal system, 'restraint' has expressed itself mainly through increased parliamentary consciousness of the impact on France's living Constitution of AAIs in particular, i.e. those APBs that, relatively speaking, enjoy most political autonomy. Recent reports and studies give voice to an attempt by the French Parliament to regain its grip on the administrative landscape.[302]

The French Council of State, Legislation Section, has arguably played a decisive role in this renewed interest and change in discourse. In 2001, the Council dedicated a part of its public report to the topic of AAIs, a report which has since then been cited extensively in studies and contributions on AAIs. Although the Council praised the benefits of administrative organization through AAIs, formulating constructive recommendations for their further development, it did simultaneously warn of the harmful consequences of some specific developments. One of the main necessities identified by the Council was the reinforcement of mechanisms by means of which AAIs would henceforth be held accountable for their actions and controlled by Parliament.[303] Suggestions were also made as to the appointment of so-called *commissaires du Gouvernement* to the board of some AAIs and as to the possibility for ministers to intervene in crisis situations and in the event of deficiencies in the performances of AAIs. These recommendations were inspired by the consideration that AAIs' independence should not place the Government and its ministers in the precarious situation in which they would not be able to intervene in situations for which they would be held accountable by the public.[304] Other recommendations concerned the creation of AAIs, since the Council observed that their emergence had been devoid of any real plan or logic.[305] Subsequently, it advised that the formula of AAIs should not be used unless in a sensible manner and the decision on whether or not to use APBs as a model of administrative organization should be embedded in a series of principles. The Council outlined some of these principles or guidelines, stressing, for instance, that neither impartiality nor expertise always require the establishment of an AAI and

---

[302] See e.g. Jacques Chevallier, 'Le statut des autorités administratives indépendantes : harmonisation ou diversification ?' [2010] RFDA 896, 896.

[303] Conseil d'État – Rapport public 2001, 364ff. This part of the Council's recommendations has been especially influential, also in later studies and doctrinal research. See e.g. the reference in Claude Rochet, Marc Cabane and Simon Formery, 'France' in OECD, *Distributed Public Governance* 71, 78.

[304] Conseil d'État – Rapport public 2001, 370–371.

[305] ibid 263.

that, because of political responsibility, AAIs should not be entrusted with decision-making powers for tasks that transcend one particular sector or that are not merely technical in nature.[306]

In 2012, in a subsequent study, the Council of State targeted another type of APB: that of *l'agence*.[307] Apart from recommendations as to the budgets and human resource management of agencies,[308] the Council drew attention to the need for a new balance and clarification regarding the relationship between central (and local) government and (their) agencies. The study, among other things, recommended that the board of directors of the agency would become a venue where dialogue between the state's representation (*l'état tuteur*) and the agency on the latter's strategy and general orientations could take place.[309] Additionally, referring to article 24 of the Constitution, the report advocated an increased role of Parliament in controlling and evaluating agencies.[310]

So how did the French Parliament react to the impulse given by its main advisory body with regard to possible APB reforms? Both the Senate and the *Assemblée Nationale* have, quite independently of each other, dedicated a thorough study to the subject of AAIs. In doing so, they have mainly adopted an evaluative and retrospective stance. One of the primary concerns has been to restore the lack of overview of the number and nature of the AAIs currently operating at the central level. This 'mapping' exercise, however, also resulted in the formulation of a set of recommendations and avenues for future action.

The first initiative was launched in 2006 by the French Senate and more particularly by its Parliamentary Office for the Evaluation of Legislation. It concerned a study performed by one of the senators, sketching the landscape of AAIs in France and identifying some topical problems. Chevallier regards the reports of the Council of State on AAIs and the Senate's report as expressions of the same concerns of rationalization and harmonization.[311] One of the main conclusions of the report was that the proliferation of AAIs and the recognition of the benefits of political independence had been accompanied by relatively weak forms of parliamentary control.[312] The report expressed the concern that the

---

306 ibid 376–378.

307 Conseil d'État, *Les agences*, 2012.

308 ibid titles 3.3 and 3.4.

309 ibid 165.

310 ibid 169.

311 Jacques Chevallier, 'Le statut des autorités administratives indépendantes: harmonisation ou diversification?' [2010] RFDA 896, 899.

312 Assemblée Nationale, *Rapport sur les AAIs*, I (2006) 5.

multiplication of AAIs would foster more distrust vis-à-vis the traditional institutions of the state in the eyes of citizens. It pleaded for the creation of AAIs not to be treated as a trivial act, but for a more principled approach to future initiatives on AAIs to be adopted.[313] The report resulted in 30 recommendations, which concerned, among other things, the rationalization of the legal regime and the organization of AAIs, and the reinforcement of democratic control on the activities of AAIs.

Important examples of such recommendations – which will not all be discussed in detail here – were:

- to assure the presence of a *commissaire du Gouvernement* in AAIs that possess rule-making powers (recommendation no. 1);[314]
- to appoint sufficient members to the boards of AAIs that have been entrusted with sanctioning powers, ensuring that the functions of prosecution and sanction can be performed separately (recommendation no. 2);[315]
- to affirm in the Constitution or in a *loi organique* supplementing article 34 of the Constitution, the legislature's competence to fix rules regarding the creation and organization of AAIs and APIs (recommendation no. 4);
- to evaluate existing AAIs on a regular basis within the competent (parliamentary) commissions (recommendation no. 6);
- to adopt a legislative framework defining the common characteristics of AAIs with regard to their independence, their sanctioning procedures and the publication of an annual report (recommendation no. 9);[316]
- to provide for the publication, by all AAIs, of an annual report addressed to, among others, the presidents of the two parliamentary assemblies (recommendation no. 27);
- to ensure the hearing of each AAI by the competent parliamentary commissions after the publication of their annual report (recommendation no. 29).

When asked how his recommendations would have to be implemented in practice, the senator spoke in favour of a framework statute (*une loi-cadre*) in order to harmonize certain aspects of the law on AAIs.[317]

---

[313] ibid 6. See also p. 7.

[314] ibid 53.

[315] Ibid 57, where reference is made to article 6(1) ECHR.

[316] ibid 81–82.

[317] ibid 8.

Up until now, no such framework legislation has been enacted in France. In 2010, doctrinal debates on the extent to which homogenization was desirable were still open.[318]

In 2010, the Senate's study was followed by an informative report of the Committee for Evaluation and Control of Public Policies of the *Assemblée Nationale*, containing, again, a total of 30 recommendations.[319] The report consisted of two main parts. Whereas the first part aimed to demonstrate why and how the acceleration of the creation of AAIs necessitated an effort of rationalization, the second main part argued that the independence of AAIs would have to go hand in hand with increased parliamentary involvement. The overall key concerns underlying the report's recommendations all involved the inroad, by the creation and functioning of AAIs, of the fundamental principles outlined in the previous section, namely legal certainty, separation of powers and democratic control.[320]

Although the report thus addressed multiple issues and problems entailed by AAIs, democratic control was undoubtedly *the* central topic. The risk of an excessive enfeeblement of the politically responsible institutions of the state was mentioned as the first reason why the subject of AAIs had been chosen as the very first topic for the newly established *Comité d'évaluation et de contrôle des politiques publiques* to study.[321] Another, related reason mentioned was the perception of members of Parliament that some AAIs were subject to insufficient democratic controls.[322]

As far as AAIs with rule-making powers are concerned, the conclusions of the report were especially firm, advocating the (re)introduction of more traditional forms of administrative oversight. More precisely, it defended the possibility for a *commissaire du Gouvernement* to be

---

[318] Vincent Lamanda, 'Les autorités administratives indépendantes: une rationalisation impossible? Colloque co-organisé le 26 mars 2010 par la Cour de cassation, l'Université de Montpellier I et le Centre d'études et de recherches de sciences administratives (CNRS – Université Paris II) – Avant-propos', [2010] RFDA 873, 874.

[319] Assemblée Nationale, *Rapport sur les AAIs*, I (2010). The report's conclusions and recommendations were based on research carried out via a series of interviews, questionnaires and visits. For a comment, see e.g. Jean-Bernard Auby, 'La façon de comprendre les AAI' [2010] *La Semaine Juridique Edition Générale* 1260.

[320] Assemblée Nationale, *Rapport sur les AAIs*, I (2010) 11.

[321] ibid 22.

[322] ibid 23–24. See also Philippe Dautry, 'Les autorités administratives indépendantes: un nouvel objet d'évaluation parlementaire' [2010] RFDA 884.

involved in procedures of rule making by an AAI, as well as a power of *homologation* for the Government vis-à-vis the rules issued by AAIs.[323] Another recommendation, related to the principle of legality, was to define precisely in the statute for each AAI entrusted with rule-making powers the scope and limits of this power.[324]

The report referred to other institutional options, apart from AAIs, that could provide an alternative in certain cases, such as *établissements publics*.[325] It recommended, moreover, that the creation and preservation of AAIs had to be properly justified.[326] Independence and impartiality (1), efficiency and reactivity (2), technicity, professionalism and proximity to the regulated sectors (3), an EU obligation (4) or new theories on the ways to exercise power (5) were considered to be acceptable motives for the creation of AAIs.[327] The report also studied some bad reasons to establish AAIs, such as a lack of political courage.[328] It was suggested that new AAIs would have to be created for a limited period of time only (for instance, five years), that existing AAIs would have to be re-evaluated periodically by the permanent commissions of Parliament and that an analysis grid would have to be drafted for the creation and periodic evaluation of AAIs.[329]

The principle that each AAI should have a *commissaire du Gouvernement* attached to it was considered not only an essential aspect of a framework created for rule-making powers of AAIs, but also as a way of ensuring 'checks and balances'. Reference was made to similar recommendations in the above-mentioned reports of the Council of State (2001) and the French Senate (2006). It was established that, despite these recommendations, a majority of AAIs still did not have a *commissaire du Gouvernement* on their boards.[330] With regard to the increased role of Parliament, both its involvement in the procedure of appointing the president and the members of the boards of AAIs and its role in ensuring AAI accountability were mentioned.[331] It was stated that all AAIs should be subject to an obligation to submit an annual report

---

[323] Assemblée Nationale, *Rapport sur les AAIs*, I (2010) 52.
[324] ibid 11.
[325] ibid 60.
[326] ibid 59–60.
[327] ibid 61–62.
[328] ibid 63–64.
[329] ibid 67–68. A proposal for such a grid was added to the report as an attachment (see p. 397).
[330] ibid 101–102.
[331] ibid 93.

(recommendation no. 25). Moreover, the relevant parliamentary commissions would have to hear the president of each AAI at least once a year (recommendation no. 27).[332]

The 2010 report was quite soon followed by a second informative report issued in 2011 by the Commission des Lois Constitutionnelles, de la Législation et de l'Administration Générale de la République, regarding the implementation of the recommendations.[333] The aim was not to offer a complete, exhaustive evaluation. Rather, the report focused on four specific topics and the recommendations related to them, i.e. the revision of the perimeter of the existing AAIs (1), the improvement of the legitimacy and functioning of the boards of AAIs (2), the intervention by a *commissaire du Gouvernement* (3) and informing Parliament on the activities of AAIs (4). The report, however, did not have much added value, since it came too soon after the 2010 study, at a time when it was obviously too early to make any real evaluation.

c. The UK

There is evidence in scholarly literature that attempts to regain a grip on APBs were already prominently on the agenda of the last Labour Government and resulted in parliamentary initiatives. One study reveals how, from 1997 on, Labour already revalued traditional mechanisms of political supervision, characteristic of the Westminster model, in order to reinforce political ministerial responsibility and tried to reconcile these with modern forms of administrative organization: 'Labour's antidote to failings in policy-making has been "joined-up government" and "improvement in service delivery" based on a model of strong central control from Number Ten and the Cabinet Office'.[334] Another study observed that the Blair Government's modernization agenda depended on 'strong policy directions from the centre of government. Modernisation aims to make services more responsive and to improve their quality, but

[332] ibid 160–165.

[333] Assemblée Nationale No 3405 – La Commission des Lois Constitutionnelles, de la Législation et de l'Administration Générale de la République – Rapport sur la mise en œuvre des recommandations du rapport du Comité d'évaluation et de contrôle des politiques publiques sur les autorités administratives indépendantes par M. Charles de la Verpillière, Député, (2011).

[334] David Richards and Martin Smith, 'The Tensions of Political Control and Administrative Autonomy: from NPM to a Reconstituted Westminster Model' in Tom Christensen and Per Lægreid (eds), *Autonomy and Regulation, Coping with Agencies in the Modern State* (Edward Elgar Publishing 2006) 181, 187.

in contrast to Next Steps which pursues this objective through fragmentation, it does so through policy and organisational integration. Moreover, instead of separating policy from operations, modernization wants them joined.'[335]

Much of the more general parliamentary debate on APBs in the UK that forms an expression of the trend of 'national restraint' has, however, taken place around the enactment of the Public Bodies Act (PBA) 2011, the UK's framework legislation on APBs. However, at least one report on a specific type of APBs, preceding the debates on the Public Bodies Bill (PBB), should be mentioned. On 6 May 2004, the House of Lords Select Committee on the Constitution published its – since then often-cited and influential – report on the subject of the accountability of the regulatory state.[336] The main focus of the report was the need for increased, consistent and coherent parliamentary scrutiny of regulation and regulators.[337] One of the report's recommendations was that the Government would explicitly have to accept overall responsibility and accountability for regulatory policy and the regulatory framework, while devolving responsibility under defined circumstances to independent regulators.[338] According to the committee, a dedicated parliamentary committee had to be established to scrutinize the regulatory state, which would preferably be a joint committee of both Houses.[339] However, the committee did not exclude or discard increased parliamentary scrutiny via political ministerial responsibility. According to the committee, independent regulators are accountable to ministers 'for the independence and effectiveness of the regulation that they were appointed to carry out, and Ministers are jointly accountable with the regulators to Parliament for the consequences of those regulatory decisions'. Therefore, the committee disagreed 'with the line of argument that regulation implies that Ministers are absolved of all accountability to Parliament for the conduct of independent regulators. Both need to be held accountable with respect to

[335] Allen Schick, 'Agencies in Search of Principles' in OECD, *Distributed Public Governance* 33, 50.
[336] Select Committee on the Constitution, *The Regulatory State: Ensuring its Accountability* (HL 2003-01, 68-I).
[337] ibid 7.
[338] ibid 8 and 43.
[339] ibid 10.

the particular roles and responsibilities that they discharge in the regulatory framework as a whole.'[340] Other recommendations involved regulators' procedural,[341] judicial[342] and financial[343] accountability. Eventually, the committee argued, regulators have to be subject to 'a 360° view of accountability'.[344] Following the recommendations formulated by the House of Lords, parliamentary scrutiny of the regulatory state, especially via select committees, was indeed reinforced and regulators have been made subject to many obligations in terms of transparency, consultation etc.

B. M&As or 'Mergers and Abolitions'

Another way in which national Governments and Parliaments can express their restraint towards the creation and proliferation of APBs is by abolishing or merging existing APBs. It is, however, often difficult to identify the precise rationale behind such operations. Given the fact that, often, no reasons are provided for individual initiatives of abolishment, one cannot presume that they have all been inspired by aspirations of rationalization or democratization. Other reasons, such as financial motives, may have played a decisive role. However, there is evidence that some recent initiatives have indeed been inspired by the rationales underlying the trend of national restraint, i.e. a revaluation of fundamental, constitutional principles, relating to the democratic legitimacy of the administration in particular.

a. The Netherlands

In January 2014, a report was issued containing the results of a study regarding the 're-positioning' of ZBOs,[345] most often referred to as the '*de Leeuw* report'. The report screened all existing ZBOs operating in the Netherlands. It was ordered after the Dutch coalition agreement had

---

340 ibid 43.

341 ibid 56.

342 ibid 10–11, 31–32 and 71ff.

343 ibid 13.

344 ibid 21.

345 Algemene Bestuursdienst Ministerie van Binnenlandse Zaken en Koninkrijksrelaties, 'Onderzoek naar de herpositionering van zbo's', http://www.rijksoverheid.nl/documenten-en-publicaties/rapporten/2014/01/22/rapport-herpositionering-zbo-s.html, Kamerstukken II 2013/14, 25.268, nr. 79.

announced an evaluation of the ZBO landscape.[346] The coalition expressed the intention henceforth to entrust the performance of government tasks to *agentschappen*. Alternatively, ZBOs would be established, but only the management/directors of the organization would receive this status.[347] The central value against which the report judged the existence and institutional design of ZBOs was that of political ministerial responsibility.[348] Other perspectives that guided the report were the 'ordering' of the administrative landscape, 'cost savings' and 'professionalization'. The study screened all (clusters of) ZBOs and investigated, for each of them, whether their ZBO status needed to be retained, whether their tasks had to be privatized or whether they had to be entrusted to an *agentschap*, to a part of the civil service or to another type of body. This resulted in a series of (non-binding) recommendations, the implementation of which would subsequently have to be considered by the Government. The study contained a 'decision tree', meant to assist in the actual evaluation of the various ZBOs.[349] The report suggested a much stricter approach to the motives behind ZBO creation anchored in the KWZBO. The outcome of the screening was that 59 of the 118 existing ZBOs could be retained: the remaining ZBOs could be abolished. In other words: only half of the existing ZBOs survived the screening. In its reaction to the report, the Government remained vague about its intentions with regard to implementation.[350] It is clear, however, that the Government is not inclined to adjust the list of motives for establishment anchored in the *Kaderwet*, discussed in Section 5.[351]

b. The UK

The enactment of the UK's PBA, i.e. the framework legislation discussed in Section 5, was preceded by a series of announcements all concerning

---

[346] See Sjoerd E Zijlstra, 'De maakbare overheid. Nieuw beleid inzake zelfstandige bestuursorganen' [2014] Nederlands Tijdschrift voor Bestuursrecht, 279.

[347] 'Bruggen Slaan', Regeerakkoord VVD-PvdA 29 October 2012, http://www.rijksoverheid.nl/documenten-en-publicaties/rapporten/2012/10/29/regeerakkoord.html.

[348] Page 5.

[349] See attachment 2 on pp. 199–205.

[350] Kamerstukken II 2013/14, 25 268, nr. 83.

[351] The Government did clarify, however, that these criteria are necessary, but not sufficient to justify the creation of a ZBO. Additional reasons are required, such as an obligation in international law. See also Sjoerd E Zijlstra, 'De maakbare overheid. Nieuw beleid inzake zelfstandige bestuursorganen' [2014] Nederlands Tijdschrift voor Bestuursrecht 279.

the Government's plans to tackle problems and criticism surrounding quangos. In July 2009, the leader of the UK's Conservative party David Cameron, promised, if elected, to abolish a number of quangos and to make sure that democratic accountability through ministers would be restored, stating that there would be 'no more hiding behind the cloak of quango independence'. According to Cameron, the problem was that 'too much of what government does [was] actually done by people that no-one can vote out'.[352] The campaign preceding the PBB reached its culmination in October 2010, only months after the election, when Francis Maude, Minister for the Cabinet Office, presented in the House of Commons the diagnosis of an investigation that his administration had been carrying out on the subject of quangos in the UK.[353] To this end, the Cabinet Office published a document with the title 'Public Bodies Reform – Proposals for Change',[354] giving a detailed overview of a total of 901 reviewed quangos and the Government's proposals to retain, abolish or reform each one of them. On that occasion, the minister also presented the tests that would have to assist the Government in determining whether the creation or the continued existence of a quango would be justified. In a first stage, the Government assessed whether the functions performed by the bodies under review were needed (as government functions, that is). Only if the answer were affirmative would the question arise as to whether the body entrusted with that task would have to continue to operate at arm's length from the Government.[355] Three valid reasons for the continued operation of ALBs were distinguished: the case in which a body carries out a highly technical activity; the situation where there is need for political impartiality; and the case in which the body needs to act independently to establish facts. 'Public bodies that passed at least one of these three tests were retained and, where appropriate, reformed to increase efficiency and ensure appropriate accountability to taxpayers', the report of the Cabinet Office

---

352 See Nicholas Watt, 'David Cameron plans to save millions by cutting quangos – and pay', *The Guardian* (6 July 2009); James Chapman, 'Cameron vows to slash number of quangos and cut Ofcom's power', *Mail Online* [*Daily Mail*] (7 July 2009).

353 HC Deb 14 October 2010, col 505; Colin Turpin and Adam Tomkins, *British Government and the Constitution* (7th edn, Cambridge University Press 2011) 436.

354 https://www.gov.uk/government/publications/public-bodies-reform-reports.

355 Cabinet Office, 'Public Bodies 2012', https://www.gov.uk/government/publications/public-bodies-reports, 7.

explained.[356] This triple test, although considered a 'central feature of the coalition government's approach to reforming the quango state', has been criticized for its indeterminacy and was said to be responsible for inconsistent outcomes in the Government's review.[357]

It has been argued that the originality of the reforms initiated by the Coalition Government should be put in some perspective. In its report 'Shrinking the Quango State', the House of Commons Public Administration Select Committee, scrutinizing the Government's reform plans, pointed out that these were 'not new promises for an incoming Government to make; in 1979, Margaret Thatcher was elected on a promise of a "bonfire of quangos" and in 1997 Tony Blair came to office with similar pledges'.[358] There have indeed been earlier waves of quango criticism and attempts at reform by those in office from as early as (the late) 1970s.[359] Both the Conservatives and Labour are considered to have played a particularly ambiguous role in the growth of the number of APBs in the UK over the past 40 years or so. Margaret Thatcher is regarded at the same time as the founding mother of the (generally considered successful) 'Next Steps Agencies' initiative and the initiator of thorough counts and cuts of NDPBs with the aim of rationalizing the public body landscape. Her plans for reforms resulted in the famous Pliatsky report ('Report on Non-Departmental Public Bodies'), published in 1980.[360] As an immediate result of this report, a substantial number of bodies were abolished for reasons of lack of democratic control[361] although many were also retained and the Government established new

---

[356] ibid 7.

[357] Matthew Flinders and Chris Skelcher, 'Shrinking the Quango State: Five Challenges in Reforming Quangos' (2012) 32(5) Public Money & Management 327, 330.

[358] Public Administration Select Committee, *Smaller Government: Shrinking the Quango State* (HC 2010–11, 537) 5.

[359] See e.g. Tony Stott, '"Snouts in the Trough": The Politics of Quangos' (1995) 48(2) Parliam Aff 323. A complete historical overview can be found in Matthew Flinders, *Delegated Governance and the British State: Walking without Order* (Oxford University Press 2008) 62ff. See also Richard Wilding, 'A Triangular Effect: Quangos, Ministers, and MPs' in Anthony Barker (ed), *Quangos in Britain. Government and the Networks of Public Policy-Making* (Palgrave Macmillan 1982) 34, 34.

[360] See e.g. RT Hon David Hunt, 'Worthwhile Bodies' (1995) 48(2) Parliam Aff 181, 192, 194.

[361] J F Garner, 'After Privatisation: Quis Custodiet Ipsos Custodes?' (1990) Public Law 329, 329–330.

ones as well.[362] As far as the Labour Government was concerned, declarations on quango reforms followed rapidly after elections in 1997, Flinders observes. However, the author discerns a discrepancy between the 'pre-election "anti-quango" polemics' and the rather weak statements and reforms that followed. 'The government's proposals set out a soft-law (i.e. non statutory) guidance framework rather than a statute-based hard-law system that would empower the public with legally enforceable rights and powers.'[363] Regardless of the substantive quality of the reforms, other literature observes that 13 years of Labour Government indeed resulted in a 10 per cent reduction in the number of quangos.[364]

Despite the competition from earlier programmes that the Coalition Government's reforms faced, it could be argued that the reforms were both more thorough in quantitative terms and more substantiated in qualitative terms, based on a pre-established set of tests and criteria anchored in a single legislative framework (*infra*), which made the approach more systematic than it appears ever to have been before.[365] One author describes the programme as 'perhaps the most challenging review so far of a form of government that has attracted much attention over the last 30 years'.[366] Acknowledging that previous Governments had also launched initiatives to reduce the number of public bodies, the Minister for the Cabinet Office claimed that his approach 'constitute[d] a more ambitious programme to realise significant and lasting improvements to the public bodies landscape'.[367] Referring to pledges of previous governments, the minister submitted that '[t]he reality has rarely matched the rhetoric' and vowed that his would be 'a Government that makes

---

[362] Colin Turpin and Adam Tomkins, *British Government and the Constitution* (7th edn, Cambridge University Press 2011) 435–436.

[363] Matthew Flinders, 'MPs and Icebergs: Parliament and Delegated Governance' (2004) 57(4) Parliam Aff 767, 776.

[364] Colin Turpin and Adam Tomkins, *British Government and the Constitution* (7th edn, Cambridge University Press 2011) 435–436.

[365] An early call for such an approach was made in Nevil Johnson, 'Accountability, Control and Complexity: Moving Beyond Ministerial Responsibility' in Anthony Barker (ed), *Quangos in Britain. Government and the Networks of Public Policy-Making* (Palgrave Macmillan 1982) 206, 218.

[366] Richard Kirkham, 'Quangos, Coalition Government and the Ombudsmen' (2010) 32(4) Journal of Social Welfare & Family Law 411, 411.

[367] HC Deb 25 October 2011, col 274 (The Minister for the Cabinet Office and Paymaster General Mr Francis Maude).

good on its promises'.[368] Others discern a 'renewed and more radical commitment' to reduce the number of NDPBs, but remain sceptical, speaking of both 'real and inflated concerns' about the role of these bodies being at the basis of the reforms.[369]

The 'quango cull' is not confined to the central level in the UK. Since the millennium change, 'quango reduction policies'[370] have been introduced in Scotland, Northern Ireland and Wales as well. In 2001, the Scottish Government published a review of public bodies, leading to proposals to abolish 52 of them.[371] The real innovation of the review, however, was located in the introduction of principles:

> against which to assess the retention of existing public bodies and the creation of new ones. Whilst acknowledging the important role that arm's length public bodies have to play in the governance of devolved Scotland, these principles placed very strong emphasis on the need to maintain the direct accountability of Scottish Ministers for the overall policy and strategic framework within which all devolved functions are carried out.[372]

C. Soft Law Instruments as Frameworks for Assessment

The phenomenon of framework legislation as defined and discussed in the next section concerns actual statutory frameworks. Increasingly, however, soft law instruments, anchoring similar principles and inspired by similar goals, are enacted or their development is advocated.

a. The Netherlands

In the Netherlands, the enactment of framework legislation was preceded by the so-called 'Directions for Legislation on ZBOs'.[373] The Directions,

---

[368] Minister for the Cabinet Office, *Government Response to the Public Administration Select Committee Report, 'Smaller Government: Shrinking the Quango State'* (Cm 8044, 2011) para 11.

[369] Colin Turpin and Adam Tomkins, *British Government and the Constitution* (7th edn, Cambridge University Press 2011) 436.

[370] Aileen McHarg, 'Devolution in the Regulatory State: Constraints and Opportunities' in Dawn Oliver, Tony Prosser and Richard Rawlings (eds), *The Regulatory State: Constitutional Implications* (Oxford University Press 2010) 5, 82.

[371] ibid 83.

[372] ibid 83. See also Matthew Flinders, 'MPs and Icebergs: Parliament and Delegated Governance' (2004) 57(4) Parliam Aff 767, 782–783. The financial crisis has become a second driver for the de-agencification process in the UK in general and it has had an accelerating effect.

[373] *Aanwijzingen voor de Regelgeving inzake ZBOs.*

issued in 1996, aimed to bring some unity to the Dutch ZBO landscape. They are part of a larger complex of Directions for Legislation, which serve as guidelines for high-quality legislation. They are not binding on the legislature, even though they do enjoy considerable authority.[374] They are, however, binding on the civil servants who prepare the legislation.[375] The specific 'Directions for ZBOs' still exist in a 'downsized' version and complement the KWZBO. Part of the Directions for ZBOs were later written into the Dutch framework legislation and disappeared from the Directions. For those issues that are not arranged in the statutory framework, the Directions remain relevant. Important requirements or restrictions that are still enshrined in the Directions are a duty to give reasons in the explanatory memorandum with regard to the creation of ZBOs or their investment with a new task,[376] the requirement of a statutory basis for the creation of ZBOs (inspired by the consideration that it detracts from political ministerial responsibility)[377] and the formulation of conditions that have to be fulfilled before investing a ZBO with rule-making powers or advisory tasks.[378]

b. The UK

One could argue that in the UK the devolved countries have been more active and above all faster than the UK (Westminster) Government and Parliament in their attempts to 'recentralize' their administrations. 'In the lead-up to devolution in each country the reversal of the proliferation of quangos became identified as a key policy objective', Birrell points out.[379] According to Flinders, '[d]evolution has ... led to the imposition of new procedures that limit the flexibility of members of the executive to create new bodies with the intention of avoiding the "institutionalitis" (i.e. frequent and *ad hoc* institutional creation) that is often problematic

---

[374] Ministerie van Justitie, Directie Wetgeving (ed), *Aanwijzingen voor de regelgeving, Aanwijzingen voor convenanten, Praktijkvoorschriften voor ontwerpers van regelingen en convenanten van de Rijksoverheid* (Sdu Uitgevers 1996) 12–13.

[375] H J de Ru, 'Publiekrechtelijke of privaatrechtelijke rechtspersonen' [2002] NJB 1099, 1101

[376] Direction 124a.

[377] Direction 124b. This requirement is not absolute: the text further specifies when exceptions are possible.

[378] Direction 124c.

[379] Derek Birrell, 'Devolution and Quangos in the United Kingdom: The Implementation of Principles and Policies for Rationalization and Democratization' (2008) 29(1) Policy Studies 35, 37.

at the national level'.[380] This especially seems the case for Scotland. Scotland has not, like the UK Parliament, enacted a statutory framework with the aim of keeping quangos (or their creators) under control. It has, however, developed a substantial policy framework on how to handle these bodies.

In June 2001, 'Public Bodies: Proposals for Change'[381] was published, a document that would later be used as the basis for a review resulting in significant APB reforms. It was preceded by a discussion paper that aimed to boost the debate on quangos and, eventually, lead to a public consultation on a list of quangos that the government intended to abolish. One of the objectives of the review was 'to devise a set of principles that takes account of the fundamental changes brought about by devolution, and to use these principles to test whether existing public bodies should be abolished and to test any future proposals for new public bodies'.[382] Another was 'to ensure that those public bodies that remain operate effectively and are genuinely and appropriately accountable to Ministers and Parliament and have legitimacy in the eyes of the public'.[383] Annex C of the discussion paper introduced a proposal for a 'set of principles against which to test public bodies'. It affirmed that 'Scottish Ministers [were] expected to, and expect to be, directly accountable to Parliament and the public for all that happens in their portfolios'.[384] It then proposed three questions to be asked for each public body: whether the function was necessary; whether it could be put under local democratic control; or whether a public body was required to carry out the function. Four valid arguments for entrusting a function to an arm's-length body were suggested.[385]

---

[380] Matthew Flinders, 'Devolution, Delegation and the Westminster Model: A Comparative Analysis of Developments Within the UK, 1998–2009' (2011) 4(1) Commonwealth & Comparative Politics 1, 9–10.

[381] http://www.gov.scot/Resource/Doc/158633/0043032.pdf.

[382] Scottish Executive, *Review of Public Bodies – Discussion Paper*, January 2001, 2, *http://www.gov.scot/Resource/Doc/156334/0041936.pdf.*

[383] ibid 9 (Annex B).

[384] ibid 13 (Annex C).

[385] ibid 14 (Annex C). These were: compliance with 'European Convention on Human Rights-type requirements (i.e. to distance Ministers from certain decisions for legal reasons)'; efficiency gains (described as enabling 'a body to focus on a particular task and to bring a more innovative approach to bear'); other overriding policy reasons to do so (the example given is that of easier interaction with NGOs or educational institutions compared with ministers); and, finally, 'to make it easier to attract funding from non-government sources'.

As Flinders points out, the significance of the Scottish Executive's initiative is not in the cull of APBs, but in the principles that have been put forward to evaluate the use of this model of governance.[386] The document also announced that the Scottish Parliament (or its committees) would have to be notified when the Executive aspired to establish a new quango. Moreover, a duty to give reasons was introduced, since 'Scottish ministers [would] also have to provide an explanation for this decision with reference to the set of principles'. The 'Proposals for Change' targeted both existing quangos (promising a review of each body at least once every five years) and future proposals, claiming that '[a] public body will only be set up if there is an absolutely clear and widely recognised need for one'.[387]

The document defined four reasons for establishing or maintaining (accountable) quangos as an alternative to entrusting tasks to the Scottish Executive. A first one is the possibility for ministers and the core Scottish Executive to focus on strategic direction or policy making rather than carrying out executive functions or detailed casework. The second valid motive is that of 'bringing expertise or experience to bear on the delivery of certain functions, securing specialist advice for Ministers' or 'dealing with complex casework in detailed areas where it would be impractical or disproportionate to retain expertise within the Executive', or 'where it would be unreasonable to expect Ministers to be directly involved or to take a view'. A third situation in which quangos are justified is:

> when quasi-judicial decisions need to be made or appeals decided and independent judgment must be guaranteed (e.g. tribunals) and where there is a consensus within society that decisions should not be taken by politicians (e.g. mechanisms for the distribution of lottery funds). A fourth and final motive is that of drawing a wider cross section of society into the processes of government and thereby extending civic participation.[388]

As far as the obligation to justify initiatives to establish new public bodies is concerned, the 'Proposals for Change' put forward that the relevant minister:

---

386 Matthew Flinders, 'MPs and Icebergs: Parliament and Delegated Governance' (2004) 57(4) Parliam Aff 767, 782–783; Matthew Flinders, 'Devolution, Delegation and the Westminster Model: A Comparative Analysis of Developments Within the UK, 1998–2009' (2011) 4(1) Commonwealth & Comparative Politics 1, 8–9.

387 Scottish Executive, *Public Bodies: Proposals for Change*, June 2001, 3.

388 ibid 7.

> should explain how the proposal is consistent with the underpinning principles and what alternative arrangements have been examined, including delivery of the function by civil servants in the core of the Executive or in an executive agency or by an existing public body or by one or more local authorities or in the private, voluntary or community sectors.[389]

This suggests that a sort of cascade system has to be followed, making sure that ministers consider alternatives that derogate from the premise of political accountability to the least possible extent. As for supervision, it was stated that:

> [m]inisters need to explain clearly to each public body through regular guidance what they expect them to achieve in terms of outcomes, and how they intend to monitor them and generally interact with them. They need to describe the sorts of circumstances in which they would generally intervene or use powers of direction (such an explanation cannot be exhaustive because not every set of circumstances can be foreseen). This guidance should be made available to Parliament and to the wider public.[390]

The Scottish policy framework offers a clear set of principles on the basis of which decisions regarding APBs will have to be made in the future. These can be qualified as a form of 'soft law', binding, as instructions, on civil servants working in departments and preparing legislation or decisions only. In this regard, they are comparable to the 'Guide for Departments' on NDPBs existing at the UK level. The Guide was first published in 1981 and has been regularly updated ever since. Its expanded 1985 version was referred to by one author as 'the nearest thing Britain has to a "constitution" for quangos, although of course, it has no formal legal status and is addressed to civil servants'.[391] Compared to the Dutch Directions for Legislation, discussed earlier, the guidelines are not formulated as rules, but rather as a checklist for the departments that prepare initiatives to create NDPBs. For instance, they remind departments that '[t]he statute or instrument creating the NDPB or conferring the relevant functions on it, should normally provide suitable powers of appointment and dismissal over the Chairman and board members' and give examples of typical grounds for dismissal. They suggest that ministers could be entrusted with additional supervisory powers, such as powers of guidance or (general or specific) direction and indicate that '[t]he nature of controls will depend both on

---

[389] ibid 8.
[390] ibid 9.
[391] Ian Harden, 'A Constitution for Quangos?' [1987] Public Law 27, 28.

the NDPB's functions, and on the closeness of supervision which ministers wish to exercise'.[392]

c. France

In its 2012 study on *agences* in the French legal order, the Council of State not only aimed to increase knowledge about the phenomenon of agencies, but also to offer a *cadre de référence* for these entities and to bring certain concerns, for instance that of parliamentary control, to the attention of politics and the public. The diversity of agencies, the lack of unity and the need for clear guidelines for the government regarding the creation of agencies were at the basis of the study,[393] the main ambition of which was, according to the Council, to restore order.[394] The Council indeed regarded the lack of any systematic development and theoretical embedding of *les agences* as especially problematic.[395] One of the main proposals was consequently to evolve towards 'an appropriate recourse to agencies', which meant that their creation would have to be 'framed'.[396]

To that end, the Council formulated suggestions as to the permissible motives for the creation of *agences*.[397] Another recommendation concerned the choice as regards the legal status of the agency: each of the possible types was linked to a specific goal, facilitating and rationalizing the choice for a particular form.[398] In order to make these assessments effective, the Council suggested that every initiative concerning the creation of an agency would have to be preceded by an impact analysis that would have to reveal that recourse to an agency is indeed the preferable option.[399]

Whereas the Council indicated that the introduction of an obligation for such a prior impact analysis would require a legislative basis,[400] it opposed the legislative anchoring of both the criteria justifying the creation of an agency as well as the guidelines with regard to the choice for a specific legal status. The Council considered it undesirable that the

---

[392] Cabinet Office, 'Public Bodies: A Guide for Departments. Chapter 3: Setting up a new Public Body – The Legislative Requirements', https://www.gov.uk/government/uploads/system/uploads/attachment_data/file/80080/PublicBodiesGuide2006_3_setting_upv2_0.pdf, 10.

[393] See the 'avant-propos' by Sauvé at 7–9.

[394] Conseil d'État, *Les agences*, 2012, 23.

[395] ibid 11.

[396] ibid 14.

[397] ibid 14 and 120.

[398] ibid 126.

[399] ibid 129.

[400] ibid 129.

administrative or constitutional court(s) would be able to test establishing legislation against these criteria.[401] This, however, could not mean that these rules or guidelines would be entirely non-committal. According to the Council, they would have a legal status similar to that of circulars issued by the Prime Minister.[402]

To that end, the Council suggested that a new type of instrument would be introduced in French administrative law: a *directive d'organisation et de gestion administrative*. Such a directive would be issued by the Prime Minister and would address the Government ministers. Deviation from the 'general orientations' in the directive would remain possible for reasons of general interest in particular cases. Compliance with the directive would be ensured via a *Comité interministériel d'évaluation des agences*, which would assemble every time an agency was created and would publish its advice.[403]

In 2010, the French Prime Minister had already issued a circular 'relative au pilotage stratégique des opérateurs de l'État'.[404] The circular concerned the political steering of *opérateurs*, a sub-category within the broader group of *établissements publics*. The main goal was to encourage the drafting of agreements between ministers and *opérateurs*, containing clear policy goals that would have to be achieved[405] in order to reinforce the strategic dimension of the *tutelle* applicable to this type of APB.[406] Although the circular did not as such concern the establishment or evaluation of operators, it did instruct that every proposal concerning the creation of a new APB of this type would have to be preceded by an impact study. According to the Council of State's 2012 report, this initiative constituted a first, but incomplete step towards the more general framework that it envisaged.[407]

D. Conclusion

The previous paragraphs aimed to demonstrate how national constitutional bodies (Parliaments, Governments and their advisors, such as the

---

[401] ibid 130.

[402] ibid 131.

[403] ibid 15 and 131–132.

[404] Circulaire relative au pilotage stratégique des opérateurs de l'État, 26 March 2010 (Le Premier Ministre), http://circulaire.legifrance.gouv.fr/pdf/2010/04/cir_30853.pdf.

[405] ibid 2.

[406] ibid 1.

[407] Conseil d'État, *Les agences*, 2012, 119.

French Council of State) in Europe have (recently) engaged in initiatives to rationalize the creation as well as the institutional embedment and design of APBs. In the discourse surrounding these efforts the same aspirations and concerns keep reappearing: bringing order to the chaos caused by the uncontrolled creation of APBs in recent years, reflecting on proper justifications for recourse to APBs, and reinforcing the role of representative democracy in the process of establishing APBs and overseeing their performance. It remains to be seen whether the intentions expressed in the studies, reports, soft law instruments etc. mentioned will lead to (continued) effective action and/or will be adhered to in the future. What seems crucial, however, is the recognition of the role played by constitutional principles in decisions on APB creation and design. A number of propositions and recommendations furthermore point at the introduction of further constraints, defined by law (via statutory or soft law frameworks) on the use of APBs. Traditional legal instruments intended to steer or supervise APBs, such as the role of the French *commissaire du Gouvernement*, the procedure of ministerial *homologation* in France or the UK's ministerial powers of 'guidance and directions' are revisited and advocated as ways to confine APBs' powers.

5. FRAMEWORK LEGISLATION AS AN INNOVATIVE INSTRUMENT FOR RATIONALIZATION

A. Introduction

This section discusses the emergence of statutory frameworks containing general rules and conditions that aim to rationalize the creation, preservation and/or functioning of APBs in order to square the APB landscape with (one or more of) the constitutional objections that it is currently believed to entail. Via the enactment of framework legislation, the legislature endeavours to transform APBs into a manageable and controllable phenomenon, embedded in, and constrained by, a set of rules and principles that ensure conformity with fundamental principles governing administrative organization.

Three of the four systems studied in this book have adopted framework legislation. The first system to enact such a framework was Flanders: since 2003, the large majority of Flemish APBs has been governed by the so-called *Kaderdecreet Bestuurlijk Beleid* (hereinafter KDBB). Three years' later, in 2006, the Netherlands adopted their statutory framework, the *Kaderwet Zelfstandige Bestuursorganen* (hereinafter KWZBO). It entered into force in 2007. In 2011, the UK's Public Bodies Act (hereinafter PBA) was enacted.

France is the odd one out in the selection of legal systems, since it has not (yet) enacted framework legislation. The idea of enacting such a framework for AAIs was advocated in a study by Frison-Roche, attached to the 2006 parliamentary report discussed earlier.[408] The actual 2006 report welcomed the idea of such a legislative framework.[409] So far, however, no initiatives have been taken in this direction.

Framework legislation on APBs is becoming popular both in and outside the European legal sphere. New Zealand, for instance, enacted in 2004 its Crown Entities Act, which anchors a typology of agencies 'ranked in order of an increasing distance from government and increasing levels of autonomy, with the different types linked to specific tasks agencies may fulfil'.[410] The EU has a framework for its own executive agencies[411] but a Commission initiative to enact an 'institutional agreement on the operating framework for European regulatory agencies' (dating from 2005) was eventually dismissed.[412] In 2012, a 'common

---

[408] Marie-Anne Frison-Roche, 'Étude dressant un bilan des autorités administratives indépendantes' in Assemblée Nationale, *Rapport sur les AAIs*, I (2006) 11.

[409] As does some doctrine. See e.g. Jean-Bernard Auby, 'Remarques terminales' [2010] RFDA 931, 932.

[410] Sandra Van Thiel, Koen Verhoest, Geert Bouckaert and Per Lægreid, 'Lessons and Recommendations for the Practice of Agencification' in Koen Verhoest, Sandra Van Thiel, Geert Bouckaert and Per Lægreid (eds), *Government Agencies. Practices and Lessons from 30 Countries* (Palgrave Macmillan 2012) 413, 418 and the references therein.

[411] Council Regulation 58/2003/EC of 19 December 2002 laying down the statute for executive agencies to be entrusted with certain tasks in the management of Community programmes [2003] OJ L11, 1–8.

[412] See e.g. Paul James Cardwell, 'The Changing Nature of European Regulatory Governance' in David Levi-Faur (ed), *Handbook on the Politics of Regulation* (Edward Elgar Publishing 2011) 536, 542; Merijn Chamon, 'EU Agencies: Does the Meroni Doctrine Make Sense?' (2010) 17(3) Maastricht Journal of European and Comparative Law 281, 281ff; Michelle Everson, 'Agencies: The 'Dark Hour' of the Executive?' in Herwig C H Hofmann and Alexander H Türk (eds), *Legal Challenges in EU Administrative Law* (Edward Elgar Publishing 2009) 116, especially 126ff; Stefan Griller and Andreas Orator, 'Everything Under Control? The "Way Forward" for European Agencies in the Footsteps of the Meroni Doctrine' (2010) 35(1) European Law Review 3, 5; Jens-Peter Schneider, 'A Common Framework for Decentralized EU Agencies and the Meroni Doctrine' in Herwig C H Hofmann and Russell L Weaver (eds), *Transatlantic Perspectives on Administrative Law* (Bruylant 2011) 203, 206ff.

approach' to EU agencies was developed. This document, however, does not have any binding legal status.[413]

B. A Comparison of the Flemish KDBB, The Dutch KWZBO and the UK'S PBA

a. Purpose

The three statutory frameworks discussed here differ as to their scope, contents and approach. What unites them, despite these differences, are the goals that they have in common.

All three statutory instruments aim to rationalize the decision of creating APBs, offering a framework for assessment in which the benefits of political autonomy are weighed against the risks for democratic legitimacy. Rationalization with a view on democratization is the shared, general and overall purpose of the frameworks studied. Framework legislation constitutes a legislative reaction to the uncurbed rise of APBs in the previous decades, associated with a lack of rational contemplation on their institutional embedment within the existing constitutional framework. By linking conditions and restrictions to the conferral of political autonomy on public bodies, framework legislation gives a statutory anchoring to the principle of centrality and its derivatives. Political ministerial responsibility is in turn revalued by a renewed emphasis on (intensive or moderate forms of) political supervision of the decisions made by APBs.

A second objective, however, is the enhancement of transparency in the APB landscape. Framework legislation offers a general and abstract picture of the rules and principles that govern pivotal aspects of APBs' creation and/or institutional design. It allows citizens and other administrations to orient themselves in the labyrinth of APBs since it streamlines initiatives regarding the creation, preservation and/or abolishment of APBs. A recent comparative study on agencies linked the emergence of (statutory and other) frameworks governing the creation of APBs to the goal of 'limiting institutional variety'.[414]

Both objectives are expressed in the explanatory memoranda or (written reports of the) parliamentary debates of all three frameworks.

---

[413] See http://europa.eu/about-eu/agencies/overhaul/index_en.htm.

[414] Sandra Van Thiel, Koen Verhoest, Geert Bouckaert and Per Lægreid, 'Lessons and Recommendations for the Practice of Agencification' in Koen Verhoest, Sandra Van Thiel, Geert Bouckaert and Per Lægreid (eds), *Government Agencies. Practices and Lessons from 30 Countries* (Palgrave Macmillan 2012) 413, 417–418.

The explanatory memorandum of the KDBB refers to the importance of (restoring) the primacy of politics in administrative decision making as well as to the preservation of the principle of political ministerial responsibility,[415] which are regarded as strongly intertwined values.[416] The Flemish KDBB originated from the concern that Flemish APBs suffered from a steering and control deficit and from a belief that this hollowed the principle of ministerial responsibility, a criticism that began to grow in the 1990s.[417] As a second goal, the explanatory memorandum mentions the enhancement of transparency with regard to the typology of APBs.[418]

The KWZBO's explanatory memorandum invokes the very same principles as justifications for its enactment.[419] More precisely, it distinguishes between two greater denominators under which to subsume the more specific goals of the act: the harmonization of the law on the organization of ZBOs on the one hand and the regulation of the primacy of politics on the other.[420] In the explanatory memorandum, the Dutch Government expressed its aspiration to provide clarity on the extent to which ministers remain politically responsible. As long as uncertainty as to the scope of ministerial responsibility with regard to ZBOs persisted, democratic control would be jeopardized. In order to meet these concerns, the KWZBO would have to contain a catalogue of ministerial supervision and steering instruments.[421] Providing more clarity as to the financial control on ZBOs was regarded as a linked, but separate pivotal motive behind the KWZBO. To this end, the framework would have to contain basic rules regarding budgets and accountability.[422] Secondly, the Dutch legislature hoped to remediate the 'non-transparent structure' of differing arrangements for ZBOs. To that end, the KWZBO would have to contain a 'number of harmonizing organizational provisions regarding ZBOs', while differentiation would remain possible when required.[423]

415 *Parl.St.* Vl.Parl. 2002–03, nr. 1612/1, 4–10.

416 ibid 5–6.

417 Koen Verhoest, Frederik Vandendriessche and Jan Rommel, 'Verzelfstandiging in Vlaanderen: theorie en praktijk' in Pierre Jadoul, Bruno Lombaert and François Tulkens (eds), *Le paraétatisme. Nouveaux régards sur la décentralisation fonctionnelle en Belgique et dans les institutions européennes* (la Charte 2010) 369, 380–381.

418 *Parl.St.* Vl.Parl. 2002–03, nr. 1612/1, 9.

419 Tweede Kamer 2000–2001, 27 426, nr. 3, 1 and 4 particularly.

420 ibid 4.

421 ibid 1 and 4.

422 ibid 5.

423 Tweede Kamer 2000–2001, 27 426, nr. 3, 1.

According to the Government, the Dutch KWZBO intended to bring order to the various ad hoc organizational arrangements governing single ZBOs.[424] The KWZBO, moreover, wishes to increase public insight in both the appearance and functioning of ZBOs. It therefore provides for the creation of a public register in which all existing ZBOs are listed, as well as for an evaluation of the functioning of ZBOs every five years.[425]

As far as the PBA is concerned, some controversy has emerged over the primary incentive behind its enactment. The opposition criticized the many contradictory declarations as to what precisely the PBA had to achieve.[426] According to the official declarations made by the Government in the press and during the parliamentary debates, the act was devised as an instrument to increase democratic accountability by re-evaluating whether and to what extent public functions had to be exercised at arm's length from ministers. To the House of Commons, the minister explained that the Bill was essentially about the House's power and right to hold the executive to account. 'It will enlarge the scope of the state – the public realm – which this House and Parliament can hold to account, and reduce the scope of quangos and non-departmental public bodies and the range of public state entities that are not accountable to a democratic authority.'[427] A closely related objective was that of increasing transparency, by presenting to citizens an organized administrative landscape with clear lines of accountability running between ministers, departments and public bodies. The Government, however, did not deny that the enactment of the PBA (and the public bodies review preceding it) had also been inspired by financial considerations: abolishing public bodies was regarded as a way to achieve savings in public expenditure. Hence, the UK Government's reform programme on public bodies, including the PBA itself, 'has been driven in part by the need to cut costs

---

[424] Tweede Kamer 2000–2001, 27 426, nr. 5, 24.

[425] Tweede Kamer 2000–2001, 27 426, nr. 3, 5.

[426] See e.g. HC Deb 12 July 2011, col 242 (Mr Jon Trickett). The House of Commons Public Administration Select Committee expressed similar doubts: Public Administration Select Committee, *Smaller Government: Shrinking the Quango State* (HC 2010–11, 537) 27ff. See the reaction in Minister for the Cabinet Office, *Government Response to the Public Administration Select Committee Report, 'Smaller Government: Shrinking the Quango State'* (Cm 8044, 2011) paras 2–3.

[427] HC Deb 12 July 2011, col 212 (The Minister for the Cabinet Office and Paymaster General Mr Francis Maude). See also HC Deb 25 October 2011, col 272 (The Minister for the Cabinet Office and Paymaster General Mr Francis Maude).

in the wake of the financial crisis, and in part by normative precepts'.[428] The Cabinet Office, however, emphasized on multiple occasions that restoring democratic accountability through political ministerial responsibility was the primary motive behind the reform, whereas financial gains constituted only a second order concern.[429] According to Prosser, the PBA 'is based on the belief that accountability is best secured by policy and discretionary decisions being taken within core government subject to ministerial responsibility to Parliament',[430] which fits the conclusion reached earlier as to the shared aspiration behind the trend of 'national restraint'. For the members of the Coalition Government defending the PBA before Parliament, the restoration of 'democratic accountability' as they conceived it revolved around the person of the minister responsible to Parliament. As pointed out earlier, there is a long-standing debate in the UK among academics as well as politicians about the effect that the creation of APBs has on the political responsibility of ministers. The current status quo that this debate seems to have reached, with the rejection by the House of Lords Select Committee on the Constitution of the accountability–responsibility dichotomy, may explain why minsters may wish to recentralize certain government tasks or tighten their relationship with APBs via initiatives such as the PBA. The opacity of the administrative landscape owing to the largely uncontrolled rise of APBs during the last decade also inspired the UK Government to enact the PBA. During the parliamentary debates, an MP declared that, in his constituency, 'people [were] deeply frustrated by how complex and expensive government has become. They would like it to be simplified and for it to be easier to find out who is in charge.'[431] The aim of achieving a transparent system of administrative organization was, moreover, strongly linked to the revaluation of the principle of ministerial accountability and, therefore, to the aim of enhancing accountability.[432] Francis Maude declared that:

---

[428] Paul Craig, *Administrative Law* (Sweet & Maxwell 2012) 80.

[429] Cabinet Office, 'Public Bodies 2012', https://www.gov.uk/government/publications/public-bodies-reports, 4; Public Administration Select Committee, *Smaller Government: Shrinking the Quango State* (HC 2010–11, 537) 28–29.

[430] Tony Prosser, 'Regulation and Legitimacy' in Jeffrey Jowell and Dawn Oliver (eds), *The Changing Constitution* (7th edn, Oxford University Press 2011) 312, 331.

[431] HC Deb 12 July 2011, col 267 (The Parliamentary Secretary, Cabinet Office, Mr Nick Hurd).

[432] HL Deb 9 November 2010, col 63.

> The public are right to expect a system in which Ministers are accountable for what the Government does and for how taxpayers' money is spent. For too long, there has been the proliferation of a complex network of public bodies, which has worked against that expectation by blurring the lines of accountability and disguising inefficiency and duplication in the delivery of public services.[433]

Examining the parliamentary debates on the PBB in both chambers of the UK Parliament, one may get the impression that parliamentary support for the Bill was rather limited. The (sometimes harsh) criticism of the Bill, however, mainly resulted from concerns about the extent to which it enabled ministers to amend primary legislation. Moreover, many peers and MPs declared an interest in one or more of the quangos featuring on the Government's list and thus facing the threat of being reformed or disappearing altogether. This led to a long list of interventions concerning the virtues and necessary preservation of specific bodies, although many of their defenders did not omit to stress that, in principle, they supported the Government's intent to put a stop to the rule of the 'quangocrats'.[434] Despite objections, it was felt by many that the objectives behind the PBA were to be welcomed. One member of the House of Lords, for instance, offered 'a very warm measure of support for the Government's objectives in this Bill' and declared that, like other peers, he distinguished the objectives of the Bill from its means.[435] Similarly, another member declared the Bill was flawed and had to be improved, but believed that 'the intentions behind it [were] sound and action [was] well overdue'.[436] Yet another of the peers welcomed the initiative, noting that:

> It is an anachronism that in this Chamber and in the other place one cannot directly question a Minister about the performance of a non-departmental public body, although obviously there can be correspondence. As a democrat I am in favour of improving that ministerial responsibility, and under the Bill that will happen.[437]

---

433 HC Deb 12 July 2011, col 212 (The Minister for the Cabinet Office and Paymaster General Mr Francis Maude).

434 As Lord Kirkwood of Kirkhope pointed out: 'even when people agree with the policy intent, they all have their little lists of complaints about bodies that they want to protect. They say, "In principle, it's really great; in practice, not in my backyard"' (HL Deb 9 November 2010), col 126. See also HL Deb 9 November 2010, col 178 (Lord Kirkwood of Kirkhope).

435 HL Deb 9 November 2010, col 94 (Lord Mayhew of Twysden).

436 ibid, col 126 (Lord Marlesford). See also HL Deb 9 November 2010, cols 177–178 (Lord Kirkwood of Kirkhope).

437 ibid, col 85 (Lord Freeman).

b. General approach and contents

The following paragraphs compare the three statutory frameworks and outline both similarities and differences. Without scrutinizing the details, they evaluate some of the main differences between the choices made by the three legislatures.

Approach There is one important way in which the approach of the PBA differs from that of its Dutch and Flemish counterpart. It was clear from the very beginning that the PBA was meant to be the Government's tool or instrument to facilitate the 'bonfire' that it had announced after its review in 2010. The UK government may take credit for writing the PBA as an Act intended to give ministers the opportunity to reverse past initiatives of entrusting public tasks to APBs. The PBA is an example of so-called 'enabling legislation', containing powers delegated to ministers, called 'Henry VIII clauses'. Ministers are empowered to use these by means of orders, being a form of secondary legislation, even when the original framework governing the body's creation and institutional design is enshrined in primary legislation. The PBA includes powers to abolish (section 1) or merge (section 2) certain public bodies, to modify the constitutional arrangements applicable to them (section 3) or their funding arrangements (section 4) or to modify or transfer their functions (section 5). The powers to abolish or merge bodies both include a power to transfer the functions of these bodies to an 'eligible person' (subsections 2 and 3 of sections 1 and 2 respectively). The persons who qualify as 'eligible persons' are listed (section 1, subsection 3) and can, for instance, be ministers themselves. Section 3, on the power to modify constitutional arrangements, contains what seems to be a non-limitative list of examples, such as, as far as 'bodies' are concerned,[438] matters relating to the provisions governing (the appointment and functions of) the chair of the body (subsection 2)(b) and its governing procedures and arrangements (subsection 2)(f). More significantly in the light of the objectives of the PBA, it also includes matters relating to the extent to which the body is accountable to ministers (subsection 2)(h).[439]

Just like its Flemish and Dutch counterparts, the PBA is meant to help central government to regain its grip on the phenomenon of APBs by setting certain standards. Instead of de-facilitating the creation of APBs, however, the PBA facilitates their dissolution or disempowerment. The

---

[438] Section 3 distinguishes between the constitutional arrangements of a *body* and those of an *office*.

[439] And for office-holders: (subsection 3)(e).

KDBB and KWZBO, on the other hand, have been written from the perspective of central government creating APBs or entrusting them with (new) government tasks instead of abolishing them or reconsidering their status. Admittedly, both the Flemish and the Dutch frameworks have been used for evaluations of existing bodies as well. However, they were not as such designed as instruments containing guidelines and procedures that were primarily intended to assist ministers in bringing public missions closer to departments again.

APBs targeted by the framework legislation A second important difference between the three statutory frameworks concerns their scope *ratione personae*, i.e. the definition of the range of APBs to which the framework applies. Compared to the KWZBO and the PBA, the Flemish KDBB is the product of a more ambitious undertaking in this respect. The coverage of the Flemish framework is more extensive than that of its counterparts in two ways. First, the Flemish legislature has aimed to create an organizational framework for the entire Flemish administration and not only for the APBs that are part of it. The KDBB, for instance, anchors the principle of homogeneous policy domains, each one individually correlating with one Flemish ministry, consisting of a department and one or more agencies without legal personality. One policy board exists per policy domain, and advisory boards can be established as well.[440] APBs with legal personality can be added to this organogram if the conditions outlined in the KDBB are fulfilled.[441] Secondly, the KDBB has the ambition to serve as a framework for all APBs established and operating in Flanders (both departmental and non-departmental), whereas the other two frameworks target only a limited number of APBs.

In the Netherlands, no general organizational framework for central administration exists. The KWZBO endeavours to offer a framework for the use and functioning of ZBOs exclusively, it does not concern ministries and their central administrations, nor does it apply to other APBs. Consequently, it does not include the so-called *agentschappen* (APBs of the departmental, executive type). The restriction of the act's personal scope to ZBOs that are invested with 'public authority' (*openbaar gezag*)[442] implies that only ZBOs that have been invested with the power to take unilateral decisions of a binding nature fall within the

[440] In practice, deviations from this ideal scheme exist.
[441] Article 3 KDBB.
[442] Article 1(a) KWZBO.

scope of the statutory framework.[443] Although APBs that have been invested with such coercive powers are indeed the most problematic ones from a democratic viewpoint, this restriction, combined with the fact that the KWZBO does not see to the so-called *agentschappen*, implies that the personal scope of the Dutch framework is rather limited.

Central to the PBA is the notion of 'public bodies', a term that is not defined by the Act itself. The Act has no need for general criteria to identify the bodies that fall within its personal scope, because it contains lists (schedules) of specific public bodies to which each of the powers entrusted to ministers apply. The exercise of each power is thus confined to a number of specific bodies. One of the problems with the Act's scope in this regard is probably that the schedules also contain bodies that perform only advisory tasks or bodies with a judicial mission, i.e. the so-called 'tribunals'. A substantial part of the parliamentary debate on the Act consisted of MPs and peers justifying the continued existence of 'their' quangos, i.e. APBs in which they occupied a seat on the board, for instance. Many, though not all, of the bodies mentioned in these defences, were indeed advisory boards or tribunals, which puts these interventions into perspective and arguably makes them more understandable. For many of these bodies, the objective of enlarging the minister's influence over them indeed seemed unnecessary, inappropriate or even unconstitutional. One of the Lords rightfully noted that:

> There has been no taxonomy of the bodies affected by the Bill – that is, there has been no proper analysis or classification of their similarities and differences. Instead, the Bill seeks sweepingly broad executive powers and the inclusion of a long list of all the quangos which might become subject to ministerial interference, control or abolition.[444]

The nature of the rules and conditions enshrined in the acts Both the KDBB and the KWZBO contain two categories of conditions. On the one hand, a number of provisions concern the decision to create APBs. They determine under what conditions and on the basis of which justifications a decision to establish an APB can be made, which forms of APBs can be chosen and which further options exist in terms of institutional design. On the other hand, the Flemish and Dutch framework legislation contains provisions governing the functioning of APBs. These determine which issues have to be dealt with in the agreement between the minister and

---

443 See Eerste Kamer 2001–2002, 27 426, nr. 276c, 6. See also Tweede Kamer 2000–2001, 27 426, nr. 5, 44.

444 HL Deb 9 November 2010, cols 99–100 (Lord Lester of Herne Hill).

the APB (Flanders), how APBs will be controlled, the way in which they will hire their personnel etc.

The original project of the Dutch KWZBO focused exclusively on constraining the internal organization and functioning of ZBOs and did not address the decision to create ZBOs. It primarily wanted to reinforce ministerial responsibility and hence democratic control by enacting uniform rules on supervision and accountability. That ZBOs existed and would continue to exist (and multiply) was as such accepted and uncontested. As far as the issue of creating ZBOs is concerned, the explanatory memorandum referred to the Directions for Legislation.[445] Eventually, the project of the KWZBO was amended and the current version contains provisions on both the creation and the institutional design of ZBOs invested with public authority. Several Members of Parliament indeed insisted that criteria regarding the creation of ZBOs be included in the statutory framework itself and eventually put forward sufficiently convincing arguments for the Government to change its mind.

In practice, both the KWZBO and the KDBB up until now seem to have inspired more reforms of existing initiatives than establishments of new APBs.

The PBA does not aim to define criteria for the creation of new public bodies. However, it contains conditions and motives against which ministers have to test their intention to abolish or modify the status of public bodies. By doing so, it automatically sets criteria for the continued existence of APBs, which can – up to a certain point – be compared to the conditions anchored in the KDBB and KWZBO for APB creation. The PBA does not as such contain any provisions on the institutional design and/or functioning of APBs. It can, however, constitute a source of indirect reform in this regard, for instance when a minister uses its power to modify a body's constitutional arrangements (section 3).

c. Focus on some specific features and provisions of particular importance in the light of the goals behind framework legislation

Typology and gradual use of APBs The most important innovation of the Flemish KDBB was the introduction of a typology of agencies and the gradual system attached to this typology. An important criticism regarding the creation of APBs in many jurisdictions is precisely the lack of any coherent catalogue of 'models' from which Parliament or the

---

[445] Tweede Kamer 2000–2001, 27 426, nr. 3, 21.

government can choose when it establishes or reforms APBs.[446] Too great a variety in the landscape of APBs leads to an overall loss of transparency in the governmental organization chart. This causes a threat to accountability 'as it is less clear who is responsible for what' and may lead to inequalities as well.[447]

The KDBB distinguishes four types of APBs:

- internally autonomized agencies (IVAs) without legal personality;
- internally autonomized agencies (IVAs) with legal personality;
- externally autonomized agencies (EVAs) established on the basis of public law;
- externally autonomized agencies (EVAs) established on the basis of private law.

IVAs without legal personality are established by the Flemish Government, whereas IVAs with legal personality are set up by the Flemish legislature. Both forms of internal autonomization are characterized by the preservation of (ministerial) hierarchical authority. EVAs in public law form, established by the legislature, have legal personality.[448] EVAs in private law form, established by the Government after a legislative authorization has been issued, have legal personality as well.[449] They are established on the basis of private law and may not deviate from its compulsory provisions.[450] The criterion that is used to differentiate between the four categories of agencies is that of the distance from the core administration or the political centre of power in terms of possibilities for steering and supervision. This is directly linked to the system of justification for establishment: as the distance from the core administration increases, additional reasons or motives are required for the creation of the agency.[451] Each single type of agency thus represents a

[446] See e.g. Sandra Van Thiel, Koen Verhoest, Geert Bouckaert and Per Lægreid, 'Lessons and Recommendations for the Practice of Agencification' in Koen Verhoest, Sandra Van Thiel, Geert Bouckaert and Per Lægreid (eds), *Government Agencies. Practices and Lessons from 30 Countries* (Palgrave Macmillan 2012) 413, 416–417.

[447] ibid 417.

[448] Article 13 KDBB.

[449] Article 30 KDBB.

[450] Article 29 KDBB.

[451] Articles 10, §3, 11, §3 and 29 KDBB.

particular degree of autonomy and *more* autonomy requires *greater* justification.

For the Netherlands, the situation is slightly different. Because the KWZBO only regulates the creation, design and functioning of ZBOs, its typology is more limited. The Dutch framework distinguishes two types of ZBOs: those established on the basis of public law on the one hand and those established on the basis of private law on the other. It does so by attaching additional conditions to the investment of a 'legal person, established on the basis of private law' with public authority.[452] The Dutch KWZBO thus has in common with the Flemish KDBB that it links a cascade system to its twofold typology. Hence, both legislative frameworks incorporate the principle that the weakest type of APB (in terms of political autonomy) is always the one that has to be considered as the first option. The choice of a more far-reaching form (implying *more* autonomy and less control) requires sufficiently convincing reasons. The cascade system consequently aims to render APBs the result of a conscious decision-making process. It prevents decision makers from automatically choosing the most far-reaching forms of political independence, as if it were a question of 'all or nothing'.

Unlike the KDBB and the KWZBO, the PBA does not anchor any typology or taxonomy of public bodies. A problem that is related to both the personal scope of the PBA and this absence of a taxonomy is the lack of an answer to the question how executive agencies fit the Government's intentions. This was one of the remarks made by the Public Administration Select Committee with regard to the PBB in its report *Smaller Government: Shrinking the Quango State*. Whereas the committee 'sympathise[d] with ministers' desire to be able to influence decisions they will ultimately be held responsible for', it also noted that '[s]takeholders and civil society play an important role providing challenge and criticism to public bodies on a day to day basis and it is easiest for them to perform this role when they have a clearly identified body to engage with, not a homogeneous central department'. The committee submitted that '[t]here [was] a way to meet both demands: set these bodies up as executive agencies – this provides a clearly identifiable organisation for stakeholders to engage with, while leaving ultimate responsibility with the Minister'.[453] According to the committee, bringing functions back

[452] Article 4.2 KWZBO.

[453] Public Administration Select Committee, *Smaller Government: Shrinking the Quango State* (HC 2010–11, 537) 3 and 47.

into sponsor departments not only threatened to undermine the role of relevant stakeholder groups, but also risked 'leaving policies fighting numerous other priorities for ministerial attention', which would mean 'less effective accountability and challenge on a day-to-day basis'.[454] It therefore recommended 'that the Government consider converting those organisations which it intends to retain and move into Government departments into Executive Agencies'.[455] The Minister for the Cabinet Office responded to this concern by assuring the select committee that a number of public bodies would indeed be converted to executive agencies 'precisely to make them democratically accountable through a Minister'.[456]

The 'Guidance on Reviews of Non Departmental Public Bodies', however, requires departments to examine a wide range of delivery options when assessing how functions should be delivered in the case of a review. For that purpose, an annex to the document contains a 'checklist of delivery options', outlining various options, such as 'abolish', 'move out of Central Government', 'bring In-House', 'merge with another body', 'delivery by a new Executive Agency' and 'continued delivery by a NDPB'.[457] Far from representing a taxonomy, this guidance indicates that the idea of thinking in terms of a gradation when it comes to empowering APBs is currently explored in the UK as well. When creating new NDPBs, departments are similarly obliged to 'consider all possible delivery models when exploring options for delivering new services or functions' and the Cabinet Office has compiled a list of options that should be explored as a minimum, including e.g. the establishment of an executive agency.[458]

Conditions and motives for the creation and preservation of APBs APBs are increasingly regarded as institutions that have to remain exceptions to

---

[454] ibid 34.

[455] ibid 34.

[456] Minister for the Cabinet Office, *Government Response to the Public Administration Select Committee Report, 'Smaller Government: Shrinking the Quango State'* (Cm 8044, 2011) para 3.

[457] Cabinet Office, 'Triennial Reviews: Guidance on Reviews of Non Departmental Public Bodies', https://www.gov.uk/government/uploads/system/uploads/attachment_data/file/332147/Triennial_Reviews_Guidance.pdf, paras 4.5 and 4.7 and respectively Annex A.

[458] Cabinet Office, 'The Approval Process for the Creation of Non Departmental Public Bodies', https://www.gov.uk/government/uploads/system/uploads/attachment_data/file/80074/Approval_process_for_the_creation_of_NDPBs_Dec 12_0.pdf, 8–10.

the rule that the administration functions under the hierarchical command of ministers that are either elected or controlled by an elected assembly. Framework legislation conceives the use of APBs as an exception that requires sufficiently convincing reasons. The three frameworks have in common that they start from the premise 'that public bodies should only exist at arm's length from ministers where there is a compelling reason for their functions to be carried out by an independent body'.[459] The cascade linked to the typology of both the KDBB and KWZBO indeed works on the basis of a system of conditions and proper motives for establishment.[460]

Whereas the PBA does not as such contain rules that condition the decision to create APBs, it does enshrine criteria against which ministers have to consider their preservation or continued existence. The powers entrusted by the PBA to ministers to decide on the fate of the public bodies listed in the Act are qualified: they are subject to conditions enshrined in the PBA itself. To that end, section 7 of the PBA provides that the modification or transfer of a function by an order under sections 1 to 5 must not prevent it (to the extent that it continues to be exercisable) from being exercised independently of ministers in any of the cases mentioned in subsection 2. Those cases are:

(a) where the function is a judicial function (whether or not exercised by a court or a tribunal);
(b) where the function's exercise involves enforcement activities[461] in relation to obligations imposed on a Minister;
(c) where the function's exercise otherwise constitutes the exercise of oversight or scrutiny of the actions of a Minister.

Pursuant to section 7, subsection 3, provisions made by an order under sections 1 to 5 must, moreover, be proportionate to the reasons underlying them.

Section 7 thus anchors situations in which the bodies enumerated in the Act cannot be deprived of their independent status. Whereas these situations indeed correspond to valid motives for the preservation of political autonomy and thus as justifications for APBs, section 7 does not constitute a comprehensive catalogue of valid reasons for the creation of

---

[459] Cabinet Office, 'Public Bodies 2012', https://www.gov.uk/government/publications/public-bodies-reports, 7. See also HC Deb 12 July 2011, col 215 (The Minister for the Cabinet Office and Paymaster General Mr Francis Maude).

[460] See in particular articles 4, §2, 10, §3, 11, §3 and 29 KDBB; articles 3 and 4 KWZBO.

[461] These are defined in subsection 4.

APBs. In other words: section 7 anchors situations in which the preservation of political autonomy is compulsory, but does not mention other conditions, motives or situations in which the preservation of political autonomy would otherwise be valid.

The considerations that qualify as valid motives for the exercise of the powers entrusted by the PBA are in turn enshrined in section 8 ('Purpose and conditions'). A minister can only use these powers if he considers that the order serves the purpose of improving the exercise of public functions, having regard to four values or purposes, being efficiency (a), effectiveness (b), economy (c) and securing appropriate accountability to ministers (d). Initially, the Bill did not contain such clear-cut restrictions as to the motives that could inspire ministerial action: it only expected ministers to 'have regard to' the motives mentioned in section 8. Concerns were expressed regarding the discretion given to ministers by this clause and its unsuitability to being applied in cases of judicial review.[462] After amendment, the clause was replaced. Now, the PBA clearly suggests that these motives are limitative, in the sense that ministers have to make sure that their initiative complies with at least one of them. The second subsection of section 8, moreover, provides that a minister may make an order under sections 1–5 only if he considers that the order does not remove any necessary protection (a) and the order does not prevent any person from continuing to exercise any right or freedom which that person might reasonably expect to continue to exercise (b).

The indeterminacy of the objectives of efficiency, effectiveness, economy and accountability featuring in section 8 of the Bill was criticized.[463] An amendment that aimed to add to the list of objectives of section 8 the objectives of fairness, openness, transparency and justice was rejected in the end because these values were deemed too abstract and therefore hard to define and apply.[464] Questions were also raised as to why the set of principles that would have to govern changes to public bodies in clause 8 of the Act did not mention independence, since, in a member of the House of Lords' view '[m]any public interests must not be subject to the party-political ebb and flow or to the opinion of the

---

[462] HL Deb 9 November 2010, col 99 (Lord Lester of Herne Hill).

[463] E.g. HL Deb 4 April 2011, 1533–1535 (Lord Soley and Lord Phillips of Sudbury) and 1541 (Lord Taylor of Holbeach); HC Deb 12 July 2011, col 240 (Mr Bernard Jenkin).

[464] See the debates in HL Deb 4 April 2011, 1530–1531 (Lord Taylor of Holbeach) 1537 (Lord Pannick) 1539–1540 (Baroness Royall of Blaisdon) 1541 (Lord Taylor of Holbeach).

Minister of the day nor should they be captured by well-funded lobbies'. Another obvious rationale for ALBs that this intervener could not find in the list was that of expertise.[465]

Since they are meant to serve as justifications for the use of the ministerial powers anchored in the PBA, the motives enshrined in section 8 should primarily be conceived as arguments for less far-reaching forms of APBs, rather than as motives that justify their creation or preservation. Remarkably, efficiency and effectiveness, core values of NPM reforms that inspired many initiatives to establish APBs in the 1980s and 1990s are now the first two motives mentioned as justifications for actions targeted at achieving precisely the opposite result.

As explained earlier, on 14 October 2010 the UK's Cabinet Office presented a test that would have to assist the Government in deciding on the destiny of the public bodies that would be submitted to review. The second part of the test consisted of three criteria, representing valid reasons for political independence of public bodies: the exercise of a technical activity; the need for political impartiality; and the need to act independently to establish facts. The question arises why these criteria were not anchored in the Bill,[466] Act or – at least – the explanatory memorandum[467] and why the Government instead opted for a reference to the vague goals of efficiency, effectiveness, economy and accountability in section 8 of the PBA.[468] The Public Administration Select Committee expressed concerns that this would lead to confusion.[469] In its response to the Public Administration Select Committee Report *Smaller Government: Shrinking the Quango State*,[470] the Government confirmed that the criteria used in the review were different from those that would guide the powers attributed to the Government via the PBA, declaring that '[t]he Bill is a vehicle for the implementation of the decisions made through the review, not a mechanism for making those decisions once

---

[465] HL Deb 9 November 2010, col 104.

[466] HC Deb 12 July 2011, col 240 (Mr Bernard Jenkin).

[467] HL Deb 9 November 2010, cols 99–100 (Lord Lester of Herne Hill).

[468] E.g. Matthew Flinders and Chris Skelcher, 'Shrinking the Quango State: Five Challenges in Reforming Quangos' (2012) 32(5) Public Money & Management 327, 330.

[469] Public Administration Select Committee, *Smaller Government: Shrinking the Quango State* (HC 2010–11, 537) 11.

[470] See the BBC's interpretation of the report in 'Quango Reduction Plan Botched, say MPs' *BBC News* (7 January 2011).

again'.[471] However, no explanation was given as to why different tests had to be used in both stages.

More confusion as to the proper motives for the creation or continued existence of NDPBs in the UK is created by the Guide for Departments on Public Bodies, Chapter 2 on 'Policy and characteristics of a Public Body', last updated in June 2006. This document presents five cases in which an NDPB will be 'the appropriate model': if the function needs to be carried out at arm's length from ministers (e.g. regulatory functions) (1), when expert advice is required by ministers on technical/specialized issues (2), if a body needs to be set up to deal with appeals (3), when a partnership needs to be formed between government and other interests (4) and when a body is required to carry out a range of commercial activities where board members need a degree of independence from government to make decisions.[472] It is unclear how this list relates to the 'triple test' mentioned above and to the reasons for preservation enshrined in the PBA.

During the debates in the House of Lords, one member wanted to learn whether the explanatory memoranda of the implementing Bills would contain evidence as to the necessity of the measures intended. Lord Taylor of Holbeach replied that the explanatory documents would be 'properly reasoned and describe not just what a statutory instrument proposes but the reasoning behind the change'.[473] As for the creation of new APBs and more particularly NDPBs, the Cabinet Office in its Guide for Departments stresses that new NDPBs 'should only be established as an absolute last resort' and that '[a]ny proposal to set up a new NDPB must be accompanied by a robust and fully costed business case'. This process of justification involves assessing the function or activity against the triple test announced by the Cabinet Office on 14 October 2010, but currently not featuring in the PBA.[474]

---

[471] Minister for the Cabinet Office, *Government Response to the Public Administration Select Committee Report, 'Smaller Government: Shrinking the Quango State'* (Cm 8044, 2011) para 34.

[472] Cabinet Office, 'Public Bodies: A Guide for Departments. Chapter 2: Policy and characteristics of a Public Body', https://www.gov.uk/government/uploads/system/uploads/attachment_data/file/80079/PublicBodiesGuide2006_2_policy_Characteristics_0.pdf, 3.

[473] HL Deb 7 March 2011, col 1411.

[474] Cabinet Office, 'Categories of Public Bodies: A Guide for Departments'. This was the Cabinet Office's position in its guidance document 'Categories of Public Bodies: A Guide for Departments', issued in 2012. In 2016, this document was replaced by 'Classification of Public Bodies: Guidance For Departments'

Political supervision and accountability Both the Flemish KDBB and the Dutch KWZBO provide clarity as to the powers of supervision available to political principals for the types of APBs that they cover. Both frameworks contain a series of provisions on the financial supervision of externally autonomized agencies. More important from the viewpoint of the principal–agent model as well as from that of the definition of APBs used in this book, however, are the provisions regarding political supervision of the substantive decisions of the APBs and of the discretionary powers that they exercise. The principal–agent model suggests that principals who delegate powers to agents are duly aware of the risk of so-called 'agency losses', i.e. outcomes generated by policy preferences of the agent that differ from those of the principal. Consequently, principals will anticipate this undesired situation, either by restricting the powers conferred on the agent or by providing mechanisms for supervision.

> Institutional design is an exercise in choosing from a menu of both *ex ante* and *ex post* (that is, ongoing) controls. Yet, because the benefits of delegation decline the more the principal limits the agency's discretion, the trick is to delegate just the amount of power to enable agents to achieve desired outcomes with minimal agency losses.[475]

The KDBB and KWZBO have in common that they aim to restore the mechanism of political ministerial responsibility by giving ministers powers of intervention that enable them to assume responsibility before Parliament. Both frameworks consequently regard the role of the competent minister as key when it comes to ensuring the democratic accountability of APBs. Only the KWZBO contains provisions anchoring an obligation to report to Parliament directly.[476]

Since the Flemish EVAs and the Dutch ZBOs are characterized and defined by a lack of hierarchical supervision exercised by the competent minister, the framework legislation anchors alternative and less intrusive

---

(https://www.gov.uk/government/publications/classification-of-public-bodies-information-and-guidance). The guidance presents a new classification of public bodies. Within the category of 'arm's-length bodies', it distinguishes between executive agencies, NDPBs and Non-Ministerial Departments. It contains a chart that should help departments in deciding which type to choose (if the creation of a new public body is necessary). See pp. 11ff.

[475] Mark Thatcher and Alec Stone Sweet, 'Theory and Practice of Delegation to Non-Majoritarian Institutions' 25(1) (2002) West European Politics 1, 4–5 with references.

[476] Article 18 KWZBO.

forms of supervision in order to enable the minister to assume political responsibility. Compared to the KDBB, the Dutch KWZBO contains a much more refined catalogue of control mechanisms for the competent minister. These are found in articles 17–23 KWZBO and they apply to ZBOs established on the basis of both public and private law. The KDBB, on the other hand, only provides for one single mechanism of comparable nature: the power of annulment, anchored in article 23, which applies to EVAs in public law form only.[477] The supervision of EVAs established on the basis of private law is not as such arranged in the KDBB, it depends on the available mechanisms anchored in private law.[478] The power of annulment is a traditional attribute of a system of control of APBs in public law form that the Belgian literature labels 'general administrative oversight'. This system typically involves a Government's commissioner or representative, who has a seat on the board of directors of the APB in an advisory capacity. This representative can decide to suspend a decision and to notify the competent minister, who can in turn decide to annul the decision. In the original KDBB, as it entered into force in 2003, no such form of administrative oversight was prescribed for the decisions of EVAs established on the basis of public law, a deletion that meant quite a trend reversal. Supervision of these authorities would be assured via the evaluation of a management agreement concluded between the political principal and the APB. The Council of State, Legislation Section expressed its concern with regard to this lacuna. The Council did not as such oppose the introduction of new, less traditional forms of supervision, but it did point out that the legislature had to ensure that some sort of supervision would effectively be provided.[479] Even though these concerns were supported by, among others, the Court of Audit[480] and concerned members of Parliament, the decree was passed without the introduction of additional forms of political supervision.

---

[477] The same article (§6) also provides for a possibility for the minister or the Government representative to oblige the agency to deliberate on any matter that he deems fit within a certain period of time. This is only possible insofar as compliance with statutory law or regulations or the statutes of the agency or the management agreement require the agency to do so.

[478] *Parl.St.* Vl.Parl. 2002–03, nr. 1612/4, 10.

[479] *Parl.St.* Vl.Parl. 2002–03, nr. 1612/1, 96.

[480] *Parl.St.* Vl.Parl. 2002–03, nr. 1612/2, 27.

In 2007, the Flemish legislature modified article 23 of the KDBB, giving it its current content and anchoring a system of general administrative oversight.[481] According to the explanatory memorandum, the supervisory powers of the Flemish Government on EVAs, which were limited to a right of consultation of the agencies' documents and a right to ask for an explanation, represented a 'very minimal form of supervision', which was inadequate and lacked efficacy. It was argued that an adequate form of supervision required that the Flemish Government would be able to ensure that the agency pursued the general interest and that it complied with the law, as well as with its own by-laws and management agreement. The purpose of the introduction of a system of administrative oversight was the compensation of the lack of direct steering powers of the Flemish Government as well as the wish to meet 'the expectations of the people regarding adequate controls on autonomized agencies (element of democratic legitimacy)'.[482]

The Dutch KWZBO enshrines an annulment power for the competent minister[483] but also adds other mechanisms that enable the minister to intervene in the decision-making process of ZBOs. These are a compulsory ministerial approval for ZBOs competent to fix tariffs as to the amount of the tariff (if no maximum is provided),[484] an obligation for the ZBO to issue an annual report that is sent to the competent minister and to both chambers of Parliament,[485] a power for the competent minister to issue so-called 'policy rules' (*beleidsregels*, i.e. instruments of ministerial guidance) with regard to the task of the ZBO[486] and a possibility for the minister to intervene in case of serious neglect of duty by a ZBO.[487] The legislature is free to declare some of the supervisory mechanisms non-applicable to certain ZBOs in their establishing legislation. The explanatory memorandum points out that, by doing so, Parliament limits ministerial responsibility and, consequently, also its own possibility to hold the minister accountable for the acts of ZBOs.[488]

---

481 Decreet 27 april 2007 tot wijziging van het kaderdecreet bestuurlijk beleid van 18 juli 2003 op het vlak van het toezicht van de Vlaamse Regering op de publiekrechtelijk vormgegeven extern verzelfstandigde agentschappen, *BS* 29 juni 2007.

482 *Parl.St.* Vl.Parl. 2006–07, nr. 1098/1, 3.

483 Article 22 KWZBO.

484 Article 17 KWZBO.

485 Article 18 KWZBO.

486 Article 21 KWZBO.

487 Article 23 KWZBO.

488 Tweede Kamer 2000–2001, 27 426, nr. 3, 4.

The PBA aims to enhance the accountability of the administration and offers ministers the opportunity to change the conditions that the bodies are subject to, also with regard to their accountability. It does not, however, provide ministers with a catalogue of tools of supervision or accountability. In its report 'Read before Burning', the Institute for Government pointed out that, as far as areas for further investigation on ALBs were concerned, the main question was 'the need to more fundamentally consider how ministers and Parliament can execute their scrutiny functions in relation to ALBs ... The doctrine of ministerial responsibility was developed at a time when government's responsibilities were far smaller, meaning that such an assessment is urgently needed.'[489]

Primacy of the democratically elected legislature in decisions regarding APBs Both the KDBB and the KWZBO adhere to the principle that the creation of APBs that are no longer subject to ministerial hierarchical authority always requires a statutory basis. During the parliamentary debates on the KWZBO, a debate arose as to the possibility of entrusting ZBOs with public authority via subordinate legislation, issued by the Government.[490] Article 5 KWZBO now provides for the compulsory involvement of Parliament in such cases.

In the UK, where parliamentary sovereignty is highly valued, debates on the primacy of the legislature when it comes to decisions regarding APBs became particularly fierce in the process leading to the enactment of the PBA. Especially the House of Lords questioned or opposed the use of so-called 'Henry VIII clauses', which would allow the Government to amend primary legislation by means of orders.[491] According to Lord Soley, it was 'as though Henry VIII has risen from the grave disguised as a parliamentary draftsman'.[492] The original Bill provided for ministerial orders to follow the simple affirmative procedure. After lengthy parliamentary debates it was decided that, next to the regular procedure, an alternative, reinforced procedure[493] would be provided, which would allow Parliament to become involved to a greater extent.

---

[489] Institute for Government, 'Read before Burning', http://www.instituteforgovernment.org.uk/publications/read-burning, 62.

[490] Tweede Kamer 2001–2002, 27 426, nr. 34; Tweede Kamer, 27 Februari 2002, Handelingen 2001–2002, nr. 50, 3560.

[491] E.g. HL Deb 9 November 2010, cols 71–72 (Baroness Royall of Blaisdon). Cf HL Deb 9 November 2010, col 108 (Lord Blackwell).

[492] HL Deb 9 November 2010, col 149.

[493] Section 11 PBA.

C. Evaluation of the Potential of Framework Legislation

a. The authority of framework legislation and its potential to bind the legislature

Since the PBA is a piece of enabling legislation, it addresses ministers, who obtain the power to amend primary legislation and, consequently, to decide on the destiny of public bodies whose existence and status would otherwise fall within the exclusive competence of the legislature. The Flemish and Dutch frameworks, on the other hand, both contain obligations that intend to constrain the statutory powers of the legislature. To the extent that the KDBB and KWZBO indeed address the legislature, the question arises whether the latter should feel constrained by the framework. This is so because the legislation that will implement the general rules anchored in these acts will occupy the same position in the hierarchy of norms as the framework legislation itself. Neither the KDBB nor the KWZBO are invested with a special weight or priority vis-à-vis other statutory acts, they occupy the same position in the system of the hierarchy of norms. To what extent, then, is framework legislation enforceable vis-à-vis the legislature itself?

In its advice on the original project of the KDBB, the Legislation Section of the Belgian Council of State noted that the provisions of the KDBB could not bind the Flemish legislature. At most, they could express an intention of the legislature that adopted them, but they could not prevent future legislatures, which remain sovereign as to their ability to judge how to make use of their powers regarding administrative organization, from deciding to establish agencies on the basis of motives other than those enshrined in the KDBB. According to the Council, the provisions on the creation of IVAs and EVAs did not, consequently, belong in a normative text and could better be reserved for the explanatory memorandum.[494] In the explanatory memorandum, the Government replied that the KDBB wished to create a uniform and coherent structure. The provisions regarding the creation of agencies by the legislature were, according to the Government, essential elements in the assessment that has to be made in order to achieve an optimal organizational form.[495] The literature, however, regards the non-binding nature of the KDBB for the legislature as 'an important weakness'.[496]

---

494 *Parl.St.* Vl.Parl. 2002–03, nr. 1612/1, 94.

495 *Parl.St.* Vl.Parl. 2002–03, nr. 1612/1, 20–21.

496 See Koen Verhoest, Frederik Vandendriessche and Jan Rommel, 'Verzelfstandiging in Vlaanderen: theorie en praktijk' in Pierre Jadoul, Bruno Lombaert

In the explanatory memorandum of the Dutch KWZBO, it was repeated several times that, despite the wish for a uniform framework, there had to be room for differentiation and tailoring.[497] Some members of Parliament worried that, because of the possibility to deviate, the KWZBO would lose its capacity to create order.[498] As mentioned earlier, the initial Bill of the KWZBO did not contain any provisions on the conditions or motives that would have to be fulfilled before a ZBO could be established. The reason why the Government was reluctant to include such provisions, despite persisting parliamentary opposition,[499] was threefold: apart from the argument that this was deemed a political rather than a legal question and that it was impossible to foresee all cases in which the establishment of a ZBO would be reasonable beforehand, the Government was convinced that a statutory framework could never bind the legislature, so that these provisions would have no effect in any case.[500]

It could be argued that the value of framework legislation is not exclusively, nor primarily, dependent on its ability to offer a rigorous set of rules and principles that require compliance at all times. An important asset of framework legislation is located in its informative value. The KDBB sketches the rough lines of administrative organization and allows for legal subjects to orientate themselves in the Flemish administrative landscape. The KWZBO is more modest in its scope, since it does not govern the entire Dutch administrative organization, but only ZBOs. Nonetheless, it contains an overview of rules and principles applicable to a majority of the ZBOs that fall under its scope and contributes to legal certainty since it fills lacunae when the legislation on a particular ZBO is incomplete. Framework legislation has made administrative organization in general, and the APB landscape in particular, more comprehensible and digestible. Because they are not strictly binding, the KDBB and the KWZBO may be considered instruments with shortcomings, but they do have added value. After all, one of the most important rationales behind the enactment of both frameworks has been the aim of offering more transparency by designing a single frame of reference. Moreover, it seems reasonable that the aspiration of uniformity should sometimes give

and François Tulkens (eds), *Le paraétatisme. Nouveaux régards sur la décentralisation fonctionnelle en Belgique et dans les institutions européennes* (la Charte 2010) 369, 390–391.

497 Tweede Kamer 2000–2001, 27 426, nr. 3, see e.g. 1 and 4.

498 Tweede Kamer 2000–2001, 27 426, nr. 4, 5 and 11.

499 Tweede Kamer 2000–2001, 27 426, nr. 8, 2.

500 Tweede Kamer 2000–2001, 27 426, nr. 5, 24.

way to the precept that proper and efficient governance may also require tailoring and flexibility. Apart from informative value, framework legislation also has a high symbolic value moreover. Whereas some soft law frameworks may be equally effective in achieving goals such as harmonization and transparency, they lack the status of rules enacted by an elected assembly. The status of a statutory framework may make Governments and civil servants preparing legislative initiatives on APBs more inclined to take into account the principles of the framework and more careful or reluctant to propose deviations.

This more nuanced approach towards the role and importance of the binding nature of framework legislation does not suggest that these statutory frameworks are entirely non-committal for the legislature. Flemish literature suggests that the principle of equality, which has constitutional value, could play a role for the legal enforceability of the rules of the KDBB. This principle would require an equal treatment of all APBs, under the condition that they are sufficiently comparable and if there is no objective or reasonable justification for differentiation.[501] The Flemish legislature, however, enjoys substantial discretion in these matters. Moreover, it is not subject to any formal duty to give reasons, so that any justification for a deviation leading to inequality can always be offered *a posteriori*.[502] In the Netherlands, where judicial review of statutory law is not permissible, no legal remedy exists against a deviation from the KWZBO. Some Members of Parliament, however, did interrogate the minister on the possible consequences of the principle of equality for Parliament's room for manoeuvre. In the minister's opinion, this principle was irrelevant for the KWZBO, since no one ZBO is similar or to such an extent comparable to another that Parliament would have to feel obliged to limit itself in its political assessment when enacting establishing legislation.[503] According to the Belgian constitutionalist Popelier, the legislature is under a duty to give reasons for any deviation from a general act in a more specific act by means of

---

[501] Koen Verhoest, Frederik Vandendriessche and Jan Rommel, 'Verzelfstandiging in Vlaanderen: theorie en praktijk' in Pierre Jadoul, Bruno Lombaert and François Tulkens (eds), *Le paraétatisme. Nouveaux régards sur la décentralisation fonctionnelle en Belgique et dans les institutions européennes* (la Charte 2010) 369, 392.

[502] ibid 392.

[503] Eerste Kamer 2001–2002, 27 426, nr. 276c, 22.

reasonable arguments, which are objectively justifiable.[504] The author links quite a severe consequence to an unjustified deviation: in the event of an irreconcilability that has not been motivated, the general rule A has priority.[505] In her argumentation, Popelier refers to the importance of coherence. A different conclusion would, according to the author, be 'little conducive for the accessibility of legislation, which precisely depends on the coherence that is based on the general framework that serves as an interpretative framework for more precise rules'.[506]

This brings us to another principle that plays a role in the debate on the enforceability of the KDBB and KWZBO: that of legal certainty. As one of the principles of proper legislation, legal certainty attaches certain consequences to the existence of framework legislation. Framework legislation intends to offer a uniform framework, contributing to the aim of coherent legislation. Every deviation slightly detracts from that goal and therefore also contributes to legal uncertainty. The Flemish and the Dutch legislatures create a lawful expectation that Flemish agencies and Dutch ZBOs respectively are established and designed in accordance with the principles anchored in the framework. In a *Rechtsstaat*, it is justified to expect from the legislature that it respects the law that it enacts when and as long as it is kept in force.

In the past, the Belgian Constitutional Court has already ruled that the legislature cannot deviate from a general act, especially one that was enacted with the aim of providing legal certainty, if it does not provide a relevant specific justification for such a deviation. In this judgment, such a justification was lacking and the court concluded that the constitutional principle of equality had been violated.[507]

For the Netherlands, reference can also be made to direction 49 of the Dutch Directions for Legislation. Pursuant to direction 49, the deviation from general acts in specific acts is only permissible if necessary. The reasons for deviation have to be mentioned in the explanatory memorandum. The KWZBO is explicitly mentioned as a 'general act'. During the parliamentary process leading to the KWZBO, some Members of Parliament argued that a deviation from the KWZBO would have to be

---

504 Patricia Popelier, *De wet juridisch bekeken* (die Keure 2004) 348 with reference to Patricia Popelier, *Rechtszekerheid als beginsel voor behoorlijke regelgeving* (Intersentia 1997) 559.

505 Patricia Popelier, *Rechtszekerheid als beginsel voor behoorlijke regelgeving* (Intersentia 1997) 559.

506 ibid 559.

507 GwH 4 March 2008, no 35/2008.

reasoned.[508] The explanatory memorandum of the KWZBO suggests that the explanatory memoranda of the special (implementing) acts could contain a justification for that deviation.[509]

b. The effects of framework legislation in practice

Up until now, no official evaluation of the implementation of, and adherence to, the KDBB has been issued by the Government or by the Flemish Parliament or its committees. In 2010, the Flemish literature ascertained that legislation on APBs that had been reformed to IVAs or EVAs frequently deviated from the KDBB. For some Flemish APBs, it has moreover become apparent that the political will to convert them to IVAs or EVAs was lacking. A particular difficulty concerns the extent to which the establishing acts comply with the conditions and motives for establishment enshrined in the KDBB.[510] A full and comprehensive empirical study of the extent to which the current Flemish APB landscape complies with the KDBB falls beyond the scope of this book. Case studies looking at randomly selected agencies and their establishing acts have revealed that the KDBB is generally adhered to. These case studies more specifically confirmed that the legislature currently justifies its decision for entrusting public tasks to an APB in the explanatory memorandum of the establishing act.[511]

In 2007, the so-called *Begeleidingsteam Kaderwet zbo's* (Supporting Team KWZBO) issued a report entitled *ZBO's binnen kaders*.[512] The team was established to support ministers who would have to decide on the future of ZBOs and on the adjustment of their establishing legislation in order to comply with the KWZBO. The Commission indicated that it would give a restrictive interpretation to the motives for establishing ZBOs anchored in the KWZBO and announced a strict scrutiny of

---

508 Tweede Kamer 2000–2001, 27 426, nr. 16; Tweede Kamer, 27 Februari 2002, Handelingen 2001–2002, nr. 50, 3532. See also Sjoerd E Zijlstra, *Bestuurlijk Organisatierecht* (Kluwer 2009) 204.

509 Tweede Kamer 2000–2001, 27 426, nr. 3, 6.

510 See Koen Verhoest, Frederik Vandendriessche and Jan Rommel, 'Verzelfstandiging in Vlaanderen: theorie en praktijk' in Pierre Jadoul, Bruno Lombaert and François Tulkens (eds), *Le paraétatisme. Nouveaux régards sur la décentralisation fonctionnelle en Belgique et dans les institutions européennes* (la Charte 2010) 369, 389–391.

511 Stéphanie De Somer, *The Creation of Autonomous Public Bodies from a European Comparative Legal Perspective: International Impulse, National Restraint and How to Reconcile These Trends*, unedited PhD thesis in Law 2014, 291–295.

512 Tweede Kamer, 23 Augustus 2007, H.

proposals that deviated from the provisions regarding ministerial (supervisory) powers (such as the annulment power and the power to issue policy rules), responsibilities of the board and accountability. The question arises whether the Commission's rigid advice has resulted in an equally rigid implementation of the KWZBO.

Unlike the KDBB, the KWZBO does anchor an official mechanism of evaluation. Pursuant to article 39.2 of the KWZBO, a report on the efficiency and the effects of the framework act in practice has to be handed to both chambers of Parliament on a quinquennial basis. The KWZBO entered into force on 1 February 2007. On 17 January 2012, and thus after a first period of five years, a first report was indeed submitted. The report reveals that, by that time, 34 of the ZBOs that had already existed at the time that the KWZBO was enacted had been brought under the system of the KWZBO and that legislation was being prepared for 28 others to achieve the same result. For 37 ZBOs who were or would be retained, it was decided not to bring them under the scope of the KWZBO. Different reasons were mentioned. Five new ZBOs had been established and five were still in the process of being established (among which existing ZBOs whose founding act would be replaced and/or that would receive a new name). Some of these ZBOs were, moreover, the result of a merger. For six ZBOs, it was not yet decided whether they would be submitted to the regime of the KWZBO.[513]

The report focused to an important extent precisely on the possibility of deviating from certain provisions of the KWZBO in a reasoned way. The report's conclusion was that this had been done to a limited extent. The article that was most often deviated from was article 22 of the KWZBO, anchoring the annulment power. All deviations from this provision were systematically applied to ZBOs established on the basis of the motive anchored in article 3, §1, a, KWZBO, being the need 'for independent judgments on the basis of specific expertise'.[514] Also in 2012, the precited report *Verbinding Verbroken* concluded that the KWZBO would have to be revised and sharpened in order to reinforce

---

[513] See Evaluatie Kaderwet zelfstandige bestuursorganen 2012, 4 and 9–10; Brief aan de voorzitter van de Tweede Kamer der Staten-Generaal d.d. 17 januari 2012 betreffende Evaluatie Kaderwet ZBO's, uitgaande van de minister van Binnenlandse Zaken en Koninkrijkrelaties, http://www.rijksoverheid.nl/documenten-en-publicaties/kamerstukken/2012/01/17/kamerbrief-evaluatie-kaderwet-zelfstandige-bestuursorganen.html. A revised version was launched on 19 April 2012.

[514] See Evaluatie Kaderwet zelfstandige bestuursorganen 2012, 11.

uniformity and transparency in the ZBO landscape.[515] A report of the General Chamber of Auditors of 2012 on the scope and implementation of the KWZBO[516] expressed its concern that too large a number of ZBOs had been excluded from the KWZBO's scope *ratione personae* and that, for those that had been brought under its scope, large numbers of deviations existed.

Even though the PBA does not suffer from any uncertainties regarding compliance of the same nature as the KDBB and KWZBO, its actual effect, i.e. the extent to which it results in APB reforms, is dependent on the extent to which the Government is prepared to use the powers that it has been invested with. The Cabinet Office publishes annual reviews containing a *status quaestionis* regarding UK public bodies.

In 2013, the House of Lords Secondary Legislation Scrutiny Committee published its *Special Report Public Bodies Act 2011: Two Years On*.[517] The committee ascertained that progress was reasonable, since '[o]rders laid to date represent just under 40% of the total envisaged after 40% of the time available has elapsed'.[518] It also concluded that some bodies originally scheduled for abolition in the PBA would eventually be retained. This made the committee wonder 'whether the Government had undertaken sufficient consultation with relevant parties before deciding to include them in the Act'.[519] The committee stressed that the '[t]he Government were not given an unfettered power to reform the organisations included in the 2011 Act. The statutory tests require a rigorous examination of the costs and benefits of these reform proposals'.[520] It acknowledged that the Government had already made progress when it came to 'the standard of supporting evidence' for the orders, but emphasized that all the statutory tests that the minister must meet before making an order would have to be addressed in the explanation of the future orders: 'The responsibility lies with the Minister to put a convincing case to Parliament (where possible with evidence) on how the

---

515 Eerste Kamer der Staten-Generaal, Parlementaire Onderzoekscommissie Privatisering/Verzelfstandiging Overheidsdiensten, 'Verbinding Verbroken? Onderzoek naar de parlementaire besluitvorming over de privatisering en verzelfstandiging van overheidsdiensten', 86.

516 Algemene Rekenkamer, *Kaderwet zbo's: reikwijdte en implementatie*, 2012, http://www.rekenkamer.nl/Publicaties/Onderzoeksrapporten/Introducties/2012/06/Kaderwet_zbo_s.

517 HL 2013–14, 98.

518 ibid 4.

519 ibid 4–5.

520 ibid 8.

proposal complies with the Act's requirements; it is not sufficient for the Explanatory Document simply to assert that the tests have been met.'[521] The committee also expected the Government to ensure that adequate consultation would take place with bodies under review, as well as with their constituency.[522]

In the 2014 Public Bodies Reform Progress Update, it was announced that, since May 2010, the number of ALBs had been reduced by over 285. Transparency had been increased (94 per cent of NDPBs were reported to publish an annual report) and the functions of over 75 bodies had been 'moved closer to elected representatives, increasing accountability'.[523] Critics have noticed, however, that the majority of quangos that the Coalition Government intended to (and had up until 2012) axe(d) were advisory, not executive NDPBs.[524]

The enactment of an instrument like the PBA was atypical for UK constitutional and administrative law, which is not in the habit of creating general frameworks to govern the organization or functioning of the public sector. Nevertheless, further pleas for rationalization have been expressed. Some of these suggestions, moreover, point at the implementation of further measures via statutory or other legal instruments of a general nature. Craig does not advocate that APBs 'should be forced into some administrative straitjacket', but points out that 'a significant spectrum [is] running between the pure ad hoc and institutional rigidity'. His proposal for a framework, for instance, addresses APBs' relationship with their parent departments and Parliament, pointing out that the issue of ministerial power over agencies is also present in relation to NDPBs (for executive agencies, the Framework Document streamlines this particular relationship).[525]

Other proposals for reform seem more neutral as to the legal instrument used for implementation, but, when adopted, would contribute to the revaluation of one or more of the meta values and legal principles that are currently central in the 'national restraint' movement. One of these proposals is the one launched by the Institute for Government in its 2010 research report. The report, titled 'Read before Burning', established that

---

[521] ibid 8.

[522] ibid 8.

[523] Cabinet Office, 'Public Bodies 2014', https://www.gov.uk/government/publications/public-bodies-2014, 8.

[524] Matthew Flinders and Chris Skelcher, 'Shrinking the Quango State: Five Challenges in Reforming Quangos' (2012) 32(5) Public Money & Management 327, 331.

[525] Paul Craig, *Administrative Law* (Sweet & Maxwell 2012) 105.

ALBs are perceived by both politicians and the public not only as 'unaccountable and inefficient', but also as 'incredibly confusing', the policy on the creation of ALBs and their institutional design lacking consistency and coherence. In the foreword, Lord Bichard of Nailsworth pointed out that 'degrees of necessary independence differ, which should be reflected in the way ALBs are formed and managed'.[526] The report furthermore notes that '[t]here is often little theoretical or empirical justification for the degree of freedom enjoyed by specific ALBs'.[527] The report advises that 'reform of arm's length government must go beyond a simple "numbers game", the traditional post-election cull of ALBs'.[528] More specific recommendations involve e.g. the introduction of sunset clauses in legislation creating ALBs, the introduction of Governance and Performance (GAP) reviews, the provision of a complete list of ALBs and an obligation for these bodies to publish transparent information on their role, relationship to government, funding and performance.[529]

The 10th and final recommendation,[530] however, is probably the most promising one (the Institute itself labels it as a 'programme for radical change'). It is meant to further rationalize the quango landscape and to 'set arm's length government on a more stable long-term footing'. It suggests that the Government should implement a new, simpler taxonomy for ALBs. The Institute, moreover, proposes a possible model for such a taxonomy, which it presents in a pyramidal structure. The basic idea behind this taxonomy is that the governance of a specific body should be related to its task or function. The classification itself is consequently 'determined by the degree of freedom from executive control on appointments, strategy, decision and budget, which the body needs to be able to discharge its functions'.[531] Bodies with mere advisory functions are excluded from the taxonomy. The Institute further distinguishes between four different functions and four corresponding types or forms of bodies. The first function is 'constitutional oversight' and is performed by 'constitutional bodies'. These are free from executive control and primarily accountable to Parliament, not to ministers. An example would be the Electoral Commission. The second function is that

---

[526] Institute for Government, 'Read before Burning', http://www.instituteforgovernment.org.uk/publications/read-burning, 2.

[527] ibid 39.

[528] ibid 10.

[529] See ibid 12–14 and 52–60 for a complete overview of all 10 recommendations.

[530] ibid 14 and 55–60.

[531] ibid 55.

of 'regulatory regime setters', 'guarantors of standards' and 'independent watchdogs', which are labelled 'independent public interest bodies' and are regarded as bodies 'whose credibility depends on them being clearly insulated from ministerial interference'. These are entitled to set their own strategy within a statutory framework but '[m]inisters would be able to provide guidance and, if set down in the founding legislation, be able to override the body on policy – but only with parliamentary oversight through the relevant select committee'. Examples are Ofcom and Ofgem, the Food Standards Agency and the Climate Change Committee. For these bodies, there is a potential for 'limited power of direction with parliamentary oversight'. A third set of functions involves 'discretionary grant-giving', 'discretionary enforcement & inspection' and 'stewardship of national assets'. They are performed by 'departmental sponsored bodies', whose business plan is signed off by a government department and who can be heard by Parliament. Building independent technical expertise was mentioned as a possible motive behind the establishment of these bodies, but the 'stewards of national assets', such as museums and galleries, were mentioned as examples as well. The last category of ALBs is in charge of 'delegated implementation of government policy' and holds the well-known name of 'executive agencies'. These are constitutionally part of the department and operate under civil service terms and conditions. Ministers are fully accountable for their performance. The Institute estimates that most executive NDPBs would become departmental-sponsored bodies in the new scheme, 'although some would be reclassified as executive agencies'.[532]

The report further distinguishes two possible ways in which the taxonomy could be implemented legally. A first possibility (this would mean, according to the report, a 'big bang approach', providing clarity to the landscape rapidly) would be that Parliament would either enact 'specific primary legislation, to give reorganisation powers, backed up by a raft of primary legislation' (enabling legislation), or a small number of Bills in order to reclassify the organizations. A second possibility would be 'to migrate bodies gradually to the new status, taking legislative powers as necessary as the opportunity arises and applying it to new bodies created'.[533] During the parliamentary debates on the PBA, the report was mentioned by a member of the House of Lords, who pointed out that it set out 'the case for reform, but it is thoughtful, rooted in reality and sets out a road map for bringing these bodies into a more

---

[532] ibid 57.
[533] ibid 14 and 60.

rational framework over time'.[534] The proposal for a taxonomy was also welcomed in the literature.[535]

In its report *Smaller Government: Shrinking the Quango State*, the House of Commons Public Administration Select Committee also referred to 'Read Before Burning', pointing out that its 'research revealed a muddled picture of governance arrangements with similar bodies having different governance and freedoms for no apparent reason'.[536] The minister agreed that the untidiness of the current system was a fact and that this was the result of 'a random process', but he declared himself to be 'temperamentally slightly allergic to trying to create a top-down overall scheme of arrangement for all of this', although he supported simplification as such. The committee itself concluded that the nature of the public bodies' landscape was complex and confusing and that simplification was:

> not a matter of administrative tidiness but a necessary step to ensure the accountability and effectiveness of these organisations. The current system is chaotic, making it difficult to understand why different types of bodies exist and what these variations mean in practice. We recommend that the Government use its triennial review process to re-examine the proper governance arrangements for each public body and place them in a new simplified taxonomy.[537]

Similarly to some of the statements about the goal of the PBA made in the course of the parliamentary process (*supra*), the committee linked the problem of 'administrative' untidiness (and, thus, opacity) to that of the lack of democratic accountability.[538]

In its response to the committee's report, the Government reiterated, however, that it was not 'persuaded that the solution to this is to invest taxpayers' money [in] the introduction of a whole new taxonomy at this

---

534 HL Deb 9 November 2010, cols 130–131 (Baroness Scott of Needham Market).

535 Matthew Flinders and Chris Skelcher, 'Shrinking the Quango State: Five Challenges in Reforming Quangos' (2012) 32(5) Public Money & Management 327, 334.

536 Public Administration Select Committee, *Smaller Government: Shrinking the Quango State* (HC 2010–11, 537) 41.

537 ibid 44.

538 ibid 44.

stage'.[539] In December 2012, the Cabinet Office nevertheless published a Guide for Departments on the 'Categories of Public Bodies'. The Guide was meant to 'set out broad definitions of the key types of body in the public landscape'.[540] Rather than designing a new taxonomy, the document delineated the scope and meaning of existing denominations for certain bodies in order to facilitate the work of the departments who would have to deal with future reform initiatives. Only the future will tell whether the PBA has indeed been the first, but also final piece of generic legislation on APBs or whether it is merely the pioneer in perhaps a series of legislative initiatives that aim to rationalize the creation, design and functioning of ALBs in the UK.

6. CONCLUSION

This chapter has argued that we are witnessing, at the domestic level in the European legal sphere, a trend of 'national restraint'. This legal movement initiates from a process of retrospective contemplation about the rise of APBs in the past decades, the desirability of this trend and – above all – its reconciliation with fundamental constitutional principles. The chapter relied on comparative legal research in order to construct a common denominator of these constitutional principles in Belgium, France, the Netherlands and the UK. The hypothesis was that APBs pose a threat to three distinct meta values of modern public law: constitutionalism, the rule of law and democracy. For each of these meta values, one or more specific fundamental principles that seem particularly affected by the emergence of APBs were selected. As far as constitutionalism is concerned, the relationship between APBs and separation of powers was studied. The principles of legal certainty and publicity or transparency were subsumed under the 'rule of law'. The meta value of democracy was subdivided into the principles of legality, political ministerial

---

[539] Minister for the Cabinet Office, *Government Response to the Public Administration Select Committee Report, 'Smaller Government: Shrinking the Quango State'* (Cm 8044, 2011) para 105.

[540] In 2016, this document was replaced with 'Classification of Public Bodies: Guidance For Departments' (https://www.gov.uk/government/publications/classification-of-public-bodies-information-and-guidance). This document not only aims to enhance conceptual clarity, but also contains guidance on the decision-making process that departments have to follow for establishing public bodies.

responsibility, democratic control of the administration by elected representatives and centrality. The analysis demonstrated how APBs have become a detriment to these principles in the selected legal systems. Certainly, there are differences in emphasis across the four systems studied. Nonetheless, they have in common that democratic concerns are central to the criticism expressed to question the constitutionality of APBs in a contemporary context. The shared democratic argument against APBs is that they distance administrative decisions of a discretionary and thus political nature from the system of representative democracy.

As a reaction to those concerns, states have been attempting to confine the unlimited spread of APBs and to rationalize the decision as to their creation. Hence, a balance is sought between upholding the above-mentioned principles and acknowledging the benefits of granting political autonomy to parts of the administration. Legislatures and Governments have recently embarked on initiatives to counteract the criticism regarding their past disregard for the constitutional concerns regarding APBs. Governments, parliaments and the constitutional bodies that advise them have thus made attempts to 'reinvent' APBs in the light of the concerns distinguished in the foregoing analysis. A distinction was made between four phenomena: a change in the discourse of these institutions vis-à-vis APBs; initiatives to 'streamline' the APB landscape (by means of abolition, mergers etc.); the drafting of soft law instruments that serve as frameworks for assessment; and, finally, the enactment of framework legislation.

Because of its originality and special importance from a legal viewpoint, the phenomenon of framework legislation received special attention in this chapter. Framework legislation contains rules and conditions with regard to the creation or retention and institutional design of APBs. On the one hand, it takes the principle of centrality as a starting point for administrative organization once more. It encourages Governments and legislatures to contemplate past and future initiatives to create APBs and/or on their institutional design and to justify their decisions accordingly. Thus, framework legislation is conducive to a more cautious attitude towards the creation of APBs, which is conceived as a decision that should never be taken lightly. It thereby contributes to a process of rationalization and democratization. On the other hand, framework legislation aims to bring order to the chaos in the current APB landscape of the three systems studied by providing more transparency on (decisions regarding) the creation of APBs and by bringing more uniformity to administrative organization.

An in-depth study of the KDBB, KWZBO and PBA, however, also demonstrates that these goals can be pursued in different ways, using different approaches and legislative techniques. All have their benefits and pitfalls and raise their own, specific legal questions. For instance, both the KDBB and KWZBO are subject to important uncertainties regarding their binding nature and enforceability. The success of the PBA, on the other hand, depends on the extent to which the UK Government will deem it necessary or expedient to use the powers it has been entrusted with by the legislature.

4. Conflict

1. DEFINING THE CONFLICT(S) BETWEEN 'EU IMPULSE' AND 'NATIONAL RESTRAINT'

> [a]s far as some of the most important developments with respect to European integration are concerned, many legal scholars are not asking the right questions simply because they focus too much on EU lawmakers who see European integration as an ongoing process with no horizon and few constitutional limits.[1]

Chapters 2 and 3 of this book identified two contemporary trends that characterize the law on APBs in a contemporary European context. Whereas APBs with substantial autonomy gain popularity in EU law as an appropriate design for national administrative authorities implementing supranational legislation, they are increasingly refuted as a preferred model for administrative organization by national scholars, politicians, parliaments and their advisory bodies. Unsurprisingly, this attitude is also reflected in the way that national Parliaments and Governments deal with the implementation of supranational obligations to create APBs. In 2012, Ottow and Lavrijssen ascertained that many European Member States were reluctant to give a far-reaching interpretation to the existing EU independence requirements, which, according to the authors, made independence quite a 'fragile concept' within Europe.[2] They referred to recent examples in various Members States, illustrating 'that in politically

[1] Rob Van Gestel and Hans-W Micklitz, 'Revitalising Doctrinal Legal Research in Europe: What About Methodology?' in Ulla Neergaard, Ruth Nielsen and Lyn Roseberry (eds), *European Legal Method Paradoxes and Revitilisation* (DJØF Publishing 2011) 25, 34.

[2] Saskia Lavrijssen and Annetje Ottow, 'Independent Supervisory Authorities: A Fragile Concept' (2012) 39(4) Legal Issues of Economic Integration 419, 431; Annetje Ottow, 'The Different Levels of Protection of National Supervisors' Independence in the European Landscape' in Suzanne Comptois and Kars J de Graaf (eds), *On Judicial and Quasi-judicial Independence* (Boom Juridische Uitgevers 2013) 139, 143ff.

sensitive issues or sectors, governments tend to interfere in the regulators' legal and political independence'.[3]

This chapter addresses the tension that exists between the EU requirements with regard to NRAs and DPAs and current national attitudes towards APBs, which originate from democratic concerns. It also looks at the way in which the European Court of Justice has dealt with this tension.

2. EXAMPLES OF CONFLICT AT MEMBER STATE LEVEL

Chapter 3 concluded that the four European legal systems studied in this book have all recently engaged in efforts to achieve a shared aspiration: to ensure that administrative decisions that involve discretionary power remain embedded in the system of representative democracy. It demonstrated that there are differences in opinion and approach as to how to achieve this result. Two main avenues can be distinguished. A first is to define strict limits with regard to the legality of the powers conferred on APBs, implying that these powers should have a (sufficiently elaborate) basis in statutory law. This is the main approach that the French *Conseil Constitutionnel* has adopted in its case law on AAIs. Secondly, one may accept the conferral of broad powers on APBs, but emphasize the need for political supervision of the decisions that result from the exercise of these powers. This has been the primary strategy adopted by the Belgian Council of State, Legislation Section. In other words: political input can be assured *ex ante*, in the phase of defining APBs' powers, or *ex post*, in the phase of the exercise of these powers.

Chapter 2 established that the current EU requirements combine a demand for broad, discretionary powers – as opposed to well-defined powers – with a prohibition on providing mechanisms that allow for day-to-day political supervision. In doing so, they deprive the institutions of representative democracy of the possibility to decide on the political considerations and consequences entailed by the administrative decisions made by the APBs in question. Here lies the primary conflict between the current EU requirements and the requirements flowing from the meta value of democracy as defined in Chapter 3.

[3] Saskia Lavrijssen and Annetje Ottow, 'Independent Supervisory Authorities: A Fragile Concept' (2012) 39(4) Legal Issues of Economic Integration 419, 432.

A. Belgium

Two judgments of the Belgian Constitutional Court address the tension between the EU independence requirements addressed in Chapter 2 and the democratic concerns outlined in Chapter 3. In 2010, the court was invited to rule on the constitutionality of the independent status of the federal energy regulator.[4] The origin of the court's judgment was a preliminary question formulated by the Council of State, Administrative Litigation Section. The case pending before the administrative judge concerned an administrative fine imposed by the energy regulator. The claimant asked the Council of State to annul the fine. Its main arguments concerned the incompatibility of the regulator's status, as anchored in the Belgian Electricity Act, with the Constitution. The challenged provisions invested the regulator with the power to control the accounts of enterprises operating in the electricity sector and to impose administrative fines. According to the claimant, they violated the Constitution, because the persons affected by the regulator's decisions did not enjoy the guarantee that this decision was made under the ultimate control of the political executive, which assumes responsibility before Parliament.

In its judgment, the Constitutional Court referred to the European directives on energy regulation and ascertained that the federal energy regulator had been established as a consequence thereof. Turning to the Belgian Constitution, the court ruled that the legislature can entrust specific executive powers in a well-defined technical matter to an autonomous administrative authority that remains subject to both judicial review and parliamentary control. Thus, the lack of hierarchical or administrative oversight was not deemed unconstitutional. Reference was further made to recital 34 of Directive 2009/72/EC, which precludes neither judicial review nor parliamentary supervision in accordance with the constitutional laws of the Member States. As far as supervision by Parliament is concerned, the court took into account the fact that the legislature defines the tasks and the functioning of the regulator (within the limits set by EU law) and approves its budget. The regulator has to issue an annual report concerning, among other things, the performance of its tasks and hand it to the competent minister, who in turn presents it to the federal legislative chambers and to the regional Governments. The legislative chambers have the possibility to call the competent ministers or the federal Government to account, via measures of control. Consequently, the court was satisfied that the regulator's status did not violate

[4] GwH 18 November 2010, no 2010/130.

the Constitution and that the lack of any form of direct political control on its decisions was not problematic from the viewpoint of parliamentary control.

Nonetheless, the court decided to develop an additional argument 'insofar as the foregoing would not suffice'.[5] The far-reaching independence of the regulatory authority and a possible conflict with the Constitution, could, according to the court, in any case be justified on the grounds of article 34 of the Belgian Constitution, providing that the exercise of certain powers can be entrusted to institutions of international law by means of a treaty or by statute. Although legal doctrine is not unanimous, this article is often regarded as the constitutional basis for the principle of the primacy of international law with direct effect over the national Constitution.[6] It is not entirely clear whether this last argument was developed in subordinate order or whether it was an essential additional condition for the court to answer the preliminary question negatively. In other words: in the absence of an EU directive, would the court still deem a similar degree of political independence reconcilable with the Belgian Constitution?

In 2013, the court was faced with EU legislation from which it derived a requirement for political independence.[7] This judgment, which was already briefly addressed in Chapter 2, concerned the Belgian federal authority entrusted with the investigation of accidents in the maritime transport sector. The court referred to its earlier judgment on the energy

---

[5] Para B.8.1. of the judgment.

[6] See e.g. Jan Velaers, *De Grondwet en de Raad van State, Afdeling Wetgeving* (Maklu 1999) 238; André Alen, 'De grondwet, hoogste rechtsnorm?', Patricia Popelier, 'De verhouding tussen de Belgische Grondwet en het internationale recht' and Pierre Vandernoot, 'Regards du Conseil d'Etat sur une disposition orpheline: l'article 34 de la Constitution', all three in *En hommage à Francis Delpérée. Itinéraires d'un constitutionnaliste* (Bruylant 2007) 105, 1231 and 1599 respectively. In a recent judgment, the Court, however, has ruled that article 34 of the Constitution does not allow for deviations 'of the national identity that is enshrined in the political and constitutional basic structures or core values of the protection that the Constitution offers to citizens'. See GwH 28 April 2016, no 62/2016, para B.8.7. Some literature has been pleading for a more critical attitude of the Constitutional Court towards European legislation that is difficult to reconcile with national constitutional principles. Such criticism may result in a dialogue with the European institutions, which may lead to solutions: see Patricia Popelier and Werner Vandenbruwaene, 'La Belgique et le projet d'intégration européenne: plaidoyer pour une stratégie constitutionnelle' [2014] Revue belge de droit constitutionnel 410.

[7] GwH 21 November 2013, no 158/2013.

regulator and to the paragraph on the existence of a 'well-defined technical matter' in order to substantiate its conclusion that the delegation was not contrary to the Constitution. It did not refer to article 34 of the Constitution. The court did not provide any further explanation as to why it believed that the APB's missions in this case were indeed 'technical' and 'well-defined'. This raises the question of whether the court does not adopt a more flexible approach when confronted with EU legislation.[8]

An approach that seems less accommodating to the demands of EU law than that of the Constitutional Court is the one adopted by the Belgian Council of State, Legislation Section. In 2003, the Council issued an opinion regarding one of the so-called 'sectorial committees' pertaining to the Commission for the Protection of Privacy (the Belgian DPA), namely the Sectorial Committee for the National Registry.[9] Pursuant to the Belgian Data Protection Act, sectorial committees, established by means of statutes, are competent to investigate and decide on applications with regard to the processing or communication of data to which special legislation is applicable within the limits fixed by the law.[10] The Council reminded the legislature that the delegation of administrative tasks to authorities without any form of administrative oversight had to go hand in hand with a statement of reasons, in the explanatory memorandum, explaining why it was necessary to deviate from the constitutional principles regarding transfer of powers and control by the political executive. The Council of State observed that the decision-making power of the sectorial committee would in certain cases imply a large discretionary power. It invited the legislature to ensure that the tasks of the committee would be better defined. Furthermore, the Council suggested entrusting the King or his minister with the actual decision-making power, under the condition that the prior advice of the sectorial committee would be sought. According to the Council, this solution would conflict to a lesser extent with the constitutional principle of political ministerial responsibility. In the light of the case law of the ECJ on the notion of 'complete independence', which was discussed in

[8] In a later case, where an EU dimension was lacking, the court demonstrated in a more convincing manner that the powers delegated to the authority in question did not involve discretionary choices and were mere 'modalities of execution with a limited and technical scope': GwH 10 November 2011, no 166/2011.

[9] *Parl.St.* Kamer 2002–03, nr. 2226/3.

[10] The sectorial committees are part of the Commission, which is in turn established as an institution of the Chamber of Representatives, in order to protect its independence.

Chapter 2 and will further be addressed in Section 3 of this chapter, serious doubts can be raised about whether this solution would have been reconcilable with article 28 of the Data Protection Directive. The Council of State itself acknowledged that the sectorial committees were public supervisory authorities in the sense of article 28 of the Data Protection Directive and, in that regard, have to enjoy a sufficient degree of independence. As an alternative, it therefore suggested that the Government could be granted a right of appeal against the decisions of the committee, for the sake of (maintaining) the law. Thus, the Council of State advised the Government to adapt its proposed initiative in order to square it both with requirements related to the principle of legality (a sufficient definition of the body's powers by the legislature) and to that of political ministerial responsibility (which requires political supervision).

Another significant opinion was issued in 2011, on the occasion of a legislative initiative that aimed to adapt Belgian legislation to recent European initiatives with regard to the sector of electronic communications, among which Directive 2009/140/EC, amending the Framework Directive.[11] The Council was critical of the removal of the power of the Cabinet[12] (as an emanation of the political executive) to suspend the execution of certain decisions of the Belgian telecom and postal regulator. The grounds for a possible suspension were both the violation of the law and the damage done to the general interest, making the power of suspension an instrument for supervision on grounds of both legality and policy.

Interestingly, the Council of State studied the proposed provisions in the light of the judgment of the Belgian Constitutional Court regarding the federal energy regulator. It referred to the reinforced independence requirements introduced by Directive 2009/140 and saw a parallel with the evolutions that had taken place in EU energy law. At the same time, however, the Council was not persuaded that the requirements enshrined in Directive 2009/140 were formulated in an equally strict wording as those used in the energy sector. The Council took into account that the prohibitions on seeking or receiving any instructions in the third Electricity Directive explicitly mention instructions by governments, whereas this specification does not feature in the parallel provisions of Directive 2009/140. Even more significant, the Council pointed out, is the explicit

---

11 *Parl.St.* Kamer 2011-12, nr. 2143/1, 173–189.

12 I.e. the joint assembly of all government ministers, excluding the secretaries of state.

mention in the revised Framework Directive that the regulator's independence does not constitute any objection to supervision in accordance with the national Constitution. Consequently, the Council concluded, the current Framework Directive does not explicitly prohibit governmental supervision of the regulatory authority if this is required by the constitutional law of the Member State, whereas such forms of supervision are explicitly excluded as far as the energy regulator is concerned.[13]

According to the Council, the judgment of the Constitutional Court did not, moreover, provide a clear answer to two important questions.[14] First, the Council wondered what had been the precise significance of the arguments developed by the court as to the role of article 34 of the Belgian Constitution. According to the Council, it was unclear whether these arguments had actually been superfluous, or whether they had been genuine conditions for the court to accept the constitutionality of the lack of any form of political supervision. Secondly, the Council wondered whether the reasoning developed by the Constitutional Court could also be applied to the rule-making powers of the regulators. The judgment of the Constitutional Court had after all been pronounced following a preliminary question in a case in which an administrative fine was challenged, i.e. a decision with an individual scope.[15] Considering these uncertainties as to the lessons to be drawn from the judgment of the Constitutional Court, the Council advised the legislature to be cautious and to reconsider the removal of the power of suspension. The Council thus encouraged the Belgian legislature to implement EU law in a way that made the legal design of APBs reconcilable with the Constitution to the best extent possible. In the light of the Council's advice, the Cabinet's power of suspension was not entirely removed: it remained applicable to those decisions that did not involve *ex ante* regulation or dispute resolution between companies.

In April 2014, however, the European Commission brought infringement procedures against Belgium before the ECJ. The Commission more precisely did not agree with Belgium's solution to limit the suspension power to the decisions mentioned. According to the Commission, none of the regulator's decisions may be subject to such powers, in order to avoid

---

13 Page 184 of the opinion. In a later opinion, with regard to the adjustment of the Belgian Electricity Act and Gas Act to the third generation of energy liberalization directives, issued before the advice discussed here, the Council was silent on the lack of political supervision provided (see *Parl.St.* Kamer 2010–11, nr. 1725/1, 262–329).

14 Pages 185–189 of the advice.

15 Pages 188–189 of the advice.

any indirect external influence that would hamper the regulator's functional independence.[16] As a consequence, the federal legislature decided to remove the power of suspension altogether.

B. France

A recent article established that in France 'the expanded mandates of independent agencies in response to EU policies ... reveal tensions between constitutional principle and EU law'.[17] More precisely, these agencies are 'central to many ongoing debates between France and the EU'.[18]

The following case illustrates how one particular measure that has been advocated in many of the studies and reports discussed in Chapter 3, i.e. the appointment of *commissaires du Gouvernement* in all AAIs, could eventually not be implemented with regard to a specific AAI because it was subject to independence requirements anchored in EU law. The 2011 report on the implementation of the recommendations made by the 2010 study of the Assemblée Nationale on AAIs contained a warning that, although the recommendation of systematically appointing *commissaires du Gouvernement* in AAIs could be welcomed, requirements of EU law would have to be respected.[19]

In 2011, on the occasion of the implementation of Directive 2009/140 into French law,[20] the French Government proposed to appoint a *commissaire du Gouvernement* to the board of the ARCEP (l'Autorité de Régulation des Communications Électroniques des Postes).[21] This representative would have to inform the authority about the Government's

---

[16] See the explanatory memorandum and the opinion of the Council of State in *Parl.St.* Kamer 2014–15, nr. 875/1.

[17] Susan Rose-Ackerman and Thomas Perroud, 'Policymaking and Public Law in France: Public Participation, Agency Independence, and Impact Assessment' [2013] Colum. J. Eur. L. 225, 237.

[18] ibid 311.

[19] Assemblée Nationale No 3405 – La Commission des Lois Constitutionnelles, de la Législation et de l'Administration Générale de la République – Rapport sur la mise en œuvre des recommandations du rapport du Comité d'évaluation et de contrôle des politiques publiques sur les autorités administratives indépendantes par M. Charles de la Verpillière, Député (2011) 32–33.

[20] Loi no 2011-302 du 22 Mars 2011 portant diverses dispositions d'adaption de la législation au droit de l'Union européenne en matière de santé, de travail et de communications électroniques.

[21] The case is also discussed in Annetje Ottow, 'The Different Levels of Protection of National Supervisors' Independence in the European Landscape' in

preferences with regard to policies in matters of postal services and electronic communications. He would have the power to make the authority discuss all questions that he deemed of interest, a request that could not be refused. The Assemblée Nationale endorsed the Government's proposal by adopting a legislative amendment. Using the same expression as Ottow and Lavrijssen in one of their contributions on the subject,[22] a French commentator argued that this initiative illustrated the fragility of the legal rules on the regulator's independence.[23]

Fierce protests by the ARCEP and its top management and a warning of the European Commission (even after amendments had been made to the initial proposal in order to secure the authority's independence)[24] eventually led to a rejection of the proposal by the French Senate. Subsequently, the *Commission mixte paritaire*, which intervenes in the case of a difference of opinion between both Houses of the French Parliament, decided to drop the proposal as well. The provisions of EU law on the NRA's political independence formed the basis of this outcome. In its reply to the European Commission, the French Government had nevertheless made every effort to defend (the reasonableness of) its position. It indicated that the objective of the initiative was to contribute to the reinforcement of a dialogue between the Government and the ARCEP, but that the *commissaire* would not take part in the deliberations of the ARCEP, let alone give instructions to the authority. In a reply to a senator's question after the proposal had already been discarded, the competent ministry declared that the Government remained convinced that the appointment of a *commissaire du Gouvernement* would not have violated EU law, but would have contributed significantly to the coherence of public action in matters of electronic communications and, consequently, to the efficiency of the implementation of EU telecom legislation.[25]

Suzanne Comptois and Kars J de Graaf (eds), *On Judicial and Quasi-judicial Independence* (Boom Juridische Uitgevers 2013) 139, 151–152.

22 Saskia Lavrijssen and Annetje Ottow, 'Independent Supervisory Authorities: A Fragile Concept' (2012) 39(4) Legal Issues of Economic Integration 419.

23 Gabriel Eckert, 'L'indépendance des autorités de régulation économique à l'égard du pouvoir politique' [2012] RFAP 629, 639.

24 See e.g. 'Un représentant de l'Etat au sein de l'Arcep: le gouvernement persiste' *Le Monde* (8–9 February 2011).

25 See Question écrite no 17046 de M. Michel Sergent, JO Sénat 3 février 2011, 231 and Réponse du Ministère chargé de l'industrie, de l'énergie et de l'économie numérique, JO Sénat 28 Avril 2011, 1108. See also Susan Rose-Ackerman and Thomas Perroud, 'Policymaking and Public Law in France:

French doctrine has more generally discerned increasing legislative reluctance to entrust AAIs, including those subject to EU independence requirements, with broad (discretionary) powers or missions.[26]

C. The Netherlands

In the Netherlands, a recent merger of regulatory bodies in one joined institution called *Autoriteit Consument en Markt* (Authority Consumer and Market, ACM) reanimated the debate on the political supervision of regulatory bodies. In its opinion on the legislative draft[27] the Dutch Council of State, Advisory Section dedicated a separate section to 'the constitutional position of the ACM'. The ACM being a ZBO, the Council reminded the Government that sufficient possibilities for political accountability had to be anchored in the statute. It linked this requirement to the constitutional principle of ministerial responsibility. As for the impact of EU law, it noted that the various provisions in the European directives on the independence of market regulators were accompanied by a clause specifying that supervision in accordance with national constitutional law remained possible. Hence, the Council concluded, ministers could still hold supervisory powers vis-à-vis the ACM in order to assume responsibility for the policy implemented by the regulator. At the same time, the Council acknowledged that EU legislation imposed certain limits in this regard. It therefore advised the legislature to explore the limits of EU law and to retain as much political supervision as possible.

In that regard, the Council wondered why the power of ministerial approval vis-à-vis so-called 'policy rules' (soft law instruments) issued by the ACM had been removed from the original draft, since this power would have allowed the competent minister to assume responsibility for these acts. The Council did not find it prima facie clear that EU law excluded this form of supervision. It invited the Government to investigate this further and – if applicable – to adapt the legislative proposal. It formulated a similar remark with regard to the power of annulment anchored in the proposal. The Bill envisaged that this power would be limited to acts with a general scope and to the situation in which the ACM would lack competence to take a certain decision, so that it would

Public Participation, Agency Independence, and Impact Assessment' [2013] Colum. J. Eur. L. 225, 284–285.

26 Jean-Louis Autin, 'Le devenir des autorités administratives indépendantes' [2010] RFDA 875, 877.

27 Tweede Kamer, vergaderjaar 2011–2012, 33 186, nr. 4, 5ff.

exceed its powers. Under normal circumstances and pursuant to both article 22 KWZBO and article 10:35 of the Dutch Act on Administrative Law, there are two grounds for annulment, being violation of the law and violation of the public interest. Limiting the reasons for annulment was, according to the Council, undesirable unless compelling reasons existed that could justify such a choice. Again, the Council advised the Government to investigate the issue more thoroughly and to revise its proposal accordingly.

The competent minister, however, rejected the Council's suggestions. He referred to the case law of the ECJ in a case against Belgium, which in his opinion demonstrated 'that the Court takes the independence flowing from European law very seriously'.[28]

In the subsequent (written and oral) debates between Parliament and the competent minister, many questions formulated by Members of Parliament related to the supervision of the new regulatory body as well.[29] The minister, however, continued to refer to EU law as the reason why no further mechanisms of (ministerial) oversight could be installed. This provoked the impression, for one Member of Parliament, that the minister was 'hiding' behind the European rules to ignore the advice of the Council of State, which had expressed doubts as to whether EU law really required such a far-reaching independence.[30] Another member was not convinced that EU law really demanded such a limited degree of oversight and wanted to know how it would be ensured that Parliament would have sufficient contacts with the NRA.[31]

Eventually, these parliamentary concerns resulted in two amendments to the Government's initial proposal, which aimed to reinvigorate political control.[32] Both amendments were declined, because they were deemed to violate the EU independence requirements in the fields of energy and electronic communications. The minister warned that, lately, the European Commission had been very strict as to the compliance by Member States with the requirements of independence for NRAs and

---

[28] Tweede Kamer, vergaderjaar 2011–2012, 33 186, nr. 4, 9 with reference to Case C-474/08, *Commission/Belgium* [2009] ECR I-175.

[29] Tweede Kamer, vergaderjaar 2011–2012, 33 186, nr. 6. See also Eerste Kamer, vergaderjaar 2012–2013, 33 186, C.

[30] Tweede Kamer, 26 September 2012, Handelingen 2012–2013, nr. 5, item 6, 30.

[31] ibid 34 and 35.

[32] Tweede Kamer, vergaderjaar 2012–2013, 33 186, nos 10 and 11.

would certainly not flinch to start infringement proceedings against the Netherlands.[33]

In 2014, the act was, moreover, adapted, further limiting the minister's power of annulment with regard to matters of energy, postal services, telecommunication and transport. As far as the decisions taken within the framework of sector-specific regulation are concerned, the application of article 22(1) KWZBO, anchoring the annulment power, was excluded entirely.[34] Decisions regarding compliance with competition law, as well as consumer protection, are still subject to the possibility of annulment.

The increased independence of national network regulators from the Dutch political arena has provoked calls in the literature for a reflection on how to ensure that regulatory decisions remain legitimate in the eyes of national stakeholders.[35]

D. The UK

Recent reforms regarding the functioning of the UK's energy regulator Ofgem demonstrate how the Government has felt the need to respond to the regulator's ever-increasing discretionary powers with a possibility of governmental input. Within the European legal sphere, the UK has undoubtedly been the motherland of independent regulatory bodies in all network sectors and their legitimacy has long been almost uncontested. In 2011, Prosser pointed out that reform initiatives such as the PBA had left regulatory bodies largely unaffected.[36] A recent study performed by Greasley and Hanretty on the lifespan and risk termination of APBs in the UK between 1985 and 2008 revealed that APBs intended to generate credible commitments in regulation were less likely than others to be

[33] Tweede Kamer, 26 September 2012, Handelingen 2012–2013, nr. 5, item 6, 51.

[34] Article I, G Wet van 25 Juni 2014 tot wijziging van de Instellingswet Autoriteit Consument en Markt en enige andere wetten in verband met de stroomlijning van het door de Autoriteit Consument en Markt te houden markttoezicht.

[35] E.g. Martijn Groenleer, 'Toezicht op de energiesector: tussen nationale belangen en Europese invloed' [2015] Tijdschrift voor Europees en economisch recht 385.

[36] Tony Prosser, 'Regulation and Legitimacy' in Jeffrey Jowell and Dawn Oliver (eds), *The Changing Constitution* (7th edn, Oxford University Press 2011) 312, 331.

terminated in any given year,[37] meaning that they have hardly been affected by 'quango culls' in the past either. Recent initiatives, however, begin to reveal that the rationalization process resulting from the trend of 'national restraint' is affecting the regulatory regime as well. An example is found in the Energy Act 2013, which now grants a power to the Secretary of State to issue a so-called 'Strategy and Policy Statement'. The introduction of this new instrument aims 'to improve alignment between the Government's strategic energy objectives and regulation of electricity and gas markets by the independent regulator'.[38] The instrument should not necessarily be regarded as a reaction to the EU's obligations regarding regulatory independence. However, the rationale behind it is the ever-expanding mission of energy regulators, which is to an important extent driven by further specifications in EU legislation with regard to the policy goals that have to be pursued by NRAs in this field.

The basis of the introduction of the 'Strategy and Policy Statement' is indeed the recognition that the role of the regulator has evolved, in the sense that regulatory bodies are increasingly faced with decisions that require policy trade-offs. In 2012, the author of an economic analysis of the role of Ofgem pointed out that 'an energy policy that previously leaned mainly to facilitating the workings of competitive markets is now concerned with fostering environmental and social outcomes that substantially conflict with what competitive markets, left to themselves, would deliver, not least because of the currently poor relative economics of most low-carbon electricity generation technologies'.[39] In the UK, this has resulted in 'successive revisions of Ofgem's duty in primary legislation, the main effect of which has been to incorporate security of supply and the reduction of greenhouse gas emissions explicitly into Ofgem's primary obligation to protect the interests of existing and future consumers'. Primary legislation, however, 'offers no further clues as to how Ofgem should balance the different interests of consumers, particularly the short-term cost of gas and electricity relative to longer-term costs or

---

37 Stephen Greasley and Chris Hanretty, 'Credibility and Agency Termination under Parliamentarism' [2016] *Journal of Public Administration Research and Theory* 159.

38 Energy Bill Provisions for Ofgem Strategy and Policy Statement – Background note (November 2012), https://www.gov.uk/government/uploads/system/uploads/attachment_data/file/65669/7202-energy-bill-provisions-for-ofgem-strategy-and-supp.pdf, p. 4.

39 Tim Tutton, 'Does Ofgem Have a Future?', Oxera Agenda May 2012 (1) 3–4.

relative to security of supply and emissions reduction'.[40] Just months before this new instrument was introduced, the same article ascertained that 'primary legislation oblige[d] Ofgem to protect a number of dimensions of the interests of both existing and future consumers, without any clear guidance as to how it should make trade-offs between these dimensions'. Previous attempts to offer guidance on how to balance policy objectives via the instrument of 'Social and Environmental Guidance' (enshrined in the Utilities Act 2000) had failed because the Government did not provide any ranking for the different policy objectives to be pursued. The conclusion was that 'the conflict between multiple politically sensitive objectives [was] obvious' and that clear guidance for Ofgem on how to balance these objectives was lacking.[41] The author predicted that the future would bring a reshuffling of duties and powers between central government services and Ofgem, (at least partly) stripping Ofgem of its policy-making powers, adding that '[n]one of this is necessarily "wrong". Energy is now a much more political area than it was in the 1990s, and the House of Lords Select Committee on Regulators is not alone in thinking that political decisions should be taken by politicians.'[42]

The reference made to the House of Lords Select Committee on Regulators relates to a 2007 report on 'UK Economic Regulators'.[43] The committee was set up following the recommendation formulated in the 2004 report of the House of Lords Select Committee on the Constitution on regulatory accountability[44] (discussed in Chapter 3), but labelled itself the 'unwished child' of that committee, since it was not the permanent, joint committee that the report had envisaged.[45] The committee warned the Government to be careful 'not to offload political policy issues onto unelected regulators'.[46] It invited the Government to 'be explicit in the political decisions it makes and the consequent guidance it issues to regulators'[47] and advised that 'an effective and transparent mechanism [needed] to be put in place for resolving potential policy conflicts so that

---

[40] ibid 4.

[41] See the references in ibid 4.

[42] ibid 5.

[43] Select Committee on Regulators, *UK Economic Regulators* (HL 2006–07, 189-I) http://www.publications.parliament.uk/pa/ld200607/ldselect/ldrgltrs/189/189i.pdf.

[44] ibid 18 and 74.

[45] ibid 73.

[46] ibid 8 and 25.

[47] ibid 13.

the regulators [would be] able to carry out their economic function without interference'.[48] According to the report, the Government had to be vigilant not to expand the remits of regulators to avoid tackling politically sensitive issues itself.[49] The committee argued that the regulators' expansion of duties, including social and environmental duties, 'along with a lack of clarity about the respective roles of government and regulators, can arguably reduce the effectiveness of the regulator, create regulatory uncertainty and risk compromising the independence of the regulator'.[50]

Section 131 of the Energy Act 2013 defines the Strategy and Policy Statement as a statement prepared by the Secretary of State that sets out: (a) the strategic priorities, and other main considerations, of Her Majesty's government in formulating its energy policy for Great Britain; (b) the particular outcomes to be achieved as a result of the implementation of that policy; and (c) the roles and responsibilities of persons (whether the Secretary of State, the Authority or other persons) who are involved in implementing that policy or who have other functions that are affected by it. Pursuant to section 132(1), Ofgem 'must have regard to the strategic priorities set out in the strategy and policy statement when carrying out regulatory functions'. The statement is subject to parliamentary approval (section 135(8)). In its annual forward work plan, Ofgem has to explain its strategy to further the delivery of the policy outcomes. In its annual report for the Secretary for State and Parliament, Ofgem has to report on how it has implemented its strategy.

In a background note[51] the Department of Energy and Climate Change explained that the Government would consider the EU's Third Package in developing the statement, since the policy outcomes would express what outcome is sought, not how Ofgem would have to act. It argued that, via Ofgem's reporting duties, the statement would foster Ofgem's accountability and transparency.[52] Earlier, in its final report on the 'Ofgem Review', the Department had referred to the general feeling that 'the regulator needed to better explain its strategy as well as its decisions, and

---

[48] ibid 13 and 73.

[49] ibid 24.

[50] ibid 24–25.

[51] Energy Bill Provisions for Ofgem Strategy and Policy Statement – Background note (November 2012), https://www.gov.uk/government/uploads/system/uploads/attachment_data/file/65669/7202-energy-bill-provisions-for-ofgem-strategy-and-supp.pdf.

[52] ibid 7.

that this explanation should be subject to increased scrutiny and challenge'.[53] The broad nature of the regulator's duties implied that it was 'given considerable room for interpretation, which could result in poor alignment between the regulator and the Government's views'.[54] This was deemed problematic because 'Ofgem's duties embed a range of wider public interest issues'.[55] According to the Department, however, it was not desirable to broaden Ofgem's responsibilities. Instead, the note proclaimed that 'it is Government that should make trade-offs at the strategic level where the general interests of citizens are at stake'.[56] Henceforth, the regulatory authority would continue to consider trade-offs between economic and broader goals, but in the (better-defined) context set by the statement.[57]

The principle of political ministerial responsibility having been revalued with regard to APBs in recent years, the UK Government now acknowledges its political responsibility for policy trade-offs in the field of energy. In adopting this instrument, the UK legislature recognizes that regulatory matters are not merely 'technical' and cannot be isolated from other policy domains, such as environmental and climate matters, security of supply, social policy and so on. Therefore, it feels the need to provide the Government with an instrument to steer the NRA when necessary, something that it has denied the need for and refrained from doing before. The draft of the first Strategy and Policy Statement was issued in August 2014: a summary of responses resulting from the consultation of stakeholders was published online in March 2015.[58]

E. Conclusion

Compared to most other types of APBs, the political autonomy of economic regulators and independent supervisors (such as DPAs) has for a long time remained uncontested. This is the case in the four European legal systems studied in this book. Christensen and Lægreid recognize this contradiction and raise the question how 'the new NPM-inspired

---

[53] Ofgem Review – Final Report (July 2011), https://www.gov.uk/government/uploads/system/uploads/attachment_data/file/48134/2151-ofgem-review-final-report.pdf, 37.
[54] ibid 24.
[55] ibid 25.
[56] ibid 25.
[57] ibid 27.
[58] https://www.gov.uk/government/consultations/strategy-and-policy-statement.

regulatory model embracing agency autonomy corresponds with regulatory challenges in the post-NPM era where there has been an enhanced focus on political control'.[59] Regulatory bodies have from the very beginning been exempt from the supervision regime for EVAs anchored in article 23 KDBB (Flanders): they have equally been exempt from most supervisory mechanisms available to ministers under the KWZBO (the Netherlands); most French AAIs that fulfilled supervisory tasks have (long) escaped the appointment of a *commissaire du Gouvernement* and their independence has been advocated and endorsed by most *doctrine* (France); and the PBA left supervisory or regulatory bodies largely unaffected (UK). Nonetheless, the implementation of the EU requirements on political independence discussed in Chapter 2 goes hand in hand with attempts to restore the grip of both ministers and parliaments on these independent regulators and to mitigate their overall political autonomy. The previous paragraphs contain examples of parliaments giving vent to their concerns about the influence of representative democracy on these bodies. In consequence thereof, they (attempt to) introduce tried mechanisms (the French *commissaire du Gouvernement*) or new instruments (the UK's Strategy and Policy Statement) that allow for a balanced degree of political input. The Councils of State of both Belgium and the Netherlands take a retrograde view in their advisory practice on the transposition of the EU requirements and continue to encourage the preservation of traditional recipes of government supervision on APBs whenever possible. Despite the fact that the very principle of political autonomy for NRAs and DPAs is not contested at the national level, attempts are discernible at Member State level to square their political autonomy with the aspiration of increasing the democratic legitimacy of APBs.

Moreover, these initiatives tie in with broader reform agendas. Other, related types of APBs, of which the political independence was up until recently as good as uncontested, are now the object of democratic reforms as well. As Moran points out:

> Financial regulation in both the Eurozone and the UK had followed the principles of the regulatory state sketched by Majone: a Madisonian, technocratic ruling order which excluded democratic politicians in favor of non-majoritarian regulatory institutions. In the crisis of 2007–8 that regulatory state was weighed in the balance and found wanting. Confronted by crisis the

[59] Tom Christensen and Per Lægreid, 'The New Regulatory Orthodoxy: A Critical Assessment' in David Levi-Faur (ed), *Handbook on the Politics of Regulation* (Edward Elgar Publishing 2011) 361, 362.

> bankers and the technocratic regulators froze, petrified like rabbits before a stoat. Now, the great agents of transformation are not the central bankers and financial regulators who until recently reigned supreme. The agents of transformation are democratic governments driven by the fear of the electoral consequences of macroeconomic collapse. The crisis produced rapid learning and innovation – a common social function of any crisis. But it was politicians who learnt most rapidly, not central bankers still trapped in the mind world of the long boom. The epistemic convergence that occurred killed the old regulatory state – and is creating a new one ... Even the crown jewels of the old regulatory state – central bank independence in setting short-term interest rates – may be lost to the politicians. Old regulatory states are dying, and new, more democratically shaped, formations being born.[60]

In 2010, Oliver pointed at similar evolutions in the area of financial regulation in the UK. With regard to utilities and public services, the author did not discern a similar call for 'radical reform', but did acknowledge that there was 'a strong case for a more comprehensive system of oversight to be established'.[61] Many European states have indeed put such systems in place.

3. THE ECJ'S POSITION

The conflict between the far-reaching degree of political autonomy currently advocated by the EU legislation, and Member States' concerns over the democratic embedment of the administration has been the subject of case law of the ECJ. Chapter 2 has already discussed the ECJ's judgment in *Commission/Germany*. In this case, the court was invited by defendant Germany to test its far-reaching interpretation of the notion of 'complete independence', anchored in article 28 of Directive 95/46/EC, against 'the principle of democracy'. Germany pleaded that this principle, which is not only anchored in the German Constitution, but also in article 6(1) EU,[62] requires the administration to be subject to the instructions of the Government, which is accountable to Parliament. The *Bund* referred to the powers of intervention that DPAs hold with regard to citizens and entities outside the public sector and which were mentioned in article

---

[60] Michael Moran, 'The Rise of the Regulatory State' in David Coen, Wyn Grant and Graham Wilson (eds), *The Oxford Handbook of Business and Government* (Oxford University Press 2010) 383, 400–401.

[61] Dawn Oliver, 'Regulation, Democracy and Democratic Oversight in the UK' in Dawn Oliver, Tony Prosser and Richard Rawlings (eds), *The Regulatory State: Constitutional Implications* (Oxford University Press 2010) 243, 266.

[62] Now enshrined in article 2 TEU.

28(3) of the directive. Because of these powers, 'a heightened scrutiny of the legality of their activities by means of instruments for monitoring legality or substance is absolutely necessary', Germany submitted.[63]

The ECJ recognized that 'the principle of democracy forms part of European Community law and was expressly enshrined in Article 6(1) EU as one of the foundations of the European Union'. It furthermore confirmed that the principle of democracy 'must be taken into consideration when interpreting acts of secondary law such as Article 28 of Directive 95/46', marking this principle as 'one of the principles common to the Member States'.[64] Nevertheless, the court did not seize the opportunity to make a thorough comparison of the precise requirements that flow from the (meta) principle of democracy in the Member States in order to define some common denominators. It furthermore made no general statement on what the European principle of democracy signifies or comprises *in abstracto*. Instead, the court was satisfied with the observation, derived from existing practices in Member States, that the principle of democracy 'does not preclude the existence of public authorities outside the classic hierarchical administration and more or less independent of the government'. In order to substantiate its argument that the notion of 'complete independence' is reconcilable with the principle of democracy, the court consequently referred to the long-existing practice in Member States of establishing APBs.

> Such independent administrative authorities, as exist moreover in the German judicial system, often have regulatory functions or carry out tasks which must be free from political influence, whilst still being required to comply with the law subject to the review of the competent courts. That is precisely the case with regard to the tasks of supervisory authorities relating to the protection of data.[65]

The Court furthermore ruled that parliamentary influence on DPAs would remain possible and even indispensable and pointed out that Directive 95/46 'in no way [made] such an absence of parliamentary influence obligatory for the Member States'.[66] More specifically, it clarified that the national Parliaments or the Government are entitled to appoint the management of the supervisory authorities and that the legislature may define the powers of those authorities. Moreover, there is no objection to the supervisory authority being subject to an obligation to report its

---

[63] Para 40.
[64] Para 41.
[65] Para 42.
[66] Para 43.

activities to Parliament.[67] The court concluded that 'conferring a status independent of the general administration on the supervisory authorities responsible for the protection of individuals with regard to the processing of personal data outside the public sector does not in itself deprive those authorities of their democratic legitimacy'.[68]

According to Lavrijssen and Ottow, the ECJ interprets the independence requirement for DPAs in a teleological way. The authors, who regard this as a positive evolution, argue that this judgment has predictive value for other independence requirements that currently figure in EU legislation.[69]

The court's reasoning, however, provokes many questions and reservations. First of all, this liberal interpretation of the principle of democracy was not the only possible interpretation that could have been adopted. The court referred to the existence of APBs in the Member States as if their establishment and empowerment were entirely uncontested. The initiatives and measures taken in different Member States to restrain and rationalize the use of APBs and the revaluation of democratic principles that goes hand in hand with that trend were disregarded. Secondly, the court refers to the existence of authorities which are 'more or less independent of the government' as an established practice in the Member States, but ignores the fact that the creation of authorities enjoying a degree of independence that excludes all political influence has been the exception rather than the norm. This is especially so if these bodies are entrusted with broad, discretionary powers.[70] The court seemingly distils its legal reasoning from Member States' constitutional traditions, but does so in a piecemeal way, emphasizing solely those characteristics that lead to an interpretation favouring the development of the internal market.[71]

---

[67] Paras 44 and 45.

[68] Para 46.

[69] Saskia Lavrijssen and Annetje Ottow, 'Independent Supervisory Authorities: A Fragile Concept' (2012) 39(4) Legal Issues of Economic Integration 419, 437.

[70] *Contra*, for France: Fabienne Kauff-Gazin, 'Vers une conception européenne de l'indépendance des autorités de regulation? – À propos de l'affaire C-518/07, Commission c/ Allemagne' [2010] Europe, étude 9.

[71] The court has been known to adopt such a partisan approach to the comparative method before: e.g. Catherine Donnelly, 'Administrative Law and Multi-Level Administration: An EU and US Comparison' in Catherine Barnard and Okeoghene Odudu (eds), *Cambridge Yearbook of European Legal Studies 2008–09* (Hart Publishing 2009) 211, 239–240.

What is more striking, however, is the justification that the ECJ provides for declaring Germany's 'tried and tested system of scrutiny of supervisory authorities with regard to the processing of personal data outside the public sector' invalid.[72] The court discards the mechanisms of representative democracy in the area of data protection because of the mere possibility 'that the scrutinizing authorities, which are part of the general administration and therefore under the control of the government of their respective *Land*, are not able to act objectively when they interpret and apply the provisions relating to the processing of personal data'.[73] According to the court, the government of a *Land* 'may have an interest in not complying with the provisions with regard to the protection of personal data where the processing of such data by a non-public body is at issue':

> That government may itself be an interested party in that processing if it actually or potentially participates therein, for example, in the case of a public-private partnership or in the case of public contracts with the private sector. That government may also have a specific interest if it is necessary or even merely useful for it to have access to databases in order to fulfill certain of its functions in particular for taxation or law enforcement purposes. Furthermore, that government may also tend to favour economic interests in the application of the provisions on the protection of individuals with regard to the processing of personal data by certain companies which are economically important to the *Land* or region.[74]

These hypothetical situations hardly seem sufficient and convincing reasons to set aside the guarantees offered by representative democracy. Moreover, it looks as though the court's reasoning cannot be applied only to the field of data protection, but to almost all areas of government decision making, which makes it untenable. There are indeed numerous situations in which the government is confronted with a conflict of interest.

On top of that, it is remarkable that the court did not only declare a power to control the merits of a decision (political supervision *sensu stricto*) incompatible with the requirement of 'complete independence' anchored in the Data Protection Directive, but also opposed the power of the Government to check the legality of the DPA's decisions. The court acknowledged that Germany sought 'only to guarantee that acts of the supervisory authorities comply with the applicable national and European

72 See the wording used in para 38, where the court cites Germany.

73 Para 34

74 Para 35.

Community provisions, and that it therefore does not aim to oblige those authorities potentially to pursue political objectives inconsistent with the protection of individuals with regard to the processing of personal data and with fundamental rights'.[75] For the (hypothetical) reasons explained above, however, it deemed even this type of supervision limited to a legality check irreconcilable with the directive. The court further explained its viewpoint, observing that 'the mere risk that the supervising authorities could exercise a political influence over the decisions of the supervisory authorities is enough to hinder the latter authorities' independent performance of their tasks'. Reference was also made to the risk of 'prior compliance',[76] an argument formulated by the European Commission, as well as to the necessity of making sure that the DPAs 'as guardians of the right to private life … remain above any suspicion of partiality'.[77]

Lastly, the court was not selective and did not specifically differentiate between different types of government supervision and the (rectifying) powers that they involve. As far as the German case was concerned, the court ascertained that state scrutiny 'whatever form it takes, in principle allows the government of the respective *Land* or an administrative body subject to that government to influence, directly or indirectly, the decisions of the supervisory authorities or, as the case may be, to cancel and replace those decisions'.[78] There is, however, arguably, an important qualitative difference in terms of impact on autonomous decision making between a mere annulment power and a power to replace an authority's decision. Such nuances, however, were disregarded by the court. Advocate General Mazák, on the other hand, in his opinion preceding the court's judgment, adopted the view that independence should not be confused with the lack of opportunity for supervision.[79] The Advocate General ascertained that 'there is nothing to indicate that oversight is exercised in a way that might hinder the data protection supervisory authorities in exercising their functions with complete independence. The Commission cannot merely make assertions that this is so; it is up to it to

---

[75] Para 33.

[76] I.e. the risk that the authorities will feel hindered from deciding freely merely because a system of government supervision is in place and that they will instead anticipate the government's reaction.

[77] Para 36. Both of these considerations can also be found in Case C-614/10 *Commission/Austria* (ECJ, 16 October 2012) paras 51 and 52.

[78] Para 32.

[79] Para 29.

establish that oversight does have such effects.'[80] Mazák therefore concluded that the Commission had failed to prove the negative consequences of the oversight as regards the exercise by the DPAs of their functions with 'complete independence'.[81]

If 'independence' is a 'fragile concept' in the context of independent supervisory bodies created under the impulse of EU law, as Lavrijssen and Ottow have claimed, this judgment of the ECJ creates the impression that the concept of 'democracy' is just as precarious. The court's approach is all the more surprising in the light of the doctrine governing the establishment of APBs at the EU level itself. In its famous *Meroni* judgment[82] and subsequent case law, the ECJ developed 'criteria against which the legality and democratic legitimation of a transfer of power is to be measured'.[83] Pursuant to the *Meroni* judgment, EU agencies (an umbrella term for a variety of APBs functioning at the EU level) cannot be invested with decision-making powers that require the exercise of discretion.[84] Consequently, the *Meroni* doctrine basically prohibits 'real' regulatory agencies.[85] Although there is much debate about the scope of application of the *Meroni* doctrine and later, related judgments of the ECJ,[86] its precepts have been applied by the ECJ in a variety of cases

---

80 Para 31.

81 Para 32.

82 Case C-9/56, *Meroni & Co., Industrie Metallurgiche, SpA/High Authority of the European Coal and Steel Community* [1958] ECR 133.

83 Stefan Griller and Andreas Orator, 'Everything Under Control? The "Way Forward" for European Agencies in the Footsteps of the Meroni Doctrine' (2010) 35(1) European Law Review 3, 15.

84 See e.g. Merijn Chamon, *EU agencies: legal and political limits to the transformation of the EU administration* (Oxford University Press 2016) 175 ff; Jens-Peter Schneider, 'A Common Framework for Decentralized EU Agencies and the Meroni Doctrine' in Herwig C H Hofmann and Russell L Weaver (eds), *Transatlantic Perspectives on Administrative Law* (Bruylant 2011) 203, 209ff.

85 Miroslava Scholten, 'Independent, Hence Unaccountable? – The Need for a Broader Debate on Accountability of the Executive' [2011] Review of European Administrative Law 5, 24 and 27.

86 Case C 98/80, *Giuseppe Romano/Institut national d'assurance maladie-invalidité* [1981] ECR 1241; Merijn Chamon, 'EU Agencies between Meroni and Romani or the Devil and the Deep Blue Sea' [2011] CML Rev. 1055–1075. For a recent account of the situation, see e.g. Marta Simoncini, 'The Erosion of the *Meroni* Doctrine. The Case of the European Aviation Safety Agency (EASA)' [2015] European Public Law 309.

regarding the admissibility of delegation.[87] Certainly, the so-called 'principle of institutional balance' has inspired *Meroni*. Although its content and scope are much debated, it is often assumed that 'institutional balance' is a specific EU translation of the principle of *trias politica* or separation of powers.[88] Griller and Orator, however, (also) locate the basis for the *Meroni* doctrine in the principle of democracy currently anchored in articles 2 and 10(1) TEU, stipulating that the functioning of the Union shall be founded on representative democracy.[89] As the authors point out, this makes representative democracy 'the explicit standard of the Union'. Consequently, 'deliberative models of democratic legitimacy' or 'output-oriented democracy', whatever their value may be, 'is not the concept of democracy as enshrined in EU primary law'.[90]

4. EU IMPULSE, SEPARATION OF POWERS AND THE RULE OF LAW

Democracy is only one of the three meta values distinguished in Chapter 3. The comparative analysis revealed that APBs also pose problems in the light of the separation of powers doctrine (as a derivative of the meta value of constitutionalism) and legal certainty (as a requirement that flows from the rule of law). Chapter 5, on the reconciliation between the EU impulse and national restraint, will focus on the conflict that originates from the democratic deficit associated with the independent supervisors only. This section dedicates a few words to possible conflicts with the other two meta values and the way in which these could be addressed.

As far as legal certainty is concerned, Chapter 3 revealed concerns about the risk of confusion for public service users entailed by the differentiation in legal status of public sector organizations. This opacity caused by the proliferation of APBs primarily originates from the

---

[87] Stefan Griller and Andreas Orator, 'Everything Under Control? The "Way Forward" for European Agencies in the Footsteps of the Meroni Doctrine' (2010) 35(1) European Law Review 3, 18 ff.

[88] See e.g. Koen Lenaerts and Amaryllis Verhoeven, 'Institutional Balance as a Guarantee for Democracy in EU Governance' in Cristian Joerges and Renaud Dehousse (eds), *Good Governance in Europe's Integrated Market* (Oxford University Press 2002) 35.

[89] Stefan Griller and Andreas Orator, 'Everything Under Control? The "Way Forward" for European Agencies in the Footsteps of the Meroni Doctrine' (2010) 35(1) European Law Review 3, 15.

[90] ibid 22.

coexistence of differing forms of institutional design. The uncurbed creation of APBs in the 1980s and 1990s and the subsequent lack of coordination following their establishment are at the basis of this problem. The question arises whether the trend of 'EU impulse' contributes to these challenges in any particular way. It could be argued that EU law has introduced new types of APBs and, with that, concepts of political autonomy with autonomous meanings and implications. These do not necessarily correspond to existing national concepts or typologies. Moreover, it could be argued that the current discrepancy between the wording of the independence requirements for NRAs in different network industries causes legal uncertainty. It remains unclear why the EU legislature has opted for varying descriptions of the independence requirements for each of these sectors and whether, for instance, the relatively more vague requirements formulated for electronic communications regulators are indeed less strict than those for their counterparts in the energy and railway transport sectors. It would be advisable for the EU legislature to contemplate the development of a single model of national supervisory authority for NRAs and DPAs, with clear and aligned requirements of political autonomy. Different sectors may necessitate different conditions, but differentiation should be clearly justified.

Chapter 3 also revealed how the institutional design of APBs and/or the instruments and decision-making powers that they are invested with may sometimes also conflict with the separation of powers doctrine. These issues are intertwined with democratic concerns and some literature regards threats to the separation of powers doctrine as threats to democratic theory.[91] It is in the nature of supervisory tasks to require a combination of rule-making powers with powers of implementation and/or sanctioning (*ex officio* or in a procedure of dispute resolution).[92] According to Scott, regulation gives rise to 'a double constitutional problem': the problem of delegation to politically unaccountable agencies on the one hand and the issue of entrusting powers of rule making and adjudication (in the British sense) to institutions of the executive on the other hand. Whereas the first objection to contemporary regulation coincides with the issues flowing from the meta value of democracy, the second one is linked to concerns of constitutionalism. He suggests that approaching the subject of regulation and regulators from the viewpoint

---

[91] E.g. David Levi-Faur, 'Regulation and Regulatory Governance' in David Levi-Faur (ed), *Handbook on the Politics of Regulation* (Edward Elgar Publishing 2011) 15.

[92] Traditional definitions of regulatory agencies often mention this combination of powers as a possible defining characteristic: e.g. ibid 11–12.

of separation of powers corresponds to an American legal perspective rather than to a European one.[93]

Chapter 3 concluded that APBs' combination of powers and functions has mostly been considered a problem in France. As a semi-presidential system, France is closer to the US than the other systems studied in this book as regards the way in which the legislature and executive relate to each other. This is especially significant when it comes to the delegation of rule-making powers to APBs: even though this practice is not uncontested in either Belgium, the Netherlands or the UK either, most criticism in this respect originates from democratic concerns in these systems. The case law of the French CC, on the other hand, has also approached the problem from the viewpoint of separation of powers, protecting the Prime Minister's role against delegation of rule-making powers by Parliament to AAIs. The prevailing idea is that, apart from the President, who is entrusted with some reserved rule-making powers, only the Prime Minister, as part of the executive, is invested with rule-making powers under the Constitution. In the other three (parliamentary) systems, where Parliament and the Government are to a greater extent aligned, entrusting APBs with rule-making powers is not as such considered a threat to the systems of checks and balances. Another role currently assumed by APBs in general and supervisory bodies in particular may, in the future, give rise to problems from that very perspective in all four systems studied equally (although, currently, the problem is also primarily acknowledged in France): their quasi-judicial role, consisting of powers of dispute resolution and/or imposing penalties. The European directives discussed in Chapter 2 make NRAs responsible for dispute resolution and sometimes oblige[94] or encourage[95] Member States to

---

[93] Colin Scott, 'Regulatory Governance and the Challenge of Constitutionalism' in Dawn Oliver, Tony Prosser and Richard Rawlings (eds), *The Regulatory State: Constitutional Implications* (Oxford University Press 2010) 15, 25–26.

[94] See e.g. article 56(9) Directive 2012/34, pursuant to which 'the regulatory body shall be able to enforce its decisions with the appropriate penalties, including fines'.

[95] See e.g. article 37(4)(d) of Directive 2009/72, requiring that NRAs have the power 'to impose effective, proportionate and dissuasive penalties on electricity undertakings not complying with their obligations under the Directive or any relevant legally binding decisions of the regulatory authority or of the Agency, or to propose that a competent court impose such penalties'. This includes the power to impose or propose the imposition of penalties of up to 10 per cent of the annual turnover of the transmission system operator on the transmission system operator or of up to 10 per cent of the annual turnover of the vertically integrated undertaking on the vertically integrated undertaking, as

invest NRAs with sanctioning powers. In France, investing AAIs with quasi-judicial powers has been deemed especially problematic when tasks of investigation, persecution and sanctioning are assumed by one and the same person or group of persons within the AAI.

Behind separation of powers as a value or an ideal there is a rationale of avoidance of abuse.[96] The danger that lurks in a concentration of powers in the hands of just a single actor is arbitrariness. How can this be overcome? A possible remedy for APBs that have been invested with quasi-judicial powers is to separate the different functions and procedures that go hand in hand with their performance. One could argue that this solution can also be extended to other cases where APBs exercise multiple powers: for instance, when APBs themselves make the rules that they are subsequently expected to implement, i.e. a combination of rule-making and implementing powers. However, one could also argue against a strict separation of functions in this case and contend that a merger of powers is precisely the strength of many APBs, since it increases the coherence of their decisions. If the APB exercises its functions with integrity, the combination of powers in a well-defined area can indeed be an asset. Without proper safeguards, it could become a danger.

If the principle of legality is respected and APBs indeed have a well-circumscribed mission, most European legal systems already embody the necessary mechanisms and procedures suitable to act against APBs entrusted with multiple powers that act in arbitrary ways. As explained above, there is one particular accountability mechanism that specifically serves the purpose of protecting citizens against abuse and arbitrariness: that of legal accountability. None of the decisions taken by APBs on the basis of their coercive powers, whether they contain rules,

---

the case may be, for non-compliance with their respective obligations pursuant to this directive. The equivalent provision for gas is found in article 41(4)(d) of Directive 2009/73. See also recitals 37 and 33 of the respective directives. According to Cabeau, the latter, alternative procedure was added to the provision 'to meet constitutional concerns raised by some Member States'. See Emmanuel Cabeau, 'National Regulatory Authorities' in Christopher Jones (ed), *EU Energy Law, Vol. I, The Internal Energy Market, The Third Liberalisation Package* (Claeys & Casteels 2010) 217, 245. The Commission's interpretative note explains that '[t]his choice made by the European Union legislator has to do with the constitutional system of some Member States where independent bodies cannot impose sanctions themselves'. See Commission, interpretative note regulatory authorities, 18.

[96] E.g. Peter Leyland, *The Constitution of the United Kingdom – A Contextual Analysis* (Hart Publishing 2012) 72.

implement them or enforce them via sanctions, escape the subsequent possibility of scrutiny by the courts. This principle is strongly endorsed by the EU legislature itself with respect to NRAs.[97]

Multiple legal principles, enforceable by the courts, can be used to challenge arbitrary conduct by APBs that combine different functions:[98] equality and non-discrimination as well as impartiality, which are recognized as legal principles (under varying forms and denominations) in the four systems of administrative justice studied here, are the first that come to mind. In some cases, more specific legal remedies exist. In Belgium, for instance, the Council of State applies the adage *patere legem quam ipse fecisti* ('respect the rule that you have made yourself') as a legally enforceable principle of proper administration.[99] This principle implies that the rules issued by the authority itself have to be complied with in all the individual decisions that it takes. This rule would also apply to the possible quasi-judicial decisions taken by an APB, such as penalties and fines. These would typically have the nature of administrative decisions, signifying that the *patere legem* principle applies to them as well.

---

[97] Legal protection by the courts is a typical attribute of the rule of law, which is 'a suggested antidote for abuses of power': Martin Krygier, 'Rule of Law' in Michel Rosenfeld and András Sajó (eds), *The Oxford Handbook of Comparative Constitutional Law* (Oxford University Press 2012) 233, 243. The rule of law in this case helps to protect an ideal linked to constitutionalism, i.e. separation of powers.

[98] See also Dominique Custos, 'Independent Administrative Authorities in France: Structural and Procedural Change at the Intersection of Americanization, Europeanization and Gallicization' in Susan Rose-Ackerman and Peter L Lindseth (eds), *Comparative Administrative Law* (Edward Elgar Publishing 2010) 277, 288 with references to case law of the French *Conseil d'Etat* and the ECtHR on the separation of powers of investigation, prosecution and adjudication within the institutional design of regulatory bodies, recognizing that 'the availability of judicial review against the sanction meant that it was unnecessary to impose all the requirements derived from the fair trial principle to this type of regulatory proceedings'.

[99] See e.g. the Belgian Council of State in RvS 11 March 2013, no 222.796, Carrissemoux.

5. Reconciliation

1. SHIFTING THE FOCUS: FOUR ALLEGED ALTERNATIVES FOR DEMOCRATIC LEGITIMACY VIA POLITICAL INPUT

Majone and those who later built on his theories reject the mechanisms of representative democracy for the purpose of regulating the (liberalized) economy. However, they do not claim to promote an anti-democratic form of governance. The development of non-majoritarian institutions[1] in the field of economic regulation 'fits the pattern of what Majone calls "Madisonian" democracy – an emphasis on the technocratic settlement of policy problems through a process of adjustment between the affected parties'.[2] The principles subsumed under the meta value of democracy in Chapter 3 (legality, political ministerial responsibility, democratic control by elected representatives and centrality) indeed all relate to representative democracy, i.e. the (only) guise under which democracy emerges in the texts of most present-day Constitutions. Like Majone, however, some argue that, in order to square the world of APBs in general, and independent supervisors in particular, with the meta value of democracy, a different conception of democracy altogether should be acknowledged.[3]

Do market regulation, data protection and – by extension – the supervision of private activities more generally indeed require a different view on democratic legitimacy and does this justify the far-reaching EU requirements on independent national supervisory authorities? Or should

[1] Majone defines this concept as 'public institutions which, by design, are not directly accountable either to voters or to elected officials'. See Giandomenico Majone, 'Regulatory Legitimacy' in Giandomenico Majone and Pio Baake (eds), *Regulating Europe* (Routledge 1996) 284, 285–286.

[2] Michael Moran, 'The Rise of the Regulatory State' in David Coen, Wyn Grant and Graham Wilson (eds), *The Oxford Handbook of Business and Government* (Oxford University Press 2010) 383, 393.

[3] Giandomenico Majone, 'Regulatory Legitimacy' in Giandomenico Majone and Pio Baake (eds), *Regulating Europe* (Routledge 1996) 284, 285–286.

these be seen as a regrettable refusal of the EU legislature to take into account traditional principles on democratic administrative organization, which should be adhered to regardless of possible disadvantages from the viewpoint of economics or public administration theory? And what does a satisfactory, alternative conception of democracy look like?

The EU by no means 'invented' the concept of a politically independent regulator. Many Member States had indeed established such entities before the EU directives even mentioned them. Often, however, their political autonomy was not defined quite as rigidly as is currently the case in the EU directives. Moreover, initially, economic regulation was defined quite narrowly, as comprising a genuine watchdog function. Regulators were supposed to oversee respect for the rules of competition law in order to create a level playing field for competitors and – on a more indirect level – a favourable environment for consumers. In many states, the current trend of EU impulse in the field of regulatory bodies indeed signified both increased political autonomy and a broadened (discretionary) mandate for regulatory bodies. Nonetheless, even before these EU directives were enacted, regulators in many European states already enjoyed a more substantial degree of political autonomy than most other APBs. As a consequence thereof, a vast body of literature on alternatives for the mechanisms of representative democracy to be applied to these supervisors has developed. Central to these suggestions is the notion of 'accountability', as an alternative to (political) control, supervision or oversight in a stricter sense.[4] Craig contrasts 'control' and 'accountability' and argues that agencies' independence in decision making 'would indicate relatively little control', whereas 'it does not necessarily follow that accountability should be similarly minimal'.[5] The core idea behind this focus on accountability is that democracy is essentially about securing legitimacy. For Black, drawing on Weber, legitimacy 'rests on the acceptability and credibility of the organisation to those it seeks to govern … legitimacy is rooted in the acceptance of that organisation by others, and more particularly in the reasons for that acceptance.'[6] Bovens has identified legitimacy as the major goal of all

[4] Giorgia Nesti, 'Strengthening the Accountability of Independent Regulatory Agencies: From Performance Back to Democracy' [2016] Comparative European Politics 1, 12.

[5] Paul Craig, *Administrative Law* (Sweet & Maxwell 2012) 92 with references, e.g. to Bovens.

[6] Julia Black, 'Constructing and Contesting Legitimacy and Accountability in Polycentric Regulatory Regimes', LSE Law, Society and Economy Working Papers 2/2008, www.lse.ac.uk/collections/law/wps/wps.htm, 16.

accountability mechanisms.[7] According to Majone, 'political principals can transfer powers to their agents, within limits set by law, but they cannot transfer legitimacy in the same way'.[8] As a consequence, literature in the fields of both public administration and law has dedicated much attention to the 'dilemma of accountable independence', especially in the field of economic regulation.[9] The vast majority of these studies advocate a shift from political accountability to other, more modern and inventive forms.[10]

A recurring problem in many of these studies is the lack of a clear definition of 'accountability', despite (or, perhaps, because of) its omnipresence in the literature. According to Black, '[t]here are almost as many definitions of accountability as there are articles on the subject, if not more'.[11] Nicolaïdes defines accountability as 'the obligation of a public authority to explain and justify its decisions'.[12] A similar definition is adopted by Oliver.[13] In recent years, social or political scientists have developed more elaborate theories on the delineation and scope of the concept, discussing its constitutive elements in detail. For Bovens, whose work in this field has been particularly influential, accountability is a 'hurrah-word',[14] a concept with 'evocative powers' and therefore also an 'elusive' concept, which can mean many different things to different

---

7 See, for instance, Mark Bovens, 'Analysing and Assessing Accountability: A Conceptual Framework' (2007) 13(4) European Law Journal 447, 464.

8 Giandomenico Majone, 'The Agency Model: The Growth of Regulation and Regulatory Institutions in the European Union' (1997) 3 Eipascope 1, 5.

9 Paul Magnette, 'The Politics of Regulation in the European Union' in Damien Geradin, Rodolphe Muñoz and Nicolas Petit (eds), *Regulation through Agencies in the EU. A New Paradigm of European Governance* (Edward Elgar Publishing 2005) 3, 3.

10 ibid 11.

11 In the same sense: Julia Black, 'Constructing and Contesting Legitimacy and Accountability in Polycentric Regulatory Regimes', LSE Law, Society and Economy Working Papers 2/2008, 23.

12 Phedon Nicolaïdes, 'Regulation of Liberalised Markets: A New Role for the State?' in Damien Geradin, Rodolphe Muñoz and Nicolas Petit (eds), *Regulation through Agencies in the EU. A New Paradigm of European Governance* (Edward Elgar Publishing 2005) 23, 33.

13 See Dawn Oliver, 'Law, Politics and Accountability' [1994] Public Law 238, 246: accountability in a wide sense requires 'that a person or body explain and justify, against criteria of some kind, their decisions or actions'.

14 Mark Bovens, 'Public Accountability' in Ewan Ferlie, Laurence E Lynn and Christopher Pollit (eds), *The Oxford Handbook of Public Management* (Oxford University Press 2008) 182, 182.

people.[15] He defines accountability as 'a relationship between an actor and a forum, in which the actor has an obligation to explain and to justify his or her conduct, the forum can pose questions and pass judgment, and the actor may face consequences'.[16] Bovens furthermore distinguishes between three separate phases in account giving: the information phase (where data are provided and explanations or justifications may be rendered); the question(ing) phase (where the forum interrogates the actor); and the phase in which the forum passes judgment. Whether the possibility for the forum to sanction the actor is indispensable to speak of accountability is contested. Bovens, Mulgan[17] and Strom[18] agree that accountability requires a possibility of sanctioning.[19] However, 'the possibility of sanctions – not the actual imposition of sanctions – makes the difference between non-committal provision of information and being held to account', Bovens argues.[20] Examples of sanctions are fines, disciplinary measures, civil remedies or even penal sanctions, but more informal or unwritten sanctions also qualify. In the field of political accountability, the ultimate sanction is the dismissal of a minister by Parliament. Rawlings and Harlow propose to reformulate the requirement of sanction, using the more friendly requirement of 'reparation and

---

[15] Mark Bovens, 'Analysing and Assessing Accountability: A Conceptual Framework' (2007) 13(4) European Law Journal 447, 448.

[16] ibid 450.

[17] Richard Mulgan, *Holding Power to Account: Accountability in Modern Democracies* (Palgrave Macmillan 2003) 9.

[18] Kaare StrØm, 'Parliamentary Democracy and Delegation' in Kaare StrØm, Wolfgang C Müller and Torbjörn Bergman (eds), *Delegation and Accountability in Parliamentary Democracies* (Oxford University Press, 2008) 55, 62.

[19] See also Mark Elliot, 'Ombudsmen, Tribunals, Inquiries: Re-fashioning Accountability Beyond the Courts' in Nicholas Bamforth and Peter Leyland (eds), *Accountability in the Contemporary Constitution* (Oxford University Press 2013) 233, 235. *Contra*: Chris Hanretty, Pierre Larouche and Andreas Reindl, 'Independence, Accountability and Perceived Quality of Regulators – A CERRE Study', Brussels, 6 March 2012, http://www.cerre.eu/publications/independence-accountability-and-perceived-quality-regulators, 38.

[20] Mark Bovens, 'Two Concepts of Accountability: Accountability as a Virtue and as a Mechanism' (2010) 33(5) West European Politics 946, 952. In the words of Papadopoulos: not the utilization of sanctions, but their 'shadow' matters: Yannis Papadopoulos, 'Problems of Democratic Accountability in Network and Multilevel Governance' (2007) 13(4) European Law Journal 469, 470.

effective redress', which the authors label as 'key factors in legitimation through accountability'.[21]

Within the field of public accountability the literature discerns various subdivisions. For instance, a distinction can be made between various forms of account giving on the basis of the forum. This results in a divide between political accountability (vis-à-vis Parliament and the electorate), legal accountability (vis-à-vis the courts), administrative accountability (vis-à-vis auditors and inspectors), professional accountability (vis-à-vis professional peers) and social accountability (vis-à-vis stakeholders).[22] Another important criterion for classification is the aspect of the conduct that is being assessed. Legal accountability is about the legality of an act, whereas political accountability, for instance, involves multiple aspects of the actor's conduct. In this respect, possible further distinctions can be made between financial, procedural and product accountability.[23]

Referring to the goal of credible commitment, Magnette points out that governments are constrained to design oversight procedures that are 'soft' enough to be compatible with the autonomy of independent regulatory agencies.[24] Four main alternatives have been put forward in this regard:

- an increased focus on output or outcome legitimacy (as opposed to input legitimacy);
- an increased focus on procedural accountability;
- a reinforcement of judicial control or legal accountability;
- an increased focus on horizontal accountability, in the sense of network accountability.

A. Output or Outcome Legitimacy

Many seek the solution for the legitimacy problem of APBs in general, and independent NRAs or DPAs in particular, in an increased focus on

---

[21] Carol Harlow and Richard Rawlings, 'Promoting Accountability in Multi-level Governance: A Network Approach' (2007)13(4) European Law Journal 542, 545–546.

[22] Mark Bovens, 'Analysing and Assessing Accountability: A Conceptual Framework' (2007) 13(4) European Law Journal 447, 455–457.

[23] ibid 459–460.

[24] Paul Magnette, 'The Politics of Regulation in the European Union' in Damien Geradin, Rodolphe Muñoz and Nicolas Petit (eds), *Regulation through Agencies in the EU. A New Paradigm of European Governance* (Edward Elgar Publishing 2005) 3, 11.

'output' or 'outcome' legitimacy. This is not surprising since one of the core ideas behind the theories of NPM was the shift from accountability based on procedures to accountability based on results. These results were labelled 'outputs' or 'outcomes', terms that are often used interchangeably, although it is sometimes assumed that outputs are the specific means or measures taken to achieve outcomes (i.e. desirable effects on society).[25] The mechanisms of representative democracy are primarily based on inputs rather than outputs: decisions and actions are legitimate because they have been taken or steered by representatives or those accountable to them. Ultimately, these representatives are appointed by the people in periodical elections. Consequently, the government's legitimacy originates from procedures in which citizens (and, after elections, their representatives) deliver an input ('input legitimacy' or 'inputs-oriented legitimacy'[26]). What matters here is that procedures have been followed to appoint those responsible to adopt policies and to make sure that the final decisions are in accordance with their preferences. Legitimacy, as it were, is created via mechanisms that are anterior to the decision itself. In a system of output or outcome legitimacy, what matters, on the other hand, is the result or outcome of the decision and more precisely the extent to which stakeholders regard this as satisfactory.[27] Consequently, legitimacy is derived from the effects of a decision and is posterior to it.

Majone claims that all non-majoritarian institutions face the same legitimacy problem. They 'yield considerable power', yet they lack the element of democratic control via political representation. Therefore, they 'must be able to achieve their own legitimacy'.[28] That legitimacy is derived from the inherent value of the products that they deliver, i.e. their output.[29] Maggetti refers to 'the expected high credibility and/or efficiency of IRAs, based on the assumption that they are more proficient in producing qualitatively better policy outputs than democratic institutions'

---

[25] In this sense: Richard Mulgan, *Holding Power to Account: Accountability in Modern Democracies* (Palgrave Macmillan 2003) 157–158.

[26] Martino Maggetti, 'Legitimacy and Accountability of Independent Regulatory Agencies: A Critical Review' (2010) 2 Living Reviews in Democracy 1.

[27] See e.g. Mark Bevir, *Democratic Governance* (Princeton University Press 2010) 37. The author speaks of 'performance accountability'.

[28] Giandomenico Majone, 'The Agency Model: The Growth of Regulation and Regulatory Institutions in the European Union' (1997) 3 Eipascope 1, 5.

[29] Mark Bevir, *Democratic Governance* (Princeton University Press 2010) 107 (on Majone's theory of legitimacy).

as a means to assure their legitimacy or 'social sustainability'.[30] Chapter 3 explained how the combination of expertise and consistency is indeed constitutive of the 'credibility' associated with political independence. Because independent regulators are staffed with experts, their decisions are regarded as well thought out and duly founded. Since experts possess the necessary knowledge and skills to achieve desirable goals, it is considered likely that they will produce good (or even better) decisions. This belief in output legitimacy is also reflected in the claim that 'consensus-based decision making should be replaced by evidence-based decision making'.[31] Moreover, experts are not influenced by short-term electoral considerations. Consequently, one can expect their policies to be more consistent. These two characteristics of decision making by independent regulators would suffice to make them legitimate.[32] Maggetti observes that the legitimacy of non-elected bodies such as independent regulatory authorities 'is normally based on a large array of "non-democratic" justifications, but primarily the need for insulation from day-to-day politics and technical expertise'.[33] An inherent paradox of regulatory authorities is indeed the fact that the goal behind their establishment and more particularly behind their independence is precisely to make regulatory decisions more legitimate in the eyes of those subject to them. In the case of (network) regulation, political independence *in itself* is thus believed to lead to increased legitimacy. Establishing an independent regulator could thus be regarded as a transaction in which one type of legitimacy is swapped for another and where it is precisely the renunciation of the repelled type (political legitimacy) that allows for the other type (output legitimacy/expert legitimacy) to exist and thrive.

---

[30] Martino Maggetti, 'Legitimacy and Accountability of Independent Regulatory Agencies: A Critical Review' (2010) 2 Living Reviews in Democracy 1.

[31] Tom Christensen and Per Lægreid, 'The New Regulatory Orthodoxy: A Critical Assessment' in David Levi-Faur (ed), *Handbook on the Politics of Regulation* (Edward Elgar Publishing 2011) 361, 363.

[32] See also Mark Bovens, Deirdre Curtin and Paul 't Hart, 'The Quest for Legitimacy and Accountability in EU Governance' in Mark Bovens, Deirdre Curtin and Paul 't Hart (eds), *The Real World of EU Accountability. What Deficit?* (Oxford University Press 2010) 9, 29.

[33] Martino Maggetti, 'Legitimacy and Accountability of Independent Regulatory Agencies: A Critical Review' (2010) 2 Living Reviews in Democracy 1, with reference to Majone.

B. Procedural Accountability

Another popular answer to the question how to make APBs in general and independent supervisors in particular accountable so as to enhance their legitimacy is labelled 'procedural accountability' or 'procedural legitimacy'.[34] Procedural legitimacy combines elements of 'input' legitimacy and 'throughput' legitimacy by emphasizing both the need for participation by stakeholders and/or the general public and the quality of the procedures that consequently deal with these inputs.[35] It concerns the reinforcement of rules and principles that have to be adhered to during the administrative process.[36] It mostly involves (the enhanced or adapted application of) traditional guarantees that are already well enshrined in most European systems of administrative law, such as the duty to give reasons, the obligations to inform, consult or hear stakeholders, requirements regarding transparency in the decision-making process etc. In many European legal systems, these safeguards were primarily introduced to ensure that the government makes careful assessments, taking into account all relevant facts, data and standpoints and justifying its ultimate decision accordingly. That these guarantees have become associated with questions of accountability has something to do with the role that they play in American administrative law and more precisely in the Administrative Procedure Act (APA). In Europe, administrative law is to a large extent designed on the basis of the idea that the individual's interests require protection against the powers of the administration. US administrative law, on the other hand, is to a much greater degree regarded as a means of making the administration accountable to the public as a whole or to stakeholders more specifically. Susan Rose-Ackermann explains how administrative law transcended its role of protector of the individual rights of citizens and 'helped to mediate the exercise of public power' following the rise of the regulatory state.

---

[34] E.g. Christina Spyrelli, 'Regulating the Regulators? An Assessment of Institutional Structures and Procedural Rules of National Regulatory Authorities' [2003–04] International Journal of Communications Law and Policy 1, 33–37.

[35] On 'throughput legitimacy' see Vivien A Schmidt, 'Democracy and Legitimacy in the European Union Revisited: Input, Output *and* "Throughput"'[2013] Political Studies 2.

[36] See e.g. Dorit Rubinstein Reiss, 'Administrative Agencies as Creators of Administrative Law Norms: Evidence from the UK, France and Sweden' in Susan Rose-Ackerman and Peter Lindseth (eds), *Comparative Administrative Law* (Edward Elgar Publishing 2010) 373, containing a comparative study of the development of norms of transparency and consultation by telecommunications and electricity regulators in England, France and Sweden.

Consequently, administrative law contributes to democratic legitimacy. 'A fair and open policymaking process helps democratic citizens to hold modern government to account in the face of demands for delegation and regulation, both within and beyond the state. Thus, administrative law must be in dialogue with constitutional law as the modern state develops.'[37]

In order to substantiate their claim that procedural accountability is a valid substitute for political accountability, its proponents refer to the similarities between procedural mechanisms, especially consultation procedures, and the process of representative democracy:

> Nowadays, most political theorists agree that the major ambition of a political polity is to produce public deliberation about collective issues: a democratic constitution should organize a sound process of confrontation of different views, so as to produce the best possible policies, well informed and responding to the citizen's expectations. The 'fiduciary principles' which constrain the agents to consult the stakeholders, to weight their views, to give access to the documents they use to prepare their decisions, and to give the reasons why those decisions were taken, pursue the same deliberative ambitions.[38]

Ideas about procedural accountability are thus closely intertwined with theories of deliberative democracy.[39] Frankenberg defines deliberation in the context of democracy as a 'device for people to develop, discover and articulate their proper interests, needs, and preferences through a process of discussion, thus trying to solve the problem of "enduring disagreement" and group polarization'. Central to deliberative democracy[40] and to

---

[37] Susan Rose-Ackerman, 'The Regulatory State' in Michel Rosenfeld and András Sajó (eds), *The Oxford Handbook of Comparative Constitutional Law* (Oxford University Press 2012) 671, 684. See also Susan Rose-Ackerman and Thomas Perroud, 'Policymaking and Public Law in France: Public Participation, Agency Independence, and Impact Assessment' [2013] Colum. J. Eur. L. 225.

[38] Paul Magnette, 'The Politics of Regulation in the European Union' in Damien Geradin, Rodolphe Muñoz and Nicolas Petit (eds), *Regulation through Agencies in the EU. A New Paradigm of European Governance* (Edward Elgar Publishing 2005) 3, 13.

[39] Susan Rose-Ackerman, 'The Regulatory State' in Michel Rosenfeld and András Sajó (eds), *The Oxford Handbook of Comparative Constitutional Law* (Oxford University Press 2012) 671, 684; Tony Prosser, *The Economic Constitution* (Oxford University Press 2014) 248ff.

[40] Günter Frankenberg, 'Democracy' in Michel Rosenfeld and András Sajó (eds), *The Oxford Handbook of Comparative Constitutional Law* (Oxford University Press 2012) 250, 255–256.

the notion of procedural accountability is the balancing of different views in society.[41] As Prosser explains, a pluralist rationale underlies these theories, assuming that 'the truth (if indeed such thing exists) best emerges through the open testing of as many different conceptions of it as possible'.[42] In France, Hacquet believes that the legitimacy of regulators' rule-making powers is conditional on the dialogue that they develop with the regulatees.[43]

Interesting in this regard are the ideas developed by Lavrijssen, who dedicated a study to the constitutionality of independent economic regulators in the Netherlands. She argues that the embedment and acceptance of the role of these entities requires a shift from the theory of 'regulatory contract' to the so-called 'stakeholders approach'. Both perspectives are Anglo-Saxon in origin and lead to a different outcome for the interpretation of constitutional principles. The 'regulatory contract theory' departs from the traditional chain of delegation and the mechanism of political responsibility to ensure accountability to voters.[44] This – in the eyes of the author, more conservative – theory assumes a traditional divide in functions between the legislature and the minister, who are responsible for the definition of policy, and the independent supervisors, who are responsible for the execution of these policies. The delegation of wide discretionary powers and especially rule-making powers to the independent supervisors is deemed to be in conflict with the primacy of the legislature.[45] The 'stakeholders approach', on the other hand, makes legitimacy conditional on the question whether the regulator can take into account, in an effective manner, the interests of all stakeholders.[46] Stakeholders are defined as all citizens and entities who have an interest in a certain decision-making process or a particular form

---

[41] See also Mark Bevir, *Democratic Governance* (Princeton University Press 2010) 194.

[42] Tony Prosser, 'Regulation and Legitimacy' in Jeffrey Jowell and Dawn Oliver (eds), *The Changing Constitution* (7th edn, Oxford University Press 2011) 312, 321.

[43] Arnaud Hacquet, 'Le pouvoir réglementaire des autorités administratives indépendantes. Réflexions sur son objet et sa légitimité' [2008] RDP 393, 418–419.

[44] Saskia Lavrijssen, *Onafhankelijke mededingingstoezichthouders, regulerende bevoegdheden en de waarborgen voor good governance* (Boom Juridische uitgevers 2006) 34.

[45] ibid 519.

[46] ibid 18.

of public service.[47] If the 'stakeholders approach' is adopted, the legislature formulates flexible and open legal norms, which are further defined by the regulator in cooperation with stakeholders.[48] This participatory scheme makes independent market supervisors sufficiently accountable to the public and thus legitimate in a democratic sense. As a principle of good governance, stakeholder participation is thus able to act as an alternative to the mechanisms of representative democracy, since it achieves the same goal.

Of the four legal systems studied in this comparative analysis, the UK has to the greatest extent adopted and implemented the idea of procedural rules as democratic legitimizers. UK scholars ascertain that both the legislature and the independent regulators operating in the UK themselves have recently been investing in proper decision-making procedures, precisely with the aim of enhancing their legitimacy. At the same time, the independent regulators are also subject to the more traditional regimes that are applicable to classic government departments or to other administrative bodies, such as freedom of information and the regime of the Parliamentary Ombudsman, Prosser points out.[49] He promotes the enactment of a general Regulatory Reform Act, fixing procedures for, for instance, consultation.[50] Mulgan refers to the UK's Citizen's Charter as 'a notable pioneer' when it comes to direct accountability to the public or 'downwards accountability'.[51] Lavrijssen substantiates her argumentation on the stakeholders theory with the 2004 study of the UK House of Lords, already discussed in Chapter 3, which contains recommendations for the reinforcement of the accountability of independent regulators.[52] She furthermore points out that both the Communications Act 2003 and the Energy Act 2004 already contained explicit obligations for the

---

[47] ibid 30.

[48] ibid 33–34.

[49] Tony Prosser, 'Regulation and Legitimacy' in Jeffrey Jowell and Dawn Oliver (eds), *The Changing Constitution* (7th edn, Oxford University Press 2011) 312, 323.

[50] ibid 332.

[51] Richard Mulgan, *Holding Power to Account: Accountability in Modern Democracies* (Palgrave Macmillan 2003) 173 with reference.

[52] Saskia Lavrijssen, *Onafhankelijke mededingingstoezichthouders, regulerende bevoegdheden en de waarborgen voor good governance* (Boom Juridische uitgevers 2006) 429 with reference to House of Lords, Select Committee on the Constitution, 6th report of Session 2003–04, *The Regulatory State: Ensuring its Accountability*, volume 1, report, HL Paper 68-1, 2004.

telecommunications and energy regulators to take into account the principles of good governance.[53]

Interestingly and paradoxically, delegation to APBs is quite often associated with the idea of evading the application of compulsory rules and principles of public law, often of a procedural nature. This ties in with the trend that Talbot has named 'deregulation' or 'reregulation', which he has labelled one of the three core ideas behind the agency concept.[54] NPM precisely aimed to get rid of procedural rules and guarantees that slowed down the administrative process and made it inefficient.[55] At present, however, precisely these guarantees are often regarded as compensation for the lack of political input.

Whereas theories of output legitimacy focus on the results achieved by the APBs, regardless of the procedures followed, forms of accountability that revolve around input or throughputs accept decisions as legitimate if a certain procedure is followed, whatever the outcome.[56] Some, however, suggest a link or interrelatedness between procedural guarantees and output legitimacy, in the sense that the expected desirable outcomes that independent regulators generate, i.e. credible decisions, based on expertise and part of a consistent policy, to some extent precisely originate from the application of proper procedural guarantees.[57] Not all proponents of independent agencies, however, agree on the desirability of public participation procedures, among other things because they fear the risk of regulatory capture.[58]

At present, the reinforcement of procedural guarantees to be applied by the IRAs is strongly promoted by the EU legislature and by the European Commission. In the field of energy liberalization, for instance, article 35(4) of Directive 2009/72 and article 39(4) of Directive 2009/73 require

---

[53] ibid 446–447.

[54] Colin Talbot, 'The Agency Idea: Sometimes Old, Sometimes New, Sometimes Borrowed, Sometimes Untrue' in Christopher Pollit and Colin Talbot (eds), *Unbundled Government. A Critical Analysis of the Global Trend to Agencies, Quangos and Contractualisation* (Routledge 2004) 3, 6 and 11–14.

[55] Richard Mulgan, *Holding Power to Account: Accountability in Modern Democracies* (Palgrave Macmillan 2003) 170.

[56] Martino Maggetti, 'Legitimacy and Accountability of Independent Regulatory Agencies: A Critical Review' (2010) 2 Living Reviews in Democracy 1.

[57] Christina Spyrelli, 'Regulating the Regulators? An Assessment of Institutional Structures and Procedural Rules of National Regulatory Authorities' [2003–04] International Journal of Communications Law and Policy 1, 33.

[58] Susan Rose-Ackerman, 'The Regulatory State' in Michel Rosenfeld and András Sajó (eds), *The Oxford Handbook of Comparative Constitutional Law* (Oxford University Press 2012) 671, 676.

Member States to ensure that the NRA exercises its powers transparently. Article 37(16) and 41(16) respectively stipulate that decisions taken by regulatory authorities have to be fully reasoned and justified to allow for judicial review. The decisions shall be available to the public while preserving the confidentiality of commercially sensitive information. The directives contain specific provisions on the consultation of the actual and potential system users and the transmission system operators.[59] In the European Commission's interpretative note, emphasis is put on transparent decision making by the NRA, as a means of assuring and reinforcing its accountability. Transparency is promoted both before (in preparation of), during and after decisions have been made. First, the Commission encourages NRAs to adopt and publish rules of procedure (including at least procedures for decision making), to have contact points for stakeholders and to 'publish information on their own organization and structure'. Secondly, NRAs are asked to consult stakeholders when they take important decisions. Lastly, the NRA must make its decisions available to the public.[60]

C. Legal Accountability

A third alleged substitute for political supervision of APBs often proposed in literature is supervision by the courts. The possibility of judicial control on the decisions of regulatory agencies is regarded as a safeguard or a genuine counterweight for their independence.[61]

As far as the energy regulators are concerned, recital 34 of the preamble of Directive 2009/72 confirms that the independence of the electricity regulator does not exclude judicial review of its decisions, in accordance with the constitutional laws of the Member States.[62] Pursuant to articles 37(17) of Directive 2009/72 (electricity) and 41(17) of Directive 2009/73 (gas), Member States have to ensure that suitable mechanisms exist at the national level under which a party affected by a

---

[59] See articles 37(2) and 22(4) of Directive 2009/72 and articles 41(2) and 33(4) of Directive 2009/73.

[60] Commission, interpretative note regulatory authorities 5.

[61] E.g. Christina Spyrelli, 'Regulating the Regulators? An Assessment of Institutional Structures and Procedural Rules of National Regulatory Authorities' [2003–04] International Journal of Communications Law and Policy 1, 42–49; Tony Prosser, 'Regulation and Legitimacy' in Jeffrey Jowell and Dawn Oliver (eds), *The Changing Constitution* (7th edn, Oxford University Press 2011) 312, 321.

[62] See also (the identical) recital 30 of Directive 2009/73.

decision of a regulatory authority has a right of appeal to a body independent of the parties involved and of any government. In its interpretation of these provisions, the European Commission clarifies that 'an appeal or review procedure before the government or a ministry would not be in line with the provisions of the new Electricity and Gas Directives' and that:

> given the NRA's autonomy in decision making and given the NRA's independence from any public entity, the power to suspend NRA decisions belongs only to courts and judges or appeal mechanisms before any other bodies independent of the parties involved and of any government. Where a government does not agree with an NRA decision, it can make use of these legal actions as well.[63]

The Commission furthermore suggests that the requirement of 'suitability' of the appeal mechanisms entails an obligation to establish specific procedures for certain types of NRA decisions 'where the court (or equivalent bodies independent of the parties involved and of any government) will rule at short notice. Similarly, in urgent cases, the court can be given the power to suspend an NRA decision (typically via summary proceedings)'.[64]

As far as regulators operating in the field of electronic communications are concerned, article 4 of the Framework Directive, pursuant to which a right of appeal has to be provided against the decisions of the regulator, was discussed in Chapter 2.[65] Pursuant to article 56(10) of Directive 2012/34, Member States shall ensure that decisions taken by the regulatory body for railway transport are subject to judicial review. The appeal may have suspensive effect on the decision of the regulatory body only when the immediate effect of the regulatory body's decision may cause irretrievable or manifestly excessive damage for the appellant. This provision is without prejudice to the powers of the court hearing the appeal as conferred by constitutional law, where applicable. Article 78 of the Data Protection Regulation enshrines the right to an effective judicial remedy against (the decisions of) the supervisory authorities.

In the judgment in *Commission/Germany*, the ECJ referred to the fact that independent administrative authorities have to comply with the law

---

[63] Commission, interpretative note regulatory authorities, 19 and 20.

[64] ibid 20.

[65] See also recital 14 of the preamble of Directive 2009/140.

and that their decisions are subject to review by the competent courts in order to substantiate their legitimacy despite their political isolation.[66]

Referring to article 4 of the Framework Directive on electronic communications and discussing the requirements that flow from this provision as well as their interpretation by the ECJ, Lavrijssen and Ottow suggest that:

> although the ECJ has not explicitly made this link, one could argue that the greater possibilities for legal protection against the NRA's decisions on the basis of EU law, may compensate for the fact that European law at the same time has decreased the role of the political arena to control the way NRAs adopt specific decisions in individual cases.[67]

Providing for additional guarantees of legal accountability has been a popular solution to compensate for the autonomy of APBs throughout their entire history. In France, political supervision by ministers has often been replaced by a possibility for the competent minister to lodge an appeal with the administrative courts in order to challenge the legality of the AAI's decisions. This practice has been endorsed by the CC.[68] The recognition of the minister's right to act as a plaintiff before the courts is regarded as necessary (and sufficient) in order to safeguard the principle of ministerial responsibility before Parliament.[69] In its interpretative note, the European Commission suggests that the legal actions against the decisions of the energy regulators, provided by national law, can be used by the Government as well. In this scenario, a minister can no longer suspend or annul the decisions of the regulatory body himself, but can indirectly achieve the same result by filing a petition with the court. A similar solution was put forward in the advice of the Belgian Council of State, Legislation Section on the establishment of one of the sectorial committees of the Belgian DPA, discussed in Chapter 4.

---

[66] Para 42.

[67] Saskia Lavrijssen and Annetje Ottow, 'The Legality of Independent Regulatory Authorities' in Leonard Besselink, Frans Pennings and Sacha Prechal (eds), *The Eclipse of the Legality Principle in the European Union* (Kluwer 2011) 73, 94–95.

[68] Conseil Constitutionnel, déc. 86 217 DC du 18 Septembre 1986, para 23; Conseil Constitutionnel, déc. 93-333 DC du 21 Janvier 1994, para 14.

[69] E.g. Aalt W Heringa, 'Agencies in France. Autorités Administratives Centrales Indépendantes/National Independent Administrative Authorities' in Tom Zwart and Luc Verhey (eds), *Agencies in European and Comparative Law* (Intersentia 2003) 37, 52.

An ongoing debate regarding the legal accountability of APBs in general, and independent supervisors more specifically, concerns the intensity of judicial scrutiny. How far can and should judges go in their assessment and review of the administrative decisions of these bodies?[70] These questions on the scope of judicial scrutiny are rooted in the separation of powers doctrine, which requires that judicial control remains strictly limited to the legality of decisions. Another, related, question is whether and to what extent courts should show deference to experts and should refrain from reviewing the scientific assessments made by regulatory bodies.[71]

D. Network Accountability

A more recent idea on how to make APBs and especially independent regulators accountable is contained in the concept of network accountability. Increasingly, it is suggested that formal and informal networks of NRAs[72] can contribute to their accountability as well.[73] The idea seems to be that peers in networks are likely to put pressure on each other and may raise the need for self-justification in the light of self-preservation.[74] According to Mulgan, 'networks can be viewed as social groupings where a division of responsibilities helps the respective parties to watch each other and keep each other honest, an extension of the separation of

---

[70] E.g. Tom Zwart, 'Judicial Review of Agency Action: The Scope of Review' in Tom Zwart and Luc Verhey (eds), *Agencies in European and Comparative Law* (Intersentia 2003) 171.

[71] See e.g. Catherine Donnelly, 'Participation and Expertise: Judicial Attitudes in Comparative Perspective' in Susan Rose-Ackerman and Peter Lindseth (eds), *Comparative Administrative Law* (Elgar 2010) 357; Carol Harlow and Richard Rawlings, *Law and Administration* (7th edn, Cambridge University Press 2009) 311; Tony Prosser, 'The Powers and Accountability of Agencies and Regulators' in David Feldman (ed), *English Public Law* (Oxford University Press 2011) 241, 250.

[72] On these networks, see e.g. Saskia Lavrijssen and Leigh Hancher, 'Networks on Track: From European Regulatory Networks to European Regulatory "Network Agencies"' (2008) 34 LIEI 23, in particular 8–11; David Coen and Mark Thatcher, 'Network Governance and Multi-level Delegation: European Networks of Regulatory Agencies' (2008) 28 Journal of Public Policy 49.

[73] Martino Maggetti, 'Legitimacy and Accountability of Independent Regulatory Agencies: A Critical Review' (2010) 2 Living Reviews in Democracy 1.

[74] Yannis Papadopoulos, 'Problems of Democratic Accountability in Network and Multilevel Governance' (2007) 13(4) European Law Journal 469, 477. The author also speaks of 'accountability through embeddedness' (p. 480).

powers theory advocated by James Madison and others'.[75] Scott speaks of 'diffuse or nodal forms of democratic decision-making' or a 'diffuse mode of constitutionalism' and stresses the learning effect that meetings in networks can generate.[76]

2. EVALUATION

It has often been suggested that (a combination of) output legitimacy, procedural accountability, judicial control and network responsiveness offer(s) sufficient guarantees to counterbalance the political independence of APBs. In the following paragraphs, it is argued that none of these four alternatives are sufficiently comparable to political accountability to replace it entirely. Inspiration for this argument is drawn from the literature on the assessment of accountability regimes.

A. Towards Conceptual Clarity

It could be argued that at least two of the four alternatives discussed in the previous section are not forms of accountability in the same sense as political accountability is.

As far as output or outcome legitimacy is concerned, the processes of explanation and justification, two key elements that appear in the definitions of both Nicolaïdes and Bovens, are lacking. These are essential features of traditional expressions of political accountability, such as political ministerial responsibility. Admittedly, legitimacy does not have to originate from accountability: public institutions can derive this quality from other sources as well.[77] In other words: output or outcome legitimacy can still be functionally equivalent to accountability mechanisms. The expertise and continuity generated by APBs are believed to ensure qualitative results, which is considered a source of legitimacy as such. However, it could be argued that not only APBs, but the entire administration, should be designed in such a way as to inspire

---

[75] Richard Mulgan, *Holding Power to Account: Accountability in Modern Democracies* (Palgrave Macmillan 2003) 213 with reference.

[76] Colin Scott, 'Regulatory Governance and the Challenge of Constitutionalism' in Dawn Oliver, Tony Prosser and Richard Rawlings (eds), *The Regulatory State: Constitutional Implications* (Oxford University Press 2010) 15, 33.

[77] Julia Black, 'Constructing and Contesting Legitimacy and Acocuntability in Polycentric Regulatory Regimes', LSE Law, Society and Economy Working Papers 2/2008, 23.

confidence in its performance and to produce high-quality decisions. These qualities give public bodies their initial legitimacy, their right to be invested with government tasks and powers in the first place. However, even when the administration is designed and staffed in ways that promise a maximum chance of efficiency and quality, this does not suffice to give it continued and perpetual legitimacy: intermediate checks and moments of questioning, explanation and justification are still required. Output legitimacy cannot replace input legitimacy but can, at best, only supplement it.[78]

A similar argument applies to some of the guarantees that are subsumed under the denominator of procedural accountability. Bovens, in an attempt to define the constitutive elements of accountability, also addresses the (equally significant) question of what is *not* accountability. Transparency, the author argues, is not enough to constitute accountability, although this is often suggested. Guarantees of transparency and openness are necessary prerequisites for accountability regimes to function properly, but do not necessarily involve a dialogue between an actor and a forum.[79] For that same reason participation is not a form of accountability either, although it may enhance political legitimacy. Again, the elements of justification, judgement and consequences are lacking.[80] A similar reasoning is found in the work of Mulgan, who points out that only if those who receive the information also have the right to demand it and to seek remedies can there be talk of accountability. 'Purely voluntary or grace-and-favour transparency does not amount to accountability.'[81] The same applies to procedures that aim to involve stakeholders, since these do not always imply 'rights to demand answers and obligations to respond'.[82]

---

[78] Paul Magnette, 'The Politics of Regulation in the European Union' in Damien Geradin, Rodolphe Muñoz and Nicolas Petit (eds), *Regulation through Agencies in the EU. A New Paradigm of European Governance* (Edward Elgar Publishing 2005) 3, 3.

[79] Mark Bovens, 'Analysing and Assessing Accountability: A Conceptual Framework' (2007) 13(4) European Law Journal 447, 453.

[80] ibid 453.

[81] Richard Mulgan, *Holding Power to Account: Accountability in Modern Democracies* (Palgrave Macmillan 2003) 11.

[82] ibid 24; see also the analysis in Bram Verschuere, Koen Verhoest, Falke Meyers and B Guy Peters, 'Accountability and Accountability Arrangements in Public Agencies' in Tom Christensen and Per Lægreid (eds), *Autonomy and Regulation, Coping with Agencies in the Modern State* (Edward Elgar Publishing 2006) 268–298 and 270.

Admitting that values such as transparency and participation are de facto often referred to as forms of accountability, Bovens has introduced a distinction between 'accountability as a virtue' and 'accountability as a mechanism'. The values of transparency and accountability qualify as accountability as a virtue, but not as accountability as a mechanism, which implies the social relation to which he refers in his more traditional definition.[83] Accountability as a mechanism focuses on *ex post facto* processes, not on *ex ante* inputs. Forms of accountability as a virtue, on the other hand, relate to a 'willingness to act in transparent, fair and equitable way'[84] and actually represent principles of good (public or corporate) governance.[85] Providing transparent procedures and organizing participatory processes etc. are desirable features for the behaviour of public organizations. When accountability is used in this sense, its 'deficits manifest themselves as inappropriate behaviour, as "bad" governance or organizational deviance'.[86] Accountability as a (social) mechanism, on the other hand, requires more than that: it involves a process of a forum actively 'holding' an actor accountable for his actions.[87] Parliamentary control through ministerial responsibility (political accountability) is such an *ex post* form of accountability. Central to the interplay between the Government and Parliament is indeed interaction via the exchange of questions and answers and the possibility, for Parliament, to sanction the Government with the ultimate instrument of dismissal. Whereas procedural guarantees and especially duties of consultation and transparency indeed involve citizens in the decision-making process in a much more direct way than the procedures of representative democracy do, they often lack the element of genuine debate and interaction and always lack the element of an instant possibility to sanction those responsible for decision making.

Apart from these issues of incomparability on the level of the definition of accountability that is adopted, there are additional reasons why the value of output/outcome legitimacy and procedural accountability as substitutes for political accountability should be assessed with some reserve, particularly in the case of independent supervisors or regulators. These are related to the goal or purpose of different types of accountability.

---

[83] Mark Bovens, 'Two Concepts of Accountability: Accountability as a Virtue and as a Mechanism' (2010) 33(5) West European Politics 946.

[84] ibid 949.

[85] ibid 961.

[86] ibid 961.

[87] ibid 948.

B. Towards a Purpose-oriented Perspective on the Suitability of Accountability Arrangements

Accountability is always a means to an end. Majone has argued that any mechanism that aims to limit or control power is a source of legitimacy.[88] The author proposes a combination of different control mechanisms, none of which involve political control, in order to make independent agencies democratically accountable.[89] This results in his famous thesis that 'when a multi-pronged system of controls works properly, no one controls an independent agency, yet the agency is "under control"'.[90] Scott speaks of an 'extended accountability model' in which interdependencies among the actors involved in regulation create checks and balances and keep regulators under control, and in which several overlapping accountability mechanisms exist while no single mechanism is crucial.[91] The problem with these statements is that they fail to acknowledge that legitimacy is not a monolithic concept. Institutions do not (necessarily) derive their legitimacy from one source only and sources of legitimacy are not simply interchangeable. Various accountability arrangements serve different goals, in the sense that they contribute to different aspects of an institution's overall legitimacy. Their appropriateness can only be judged in the light of that purpose.

Both legal accountability and network accountability differ from political accountability as far as their goal or objective is concerned. The former present themselves as mechanisms that ensure that power is kept in balance, which is just one condition for the legitimacy of public actors. They serve (only) one particular purpose of accountability arrangements: the prevention of abuse of power. Bovens speaks of the constitutional

---

88 Giandomenico Majone, 'The Agency Model: The Growth of Regulation and Regulatory Institutions in the European Union' (1997) 3 Eipascope 1, 5–6.

89 These are: 'clear and narrowly defined objectives, to facilitate accountability by results; strict procedural requirements, to limit regulatory discretion; judicial review, to ensure protection of the rights of citizens; professionalism and peer review, to certify the technical quality of agency decisions; transparency and public participation, to make agencies responsive to public concerns'.

90 Giandomenico Majone, 'The Agency Model: The Growth of Regulation and Regulatory Institutions in the European Union' (1997) 3 Eipascope 1, 6.

91 See Fabrizio Gilardi, *Delegation in the Regulatory State. Independent Regulatory Agencies in Western Europe* (Edward Elgar Publishing 2008) 25–26 paraphrasing Colin Scott, 'Accountability in the Regulatory State' (2000) 27(1) Journal of Law and Society 38. See also the discussion in Carol Harlow and Richard Rawlings, *Law and Administration* (7th edn, Cambridge University Press 2009) 306–307.

perspective on the rationale behind provisions of accountability. The idea behind this rationale is the introduction of checks and balances, of 'institutional countervailing powers'.[92] Legal accountability ensures that executive authority, in this case embodied by the APB, is controlled by the judiciary, being another state power. It primarily aims to assure an equilibrium of power. It fits the idea that separation of powers above all other things requires control of all state powers over each other, in order to avoid concentration and misuse or abuse. Network accountability to a large extent serves a similar rationale. Networks generate a system of interaction that has the effect of keeping power in balance. Papadopoulos qualifies network accountability as a soft and horizontal system of checks and balances.[93] The same goes for Scott's model of 'extended accountability'. The strength of this model is deemed to lie in the fact that each actor 'has powers or capacities which constrain the capacities of the others' and consequently in 'the opposing tensions and forces generated'.[94]

Accountability, however, is not exclusively about providing a counterbalance for the exercise of power, it does not solely aim to organize a system of checks and balances. Accountability in the form of political control or oversight serves a different purpose: it relates to the democratic perspective on accountability. In Bovens' conception of democratic accountability, political actors play an important role: it is via them that account is given to the people. The central idea behind the democratic perspective is that accountability controls and legitimizes government actions by linking them effectively to the democratic chain of delegation.[95] The basis of this chain of delegation is the idea of popular sovereignty. The sovereignty of the people, whom Bovens qualifies as the primary principals in a democracy, is transferred to elected representatives. Subsequently, the executive powers are delegated to the Government. Further delegations to civil servants and APBs eventually close the loop. The accountability chain forms the mirror image of the chain of

[92] Mark Bovens, 'Analysing and Assessing Accountability. A Conceptual Framework' (2007) 13(4) European Law Journal 447, 463.

[93] Yannis Papadopoulos, 'Problems of Democratic Accountability in Network and Multilevel Governance' (2007) 13(4) European Law Journal 469, 481.

[94] Colin Scott, 'Accountability in the Regulatory State' (2000) 27(1) Journal of Law and Society 38, 52.

[95] Mark Bovens, 'Analysing and Assessing Accountability: A Conceptual Framework' (2007) 13(4) European Law Journal 447, 465.

delegation: it requires feedback from each agent to his principal and thus, eventually, to the citizens.[96]

In order to assess whether an accountability arrangement contributes to democratic goals, one should ascertain whether it adds to the possibilities open to voter, Parliament or other representative bodies to control the executive power.[97] Only mechanisms that fulfil this criterion are mechanisms of democratic accountability and can hence contribute to democratic legitimacy. Bovens summarizes the central issue of the democratic perspective in the question whether or not accountability arrangements help to provide political principals with sufficient information about the behaviour of their agents and whether they offer enough incentives to commit themselves to the agendas of their democratically elected principals.[98] Not all accountability mechanisms are suitable to achieve this goal.

The identification of these different perspectives on accountability signifies that an assessment of the quality of accountability mechanisms can lead to different results, depending on the purpose that one expects the mechanism to serve: 'accountability arrangements may score well from one perspective, but not from others'.[99]

Judicial control, resulting in legal accountability, does not aim to link APBs to the chain of delegation. On the contrary: one of the key features or even *raisons d'être* of the judiciary is its independence of that very chain, i.e. its separateness as a state power. From this characteristic flows an important limit to judicial control: courts only assess whether an act of an executive body does not violate the law. This does not mean that judicial review is anti-democratic or could not support the democratic basis of administrative decision making. Since courts control the legality of administrative decisions, they help to ensure that these decisions do not violate Parliament's wish.[100] Courts cannot, however, exercise any real policy control: they cannot assess the necessity or desirability of a decision in the light of the general interest, if that general interest has not

---

[96] ibid 463 with reference to Adam Przeworski, Susan C Stokes and Bernard Manin (eds), *Democracy, Accountability, and Representation* (Cambridge University Press 1999).

[97] Mark Bovens, 'Analysing and Assessing Accountability: A Conceptual Framework' (2007) 13(4) European Law Journal 447, 465.

[98] ibid 465.

[99] ibid 466.

[100] In this regard, see the argument developed in T R S Allan, 'Accountability to Law' in Nicholas Bamforth and Peter Leyland (eds), *Accountability in the Contemporary Constitution* (Oxford University Press 2013) 77, 103.

already been enshrined in legislation.[101] If the decision that is being challenged has been taken on the basis of discretionary powers, the courts must be careful not to substitute their own assessments for those of the administration. At most, courts can be invited to assess whether a public authority has not exercised its discretion in an (obviously) unreasonable manner.[102]

Craig and Tomkins warn that lawyers tend to overestimate the importance and the potential of judicial review[103] and advise them to 'be mindful of the importance of the political as a way of checking and controlling the exercise of executive power'.[104] According to Elliott:

> [a]ccountability can, and should, take several forms. This, in turn, demands that accountability be supplied by a range of functionally-complementary institutions applying a diversity of criteria and approaches. Against this background, the judicialization of accountability should be regarded with a degree of suspicion, as should the assumption that judicial accountability can fill the gap where other modes of accountability are found wanting.[105]

Similarly, network accountability, however valuable in the light of achieving a proper system of checks and balances, does not contribute to the democratic legitimacy of a government institution either. Papadopoulos points out that 'even if the network is pluralistic, the diversity of

---

[101] Even though literature demonstrates that courts have in fact increasingly filled the gap left by the legislature in many parliamentary systems when it comes to overseeing the executive and have adapted their viewpoints on standing and scope of review accordingly. See Tom Zwart, 'Overseeing the Executive: Is the Legislature Reclaiming Lost Territory from the Courts?' in Susan Rose-Ackerman and Peter Lindseth (eds), *Comparative Administrative Law* (Edward Elgar Publishing 2010) 148, 148–152.

[102] See e.g. Philip Norton (Lord Norton of Louth), 'Regulating the Regulatory State' (2004) 57(4) Parliam Aff 785, 792–793; Carol Harlow and Richard Rawlings, *Law and Administration* (7th edn, Cambridge University Press 2009) 311–312.

[103] Other authors as well state (and regret) that 'lawyers' love affair with the rule of law tends to place courts at the heart of the accountability system': Arthur Benz, Carol Harlow and Yannis Papadopoulos, 'Introduction' (2007) 13(4) *European Law Journal* 441, 444.

[104] Paul Craig and Adam Tomkins, 'Introduction' in Paul Craig and Adam Tomkins (eds), *The Executive and Public Law. Power and Accountability in Comparative Perspective* (Oxford University Press 2006) 1, 11–12.

[105] Mark Elliot, 'Ombudsmen, Tribunals, Inquiries: Re-fashioning Accountability Beyond the Courts' in Nicholas Bamforth and Peter Leyland (eds), *Accountability in the Contemporary Constitution* (Oxford University Press 2013) 233, 258.

perspectives does not guarantee that these perspectives are representative of society at large'.[106]

The distinct value of output and outcome legitimacy, yielded by expert decision making, is beyond doubt. Decision making by experts, however, is essentially different from political decision making. First, experts, just like courts, have no mandate to determine what is desirable in the light of the public interest. Secondly, the output/outcome legitimacy argument primarily focuses on objectivity and truth finding. Experts are often better placed than elected politicians to decide what is necessary or useful from a technical viewpoint. However, this is not what government decision making in general, and regulatory decision making in particular, are essentially, let alone exclusively, about. Democratic decision making does not primarily revolve around finding the 'truth' in a scientific meaning, it is about determining what policy is desirable and, consequently, what is necessary for the furtherance of the general well-being and welfare. In Prosser's words, 'regulatory decision making revolves around deep conflicts of social values and is not merely the outcome of technical processes'.[107]

The ostensibly most appealing alternative for political legitimacy is procedural legitimacy. This is especially the case for the procedures of participatory and deliberative democracy. Just like the political chain of accountability, participatory mechanisms create a direct line between the administration and (a part of) the public. In this way, they yield 'popular influence' on public decision making. Unlike the mechanisms of legal accountability and network accountability, which are first and foremost about keeping power in balance, participatory procedures therefore directly contribute to the democratic legitimacy of the decision-making process.

Participatory democracy offers a lot in terms of democratic legitimacy that elected democracy cannot. It allows for persons or groups who have a specific interest in a proposed decision to be identified and invited to give input. That input is important for two reasons. First, it ensures that decisions are better thought through and informed by the concerns of real people and real situations. Second, it encourages decision makers to balance the various interests that may be at stake. It especially invites them to reconcile policy objectives that serve broad societal interests with the concerns of those who are likely to be affected by their decisions

---

[106] Yannis Papadopoulos, 'Problems of Democratic Accountability in Network and Multilevel Governance' (2007) 13(4) European Law Journal 469, 481.

[107] Tony Prosser, *The Regulatory Enterprise – Government, Regulation and Legitimacy* (Oxford University Press 2010) 203.

more directly. Consequently, participation of this type contributes to the rationality of administrative decisions as well as to public support. Consultation of stakeholders has therefore become an indispensable guarantee in administrative and especially regulatory decision making. It should not be regarded as a possible *alternative* for political legitimacy when the latter is impossible or undesirable: it has become *essential* to public governance even when the political process is able to do its work to the full extent. It has, moreover, become more than a *supplement* to the political process: in many cases, it is a necessary *complement*.

Just like elected democracy, participatory democracy carries dangers as well as opportunities. On the one hand, there is a risk of so-called 'regulatory capture'.[108] This means that the political influence that APBs deliberately lack may be replaced by more subtle but nevertheless effective attempts by stakeholders to have the final say in regulatory matters.[109] These stakeholders are often (organizations consisting of or established by) the very subjects of the decisions made by the APB. Stakeholder participation can consequently lead to unhealthy situations of lobbying and bias.[110] Naturally, there are ways to overcome these obstacles or to make them less influential: participation procedures that are carefully designed can avoid undue influence and hence biased decision making. Moreover, the risk of regulatory capture is not exclusively linked to stakeholder participation: regulators subject to political accountability can be 'captured' by their political principals as well, implying that they become puppets on strings instead of APBs who develop their own, expert opinions.

Regardless of the many merits of participatory democracy, it would be wrong to look at it as a replacement for elected democracy. This is so because the interests that inspire the political process on the one hand and the participatory process on the other are different and therefore

---

[108] See e.g. Barry M Mitnick, 'Capturing "Capture": Definition and Mechanisms' in David Levi-Faur (ed), *Handbook on the Politics of Regulation* (Edward Elgar Publishing 2011) 34.

[109] See also Aalt W Heringa and Luc F M Verhey, 'Independent Agencies and Political Control' in Tom Zwart and Luc Verhey (eds), *Agencies in European and Comparative Law* (Intersentia 2003) 155, 163 and 167.

[110] See e.g. Dawn Oliver, 'Regulation, Democracy and Democratic Oversight in the UK' in Dawn Oliver, Tony Prosser and Richard Rawlings (eds), *The Regulatory State: Constitutional Implications* (Oxford University Press 2010) 243, 248–249; Dorit Rubinstein Reiss 'Administrative Agencies as Creators of Administrative Law Norms: Evidence from the UK, France and Sweden' in Susan Rose-Ackerman and Peter Lindseth (eds), *Comparative Administrative Law* (Edward Elgar Publishing 2010) 373, 384.

complementary, rather than interchangeable. Participatory democracy revolves around the interests of stakeholders. The political process, on the other hand, puts the general or public interest at centre stage. The general interest is a dynamic concept, which evolves along with society and its economic, social and ideological conceptions. In a representative democracy, these conceptions are measured via the opinions expressed and votes cast by the elected representatives of the people, who decide what serves the general interest best and what policies are needed to achieve the identified goals. Therefore, elected parliaments have 'the monopoly of expressing the popular will'.[111] Individual citizens lack this mandate of defining the public interest. So do organized interest groups of stakeholders. Consultation of, or participation by, direct stakeholders is an important guarantee and leads to more balanced, proportionate and fair decision making, but not necessarily to decision making that serves the public interest. What is in the public interest is ultimately for elected politicians to decide, often taking into account the results of participatory processes, but making their own assessment in the end.[112] Participatory mechanisms, in other words, do not offer overall democratic legitimacy, they identify partial interests and compel decision makers to take these into account. They do not, usually, aim to involve the public as a whole or a representative sample of the population in the decision-making process. This does not change if various groups of stakeholders, even with obviously opposing interests, such as the operators and consumers in the case of economic regulation, are involved. The public interest is more than a sum of all private interests that are directly affected by a specific decision. According to Fishkin, who reflects about how to reconcile deliberation and political equality as essential values of democratic theory, '[t]here is little reason to think that the minorities who self-select to become engaged in their areas of special interest would approximate the views of the rest of the electorate'.[113] In a system of representative democracy, the 'general interest' is in the end defined through the process of deliberation and vote by elected representatives. Acknowledging this reality, Black defends a 'thick conception' of proceduralization, referring to concepts of deliberative or discourse-based

---

[111] Aalt W Heringa, and Luc F M Verhey, 'Independent Agencies and Political Control' in Tom Zwart and Luc Verhey (eds), *Agencies in European and Comparative Law* (Intersentia 2003) 155, 163.

[112] See also Stuart Weir, 'Quangos: Questions of Democratic Accountability' (1995) 48(2) Parliam Aff 306, 310.

[113] James S Fishkin, *When the People Speak: Deliberative Democracy and Public Consultation* (Oxford University Press 2009) 8.

democracy and more specifically to Habermas. In such a conception, unilateral preference and interests are transcended. Black acknowledges, however, that such projects pose particular challenges with regard to procedural design and can be time-consuming and require further research and theoretical development.[114]

Finally, government decision making does not take place within isolated policy domains, each corresponding to a well-defined group of stakeholders. In a complex world characterized by interdependencies between policies, no decision is isolated, as choices in one policy domain affect other policy domains, which may have other direct stakeholders. Taking tariffs in the field of energy regulation as an example: only a limited number of interested parties will be involved in participation procedures organized to decide upon, for instance, tariff methodologies. Such decisions, however, have broad social implications. This is so because the distribution of costs among consumers (companies versus private parties: people who live in the cities versus those who live in the countryside) depends on them. Thus, each and every member of society suddenly becomes an 'interested party'. Such decisions require policy trade-offs that can simply not be taken on the basis of the input of well-defined groups of stakeholders only. For that reason, many argue that forms of participatory or deliberative democracy, however necessary as complements, cannot replace representative democracy.[115]

In sum: both representative and participatory democracy correlate with a specific sub-purpose of the wider democratic goal. They are not in competition to become *the* ultimate model of democracy, they work together to achieve a more complete account of democracy.

---

[114] Julia Black, 'Proceduralizing Regulation: Part I' (2000) Oxford Journal of Legal Studies 597; Julia Black, 'Proceduralizing Regulation: Part II' (2000) Oxford Journal of Legal Studies 33.

[115] Andreas L Paulus, 'The International Legal System as a Constitution' in Jeffrey L Dunoff and Joel P Trachtman (eds), *Ruling the World? Constitutionalism, International Law and Global Governance* (Cambridge University Press 2008) 69, 96; Armin von Bogdandy, 'Founding Principles' in Armin von Bogdandy and Jürgen Bast (eds), *Principles of European Constitutional Law* (Hart 2009) 11, 51; Mark Bevir, *Democratic Governance* (Princeton University Press 2010) 270.

3. THE WAY FORWARD

A. Philosophical Foundations of the Need for Political Accountability

> L[e] présence [des AAIs] est aujourd'hui devenue si habituelle qu'on ne s'interroge plus sur leur nature juridique et leur légitimité, ... A tort car, au-delà de leur existence, c'est de notre liberté qu'il s'agit.[116]

The legitimacy that an institution derives from its outputs or outcomes, from the procedures that it applies, from its accountability to the courts and from its participation in networks of peers, is valuable and even necessary to complement the more traditional forms of political accountability. None of these sources of legitimacy, however, are sufficiently comparable to the legitimacy that originates from political accountability to serve as a genuine substitute. More specifically, a purpose-oriented approach to accountability and legitimacy reveals that only political accountability can ensure that decisions serve the 'public' or 'general' interest. As a contribution on the accountability of independent regulatory agencies argued: '[t]he only way to strengthen the effect of accountability is to bring politics and democratic values back into the regulatory process'.[117]

Some authors, rather than placing their trust in one of the above-mentioned alternatives, suggest a combination of two or more. The existence of many diffuse mechanism of supervision and control would assure accountability.[118] This 'strength-in-numbers' argument, however, is not convincing either: it still denies the need for one source of legitimacy for which no substitutes exist: that of political representation. Black adopts the view that different 'legitimacy communities' exist with diverging demands as to what makes an institution (and a regulator

---

116 Jean-Philippe Feldman, 'Les "autorités administratives indépendantes" sont-elles légitimes? Sur les AAI en général et le Conseil supérieur de l'audiovisuel en particulier' [2010] Receuil Dalloz 2852, 2852.

117 Giorgia Nesti, 'Strengthening the Accountability of Independent Regulatory Agencies: From Performance Back to Democracy' [2016] Comparative European Politics 1, 3.

118 See, for instance, Leigh Hancher and Pierre Larouche, 'The Coming of Age of EU Regulation of Network Industries and Services of General Economic Interest' in Paul Craig and Grainne de Búrca (eds), *The Evolution of EU Law* (Oxford University Press 2011) 743, 775; Dawn Oliver, 'Regulation, Democracy and Democratic Oversight in the UK' in Dawn Oliver, Tony Prosser and Richard Rawlings (eds), *The Regulatory State: Constitutional Implications* (Oxford University Press 2010) 243, 251.

particularly) legitimate. She therefore dismisses Scott's 'extended accountability' model, 'in which different types of accountability can be substituted for another should one of them fail'. 'Substituting accountability to a political forum with an audit, for example, may be more effective in functional terms (e.g. in ensuring financial prudence and probity), but in terms of the organisation's legitimacy the substitution might be acceptable to some, deeply unacceptable to others.'[119]

The problem with the alleged alternatives for political accountability discussed in this chapter is that the central agents for each of these alleged alternatives (experts, stakeholders, judges or peers) lack the ability or quality to decide on questions of policy. Chapter 3 concluded that the core concern behind the trend of 'national restraint' in democratic terms was precisely to ensure that administrative decisions with a political dimension are embedded in the system of representative democracy. When, however, do decisions involve a political component? When do they require an opinion of what constitutes 'the public interest'? In this respect, regulatory theory disagrees with the political philosophy underlying the democratic principles and procedures anchored in most modern Constitutions.

Majone's theory of regulatory governance acknowledges the link between the definition of policies on the one hand and the process of majority voting on the other. He sees this link, however, as applying exclusively to decisions on redistribution of income and wealth. Regulatory decisions, the author argues, do not involve questions of redistribution, they are concerned with achieving efficiency, which is a matter of single preferable outcomes that have to be identified by experts.[120] Certainly, he admits that regulatory policies have redistributive consequences, but submits that redistribution is not an objective that the regulator should actively pursue.[121] Regulatory theory thus adopts a narrow conception of what is 'political' or what constitutes 'the general interest' and argues that only in the case of redistributive purposes should decisions be taken under the scrutiny of elected representatives. There is, however, no evidence that the primacy of elected principles that is upheld by modern Constitutions extends only to cases with redistributive consequences. Some authors, moreover, argue that regulatory decisions can

[119] Julia Black, 'Constructing and Contesting Legitimacy and Accountability in Polycentric Regulatory Regimes', LSE Law, Society and Economy Working Papers 2/2008, 28.

[120] Giandomenico Majone, 'Regulatory Legitimacy' in Giandomenico Majone and Pio Baake (eds), *Regulating Europe* (Routledge 1996) 284, 294.

[121] ibid 284–295.

have redistributive effects,[122] which is acknowledged by Majone as well. Gilardi suggests that all decisions, including those made by independent regulators, have some Pareto-inefficient components, which means that the actors of representative democracy remain relevant.[123]

Seventeenth- and eighteenth-century political philosophy, on the other hand, did not primarily link the need for representative government to matters of redistribution, but to the idea of coercive power. Characteristic of the state is that it has a monopoly on the instrument of unilateral decisions that bind citizens without their consent. Unilateral obligation is the exclusive prerogative of the state. However, the administration is subject to a prohibition on arbitrariness: it can only use its powers with the aim of pursuing the general interest, as defined in the legislation that it applies or executes. The right to enact this legislation and, consequently, to define the general interest, is conferred on representatives of the people via periodical elections. They decide on the *reasons* for which coercive administrative powers can be used and, thus, on the policy that underlies them.

This touches upon the very core of European conceptions of democracy and on the theories of political philosophers such as Locke and Rousseau. Rousseau's notorious work *The Social Contract* (*Du Contrat Social*) revolves around two central notions: legitimacy and freedom. Rousseau more precisely strived to find 'a morally and rationally justified basis for rule and organization'.[124] His work sought a legitimation for the deprival of a person's freedom by the authorities of the state. Rousseau found this legitimation in the expression of the 'general will'. The definition of this 'general will' had to remain an exclusive prerogative for the 'Sovereign', a collective body created by means of a voluntary act of association by the state's citizens. Precisely because of this agreement, the Sovereign has the legitimacy to make laws that are binding for all citizens. 'Since no man has a natural authority over his fellow, and force creates no right, we must conclude that conventions form the basis of all legitimate authority among men', Rousseau proclaimed.[125] Although

---

[122] See e.g. Cosmo Graham, *Regulating Public Utilities: A Constitutional Approach* (Hart Publishing 2000), 26–27; Tony Prosser, *The Regulatory Enterprise – Government, Regulation and Legitimacy* (Oxford University Press 2010) 6–7.

[123] Fabrizio Gilardi, *Delegation in the Regulatory State. Independent Regulatory Agencies in Western Europe* (Edward Elgar Publishing 2008) 25–26.

[124] Nicholas Dent, *Rousseau* (Routledge 2005) 126.

[125] Beginning of Book I, Chapter IV, English translation via http://oll.libertyfund.org/. Bertram, interpreting this paragraph in the light of the similar

there is much debate and controversy about the definition of this 'Sovereign' in Rousseau's work, he denominates the collectivity of citizens who constitute the Sovereign as the People, thus defending popular sovereignty. Rousseau argued that the vote of the majority always binds all other citizens, since this follows from the contract itself.[126]

Even though Rousseau has definitely influenced Europe's history in terms of citizens' claim to popular sovereignty, he was not the father of modern representative democracy. On the contrary: his writings suggest that the entire collectivity of citizens should sanction each and every law and do not regard lawmaking by representation as legitimate.[127] It was Immanuel Kant, whose political philosophy was to an important extent inspired by Rousseau's, who contended that 'the sovereignty of the general will has to be alienable and must be seen by those who seen themselves participating in the general will in the legitimate government'.[128] Throughout time, systems of representative democracy have increasingly been defended against more radical ideas on popular sovereignty and direct democracy. Contemporary sovereignty literature ascertains that, in a system of representative government, '[t]he will expressed by the representatives is presumed to be the expression of the general will and this is an absolute presumption, which can never be rebutted'.[129]

John Locke, whose *Two Treatises of Government* preceded Rousseau's work, situated the need for a social contract in the protection of every person's right to property. His notion of property, however, is a broad one

---

theories of Hobbes and Locke, paraphrases it as follows: 'We are born free and equal in the sense that no person has by nature the right to command any other person nor the duty to submit to the commands of another. There is no natural hierarchy in the human species, no alpha-male whom the rest of us have to put up with as the one in charge. Human beings are normally endowed with enough reason to make them adequate as masters of themselves and need not, and should not, submit to the authority of another.' (Cristopher Bertram, *Rousseau and the Social Contract* (Routledge 2003) 43).

[126] Book IV, Chapter II. On Rousseau and majority rule, see also Christopher D Wraight, *Rousseau's The Social Contract: A Reader's Guide* (Continuum 2008) 58.

[127] ibid 109.

[128] Howard Williams, 'Kant on the Social Contract' in David Boucher and Paul Kelly (eds), *The Social Contract from Hobbes to Rawls* (Routledge 1994) 134.

[129] Michel Troper, 'Sovereignty' in Michel Rosenfeld and András Sajó (eds), *The Oxford Handbook of Comparative Constitutional Law* (Oxford University Press 2012) 350, 366.

and includes a person's life, health, liberty and possessions.[130] Similarly to Rousseau, Locke argues that it is precisely to protect this property that people agree to relinquish it partially, by accepting the authority of the state. For Locke, consent is what justifies that men become subject to the political power of others and 'put on the bonds of Civil Society'.[131] The social contract to which the members of a community have agreed 'assigns to its numerical majority a *right* to make decisions … which are binding on the minority'.[132]

This focus of the social contract philosophers on the value of personal freedom as being central to (representative) democracy is adopted by contemporary authors as well. Von Bogdandy has argued that 'the phenomenon of one-sided public power [is] as the heart of every constitutional order'.[133] For Oliver, democratic oversight of regulation 'is an issue because regulation involves the limitation of freedom of activity in areas – often but not only areas of economic activity – that have a potentially large impact on the public interest or on the interests of particular individuals and enterprises'.[134]

Interestingly, in accounts of representative democracy that focus on coercive powers, the principle of democracy sometimes transcends its nature of an abstract meta value and becomes something of an individual right. A focus on the individual as the primary addressee of democratic legitimacy, can, however, be used as an argument against representative democracy as well. Legal subjects who are directly affected by coercive measures may indeed, as individuals, prefer other actors, such as experts in APBs, above elected representatives as legitimizers. It could be argued that economic actors, who are subject to decisions taken by regulatory bodies that directly address them, are perfectly happy with (only) experts as decision makers. Such an argument in favour of insulation from representative democracy, however, would be flawed, since the reasons or the policies behind coercive measures are part of a larger political agenda, in which different measures that serve the public interest are

130 See A J Pyle, *Locke* (Polity 2013) 154.

131 Inspired by the citation of *Two Treatises of Government* 330–331 in A J Pyle, *Locke* (Polity 2013) 156.

132 Willmoore Kendall, *John Locke and the Doctrine of Majority Rule* (University of Illinois Press 1965) 112.

133 Armin von Bogdandy, 'Founding Principles' in Armin von Bogdandy and Jürgen Bast (eds), *Principles of European Constitutional Law* (Hart 2009) 11, 24.

134 Dawn Oliver, 'Regulation, Democracy and Democratic Oversight in the UK' in Dawn Oliver, Tony Prosser and Richard Rawlings (eds), *The Regulatory State: Constitutional Implications* (Oxford University Press 2010) 243, 243.

coordinated. Government policies are indeed interdependent and, in order to assure that they do not conflict, but – on the contrary – work together, it is important that elected representatives do not renounce parts of their policy-making power.

In sum: not only decisions with a redistributive effect, but all decisions that produce legal effects and that involve the exercise of discretionary powers by APBs require some form of political input or accountability.[135] In modern democracies, policy making is to a large extent in the hands of the executive.[136] This means that policy is created when administrative bodies exercise their discretionary powers. Increasingly, the justification for governmental action, i.e. the policy behind it, is not expressed in legislation, voted directly by elected representatives, but is defined at the micro level, for instance when APBs make administrative decisions. Consequently, as Rose-Ackermann and Perroud point out, 'the policy-making process in the executive and in independent agencies is ultimately a political one'.[137]

Most of the APBs that are subject to the trend of 'EU impulse' described in Chapter 2 enjoy important coercive powers, which involve discretion. The European liberalization directives in the field of economic regulation, for instance, require that NRAs are entrusted with certain powers to impose obligations on the regulated parties. Pursuant to article 37(4) of Directive 2009/72 for the electricity market, the regulatory authority should have a power to issue binding decisions on electricity undertakings (a), to impose any necessary and proportionate measures to promote effective competition and ensure the proper functioning of the market (b), and to impose effective, proportionate and dissuasive penalties on electricity undertakings not complying with their obligations

---

135 See also Jacint Jordana, Andrea C Bianculli and Xavier Fernández-i-Marin, 'When Accountability Meets Regulation' in Andrea C Bianculli, Xavier Fernández-i-Marin and Jacint Jordana (eds), *Accountability and Regulatory Governance* (Palgrave Macmillan 2014) 1, 7, where the need for (democratic) accountability is linked to coercion.

136 See e.g. Susan Rose-Ackerman and Thomas Perroud, 'Policymaking and Public Law in France: Public Participation, Agency Independence, and Impact Assessment' [2013] Colum. J. Eur. L. 225, 227.

137 ibid 233–234. This is also because broad and general policy goals can often be achieved in a number of ways and all of these ways constitute political options as well. See e.g. David Richards and Martin Smith, 'The Tensions of Political Control and Administrative Autonomy: from NPM to a Reconstituted Westminster Model' in Tom Christensen and Per Lægreid (eds), *Autonomy and Regulation, Coping with Agencies in the Modern State* (Edward Elgar Publishing 2006) 181, 185.

under the Directive or any relevant legally binding decisions of the regulatory authority or of the Agency, or to propose that a competent court impose such penalties (d). Similar provisions occur in article 41(4) of Directive 2009/73 for gas.[138] The Framework Directive contains a chapter on the tasks of NRAs responsible for the field of electronic communications, but does not as such anchor an abstract list of the powers that they should be invested with in order to perform these tasks. However, specific articles do point to coercive powers. An example is found in article 13b, stipulating that Member States shall ensure that, in order to implement their tasks regarding security and integrity of networks and services, competent national regulatory authorities have the power to issue binding instructions to undertakings providing public communications networks or publicly available electronic communications services. Moreover, all NRAs (including those for the railway sector) should be invested with the power to issue a binding decision in the context of their tasks of dispute resolution.[139] Chapter 4 demonstrated that the exercise of some of the most important of these regulatory powers is not limited to the strict application of rules, but involves making discretionary assessments. Pursuant to article 58 of the Data Protection Regulation, each supervisory authority is invested with a number of investigative and corrective powers. The latter include, for instance, the imposition of temporary or definitive bans on processing or of administrative fines.

B. The Potential of Balanced Solutions for Political Supervision and Accountability of National Regulatory and Supervisory Bodies

> A main challenge is how agency autonomy and democratic accountability can be made into complementary and mutually reinforcing rather than competing values.[140]

There is a common concern in many European democracies that matters of policy definition are entrusted to APBs that are increasingly insulated from political influence. At the same time, EU legislation increasingly advocates the independence of national supervisors, particularly in the

---

[138] See also recitals 37 and 33 of the respective directives.

[139] Article 37(11) Directive 2009/72; article 41(11) Directive 2009/73; article 20(1) Framework Directive; article 56(9) Directive 2012/34.

[140] Tom Christensen and Per Lægreid, 'Agencification and Regulatory Reforms' in Tom Christensen and Per Lægreid (eds), *Autonomy and Regulation, Coping with Agencies in the Modern State* (Edward Elgar Publishing 2006) 8, 29.

fields of economic regulation and data protection. The ECJ, moreover, does not seem inclined to meet Member States' concerns by giving a mild interpretation to the independence requirements in the directives. This chapter has assessed the value of some alternatives for political accountability that have been suggested in the literature. It concluded that the various sources of administrative legitimacy discerned in modern literature constitute a complementary system. For most government decisions (and especially regulatory decisions), none of these sources can be put aside or replaced entirely by (one of) the others.

This chapter subsequently assessed the circumstances under which political accountability via representative, majoritarian institutions is an essential aspect of public accountability. It contrasted regulatory theory, which attaches central importance to the redistributive effects of administrative decisions, with the political philosophy of Rousseau and Locke, which focuses on the definition of the 'general will' by the (majority of the) people as a legitimizing device for coercive measures. This philosophy underlies the rules, principles and procedures of representative democracy and political accountability in most modern Constitutions. Many of the APBs discussed in Chapter 2 possess coercive powers and make discretionary assessments. The insulation of the contents and justifications for these decisions from the influence of representative democracy is problematic.

The diagnosis is clear, but what is the proper remedy? The purpose of this section is to launch some ideas on whether, to what extent and how the valid aspirations underlying the trend of EU impulse can be reconciled with the requirement of political accountability. Arrangements of political accountability should be well thought through and tailored to the specificities of the institution and to the task at hand. A 'one-size-fits-all' solution does not exist. Special importance should be attached to the reasons or goals behind requirements of political autonomy underlying the trend of 'EU impulse', insofar as they are valid, reasonable and evidence-based. Chapter 2 concluded that time consistency as conceived by the credibility theory is at odds with the essential alterability of government policy. Moreover, a first, tentative empirical study on market players' preferences revealed that the degree of independence required also seems unnecessarily far reaching to meet the concerns of market players or investors in terms of regulatory stability, which is the ultimate goal behind the EU requirements. More importantly, market players themselves see only a limited correlation between the political independence of regulators on the one hand and continuity or stability in regulatory matters on the other. The expert motive and the conflict of interest motive, however, respond to real concerns and constitute valid reasons for granting a degree of political autonomy to the supervisors subject to EU impulse. Both of these concerns justify the establishment of APBs in the areas of economic regulation and human rights monitoring, adjudication or implementation. Nevertheless, autonomy knows many degrees. Definitely, expert decision making in technical matters as well as avoiding conflicts of interest require a certain, and perhaps a substantial, degree of political autonomy. The question, however, is whether these concerns really exclude all forms of political supervision or influence. The following paragraphs present the results of interview research that aims to demonstrate that the opposite is true.

a. Reconciling autonomy and expertise

In both Flanders and the Netherlands, APBs established for reasons of expertise have traditionally been made subject to a form of political supervision that can ultimately result in an annulment of a decision. The Flemish EVAs in public law form, established pursuant to the KDBB, are subject to so-called 'administrative oversight', which gives ministers the power to annul their decisions (article 23 KDBB). For the Dutch ZBOs, a power of annulment has been anchored in article 22 KWZBO. Both EVAs and ZBOs are often established for reasons of expertise. Both the Flemish and the Dutch framework legislation have not deemed an annulment power as such irreconcilable with this rationale. In France, the power of annulment is part of the system of *tutelle*, applied to *agences* or *établissements publics*. International literature uses concepts such as 'quashing', 'cancellation' or 'nullification' to refer to mechanisms that are identical or similar.[141] Veto powers qualify as traditional sanctions in an accountability relationship.[142]

An annulment power locates (the possibility of) political input on the level of the actual decisions taken by the APBs. Most theories on 'accountability' regard the presence of a sanctioning mechanism as crucial. A more positive view on the element of 'sanction' in accountability arrangements is Harlow and Rawlings' condition of 'reparation and

---

[141] Gerard C Rowe, 'Administrative Supervision of Administrative Action in the European Union' in Herwig C H Hofmann and Alexander H Türk (eds), *Legal Challenges in EU Administrative Law: Towards an Integrated Administration* (Edward Elgar Publishing 2009) 179, 199.

[142] Mark Bovens, 'Analysing and Assessing Accountability: A Conceptual Framework' (2007) 13(4) European Law Journal 447, 452 with reference to Kaare Strøm, 'Parliamentary Democracy and Delegation' in Kaare Strøm, Wolfgang C Müller and Torbjörn Bergman (eds), *Delegation and Accountability in Parliamentary Democracies* (Oxford University Press, 2008) 55, 62.

effective redress', mentioned earlier in this chapter. The idea is that political principals should be able to compel APBs to take their input into account and to reconsider their decisions accordingly. This does not mean that political principals should have the means to 'punish' APBs for non-compliance, but that they can interfere whenever the decision made or the solution reached does not comply with the policies that they pursue. One of the major problems produced by the current EU legislation on independent supervisors is indeed that it allows for the definition of general policy guidelines, but does not provide, nor seems to allow, for any political remedy if NRAs or DPAs do not comply with these guidelines. Some authors, advocates of strong and independent NRAs and DPAs, are radically against forms of supervision that allow for interference on the level of the discretionary powers exercised in the actual decision-making process. According to Lavrijssen and Ottow, elected politicians are entitled (only) to issue policy guidelines that:

> relate to policy choices that are so general that they do not cause clear controversies among the different market players and do not have direct economic consequences for the different stakeholders ... However, the choice for a specific tariff method, the design of regulatory remedies, and the trade-off between different regulatory objectives, is the responsibility of the NRAs.[143]

Such an approach reduces the majoritarian institutions of representative democracy to oracles that from time to time confirm and remind APBs of some general principles and values about which hardly any meaningful disagreement exists. It is precisely on the level of representative democracy, however, that controversial policy issues should be debated and difficult trade-offs should be made. It is up to democratic institutions to overcome such important societal antitheses. Even Majone is not a proponent of broad discretionary mandates for regulatory bodies: this hampers their legitimacy, because it prevents them from being properly evaluated on the basis of their results or outcomes.[144] Mechanisms of supervision like those often applied in Belgium and the Netherlands allow for a political principal to become involved in the actual decision-making process: to give 'political input'. At the same time, they constitute a mechanism of accountability, where the APB (the actor who

[143] Saskia Lavrijssen and Annetje Ottow, 'Independent Supervisory Authorities: A Fragile Concept' (2012) 39(4) Legal Issues of Economic Integration 419, 436.

[144] Giandomenico Majone, 'Regulatory Legitimacy' in Giandomenico Majone and Pio Baake (eds), *Regulating Europe* (Routledge 1996) 284, 294.

takes the final decision) answers to the forum (the political principal) about the expediency of its acts and the extent to which it has taken prior political input of general nature into account. They furthermore respond to the criterion of 'reparation and effective redress' (Harlow and Rawlings) or 'amendatory accountability' (Turpin[145]).[146]

The interviews presented in the following paragraphs were carried out to find out whether such powers of supervision carry the characteristics necessary to strike a fair balance between the importance of expertise through autonomy and that of democratic (political) supervision. In theory, an annulment power has some promising characteristics. First, it does not allow for censorship. The independent authority issues its decision and is able to enforce it without the need for prior consent. Supervision takes place *ex post facto*. Political involvement is possible, but not compulsory. Secondly, it does not allow for substitution. The APB itself takes a new decision after annulment. An annulment gives the political principal a right to veto the decision, but does not give it the power to replace the decision with its own.

All of this, however, is based on theoretical reasoning; on a rational assessment of the desirable characteristics of a system of supervision that is supposed to fulfil a conciliatory role in the relationship between experts and politicians. But does the theory pass the test of practice? In practice, informal mechanisms could make experts in APBs feel obliged or inclined to 'give in'. The question consequently arises whether, to what extent and under what circumstances a power of annulment is either detrimental to, or reconcilable with, the role of experts in practice. Possible deficiencies can be traced by talking to the experts in the APBs that are subject to this form of supervision. Before discussing the results of these interviews, we will say something about their design.

b. Design

The aim of the interviews was to gauge the impact of political supervision in the form of an annulment power on APBs and on the role

---

145 Colin Turpin, 'Ministerial Responsibility' in Dawn Oliver and Jeffrey Jowell (eds), *The Changing Constitution* (Clarendon Press 1994) 109, 138.

146 See also the definition of 'supervision' in Gerard C Rowe, 'Administrative Supervision of Administrative Action in the European Union' in Herwig C H Hofmann and Alexander H Türk (eds), *Legal Challenges in EU Administrative Law: Towards an Integrated Administration* (Edward Elgar Publishing 2009) 179, 190: '"Supervision" is conceived of as a range of measures and actions extending from the structuring and steering of decision-making in advance through the measures for correction and error after the event.'

played by the expertise or practical experience acquired by their members in particular. The central questions that guided the interviews were:

> How does the instrument of annulment function in practice? Do the experts that are under supervision regard it as an impediment for their work? Does it frustrate technically desirable decision making? Is it often used? Is it used as a blunt instrument, or is its use preceded by dialogue, consultation … ?

The interviews were semi-structured. All the APBs that were interviewed had in common that at least one of the reasons for their establishment had been the need for expertise or the wish for participation by stakeholders for reasons of giving sufficient leeway to experience-related knowledge. Eight Dutch ZBOs were interviewed, one Belgian federal APB and five Flemish APBs. The sample contains a good mix of APBs relying on scientific or technical expertise on the one hand, and more experience-based forms of expertise on the other hand (and, often, the APBs actually combined both). It moreover contains APBs operating in different sectors. Even though most regulatory bodies in Belgium and the Netherlands are not or no longer subject to the possibility of annulment (often precisely because of EU legislation), the sample contains at least one body with a clear regulatory remit. Some APBs had been established fairly recently, others had a longer history.

Since it was the course of the process of administrative oversight and its effects that needed further investigation, the primary criterion for the person of the interviewee was his or her familiarity with, or involvement in, the procedures of administrative oversight. For that reason, the APBs were not specifically asked to provide an appointment with a staff member of their legal service or with a member of the board per se. It was left up to them to make a suggestion as to who would be able to provide the most valuable information about this topic. Consequently, people with a variety of backgrounds (lawyers, political scientists, economists) and different positions in the organization (managing directors, heads of the legal service) were interviewed. Since the interviewees would be asked about their relationships with their political principals, promising anonymity seemed the only way to ensure that the answers would be as sincere as possible.

c. Results

All interviewees agreed that the expertise or practical experience of their management and staff was of (considerable) importance for the satisfactory functioning of their decision-making process. One interviewee pointed out that the heterogeneous composition of the board of directors of the APB, involving different actors active in the sector regulated by the APB, gave the decision-making process a considerable added value.

Of all 14 APBs interviewed, only one had ever actually been confronted with an annulment by the competent minister. This, moreover, had only occurred a single time. The annulment was not pronounced because the minister discerned a violation of the law, but rather resulted from a disagreement on the policy adopted/the discretion exercised by the APB in a particular decision. Of all APBs interviewed, this APB was probably the one that relied most on scientific, technical expertise *sensu stricto*. The disagreement between the APB and the minister was consequently related to a discrepancy between what the APB deemed best from a technical viewpoint on the one hand, and what the minister regarded as expedient from a political viewpoint on the other. The annulment decision had been properly reasoned so that, according to the interviewee, it was clear to the APB why the minister had considered it necessary to use his veto. Another APB had been confronted with a Government representative who had exercised his power of suspension, but the competent minister had subsequently decided to let the decision pass and not to exercise his power of annulment. Moreover, the representative's veto revolved around a legal problem rather than a policy-related issue.

Each and every one of the interviewees pointed out that, in practice, the relationship between the APB and the minister's cabinet or department was one of formal as well as informal debate and consultation. All APBs interviewed agreed that the habit of informal consultation was key to the autonomy of the agency, since it prevented administrative oversight from being a one-sided event and precluded a culture of conflict. Most of the APBs seemed to perceive their relationship with the political principal as a partnership rather than a relationship based on a sequence of individual actions from both sides. The informal consultation between the APBs and the ministries could take various forms. Some APBs systematically contacted the ministry for important or possibly politically sensitive issues. One interviewee pointed out that important, non-routine dossiers were never put on the board's agenda without a prior informal consultation of the ministry. Another interviewee pointed out that the reason that his/her APB had never been confronted with an annulment decision was exactly the culture of constructive dialogue. According to this person, consultation between the APB and the ministry could effectively lead to decisions of better quality. Another interviewee pointed out that all strategic decisions that reached the agenda of the board of directors would already have been discussed with the ministry, so that the minister would never be faced with surprises. For this reason, it seemed quite improbable that an annulment would ever be pronounced, since possible points of disagreement would long have been – in the words of the interviewee – 'demined' through informal dialogue before the proposal reached the board's agenda.

Yet another interviewee pointed out that, on two or three occasions, they remembered receiving a telephone call from the ministry to inform the APB that the minister was not happy with a particular proposal. In those cases, the decision would either be postponed to a next meeting of the board, or there would be an exchange of arguments between the APB and the ministry. One of the interviewees declared that, as soon as there was a feeling of disagreement between the APB and the ministry, the latter would take the initiative to contact the minister or the head of the ministry itself. Another person declared that the APB strived for maximum transparency vis-à-vis the ministry, which created a feeling of trust and confidence. According to this interviewee, cases in which bad relationships existed between the ministry and an APB not infrequently resulted from a lack of transparency and deliberation. Another interviewee also declared that trust and deliberation were key in the relationship between the APB and its minister: for that reason, the APB would keep the ministry informed, especially when it expected decisions to cause political controversy. According to this interviewee, this attitude contributed to an understanding of each other's positions. However, this person also stressed that, in this process, everybody was free to express their opinion. The APB and the ministry did not always agree, but had up until then always succeeded in finding a solution on the basis of deliberation. The (Belgian) interviewee of the only APB that had been confronted with an annulment decision by the competent minister agreed with the suggestion that a statutory obligation of prior consultation between the experts within the agency and the political principal would be a positive legal innovation. 'As much dialogue as possible, has its advantages', the interviewee stressed. Yet another interviewee regarded consultation with the ministry as having a preventive function, signifying that differences in opinion would surface at an early stage and would be discussed in order to find a solution. One of the interviewees confirmed this attitude and spoke of 'conflict-avoiding behaviour'. Another interviewee would have preferred a lot more deliberation with the ministry than had been the case up until the date of the interview: this interviewee saw important advantages in the APB and ministry acting 'shoulder to shoulder' more often.

Most of the APBs assessed the current level of autonomy that they enjoyed in practice and the level of interference by the minister as quite satisfactory. For most APBs, the culture of consultation was key to this satisfaction. One interviewee acknowledged that sometimes finding a proper balance between the primacy of politics and the goals of the APB's board was not easy. Nevertheless, the interviewee declared that they understood that the APB had to live with the reality that its projects had to obtain political support and had to be politically viable. The interviewee pointed to one particular measure, which the APB had been wanting to take for some time now. Although the APB had been invested with the formal power to implement this measure (without prior approval by the minister), it was fully aware that this would create an open conflict, which it wished to avoid. Another interviewee declared that the APB could do its job in accordance with its own insights. In any case, the policies to be followed by the APB were to a large extent already established by politicians beforehand (via a management agreement). Apart from that, the expertise of the people working for the APB was sufficiently ensured in order to weigh on the decision-making process.

Yet another interviewee declared that the APB welcomed policy input, since it was fully aware that its function was essentially to execute policy and that everyone had to assume their own role. The interviewee was quite satisfied about how, through the constructive attitude of the Government's representative, who occasionally intervened to draw attention to a political concern, and the culture of informal consultation, it was ensured that politics and operational matters were in harmony. The same interviewee, however, pointed out that the evolution of more policy input *ex ante*, via rigid regulations, had started to reduce the discretion of the agency in an undesirable way. Another interviewee, however, regretted the lack of a management contract between their agency and the minister. According to this interviewee, such a contract would allow for the experts and the political principal to reach a clear agreement beforehand. Yet another interviewee pointed out that in their sector expertise and decision making on the basis of objective criteria were key, but, at the same time, the policy field in which the APB operated was one in which political involvement was indispensable and was high on the agenda of all political parties. Consequently, it was deemed very difficult to find a balance between autonomy and political interference. This interviewee, however, was also more in favour of policy input *ex ante*, via general directions and guidelines, which would allow for the APB to take into account political preferences in its decision-making process. The interviewee did not, however, discard the power of annulment that was currently applicable to his/her APB, but had preferred it to be applicable to the rule-making powers of the APB only (and not to its decisions with an individual scope). Because even the individual decisions of this APB sometimes entailed important political questions or even controversies, the legislature had, however, opted for a power of annulment extended to these individual decisions. The interviewee was of the opinion, however, that, in these individual cases, only technical and objective facts and criteria could play a role, which made political interference, via an annulment power or any other form of supervision inappropriate. An annulment of the general policy lines adopted by the APB via its rule-making powers was, however, deemed suitable. Another interviewee, on the other hand, defended the completely opposite solution, favouring policy input *ex ante* as far as its (quasi) rule-making powers were concerned, but not opposing the annulment power for decisions with an individual scope. Another interviewee observed that the criteria that their APB used to take decisions only concerned objective rules of quality anchored in legislation. However, because the outcome of this APB's decisions could affect the public interest, this interviewee deemed it appropriate that a possibility would be provided for the Government to interfere.

The interviewee of the one APB that had been confronted with an annulment decision declared that it was important that, in individual cases, political interference was absent and that the agency could, initially, give its own assessment and make a decision based on technical considerations. However, if the minister were of the opinion that, for policy reasons, another decision had to be taken, then the agency would accept this. 'After all, we live in a democracy', the interviewee concluded.

The APBs interviewed were also asked whether they regarded the mere existence of administrative oversight, i.e. the mere possibility or always-present threat that the minister could intervene, as an impediment to their free expertise-based decision making. In connection to that, they were asked whether the presence of the Government's representative, if applicable, during the board's meetings was an impediment to their free deliberation. The vast majority of them answered in the negative. One person explained that their APB maintained an open relationship with the ministry and that they felt free to express their own opinion, even if they knew that the minister did not agree. Another person described the role of general administrative oversight of the APB as 'an entirely marginal phenomenon'. The majority of the APBs indeed pointed out that the Government's representatives hardly ever intervened during the board's meetings. When they did, moreover, the aim was usually to draw attention to possible legal problems or impediments. One of the APBs pointed out that the Government's representative sometimes intervened to express the minister's political preferences or priorities, in order to make sure that the APB took these into account in its initial decision. However, the APB did not regard these interventions as orders or instructions, but rather as suggestions or questions for reflection. Another interviewee pointed out that, because the political goals that the APB had to pursue were fixed in a management agreement for a certain period of time, the Government's representative hardly ever interfered for policy reasons, except precisely when a difference of opinion arose about the interpretation of these pre-fixed policy goals. Yet another interviewee declared that, in theory, the mere existence of a power of annulment could have implied a feeling of threat, which could have led to a certain (implicit) influence. However, their APB had not adjusted its behaviour since the power of annulment had been introduced and the minister had not done so either, at least not to the extent that they had threatened the APB with the possibility of an annulment. However, the interviewee had noticed that, recently and under parliamentary pressure, the minister had felt inclined to interfere in individual cases to a greater extent, but via other (even non-statutory) instruments. The interviewee did not exclude that the existence of the annulment power in individual cases had made the minister feel more confident to do so. Another interviewee did not deem it impossible that the APB would 'explore the boundaries' of its decision-making power to a greater extent if the annulment power would not exist, although they did not genuinely regard it as a burden. Another interviewee, however, pointed out that '[the annulment power] is at most something that plays in the background. Simply: what will [the ministry] think? That is the most important question. Not because they swing a weapon that makes you afraid. That is not the way it works.'

One of the interviewees, when asked whether they perceived the annulment power as a 'sword of Damocles', replied:

> No, I even regard it as a positive thing. It simulates, it provokes a ZBO to be fully transparent in all phases. And that implies that, if the Government has the idea that things should be done differently than the ZBO has done them, it can express this concern in a very early phase. And it is just part of the work that we do, that a minister should have the possibility to say, at a given moment in time: I see this differently and take a different decision. I intervene and annul the decision that you have taken, as a ZBO.

d. Discussion

The interviews aimed to find out more about the actual effects of an annulment power as a form of political supervision of APBs. However, the interviews revealed that this power is hardly ever used. Only one interviewee could testify about what it meant to be faced with an annulment. The lack of testimony on the use of the annulment power, however, does not mean that the interviews did not lead to meaningful results. Both the APB that had been confronted with an annulment decision and the APBs that were now and then faced with remarks or objections by their ministry were understanding as to the need for this political interference. APBs are prepared to achieve solutions that are satisfactory from both a technical or experience-based viewpoint and from a political perspective. Not all APBs had an explicit opinion on what 'type' of political supervision they preferred. Some, however, had a specific preference for powers of prior approval above annulment powers, whereas others preferred it exactly the other way around. These preferences, however, seemed to have more to do with questions of efficiency than with the impact that these powers would have on their autonomy as experts.

The most notable conclusion that can be drawn is that there seems to be a great deal of preparedness from both the side of the APB and the side of ministries (as perceived by the APBs) to consult each other and to engage in a dialogue. This culture of consultation does not imply that the APBs submit themselves to their political principals and/or feel constrained in expressing their independent, expert opinions. In general, the relationship was characterized as one of mutual understanding and respect for each other's roles and concerns. Giving a power of supervision to political principals consequently does not have to lead to undue pressure or experts feeling unable to give an uncensored opinion. Sometimes, the APB feels that issues are politically sensitive and deems it best to contact the ministry before it makes a decision. In other cases, it becomes apparent that APBs and ministers have different opinions, in which case deliberation is intended to achieve a shared solution. Sometimes, the bodies themselves take the initiative to contact the ministry, sometimes the ministry consults the APB when such a decision is afoot. Gaining the trust of ministries was regarded as key, also in order to ensure that the APB kept its credibility and 'earned' its independence, so that it could perform its missions properly. Thatcher, having studied data on the use of powers to overturn decisions of certain APBs (IRAs) in Germany and the UK, comes to a similar conclusion. The author ascertains that these powers are hardly ever used either[147] and suggests that 'IRA members may have rationally anticipated their government's ability to wield controls, so that elected politicians in Europe do not even need to apply them. Instead, IRAs have engaged in positive exchange

[147] See Mark Thatcher, 'The Third Force? Independent Regulatory Agencies and Elected Politicians in Europe' 2005 18(3) Governance 347, 361–362.

relationships with governments – following their preferences and winning rewards'.[148]

Consultation and deliberation therefore seem to constitute crucial factors in the reconciliation of the expert's autonomy and the politician's right of supervision. At present, these processes, however, emerge in a spontaneous and rather informal manner. In the Netherlands, a minister who intends to use his annulment power vis-à-vis a ZBO is under a statutory obligation to consult. Pursuant to article 10:41 of the Algemene Wet Bestuursrecht (Awb – General Act Administrative Law), there can be no annulment unless the ZBO has been offered the opportunity of prior consultation (1) and the motivation of the annulment decision has to refer to the elements that have been brought forward during this consultation (2). Since most of the APBs interviewed regarded the practice of consultation and deliberation as one of the most important explanations for the fact that they had not yet been confronted with an annulment power, deliberation – as some expressed it – may have an important preventive function. Therefore, a statutory obligation of this type could have a lot of potential as an instrument to avoid annulment and to reach a mutual solution which fully respects the role of experts and political principals. As suggested above, the annulment power implies that experts and politicians need each other to reach a final solution, since neither has the power to force the other to accept a solution that they deem undesirable. Therefore, the annulment gives an incentive to cooperate. A compulsory, statutory, prior consultation may be able to speed up that process.

e. Intermediate conclusion

According to Marcou, regulation is a task that is 'shared' between regulators and politicians. On the basis of a comparative study of the regulatory function in various European countries carried out in 2006, the author concluded that, in the countries studied (among them Belgium, France, the Netherlands and the UK) there was a trend in the legislation applicable to regulatory bodies towards a reintroduction of political control in the light of democratic accountability.[149]

The model of political supervision that was investigated in the previous paragraphs has promising characteristics. Whereas experts are encouraged to take into account political concerns because they know that their

---

[148] ibid 365.

[149] Gérard Marcou, 'La notion juridique de régulation' [2006] AJDA 347, 353.

decision can be overturned, political principals also know that they can only veto particular decisions but cannot substitute the body's decision with their own. Both parties are dependent on each other's goodwill and cooperation, which may give them an incentive to act in a reasonable and constructive way. Admittedly, this could also result in paralysis. Delzangles, writing about the procedure of *homologation* in France (which gives ministers a right of veto with regard to the rules issued by some AAIs), suggests that legislatures should provide for procedural solutions to overcome situations in which no agreement is reached.[150]

The Belgian and Dutch model, of course, is not the only and overall-applicable valid configuration for the reconciliation of the democratic concerns outlined above and the need for expertise underlying the trend of 'EU impulse'. There are definitely other solutions conceivable that ensure that both representative democracy and expertise can play their own, distinct roles in administrative decision making in a positive and constructive way. If anything, this book aims to encourage further research as to proper ways of achieving precisely that goal. National legislatures, when designing a suitable model for supervision of these types of agencies, would be able to make better-informed decisions on matters of administrative organization if more such evidence were available. The same is true for the EU legislature, which would perhaps think differently about complete political insulation as a requirement for the independence of national supervisors. Proposals in this regard should also take into account the traditions of the Member States. In the UK, for instance, it is customary to entrust the competent minister or secretary of state with powers of 'approval', 'guidance' or 'direction'. In a recent contribution, the chief executive of Ofwat argued that 'strategic steers' and 'guidance' alongside other instruments of law and policy 'allow for a constructive dialogue between government and regulators that both facilitates and channels government interjections in ways that rightfully influence but do not compromise the exercise of regulators' discretion'.[151] In France, a power of *homologation* is common, especially with regard to AAIs' rule-making powers.

The results of the interviews with market players discussed in Chapter 2 revealed that they particularly value the expertise that IRAs embody. Regulatees expect expertise to play a decisive role in regulatory decision making. Satisfying that concern implies that the role of experts is

---

[150] Hubert Delzangles, 'L'indépendance de l'autorité de sûreté nucléaire, des progrès à envisager' [2013] Revue juridique de l'environnement 7, 25.

[151] Cathryn Ross, 'Independent Economic Regulation: A Tale of Two Paradoxes', Oxera Agenda November 2013.

somehow protected and that their assessments are not made subordinate to those of any other actors. Any mechanism for political accountability of APBs established for reasons of expertise should take that premise into account. Proposals of reconciliation should fully acknowledge the premise that both experts and politicians have their own, distinct roles to play in the process. They generate different 'products', i.e. expert opinions versus (reasonable and justified) political preferences. However, these products have to be combined in a single administrative decision. Because both expertise and political consent are equally indispensable ingredients of the solution, a 'reconciliation' cannot imply that, in the end, either experts or politicians 'win'. The final decision reached should meet the concerns of both. Mechanisms of political accountability should thus allow for politicians to have a final say in the policy underlying the decision, while at the same time ensuring that the decision remains technically appropriate and that experts remain the uncontested final judges of that.

Whichever power is given to the political principal, tailored and balanced forms of political input should aim to establish a form of equal partnership between regulatory bodies and experts. Such a form of supervision acknowledges the complexity of the decisions that APBs established for reasons of expertise make and that require different types of input to be equally represented and decisive for the final outcome. Deliberation between a minister and an APB does not have to be detrimental to, but can on the contrary strengthen, the latter's autonomy.[152] Since the ultimate decision should be both technically and politically desirable, dialogue between experts and politicians, in which both sides are invited to empathize with each other's viewpoints and to accept the reasonableness of each other's concerns, seems highly desirable.

f. Reconciling balanced forms of political input with the conflicts of interest rationale

Chapter 2 concluded that, apart from expertise, there is another important and valid concern behind the requirements for IRA independence in the European liberalization directives. In many European countries, government enterprises are still operating in the liberalized markets. Allowing for political interference in the regulatory process is said to entail a risk that political principals will use their powers to the sole or primary

---

[152] Philip Norton (Lord Norton of Louth), 'Regulating the Regulatory State' (2004) 57(4) Parliam Aff 785, 794.

benefit of that enterprise. As far as DPAs are concerned, it may be the government itself that is subject to the supervision of these bodies. Consequently, political principals may want to interfere with DPAs' decisions with the sole aim of avoiding 'naming and shaming'. Moreover, conflicts of interest can result from powers of political supervision even when the bodies under the scrutiny of the APB are private parties, rather than government bodies. In the ECJ's Grand Chamber judgment in *Commission/Germany*, the court addressed the possible conflicts of interest that could arise when government control is exercised on the DPAs responsible for the private sector.

To what extent are instruments of political supervision, even if they are moderate and tailored, reconcilable with these concerns of avoiding conflicts of interest? The problem with accepting the political isolation of IRAs and DPAs for reasons of avoiding conflicts of interest is that one could easily identify other policy domains in which similar risks of conflicting interests arise. Reconciling interests is in a sense part of the core business of governments.[153] Administrative bodies, in their decision-making processes, constantly balance interests on two levels. On the one hand, the individual interests of those who are 'governed' or 'administered' sometimes conflict with what is deemed expedient in the light of the general interest. On the other hand, different aspects of the general interest may interfere with each other. Conflicting interests, moreover, are especially central to EU administrative law, where non-discrimination between citizens and businesses from the various Member States is essential to ensure a properly functioning internal market. Domestic administrations that implement or oversee the application of EU law have to set aside national interests to achieve that aim. It would be unthinkable to isolate all administrative services that implement EU law from the influence of the political executive in order to preclude any undue influence from domestic concerns. In other words: political isolation is not the proper answer to the problem of conflicting interests.

What can be done to avoid conflicting interests from affecting fair and legal decision making then? First of all, EU citizens or businesses who feel that they are being discriminated against can have recourse to judicial procedures at the national and – ultimately, via the procedure of preliminary questions – EU level. These have been put in place precisely to ensure that EU law is enforced effectively and without discrimination. Secondly, modern administrative law embodies specific legal remedies

---

[153] See e.g. Jean-Bernard Auby, 'Conflits d'intérêts et droit administratif' [2010] Droit Administratif étude 24.

against government decisions that are inspired by impermissible considerations. The exercise of statutory forms of supervision typically results in an administrative decision,[154] which, pursuant to the rule of law doctrine, should also be subject to judicial review. In Belgium, the Netherlands, France and the UK, administrative acts can be challenged before the courts because they are allegedly compromised by diversion of power (*détournement de pouvoir*) or inspired by improper purposes. Diversion of power or improper purposes exist when a decision is not inspired by the public or general interest, but by ulterior motives. A minister entrusted with a veto power vis-à-vis an NRA should only use this power to act in the light of the goals that are served by regulation. A ministerial veto of a righteous decision to impose a fine on the Government's incumbent in order to avoid a deterioration of the financial situation of this company consequently constitutes diversion of power. In the same way, the annulment of a decision taken by a DPA, not because the authority has failed to strike a proper balance between the right to the protection of private life and the right to free movement of data, but merely because the commercial interests of a partner in a public–private partnership are affected and the Government wishes to protect these,[155] qualifies as diversion of power.[156]

Admittedly, it is difficult to prove diversion of power or improper purposes, which is precisely the reason why this ground for review is not often applied.[157] Other general principles or guarantees of administrative law, however, enforceable before the administrative courts, target conflicting interests as well. An example is the principle of impartiality or unbiased decision making. The duty to give reasons, as a procedural requirement, can, moreover, reinforce claims based on improper purposes, since it allows the judge to assess whether or not it is plausible that proper motives, related to regulatory goals, have inspired the political principal to use his power of intervention. An enhanced duty to give reasons seems advisable in such situations. If the political principal is

---

[154] See e.g. Gerard C Rowe, 'Administrative Supervision of Administrative Action in the European Union' in Herwig C H Hofmann and Alexander H Türk (eds), *Legal Challenges in EU Administrative Law: Towards an Integrated Administration* (Edward Elgar Publishing 2009) 179, 205.

[155] This was one of the situations put forward by the ECJ in *Commission/ Germany*.

[156] See also Sjoerd E Zijlstra, 'Zbo's, marktautoriteiten en regelgevende bevoegdheid' [2005] *Tijdschrift voor Ondernemingsbestuur* 2, 4.

[157] E.g. Jean-Bernard Auby, 'Conflits d'intérêts et droit administratif' [2010] Droit Administratif étude 24, para 56.

obliged to justify his decision to intervene in the light of general policy objectives predefined by the legislature and makes it plausible that an intervention was indeed necessary for reasons of general interest linked to regulatory objectives, it will be easier for the court to determine whether there has been diversion of power.

In sum: administrative law does not need non-majoritarian institutions to protect decision-making processes from undue political considerations. Political oversight of APBs that supervise government enterprises or institutions, however, has to be designed in such a way that intervention for improper purposes is prevented or can easily be detected.

g. The question of the appropriate political principal

Finally, the question arises who is eligible to qualify as 'the political principal'. In all four systems studied, powers of political supervision such as annulment, veto, prior approval, homologation, direction, guidance etc. are embedded in the system of political ministerial responsibility. Ministers supervise APBs and are in turn held accountable by Parliament. The ultimate goal of political supervision of APBs is indeed scrutiny by elected representatives.

However, the efficacy of political ministerial responsibility is increasingly criticized in parliamentary systems and there is an important trend in the literature to promote direct control by parliaments.[158] The question arises whether parliaments themselves could indeed organize a system of political accountability without involving middlemen such as ministers. Especially in the UK, proposals have been formulated and initiatives have been taken to make APBs in general, and independent regulators in particular, subject to direct parliamentary supervision. To that end, parliamentary select committees have been entrusted with tasks of oversight and monitoring of regulators.[159] Departmental select committees can request that regulators appear before them, but cannot force them to change their policies, although they can make recommendations.

---

[158] E.g. Margot Aelen, *Beginselen van goed markttoezicht* (Boom Juridische Uitgevers 2014) 449; Jean-Pierre Duprat, 'La soumission des régulateurs à régulation' [2006] AJDA 1203; Gabriel Eckert, 'L'indépendance des autorités de régulation économique à l'égard du pouvoir politique' [2012] RFAP 629, 640–641; Aalt W Heringa, and Luc F M Verhey, 'Independent Agencies and Political Control' in Tom Zwart and Luc Verhey (eds), *Agencies in European and Comparative Law* (Intersentia 2003) 155, 167–169.

[159] Dawn Oliver, 'Regulation, Democracy and Democratic Oversight in the UK' in Dawn Oliver, Tony Prosser and Richard Rawlings (eds), *The Regulatory State: Constitutional Implications* (Oxford University Press 2010) 243, 252–253

Chapter 3 revealed that constitutional objections may exist to parliaments questioning civil servants or members of the boards of APBs directly and that this debate has also emerged with regard to APBs. In the Netherlands, for instance, it is assumed that Parliament is entitled to pose questions to the directors of regulatory bodies, but the latter are – except in the case of a parliamentary inquiry – not obliged to answer.[160] More importantly, however, parliamentary committees controlling APBs in most Western countries seem to have in common that they have only few tools to hold APBs to account and – more precisely – that they usually lack formal sanctioning powers or powers of reparation and (effective) redress. 'Legislative committees have the right to seek information and explanations from members of the executive (*information*). They can also evaluate and make their recommendations *(discussion)* but lack the final power of *rectification*, except indirectly through the force of publicity and political pressure.'[161]

Whereas Parliaments are invested with a power to dismiss the Government or an individual minister, it is uncommon for parliamentary committees scrutinizing APBs to have similar powers vis-à-vis the boards of these bodies. As we have seen, the independence requirements emerging under the trend of EU impulse typically exclude board members from being dismissed for political reasons. Therefore, dismissal in this context cannot qualify as a sanction that is part of an arrangement of political accountability. The same is true for the power to abolish APBs: for those bodies of which the establishment is compulsory under supranational law, this possibility is no longer available for national parliaments. However, dismissal and abolishment are blunt instruments and therefore not necessarily desirable penalties. As Rawlings and Harlow argue, some form of 'reparation or redress' is sufficient for an accountability arrangement to be fully fledged. However, it is not common for parliamentary committees to have any such powers either. While there seem to be no practical objections against an elected President assuming

with reference to Tony Prosser, 'The Powers and Accountability of Agencies and Regulators' in David Feldman (ed), *English Public Law* (Oxford University Press 2009) 246–248; Julia Black, 'Calling Regulators to Account: Challenges, Capacities and Prospects' in Nicholas Bamforth and Peter Leyland (eds), *Accountability in the Contemporary Constitution* (Oxford University Press 2013) 354, 374ff.

[160] E.g. Saskia Lavrijssen, *Onafhankelijke mededingingstoezichthouders, regulerende bevoegdheden en de waarborgen voor good governance* (Boom Juridische uitgevers 2006) 96.

[161] R Richard Mulgan, *Holding Power to Account: Accountability in Modern Democracies* (Palgrave Macmillan 2003) 54–55.

these types of powers, this somehow seems different for an elected Parliament. The cumbersome structure of a parliament hardly seems to allow for the investment with supervisory powers such as the one explored above. Parliaments typically lack the administration and the tools to organize such systems of accountability.[162] '[In] relation to the final stage of *rectification*', Mulgan points out, 'the main role of the legislature is as an inducer rather than an enforcer.'[163] Some authors therefore argue for a system of parliamentary accountability of (specific types of) APBs that is closer to the US system, where Congress can, for instance, modify the content of certain rules enacted by independent agencies if these are deemed illegal or (politically) undesirable.[164] A rare example of such powers in Europe are the (veto) powers of Parliament vis-à-vis so-called secondary legislation in the UK.

Black refers to a statement made by the House of Commons Select Committee for Business and Enterprise with regard to a proposal to merge regulators and to make them subject to an accountability mechanism consisting of the submission of an annual report with subsequent scrutiny by a select committee. The committee, however, argued that select committees have no power of direction but only recommendatory power, signifying that they have 'no power to make either the government or the regulator think again'. The Committee concluded that only the Government had the resources and powers to monitor a regulator.[165]

Oliver has formulated a proposal for an intermediate form, which holds elements of direct control by Parliament and political ministerial responsibility. The author promotes the creation of a 'Standing Royal Commission on the Regulatory State'. The aim of such an expert commission and its contribution to the fulfilment of the principle of democracy would be that it informs Parliament, its committees, the government and the public

---

162 See e.g. Matthew Flinders, 'MPs and Icebergs: Parliament and Delegated Governance' (2004) 57(4) Parliam Aff 767, 778 on obstacles for parliaments to hold NDPBs to account. See also OECD, *Distributed Public Governance*, 27.

163 Richard Mulgan, *Holding Power to Account: Accountability in Modern Democracies* (Palgrave Macmillan 2003) 62.

164 Such powers are anchored in the Congressional Review Act. See Tom Zwart, 'Independent Regulatory Agencies in the US' in Tom Zwart and Luc Verhey (eds), *Agencies in European and Comparative Law* (Intersentia 2003) 3, 10.

165 Julia Black, 'Calling Regulators to Account: Challenges, Capacities and Prospects' in Nicholas Bamforth and Peter Leyland (eds), *Accountability in the Contemporary Constitution* (Oxford University Press 2013) 354, 376 with reference to House of Commons Business and Enterprise Committee, *The Postal Services Bill* 5th Report of Session 2008–09 HC 172-I, paras 96 and 97.

as a whole.[166] After receiving the Commission's reports, Parliament can further question the Government on the results that they contain.[167] Hence, the proposal seems to favour more (informed) parliamentary scrutiny, while at the same time revaluing ministerial responsibility.

Given European traditions regarding political control of the administration, the Government and its ministers will continue to play a central role when it comes to the application of mechanisms of accountability in parliamentary systems. Ministerial responsibility, moreover, has some other clear advantages as well. It is a form of what Bovens calls 'hierarchical accountability' or 'one for all-accountability'.[168] Nevertheless, the trend of parliaments assuming a more active role in scrutinizing the acts of APBs can play an important supporting and supplementary role.

---

[166] In that respect, see also Yannis Papadopoulos, 'Problems of Democratic Accountability in Network and Multilevel Governance' (2007) 13(4) European Law Journal 469, 485.

[167] Dawn Oliver, 'Regulation, Democracy and Democratic Oversight in the UK' in Dawn Oliver, Tony Prosser and Richard Rawlings (eds), *The Regulatory State: Constitutional Implications* (Oxford University Press 2010) 243, 265–266.

[168] Mark Bovens, 'Analysing and Assessing Accountability: A Conceptual Framework' (2007) 13(4) European Law Journal 447, 458.

6. Final conclusions and recommendations

1. *NIHIL EST SIMUL INVENTUM ET PERFECTUM* (CICERO)

Nothing is ever invented and perfected at the same time. This is also true for the phenomenon that was central to this book: that of autonomous public bodies. Chapter 1 defined the phenomenon of 'creating APBs' as one of 'entrusting entities distinct from the core administration, but with an organic or at least institutional tie with the government apparatus, with government tasks and letting them perform these tasks with a certain degree of autonomy in relation to elected politicians'. It is not clear when APBs were 'invented' as forms of administrative organization, it is equally unclear if and when they will reach a state of 'perfection'. The two trends studied in this book, namely those of 'EU impulse' and 'national restraint' reveal that yet another era in the history of APBs has dawned. It entails exciting new questions for academics, governments and all those involved in matters of administrative organization. Each of these trends deserves further scholarly attention as separate, stand-alone evolutions. The tension to which they give rise when the rationales that inspire them are confronted constitutes, however, a particularly challenging topic for academia to monitor in the coming years.

2. MAIN FINDINGS AND PROPOSITIONS

A. The 'Role' or 'Rule' of Law as Regards the Creation of APBs

Law and legal discourse play an increasingly important role in the process of creating APBs. The law on administrative organization is not 'neutral' or 'value free', it is embedded in a system of fundamental rules and principles. Law currently 'rules' or dominates the subject of creating APBs in a way that it has never done before. The trend of 'EU impulse' implies that creating APBs is no longer solely a question of political choice: in some cases, it has become one of legal obligation. The trend of 'national restraint', on the other hand, demonstrates that, increasingly, legislatures, Governments and scholars acknowledge that decisions related to APBs are inextricably linked to legal assessments and more precisely to trade-offs with fundamental, constitutional principles. For a long time, the logics of political and economic theories have dominated the debate on APBs, overshadowing the question of what is possible, imperative or desirable from a legal perspective. That period seems to have passed permanently.

B. The Trend of 'EU Impulse'

The law on national administrative organization no longer has the status of a domain in which nation states enjoy complete sovereignty. Increasingly, international and supranational sources of law mingle in questions of administrative design. One way in which they do so is by obliging or encouraging states to establish and empower APBs.

Chapter 2 established that the trend of 'EU impulse' is mainly discernible in two areas of government intervention: economic regulation on the one hand and human rights implementation, adjudication, monitoring or supervision on the other. In the former field, the APBs concerned are NRAs operating in network sectors such as the energy industry or the market for electronic communications. In the area of human rights protection, DPAs are the most important examples of bodies subject to the trend of 'EU impulse'.

Apart from national constitutional concerns, this evolution raises the question of whether the EU legislature is allowed to interfere with national administrative organization to the extent that it currently does. It was argued that the legal status and value of the principle of Member States' institutional autonomy is dubious. Does 'principle' in this context mean 'starting point', implying that deviations are possible? In that case, Member States are free to determine to whom they entrust the implementation of EU law, if and as long as the European legislature does not give any directions. Or is this principle more fundamental or predominant in nature, meaning that it prevails over EU legislation, which can only interfere in exceptional circumstances that require sufficiently strong reasons?[1] Furthermore, the question arises whether matters of administrative organization are not to such an extent intertwined with a state's singularity that they pertain to its 'constitutional identity'. Pursuant to

[1] Cf. Hubert Delzangles, 'L'indépendance de l'autorité de sûreté nucléaire, des progrès à envisager' [2013] Revue juridique de l'environnement 7, 10.

article 4(2) TEU 'the Union shall respect the Member States' national identities, inherent in their fundamental structures, political and constitutional, inclusive of regional and local self-government'. There is much debate, however, about the scope of this provision. Does it protect differences between Member States or principles and traditions that are common to them? And when is an institution, instrument, rule or principle so essential that it shapes Member States' identity?[2] These questions pertain to an altogether different debate from the one that was central to this study. There is work here for EU lawyers and scholars in the future, who may take an interest in this evolution and question it from the perspective of other principles, such as subsidiarity and proportionality, as well.

Typical for the national APBs that are created pursuant to EU legislation is that they enjoy broad discretionary powers. An important caveat in this respect is that government tasks that are 'technical' in nature or that require substantial scientific or experience-based knowledge should not be labelled as 'apolitical' too easily. This argument is often put forward with regard to the missions entrusted to the APBs subject to the trend of 'EU impulse' and especially with regard to IRAs. These bodies are, however, increasingly obliged to take into account a number of different objectives and considerations and to make policy trade-offs. Some literature has claimed that '[m]oving regulatory decision making to autonomous agencies is not only about non-political technical and technocratic efficiency but also involves sensitive political trade-offs and value-based choices'. It argues for a recognition of this complex reality, which exceeds technical criteria and assessments, and for a revaluation of the role of politics in regulatory matters.[3] In 2002, the OECD more generally ascertained that the use of APBs to regulate complex and politically sensitive societal problems was increasingly criticized. 'Critics claim that while independent expertise is often needed,

---

[2] See the contributions in Alejandro Saiz Arnaiz and Carina Alcoberro Llivina (eds), *National Constitutional Identity and European Integration* (Intersentia 2013). In a recent judgment, the Belgian Constitutional Court has ruled that the legislature cannot deviate from 'the national identity that is enshrined in the political and constitutional basic structures or from the core values of the protection that the Constitution offers to citizens', even if it implements treaties in the context of the EU. See GwH 28 April 2016, no 62/2016, para B.8.7.

[3] Tom Christensen and Per Lægreid, 'Agencification and Regulatory Reforms' in Tom Christensen and Per Lægreid (eds), *Autonomy and Regulation, Coping with Agencies in the Modern State* (Edward Elgar Publishing 2006) 8, 38.

these new independent entities sometimes allow governments to avoid taking political decisions or to take decisions guided only by technical expertise on issues that require a political choice and are at the core of political responsibility.'[4] Others have warned that '[d]ecisions are made no less political by delegating them to an "independent" body or making them according to a rule-based framework. In reality politics is transferred to a new arena … Depoliticization is a misnomer. The politics remain but the arena changes.'[5] Economic regulation as conceived by EU legislation incorporates political choices and trade-offs. This is even more the case today than it was at the beginning of the 1990s, when liberalization took off.

The missions entrusted to NHRIs may at first sight seem less sensitive to political choices or trade-offs. This is not always true, however. The most important human rights catalogue within Europe, the ECHR, contains a number of qualified fundamental rights, which can be limited as far as this is necessary in a democratic society to protect a number of enumerated interests. These interests touch upon policies developed at the national level. If and to the extent that the Strasbourg Court acknowledges that European states have a (large) 'margin of appreciation', it seems to allow for national political concerns to play a role in human rights interpretation and adjudication. Many other human rights instruments and bodies adopt a similar logic. DPAs, who make statements on what is permissible under the right to privacy, may also take into account the national context and, hence, make assessments in which they weigh various interests that may involve political choices.

EU obligations to establish APBs are inspired by considerations of credibility, comprising more general values such as integrity, quality and trustworthiness. Ensuring that expertise (either technical or experience-based) plays a decisive role in the decision-making process and avoiding conflicts of interest are components of this wider goal of 'credibility'. Chapter 2 further elaborated on the precise purport of these motives. As for the rationale of avoiding conflicts of interest, it was explained that economic regulation and human rights implementation, monitoring or supervision have in common that the responsible bodies sometimes supervise government institutions or politicians themselves. In the case of IRAs, government-owned enterprises, for which ministers may have to

---

[4] OECD, *Distributed Public Governance*, 22.

[5] Matthew Flinders and Jim Buller, 'Depoliticization, Democracy and Arena Shifting' in Tom Christensen and Per Lægreid (eds), *Autonomy and Regulation, Coping with Agencies in the Modern State* (Edward Elgar Publishing 2006) 53, 73.

assume responsibility, are subject to regulation as well. Ministers may face conflicting interests when they have to promote non-discriminatory regulation, while at the same time being concerned that the government's own market player performs well (or not worse than its competitors). As far as DPAs are concerned, because of the primarily vertical effect of human rights, governments themselves are often the object of the supervisory process, making governmental influence in the decision-making process hard to justify.

For economic regulation more specifically, 'time consistency' has been put forward as an imperative goal and as the major benefit of political independence by political economists and others. This argument still knows wide acclamation in academic literature and its value seems quite uncontested. Perhaps the most controversial suggestion that follows from this book is that the value of this argument is overestimated. First, from a legal-theoretical viewpoint, it was argued that the time consistency argument is at odds with an essential characteristic of the public service, being its capacity to adapt to new situations and to respond to newly emerged necessities. In French-inspired systems, this principle is enshrined in the so-called *loi du service public* of *adaptabilité* or *mutabilité*. Although these principles apply to administrative decision makers as such and may lack real constitutional value, one could argue that democracy as such requires elected politicians to be responsive to changes in society and to respond by adapting policies to what they deem in the public interest. Considering the primacy of elected politicians in administrative decision making, which was identified as a constitutional premise common to all four systems studied in this book, it in any case seems inadmissible that the legislature deprives the political executive of all opportunities to change policies as it sees fit. On top of that, it could be argued that the principle of equality is at stake here, since it may be difficult to justify that one particular sector is insulated from the possibility of undergoing political fluctuations, whereas citizens and enterprises operating outside that sector do not enjoy such a guarantee of stability.

A second basis for refuting the time consistency argument was empirical. The literature has observed that regulatory reforms with regard to institutional design have 'weak empirical foundations'.[6] Long standing theories on the expected benefits of regulatory independence, developed

[6] Tom Christensen and Per Lægreid, 'Regulatory Agencies – The Challenges of Balancing Agency Autonomy and Political Control' (2007) 20(3) Governance: An International Journal of Policy, Administration, and Institutions 499, 500.

in the fields of political science and law and economics, are mostly based on theoretical models, and require further empirical testing to assess whether and to what extent they correspond to perceptions and behaviour in 'the real world'. A series of eight in-depth interviews with Belgian market players in both energy and telecommunications pointed out that these players see only a limited correlation between the political independence of regulators on the one hand and continuity or stability in regulatory matters on the other. The expertise entailed by political independence, on the other hand, was regarded as an indispensable characteristic of IRAs by those market players.

C. The Trend of 'National Restraint'

The trend of EU impulse stimulates the creation of APBs. On the domestic level, on the other hand, many Member States have precisely put in place initiatives to stop the uncurbed rise of APBs in the administrative landscape. More particularly, attempts are being made to rationalize decisions on the creation and institutional design of APBs. These initiatives are predominantly inspired by democratic concerns. They more precisely aspire to ensure that administrative decisions that involve political choices are made under the ultimate responsibility of (those directly controlled by) the elected representatives of the people. Four national legal systems were studied in this book: Belgium, France, the Netherlands and the UK.

The 1980s and 1990s were characterized in many European states by an uncontrolled proliferation of APBs. The development of the law on APBs in European states in the 20th and 21st centuries can be seen as a process towards if not perfection, at least maturity. Whereas the ideas of NPM and related doctrines were favourably received by the majority of legislatures, Governments and academics alike in the beginning, they were later followed by much scepticism and criticism. In the course of the debates on the PBA, one of the peers in the House of Lords observed that:

> [W]e must all admit that we have been too quick in the past – and I fear we will be in future – to reach for the quango as a policy response to every problem that comes before us. I heard an expression in another context which covers it, which is, 'If you have a hammer, all problems look like nails'. I fear that that is where we are with quangos – we just create them.[7]

---

[7] HL Deb 9 November 2010, col 129 (Baroness Scott of Needham Market).

The current trend of rationalization implies that legislatures and Governments change this attitude of improvident recourse to APBs and strive to ensure that creating APBs and making decisions as to their institutional design will henceforth involve a duly thought-through and reasoned decision, based on a balanced assessment. Even though democratic concerns are undoubtedly central to the efforts of rationalization and reform that constitute the trend of 'national restraint', two other constitutional meta values are at stake as well. Because APBs often combine powers of rule making, individual decision making and sanctioning, the question arises whether and to what extent they violate the doctrine of separation of powers, as upheld and interpreted in current (European) Constitutions. Because of the rise of regulatory bodies, this question deserves further attention in the future. Nevertheless, concerns over separation of powers are often closely intertwined with – again – democratic claims. Another constitutional milestone at stake is that of the 'rule of law' and more precisely its requirements with regard to transparency and legal certainty. APBs render the administrative landscape less comprehensible and accessible for legal subjects. Many of the initiatives preconceived or taken at the national level and described in Chapter 3 precisely aim to remedy this lack of 'recognizability' of administrative organization.

The trend of 'national restraint' forces lawmakers to reflect on and conceive of new, innovative instruments that help legislatures and Governments in this effort of rationalization. Framework legislation governing the creation and institutional design of APBs has the potential to play an important role in such efforts. If it is not always able to bind legislatures, it at least offers them a clear framework for assessment and encourages them to balance the various values at stake. Chapter 3 discussed the goals, contents, merits and flaws of three statutory frameworks on APBs: the Flemish KDBB, the Dutch KWZBO and the UK's PBA. Even though these three frameworks differ in scope and approach, they have in common that they contain general rules and conditions that aim to rationalize the creation, preservation and/or functioning of APBs in order to square the APB landscape with (one or more of) the constitutional objections that it is currently believed to entail. It was established that, via the enactment of framework legislation, the legislature endeavours to transform APBs into a manageable and controllable phenomenon, embedded in, and constrained by, a set of rules and principles that ensure conformity with fundamental principles governing administrative organization

The study revealed that statutory frameworks that aim to impose rules and obligations on the legislature, such as the KDBB and the KWZBO, raise questions as to their enforceability. Since these statutes do not occupy a superior position in the hierarchy of norms compared to the statutes that create and design the APBs, the legislature seems free to deviate from the framework. It was argued that both the informative and symbolic value of a statutory framework already provide added value. At the same time, framework legislation is not entirely non-committal either. The constitutional principles of equality and legal certainty may well imply that legislatures at least have to provide sufficiently compelling reasons when they deviate from the framework.

According to Scholten, the input legitimacy of IRAs also depends on the accountability assumed by those who create IRAs. She argues that delegation to IRAs itself should be subject to restrictions, which limit the discretion of their creators (typically legislatures). Thus, people should feel involved in the decision to create and empower IRAs and the political institutions that take such decisions should be held accountable for them. She refers to general legislative frameworks, such as the Dutch KWZBO, which can foster that type of legitimacy.[8] Typical of the IRAs established on the basis of EU law is that national legislatures lack the power to decide on their life or death, on their institutional design and to some extent on their missions and powers.

D. The Tension Between (the Rationales Underlying) Both Trends: The Way Forward for the EU and for National Lawmakers

The trends of 'EU impulse' and 'national restraint' can both be studied separately, for what they are. New questions emerge, however, once the reasons or drivers that underlie them are confronted.

Chapter 4 of this book has revealed that the NRAs and DPAs whose creation and empowerment is currently mandatory under EU law have given rise to tensions with national constitutional law. Central to these tensions are concerns about the democratic accountability of these supervisory bodies. In its judgment in *Commission/Germany*, the ECJ ruled that the requirement of 'complete independence' anchored in the Data Protection Directive was not contrary to the principle of democracy enshrined in EU primary law. The court relied on the fact that APBs are already part of the administrative landscape in many Member States. It did not, however, take into account that delegation to APBs that are subject to no forms of political oversight of input whatsoever is not at all

8 Miroslava Scholten, 'Democratic Input Legitimacy of IRAs: Proposing an Assessment Framework' [2015] Utrecht Law Review 64.

common practice in Member States. The combination of such a far-reaching degree of political autonomy with large discretionary powers is particularly hard to reconcile with many national European Constitutions.

For the future, it seems advisable for the EU legislature to take into account fundamental principles governing administrative organization common to the constitutional traditions of European democracies when enacting legislation that directly affects Member States' systems of administrative organization. Similarly to what has been argued and accepted for fundamental rights and freedoms, the EU should accept these principles, which are constitutional in nature, as general and predominant principles, constituting an integral part of the EU administrative legal order. Pursuant to article 6 TEU, '[f]undamental rights, as guaranteed by the European Convention for the Protection of Human Rights and Fundamental Freedoms and as they result from the constitutional traditions common to the Member States, shall constitute general principles of the Union's law'. Before this provision featured in the Treaty, the EU legislature and the ECJ qualified fundamental (human) rights as general principles of EU law already. The question arises why the same should not be true for other common European fundamental principles with constitutional value. To that end, both the European legislature and the ECJ should engage in efforts to identify such common denominators. The trend of 'national restraint' indicates a return to a more conservative interpretation of traditional principles related to the meta values of constitutionalism, the rule of law and – most importantly – democracy. If the EU continues to influence the administrative organization of the Member States, it should be willing to adopt a bottom-up approach that takes such evolutions, coming from the base, into account.

Scholars studying the EU as a constitutional system are often preoccupied with concerns about the democratic legitimacy of the EU institutions themselves. What is often not reflected or taken into account in these analyses, however, is the democratic legitimacy of the stage that follows the legislative process, i.e. that of the implementation of EU law. In this stage, the Union still predominantly relies on the administrative apparatus of the Member States. It is therefore not surprising that EU law may wish to influence the design of national administrations and may consider it necessary to formulate certain requirements as to the features of the organizations entrusted with the implementation of substantive EU law. However, the effective and credible implementation of EU law does not justify the establishment of authorities with insufficient democratic legitimacy at the national level.

Chapter 5, finally, addressed the question of how the tension between the valid reasons behind EU law and domestic constitutional law, discussed in Chapter 4, can be reconciled. It discussed four frequently advocated alternative sources of legitimacy for APBs in general and independent supervisors, such as IRAs and DPAs, in particular: output or outcome legitimacy, procedural accountability, legal accountability and network accountability. All of these sources of legitimacy are indispensable to modern administrative decision making. It was argued, however, that neither of these are proper *substitutes* for political accountability via the chain of delegation. The problem with most suggestions on alternative forms of legitimacy or accountability for independent supervisors is that they fail to acknowledge that the legitimacy that public decision making derives from the involvement of elected politicians has its own, distinct value. No other sources of legitimacy, however valuable and even necessary as complements, can serve as genuine substitutes for that. In order to substantiate this thesis, Bovens' theoretical work on accountability was used as a frame of reference, since this has provided useful anchor points for assessments of accountability mechanisms. Particular attention was paid to those parts of his theory that proclaim that different accountability arrangements serve different goals, which largely correspond to different constitutional meta values. This resulted in a plea for a more purpose-oriented perspective on public accountability. A crucial insight that follows from this part of Bovens' theory is that not all forms of accountability automatically increase the *democratic* quality of administrative decision making. The conclusion was that political, procedural, legal and network accountability or legitimacy constitute essential, non-overlapping spheres, rather than alternatives to each other.

Definitely, one can choose to interpret constitutional rules and principles on the functioning of representative democracy in an absolute and rigid way, or one can opt for a more relative and flexible interpretation, which takes into account the evolution of ideas on governance and government legitimacy. Such interpretations can be valid, but should never detract from the core of these principles or hollow them altogether.[9] Bevir, for instance, has warned that, despite theories on alternative sources of legitimacy put forward by neoliberals, '[t]he danger of the word "non-majoritarian", ... is that it often may hide the fact that the argument being made is actually about restricting democracy'.[10]

[9] In that sense: L F M Verhey and N Verheij, 'De macht van marktmeesters, markttoezicht in constitutioneel perspectief' [2005] *Toezicht, Handelingen Nederlandse Juristenvereniging* 135, 184–185.

[10] Mark Bevir, *Democratic Governance* (Princeton University Press 2010) 106.

The inescapability of political accountability as an aspect of public legitimacy does not, however, have to lead to an unbridgeable dilemma between fulfilling the valid goals behind the trend of 'EU impulse' on the one hand and taking into account the democratic constraints on the creation of APBs central to the trend of 'national restraint' on the other. Chapter 5 has argued that ensuring that expertise plays a decisive role in administrative decision making does not presuppose political independence in the overall and complete sense that is currently advocated by EU legislation. In other words: allowing for experts to play their distinct roles, even in areas as technical as regulatory decision making, does not require complete political insulation. As Chevallier points out, persisting in such beliefs may lead to 'un gouvernement des sages', which has no more legitimacy than the 'gouvernement des juges' of which so many have warned in the past.[11]

Special attention was dedicated in this book to the possibility of conceiving models that unite the much-valued technical expertise embodied by regulatory bodies as well as DPAs and the need for political involvement. It was claimed that balanced forms of political supervision are conceivable, in which the roles of experts and elected politicians are equally and substantially protected. In this way, both experts and elected government can play their own, distinct, but complementary roles in administrative (regulatory) decision making. Thus, the legitimacy that both elected politicians and experts add to that process is merged. Some legal systems are familiar with forms of supervision that aim to achieve that aim. But do these mechanisms work, do they succeed in achieving that goal? This is an empirical, rather than a theoretical question. Open-ended interviews were carried out with a total of 14 APBs, both Belgian and Dutch, established for reasons of expertise and subject to administrative oversight with the ultimate possibility of an annulment. These revealed that these types of oversight powers were not perceived as being detrimental to the APBs' ability to give free expert opinions and to ensure that these could genuinely play a decisive role in the decision-making process. The interviews revealed that these APBs in general had a constructive relationship of mutual understanding and respect with their political principals. Consultation and deliberation between both actors ensured that conflicts were avoided and that both could play their own specific roles. These findings suggest that expertise and political input do not have to exclude each other. There are many ways conceivable to unite

[11] Jacques Chevallier, 'Réflexions sur l'institution des autorités administratives indépendantes' [1986] JCP-G I-3254.

both values in the configuration of APBs. Many avenues remain to be explored if progress is going to be made in this area: other forms of supervision and cooperation could be thought out and experimented with. What is no longer acceptable, however, is to continue to argue that expert-based decision making requires complete political autonomy. Or, to paraphrase Prosser: the way forward is that of a collaborative approach to regulation, involving both the regulator and government.[12]

Moreover, this book submitted that balanced forms of political input or supervision do not have to be ruled out in cases where political principals face conflicting interests. It stressed that (EU) administrative law is all about adverse interests and how to deal with them in acceptable ways. Many of the most prominent principles and mechanisms of administrative law in the European legal sphere, anchored in legislation or developed in the case law of administrative courts, deal with this very challenge: grounds of appeal such as *détournement de pouvoir*, the principle of equality, the duty to act in an impartial or unbiased way etc. Consequently, the risk of a minister being confronted with conflicting interests hardly seems to justify an obligation of withdrawal of all his/her influence on an aspect of administrative decision making.

This book has not argued that EU law is simply wrong to require the creation of APBs in the fields in which it currently does. However, it did submit that, when it imposes such institutional requirements, it should acknowledge the existence and consider the use of intermediate forms. It has aspired to demonstrate that models of APBs can be conceived that fit a common European denominator of 'democratic administration', while at the same time respecting the valid rationales that underlie the choice of the supranational legislature to oblige Member States to establish independent supervisory bodies. In 2006, a study on agencification and regulatory reforms concluded that the first topic that further research on regulatory reform and autonomous agencies would have to focus on was:

> to investigate the role of representative political bodies and political executives in the new regulatory state. The changing relationship between politicians and bureaucrats and ways of balancing agency autonomy with political control are research issues that deserve greater attention. In prescribing both enhanced autonomy and deregulation and more control and reregulation, regulatory reform perpetuates an enduring tension in the history of regulatory governance. The balance between autonomy and control is difficult to find

[12] Tony Prosser, *The Regulatory Enterprise – Government, Regulation and Legitimacy* (Oxford University Press 2010) 234.

> and hard to maintain, and a main challenge is to clarify under what conditions the equilibrium tends to tip one way or the other.[13]

Finally, reinstating the position and role of representative democracy with regard to the missions performed by APBs, for instance by reintroducing balanced forms of political supervision, requires that we restore confidence in political principals, such as ministers, as rational actors. In order to achieve this goal, a lot of course depends on the mentality and behaviour of political principals themselves. However, law and the legislature can contribute to this renewed confidence in the rationality of political principals, for instance by developing 'smart' procedures. This book, for example, proposed making powers of supervision for political principals on APBs go hand in hand with a statutory obligation of prior consultation. It was explained that, in the Netherlands, the prevailing legislation links such an obligation to powers of annulment entrusted to ministers. It moreover obliges ministers to refer to the elements brought forward during this consultation in the statement of reasons of the annulment decision. Such procedural guarantees oblige political principals to take duly founded decisions, based on a rational assessment of all the elements at stake. This study also suggested that precluding possible conflicts of interest from compromising public decision making does not require excluding all possibilities of political interference in the process. In these cases, legislatures could impose an enhanced duty to give reasons on the political principal, who would have to explain why he deemed it necessary to interfere (for instance, by suspending or annulling a decision). The legislature could then also specify the (public interest-related) goals for which political principals are allowed to exercise their power of intervention or supervision with regard to the APB. If these reasons are not sufficiently convincing, this could be taken into account by a court asked to rule on a complaint of improper purposes or a related ground of review.

3. AVENUES FOR FURTHER RESEARCH

As a topic of scholarly research, APBs require closer cooperation between different academic disciplines. In the last decades – and

---

[13] Tom Christensen and Per Lægreid, 'Agencification and Regulatory Reforms' in Tom Christensen and Per Lægreid (eds), *Autonomy and Regulation, Coping with Agencies in the Modern State* (Edward Elgar Publishing 2006) 8, 38.

especially since the 1980s – a vast body of theoretical and empirical research probing the desirability of various blueprints for administrative organization has been developed within the discipline of public administration. This has taken place independently from most legal research on autonomous government and its impact on the administrative landscape. Indeed, comparative and international literature in the discipline of political science has to a large extent flourished without much interaction or cross-fertilization with scholarly efforts by constitutional or administrative lawyers. This is problematic, because it detracts from the value of the often well-intended and meticulous research developed in both disciplines. Whereas lawyers are focused on studying positive law, i.e. the law as it is, and test its validity in the light of – for instance – the rules and principles of the Constitution, they are often only little aware of, or concerned with, for instance, inefficiencies caused by the prevailing configuration. Conversely, scholars in public administration sometimes make projections about what the administration could or should look like in order to function optimally, forgetting that constitutional theory, and hence law, sets limits to the extent to which one can experiment with the design of the public service. Research on APBs would particularly profit from the merger of insights, as well as methods, developed and employed in political science on the one hand and sound legal argumentation on the other.

May this book therefore lead to collaboration between disciplines, which could bring us one step nearer to perfecting our body of knowledge on the benefits, risks and conditions of delegation to APBs.

Bibliography

Ackerman, Bruce, 'Good-bye, Montesquieu' in Susan Rose-Ackerman and Peter L Lindseth (eds), *Comparative Administrative Law* (Edward Elgar Publishing 2010) 128.

Aelen, Margot, *Beginselen van goed markttoezicht* (Boom Juridische Uitgevers 2014).

Alen, André, *Poging tot een juridische begripsomschrijving van unitarisme, centralisatie, deconcentratie, decentralisatie, regionalisme, federalisme en confederatie* (U.G.A. 1975).

Alen, André, 'De grondwet, hoogste rechtsnorm?' in *En hommage à Francis Delpérée. Itinéraires d'un constitutionnaliste* (Bruylant 2007) 105.

Allan, T R S, 'Accountability to Law' in Nicholas Bamforth and Peter Leyland (eds), *Accountability in the Contemporary Constitution* (Oxford University Press 2013) 77.

Andersen, Robert, 'Les autorités administratives indépendantes en droit belge' [2008] Annuaire Européen d'administration Publique 25.

Auby, Jean-Bernard, 'Conflits d'intérêts et droit administratif' [2010] Droit Administratif Étude 24.

Auby, Jean-Bernard, 'La façon de comprendre les AAI' [2010] *La Semaine Juridique Edition Générale* 1260.

Auby, Jean-Bernard, 'Remarques terminales' [2010] RFDA 931.

Auby, Jean-Marie, 'Le pouvoir réglementaire des autorités des collectivités locales' [1984] AJDA 468.

Autin, Jean-Louis, 'Le devenir des autorités administratives indépendantes' [2010] RFDA 875.

Baldwin, R, '"The Next Steps": Ministerial Responsibility and Government by Agency' (1988) 51(5) MLR 622.

Baldwin, Robert, Martin Cave and Martin Lodge, *Understanding Regulation* (Oxford University Press 2012).

Balthasar, Alexander, '"Complete Independence" of National Data Protection Supervisory Authorities – Second Try: Comments on the Judgment of the CJEU of 16 October 2012, C-614/10 (*European Commission v. Austria*), with Due Regard to its Previous Judgment of 9 March 2010, C-518/07 (*European Commission v. Germany*)' (2013) 9(3) Utrecht Law Review 26.

Bamforth, Nicholas, 'Accountability of and to the Legislature' in Nicholas Bamforth and Peter Leyland (eds), *Accountability in the Contemporary Constitution* (Oxford University Press 2013) 259.

Baranger, Denis, 'Executive Power in France' in Paul Craig and Adam Tomkins (eds), *The Executive and Public Law. Power and Accountability in Comparative Perspective* (Oxford University Press, 2006) 217.

Barker, Anthony, 'Governmental Bodies and the Networks of Mutual Accountability' in Anthony Barker (ed), *Quangos in Britain. Government and the Networks of Public Policy-Making* (Palgrave Macmillan 1982) 3.

Belinfante, A D and J L de Reede, *Beginselen van het Nederlandse Staatsrecht* (Kluwer 2012).

Bell, John, 'Comparative Administrative Law' in Mathias Reimann and Reinhard Zimmermann (eds), *The Oxford Handbook of Comparative Law* (Oxford University Press 2006) 1259.

Ben Hadj Yahia, Sonia, 'Controverses autour des autorités de régulation' (2010) 18 La Semaine Juridique Entreprise et Affaires 17.

Benz, Arthur, Carol Harlow and Yannis Papadopoulos, 'Introduction' (2007) 13(4) European Law Journal 441.

Bertram, Cristopher, *Rousseau and the Social Contract* (Routledge 2003).

Besson, Samantha, 'Whose Constitution(s)? International Law, Constitutionalism and Democracy' in Jeffrey L Dunoff and Joel P Trachtman (eds), *Ruling the World? Constitutionalism, International Law and Global Governance* (Cambridge University Press 2008) 381.

Bevir, Mark, *Democratic Governance* (Princeton University Press 2010).

Birrell, Derek, 'Devolution and Quangos in the United Kingdom: The Implementation of Principles and Policies for Rationalization and Democratization' (2008) 29(1) Policy Studies 35.

Black, Julia, 'Proceduralizing Regulation: Part I' (2000) Oxford Journal of Legal Studies 597

Black, Julia, 'Proceduralizing Regulation: Part II' (2000) Oxford Journal of Legal Studies 33.

Black, Julia, 'Constructing and Contesting Legitimacy and Accountability in Polycentric Regulatory Regimes', LSE Law, Society and Economy Working Papers 2/2008, www.lse.ac.uk/collections/law/wps/wps.htm.

Black, Julia, 'Calling Regulators to Account: Challenges, Capacities and Prospects' in Nicholas Bamforth and Peter Leyland (eds), *Accountability in the Contemporary Constitution* (Oxford University Press 2013) 354.

den Boer, M M, 'Zelfstandige bestuursorganen uit de zelfkant van de democratie?' in C P J Goorlen, M M Den Boer and F K Buijn (eds), *Zbo's, verzelfstandiging en privatisering* (Tjeenk Willink 1997) 124.

den Boer, M M, *Preadvies verzelfstandiging van bestuurstaken op z'n Hollands* (Tjeenk Willink, 1999).

von Bogdandy, Armin, 'Founding Principles' in Armin von Bogdandy and Jürgen Bast (eds), *Principles of European Constitutional Law* (Hart 2009) 11.

von Bogdandy, Armin, 'Comparative Constitutional Law: A Contested Domain – A. Comparative Constitutional Law: A Continental Perspective' in Michel Rosenfeld and András Sajó (eds), *The Oxford Handbook of Comparative Constitutional Law* (Oxford University Press 2012) 25.

Bosco, David, 'La séparation des fonctions d'instruction et de jugement constitutionnalisée!' [2013/10] *Contrats Concurrence Consommation* 20.

Bouckaert, Geert and Guy B Peters, 'What Is Available and What Is Missing in the Study of Quangos?' in Christopher Pollit and Colin Talbot (eds), *Unbundled Government, A Critical Analysis of the Global Trend to Agencies, Quangos and Contractualisation* (Routledge 2004) 22.

Boucquey, Pascal and Pierre-Olivier de Broux, 'Les recours juridictionnels contre les décisions des autorités de régulation' in Hugues Dumont, Pierre Jadoul and Sébastien van Drooghenbroeck (eds), *La protection juridictionnelle du citoyen face à l'administration* (la Charte 2007) 209.

Bougrab, Jeannette, 'Independent Administrative Authorities in France' in Roberto Caranta, Mads Adenas and Duncan Fairgrieve (eds), *Independent Administrative Authorities* (British Institute of International and Comparative Law 2004) 47.

Bovens, Mark, 'Analysing and Assessing Accountability: A Conceptual Framework' (2007) 13(4) European Law Journal 447.

Bovens, Mark, 'Public Accountability' in Ewan Ferlie, Laurence E Lynn and Christopher Pollit (eds), *The Oxford Handbook of Public Management* (Oxford University Press 2008) 182.

Bovens, Mark, 'Two Concepts of Accountability: Accountability as a Virtue and as a Mechanism' (2010) 33(5) West European Politics 946.

Bovens, Mark, Deirdre Curtin and Paul 't Hart, 'The Quest for Legitimacy and Accountability in EU Governance' in Mark Bovens, Deirdre Curtin and Paul 't Hart (eds), *The Real World of EU Accountability. What Deficit?* (Oxford University Press 2010) 9.

Boxum, J L, J de Ridder and M Scheltema, *Zelfstandige bestuursorganen in soorten: verslag van een onderzoek naar de praktijk van zelfstandige bestuursorganen* (Kluwer 1989).

Boxum, J L, 'Ministeriële verantwoordelijkheid en zelfstandige bestuursorganen' in D J Elzinga (ed), *Ministeriële verantwoordelijkheid in Nederland* (W.E.J. Tjeenk Willink 1994) 257.

Bradley, A W and K D Ewing, *Constitutional & Administrative Law* (Longman Pearson 2011).

Broeksteeg, J L W, *Verantwoordelijkheid en aansprakelijkheid in het staatsrecht* (Kluwer 2004).

Broeksteeg, J L W, 'Ministeriële verantwoordelijkheid voor zelfstandige bestuursorganen' in J L W Broeksteeg, J Th J van den Berg and L F M Verhey (eds), *Ministeriële verantwoordelijkheid opnieuw gewogen* (Kluwer 2006) 87.

de Broux, Pierre-Olivier, 'Introduction à la décentralisation administrative: évolutions théoriques et pratiques politiques' in Pierre Jadoul, Bruno Lombaert and François Tulkens (eds), *Le paraétatisme. Nouveaux régards sur la décentralisation fonctionnelle en Belgique et dans les institutions européennes* (la Charte 2010) 1.

Burkens, M C, Henk R B M Kummeling, Ben P Vermeulen and Rob J G M Widdershoven, *Beginselen van de democratische rechtsstaat. Inleiding tot de grondslagen van het Nederlandse staats- en bestuursrecht* (Kluwer 2006).

Buttgenbach, André, *Théorie générale des modes de gestion des services publics en Belgique* (Larcier 1952).

Cabeau, Emmanuel, 'National Regulatory Authorities' in Christopher Jones (ed), *EU Energy Law, Vol. I, The Internal Energy Market, The Third Liberalisation Package* (Claeys & Casteels 2010) 217.

Cane, Peter, *Administrative Law* (5th edn, Clarendon Press 2011).

della Cananea, Giacinto, 'Administrative Law in Europe: A Historical and Comparative Perspective' [2010] Online Italian Journal of Public Law 162.

Cardenas, Sonia, 'Emerging Global Actors: The United Nations and National Human Rights Institutions' (2003) 9 Global Governance 23.

Cardwell, Paul James, 'The Changing Nature of European Regulatory Governance' in David Levi-Faur (ed), *Handbook on the Politics of Regulation* (Edward Elgar Publishing 2011) 536.

Chalmers, Damian, Gareth Davies and Giorgio Monti, *European Union Law* (Cambridge University Press 2010).

Chamon, Merijn, 'EU Agencies: Does the Meroni Doctrine Make Sense?' (2010) 17(3) Maastricht Journal of European and Comparative Law 281.

Chamon, Merijn, 'EU Agencies between Meroni and Romani or the Devil and the Deep Blue Sea' [2011] CML Rev 1055.

Chevallier, Jacques, 'Réflexions sur l'institution des autorités administratives indépendantes' [1986] JCP-G I-3254.

Chevallier, Jacques, 'Le statut des autorités administratives indépendantes: harmonisation ou diversification ?' [2010] RFDA 896.

Chrétien, Patrice and Nicolas Chifflot, *Droit Administratif* (Sirey 2012).

Christensen, Tom and Per Lægreid (eds), *Autonomy and Regulation, Coping with Agencies in the Modern State* (Edward Elgar Publishing 2006).

Christensen, Tom and Per Lægreid, 'Agencification and Regulatory Reforms' in Tom Christensen and Per Lægreid (eds), *Autonomy and Regulation, Coping with Agencies in the Modern State* (Edward Elgar Publishing 2006) 8.

Christensen, Tom and Per Lægreid, 'Rebalancing the State: Reregulation and the Reassertion of the Centre' in Tom Christensen and Per Lægreid (eds), *Autonomy and Regulation, Coping with Agencies in the Modern State* (Edward Elgar Publishing 2006) 359.

Christensen, Tom and Per Lægreid, 'Regulatory Agencies – The Challenges of Balancing Agency Autonomy and Political Control' (2007) 20(3) Governance: An International Journal of Policy, Administration, and Institutions 499.

Christensen, Tom and Per Lægreid, 'The New Regulatory Orthodoxy: A Critical Assessment' in David Levi-Faur, (ed), *Handbook on the Politics of Regulation* (Edward Elgar Publishing 2011) 361.

Christensen, Tom and Per Lægreid (eds), *Transcending New Public Management. The Transformation of Public Sector Reforms* (Ashgate 2011).

Coen, David and Mark Thatcher, 'Network Governance and Multi-level Delegation: European Networks of Regulatory Agencies' (2008) 28 Journal of Public Policy 49.

Collet, Martin, 'La création des autorités administratives indépendantes: symptôme ou remède d'un Etat en crise?' (2007) 330 Regards sur l'actualité 5.

Collet, Martin, 'Autorités de régulation économique: l'émergence d'une catégorie nouvelle?' [2008] Revue Juridique de l'économie Publique Comm. 11.

Covlosky, Salo, Roberto Pires and Susan S Silbey, 'The Pragmatic Politics of Regulatory Enforcement' in David Levi-Faur (ed), *Handbook on the Politics of Regulation* (Edward Elgar Publishing 2011) 322.

Craig, Paul, 'Shared Administration, Disbursement of Community Funds and the Regulatory State' in Herwig C H Hofmann and Alexander H Türk (eds), *Legal Challenges in EU Administrative Law. Towards an Integrated Administration* (Edward Elgar Publishing 2009) 34.

Craig, Paul, *Administrative Law* (Sweet & Maxwell 2012).

Craig, Paul and Adam Tomkins, 'Introduction' in Paul Craig and Adam Tomkins (eds), *The Executive and Public Law. Power and Accountability in Comparative Perspective* (Oxford University Press 2006) 1.

Curaj, Adrian, Peter Scott, Lazăr Vlascenau and Lesley Wilson, *European Higher Education at the Crossroads: Between the Bologna Process and National Reforms* (Springer Netherlands 2012).

Curtin, Deirdre, 'Holding (Quasi-)Autonomous EU Administrative Actors to Public Account' (2007) 13(4) European Law Journal 523.

Custos, Dominique, 'Independent Administrative Authorities in France: Structural and Procedural Change at the Intersection of Americanization, Europeanization and Gallicization' in Susan Rose-Ackerman and Peter L Lindseth (eds), *Comparative Administrative Law* (Edward Elgar Publishing 2010) 277.

Dann, Philipp, 'The Political Institutions' in Armin von Bogdandy and Jürgen Bast (eds), *Principles of European Constitutional Law* (Hart 2009) 237.

Dautry, Philippe, 'Les autorités administratives indépendantes: un nouvel objet d'évaluation parlementaire' [2010] RFDA 884.

Degoffe, Michel, 'Les autorités publiques indépendantes' [2008] AJDA 622.

Deleon, Linda, 'Public Management, Democracy, and Politics' in Ewan Ferlie, Laurence E Lynn and Christopher Pollit (eds), *The Oxford Handbook of Public Management* (Oxford University Press 2008) 102.

Delpérée, Francis, 'Synthèse. Les autorités administratives indépendantes' [2008] Annuaire Européen d'administration Publique 317.

Delvax, Denis, 'Les contrôles administratives pesant sur les autorités administratives indépendantes' (2008) 37 Revue de Droit de l'ULB 107.

Delzangles, Hubert, 'L'indépendance de l'autorité de sûreté nucléaire, des progrès à envisager' [2013] Revue Juridique de l'environnement 7.

Dent, Nicholas, *Rousseau* (Routledge 2005).

Dickson, Brice, 'The Contribution of Human Rights Commissions to the Protection of Human Rights' [2003] Public Law 272.

Döhler, Marian, 'Institutional Choice and Bureaucratic Autonomy in Germany' (2002) 25(1) West European Politics 101.

Döhler, Marian and Werner Jann, 'Germany' in OECD, *Distributed Public Governance* 97.

Donnelly, Catherine, 'Administrative Law and Multi-Level Administration: An EU and US Comparison' in Catherine Barnard and Okeoghene Odudu (eds), *Cambridge Yearbook of European Legal Studies 2008–09* (Hart Publishing 2009) 211.

Donnelly, Catherine, 'Participation and Expertise: Judicial Attitudes in Comparative Perspective' in Susan Rose-Ackerman and Peter Lindseth (eds), *Comparative Administrative Law* (Edward Elgar Publishing 2010).

Drewry, Gavin, 'Revolution in Whitehall: the Next Steps and Beyond' in Jeffrey Jowell and Dawn Oliver (eds), *The Changing Constitution* (3rd edn, Oxford University Press 1994) 155.

Drewry, Gavin, 'The Executive: Towards Accountable Government and Effective Governance?' in Jeffrey Jowell and Dawn Oliver (eds), *The Changing Constitution* (Oxford University Press 2011) 187.

Duprat, Jean-Pierre, 'La soumission des régulateurs à régulation' [2006] AJDA 1203.

Eckert, Gabriel, 'L'indépendance des autorités de régulation économique à l'égard du pouvoir politique' [2012] RFAP 629.

Egeberg, Morten, 'Europe's Executive Branch of Government in the Melting Pot: An Overview' in Morten Egeberg (ed), *Multilevel Union Administration. The Transformation of Executive Politics in Europe* (Palgrave Macmillan 2006).

Eisner, Marc Allen, 'Beyond the Logic of the Market: Toward an Institutional Analysis of Regulatory Reforms' in David Levi-Faur (ed), *Handbook on the Politics of Regulation* (Edward Elgar Publishing 2011) 129.

Elliot, Mark, 'Ombudsmen, Tribunals, Inquiries: Re-fashioning Accountability Beyond the Courts' in Nicholas Bamforth and Peter Leyland (eds), *Accountability in the Contemporary Constitution* (Oxford University Press 2013) 233.

Elzinga, D J, 'De doctrine van de politieke ministeriële verantwoordelijkheid. Over de verhouding tussen staatsrechtelijke normen en de politieke praktijk' in Interuniversitair Centrum voor Staatsrecht v.z.w. (ed), *De ministeriële verantwoordelijkheid / La responsabilité ministérielle* (Kluwer 1991) 17.

Elzinga, D J, 'De politieke ministeriële verantwoordelijkheid' in D J Elzinga (ed), *Ministeriële verantwoordelijkheid in Nederland* (W.E.J. Tjeenk Willink 1994) 31.

Everson, Michelle, 'Agencies: The "Dark Hour" of the Executive?' in Herwig C H Hofmann and Alexander H Türk (eds), *Legal Challenges in EU Administrative Law* (Edward Elgar Publishing 2009) 116.

Eymeri-Douzans, J Jean Michel and Jon Pierre, 'Conclusion' in Jean-Michel Eymeri-Douzans and Jon Pierre (eds), *Administrative Reforms and Democratic Governance* (Routledge 2011) 202.

Favoreu, Louis, Patrick Gaïa, Richard Ghevontian, Jean-Louis Mestre, Otto Piersmann, André Roux and Guy Scoffoni, *Droit constitutionnel* (Dalloz 2009).

Feldman, Jean-Philippe, 'Les "autorités administratives indépendantes" sont-elles légitimes? Sur les AAI en général et le Conseil supérieur de l'audiovisuel en particulier' [2010] Receuil Dalloz 2852.
Fellman, David, 'Constitutionalism' in Philip P Wiener (ed), *Dictionary of the History of Ideas: Studies of Selected Pivotal Ideas, vol. 1* (Charles Scribner's Sons 1974) 485.
Finger, Matthias, 'Towards a European Model of Regulatory Governance?' in David Levi-Faur (ed), *Handbook on the Politics of Regulation* (Edward Elgar Publishing 2011) 525.
Fishkin, James S, *When the People Speak: Deliberative Democracy and Public Consultation* (Oxford University Press 2009).
Flinders, Matthew V, 'Quangos: Why Do Governments Love Them?' in Matthew V Flinders and Martin J Smith (eds), *Quangos, Accountability and Reform. The Politics of Quasi-Government* (MacMillan Press Ltd 1999) 26.
Flinders, Matthew, 'MPs and Icebergs: Parliament and Delegated Governance' (2004) 57(4) Parliam Aff 767.
Flinders, Matthew, *Delegated Governance and the British State: Walking without Order* (Oxford University Press 2008).
Flinders, Matthew, 'Devolution, Delegation and the Westminster Model: A Comparative Analysis of Developments within the UK, 1998–2009' (2011) 4(1) Commonwealth & Comparative Politics 1.
Flinders, Matthew and Jim Buller, 'Depoliticization, Democracy and Arena Shifting' in Tom Christensen and Per Lægreid (eds), *Autonomy and Regulation, Coping with Agencies in the Modern State* (Edward Elgar Publishing 2006) 53.
Flinders, Matthew and Chris Skelcher, 'Shrinking the Quango State: Five Challenges in Reforming Quangos' (2012) 32(5) Public Money & Management 327.
Frankenberg, Günter, 'Democracy' in Michel Rosenfeld and András Sajó (eds), *The Oxford Handbook of Comparative Constitutional Law* (Oxford University Press 2012) 250.
Frier, Pierre-Laurent and Jacques Petit, *Précis de droit administrative* (Montchrestien 2006).
Garner, J F, 'After Privatisation: Quis Custodiet ipsos Custodes?' (1990) Public Law 329.
Gentot, Michel, *Les autorités administratives indépendantes* (Montchrestien 1994).
Georges, Philippe and Guy Siat, *Droit public* (Dalloz 2006).
van Gestel, R A J, Ph Eijlander and J A F Peters, 'The Regulatory Powers of Quangos in the Netherlands: Are Trojan Horses Invading Our Democracy?' (Paper for the Nederlandse Vereniging voor

Rechtsvergelijking/Netherlands Comparative Law Association), http://www.ejcl.org/111/abs111-9.html.

van Gestel, R A J and Hans-W Micklitz, 'Revitalising Doctrinal Legal Research in Europe: What About Methodology?' in Ulla Neergaard, Ruth Nielsen and Lyn Roseberry (eds), *European Legal Method – Paradoxes and Revitilisation* (DJØF Publishing 2011) 25.

Geurink, E, 'Ministeriële verantwoordelijkheid voor ambtenaren' in J L W Broeksteeg, J Th J van den Berg and L F M Verhey (eds), *Ministeriële verantwoordelijkheid opnieuw gewogen* (Kluwer 2006).

Geveke, Arjan, 'Improving Implementation by National Regulatory Authorities' [2003] Eipascope 26.

Gilardi, Fabrizio, 'Policy Credibility and Delegation to Independent Regulatory Agencies: A Comparative Empirical Analysis' [2002] Journal of European Public Policy 873.

Gilardi, Fabrizio, *Delegation in the Regulatory State. Independent Regulatory Agencies in Western Europe* (Edward Elgar Publishing 2008).

Gilardi, Fabrizio and Martino Maggetti, 'The Independence of Regulatory Authorities' in David Levi-Faur (ed), *Handbook on the Politics of Regulation* (Edward Elgar Publishing 2011) 201.

Graham, Cosmo, *Regulating Public Utilities: A Constitutional Approach* (Hart Publishing 2000).

Grave, Carsten, Matthew Flinders and Sandra Van Thiel, 'Quangos – What's in a Name? Defining Quangos from a Comparative Perspective' 12(2) (1999) Governance 129.

Greasley, Stephen and Chris Hanretty, 'Credibility and Agency Termination under Parliamentarism' [2016] *Journal of Public Administration Research and Theory* 159.

Griller, Stefan and Andreas Orator, 'Everything Under Control? The "Way Forward" for European Agencies in the Footsteps of the Meroni Doctrine' (2010) 35(1) European Law Review 3.

Groenleer, Martijn, 'Toezicht op de energiesector: tussen nationale belangen en Europese invloed' [2015] Tijdschrift voor Europees en economisch recht 385.

Grønnegård Christensen, Jørgen, 'Competing Theories of Regulatory Governance: Reconsidering Public Interest Theory of Regulation' in David Levi-Faur (ed), *Handbook on the Politics of Regulation* (Edward Elgar Publishing 2011) 96.

Guédon, Marie-José, *Les autorités administratives indépendantes* (Librairie générale de droit et de jurisprudence 1991).

Hacquet, Arnaud, 'Le pouvoir réglementaire des autorités administratives indépendantes. Réflexions sur son objet et sa légitimité' [2008] RDP 393.

Halberstam, Daniel, 'The Promise of Comparative Administrative Law: A Constitutional Perspective on Independent Agencies' in Susan Rose-Ackerman and Peter L Lindseth (eds), *Comparative Administrative Law* (Edward Elgar Publishing 2010) 185.

Hancher, Leigh and Pierre Larouche, 'The Coming of Age of EU Regulation of Network Industries and Services of General Economic Interest' in Paul Craig and Grainne de Búrca (eds), *The Evolution of EU Law* (Oxford University Press 2011) 743.

Hanretty, Chris, Pierre Larouche and Andreas Reindl, 'Independence, Accountability and Perceived Quality of Regulators – A CERRE Study', Brussels, 6 March 2012, http://www.cerre.eu/sites/cerre/files/120306_IndependenceAccountabilityPerceivedQualityofNRAs.pdf.

Harden, Ian, 'A Constitution for Quangos?' [1987] Public Law 27.

Harding, Andrew and Peter Leyland, 'Comparative Law in Constitutional Contexts' in Esin Örücü and David Nelken (eds), *Comparative Law. A Handbook* (Hart Publishing 2007) 313.

Harlow, Carol and Richard Rawlings, 'Promoting Accountability in Multilevel Governance: A Network Approach' (2007) 13(4) European Law Journal 542.

Harlow, Carol and Richard Rawlings, *Law and Administration* (7th edn, Cambridge University Press 2009).

Henisz, Witold J, 'The Institutional Environment for Infrastructure Investment' [2002] *Industrial and Corporate Change* 355.

Heringa, Aalt W, 'Agencies in France. Autorités Administratives Centrales Indépendantes / National Independent Administrative Authorities' in Tom Zwart and Luc Verhey (eds), *Agencies in European and Comparative Law* (Intersentia 2003) 37.

Heringa, Aalt W and Luc F M Verhey, 'Independent Agencies and Political Control' in Tom Zwart and Luc Verhey (eds), *Agencies in European and Comparative Law* (Intersentia 2003) 155.

Van Hoecke, Mark, 'Legal Doctrine: Which Method(s) for What Kind of Discipline?' in Mark Van Hoecke (ed), *Methodologies of Legal Research. Which Kind of Method for What Kind of Discipline?* (Hart Publishing 2011) 1.

Hood, Christopher, *The Blame Game: Spin, Bureaucracy, and Self-Preservation in Government* (Princeton University Press 2011).

Hood Phillips, O, Paul Jackson and Patricia Leopold, *Constitutional and Administrative Law* (Sweet & Maxwell 2001).

D'Hooghe, David and Philip De Keyser, 'Het continuïteitsbeginsel en het veranderlijkheidsbeginsel' in Ingrid Opdebeek and Marnix Van Damme (eds), *Beginselen van behoorlijk bestuur* (die Keure 2006) 363.

Hunt, David, 'Worthwhile Bodies' (1995) 48(2) Parliam Aff 181.

Jadoul, Pierre, Bruno Lombaert and François Tulkens (eds), *Le paraétatisme. Nouveaux régards sur la décentralisation fonctionnelle en Belgique et dans les institutions européennes* (la Charte 2010).

Jans, Jan H, Roel de Lange, Sacha Prechal and Rob Widdershoven, *Europeanisation of Public Law* (Europa Law Publishing 2007).

Jeffrey Jacobsohn, Gary, 'Constitutional Values and Principles' in Michel Rosenfeld and András Sajó (eds), *The Oxford Handbook of Comparative Constitutional Law* (Oxford University Press 2012) 777.

Jenkins, Kate, *Politicians and Public Services. Implementing Change in a Clash of Cultures* (Edward Elgar Publishing 2008).

Joassart, Marc, Elisabeth Willemart, Florence Piret and Raphaël Born, 'Le Conseil d'Etat, Chronique de jurisprudence 2009' [2010] RBDC 93.

Johnson, Nevil, 'Accountability, Control and Complexity: Moving Beyond Ministerial Responsibility' in Anthony Barker (ed), *Quangos in Britain. Government and the Networks of Public Policy-Making* (Palgrave Macmillan 1982) 206.

Jordana, Jacint, Andrea C Bianculli and Xavier Fernández-i-Marin, 'When Accountability Meets Regulation' in Andrea C Bianculli, Xavier Fernández-i-Marin and Jacint Jordana (eds), *Accountability and Regulatory Governance* (Palgrave Macmillan 2014) 1.

Jowell, Jeffrey, 'The Rule of Law and Its Underlying Values' in Jeffrey Jowell and Dawn Oliver (eds), *The Changing Constitution* (7th edn, Oxford University Press 2011) 11.

Kauff-Gazin, Fabienne, 'Vers une conception Européenne de l'indépendance des autorités de regulation? – À propos de l'affaire C-518/07, Commission c/ Allemagne' [2010] Europe, étude 9.

Kendall, Willmoore, *John Locke and the Doctrine of Majority Rule* (University of Illinois Press 1965).

Kirkham, Richard, 'Quangos, Coalition Government and the Ombudsmen' (2010) 32(4) Journal of Social Welfare & Family Law 411.

Krygier, Martin, 'Rule of Law' in Michel Rosenfeld and András Sajó (eds), *The Oxford Handbook of Comparative Constitutional Law* (Oxford University Press 2012) 233.

Kummeling, Henk R B M and Antonius P W Duijkersloot, 'Agencies and the Netherlands' in Tom Zwart and Luc Verhey (eds), *Agencies in European and Comparative Law* (Intersentia 2003) 79.

Lamanda, Vincent, 'Les autorités administratives indépendantes: une rationalisation impossible? Colloque co-organisé le 26 mars 2010 par la Cour de cassation, l'Université de Montpellier I et le Centre d'études et de recherches de sciences administratives (CNRS – Université Paris II) – Avant-propos' [2010] RFDA 873.

Larouche, Pierre, 'Coordination of European and Member State Regulatory Policy: Horizontal, Vertical and Transversal Aspects' in Damien Geradin, Rodolphe Muñoz and Nicolas Petit (eds), *Regulation through Agencies in the EU. A New Paradigm of European Governance* (Edward Elgar Publishing 2005) 164.

Lavrijssen, Saskia, *Onafhankelijke mededingingstoezichthouders, regulerende bevoegdheden en de waarborgen voor good governance* (Boom Juridische Uitgevers 2006).

Lavrijssen, Saskia and Leigh Hancher, 'Networks on Track: From European Regulatory Networks to European Regulatory "Network Agencies"' (2008) 34 LIEI 23.

Lavrijssen, Saskia and Thomas Nauta, 'De Europeanisering van het toezicht op de energiesector' [2012] Nederlands Tijdschrift voor energierecht 136.

Lavrijssen, Saskia and Annetje Ottow, 'The Legality of Independent Regulatory Authorities' in Leonard Besselink, Frans Pennings and Sacha Prechal (eds), *The Eclipse of the Legality Principle in the European Union* (Kluwer 2011) 73.

Lavrijssen, Saskia and Annetje Ottow, 'Independent Supervisory Authorities: A Fragile Concept' (2012) 39(4) Legal Issues of Economic Integration 419.

Lenaerts, Koenraad and Piet Van Nuffel, *Constitutional Law of the European Union* (Sweet & Maxwell 2005).

Lenaerts, Koen and Amaryllis Verhoeven, 'Institutional Balance as a Guarantee for Democracy in EU Governance' in Cristian Joerges and Renaud Dehousse (eds), *Good Governance in Europe's Integrated Market* (Oxford University Press 2002) 35.

Leus, Kaat, 'Een klassiek bestuursrechtelijke benadering van het verschijnsel "verzelfstandiging" van openbare diensten: naar een nieuw evenwicht tussen autonomie en centrale sturing' in J E Krings (ed), *Liber Amicorum Prof. Dr. G. Baeteman*, (Kluwer Rechtswetenschappen België 1997) 585.

Leus, Kaat and Sven Baeten, 'Nieuwe vormen van overheidsrechtspersonen' in Willy Van Eeckhoutte (ed), *Het Rechtspersonenrecht, XVe postuniversitaire cyclus Willy Delva 1998–1999* (Mys & Breesch 1999) 149

Levi-Faur, David, 'Regulation and Regulatory Governance' in David Levi-Faur (ed), *Handbook on the Politics of Regulation* (Edward Elgar Publishing 2011) 3.

Levi-Faur, David, 'The Regulatory State and Regulatory Capitalism: An Institutional Perspective' in David Levi-Faur (ed), *Handbook on the Politics of Regulation* (Edward Elgar Publishing 2011) 662.

Leyland, Peter, *The Constitution of the United Kingdom – A Contextual Analysis* (Hart Publishing 2012).

Leyland, Peter and Gordon Anthony, *Textbook on Administrative Law* (Oxford University Press 2009) 42.

Lindseth, Peter L, *Power and Legitimacy: Reconciling Europe and the Nation State* (Oxford University Press 2010).

Liu, Margaret L, 'Ministerial Responsibility and Constitutional Law' (2002) 7(2) Coventry Law Journal 25.

Lombard, Martine, 'Institutions de régulation économique et démocratie politique' [2005] AJDA 530.

Lubberdink, H G, *De betekenis van de ministeriële verantwoordelijkheid voor de organisatie van het openbaar bestuur* (Kluwer 1982).

Luppi, Philippe, 'L'unité du pouvoir réglementaire du Premier ministre et son caractère *ab initio*' [2007] AJDA 1643.

Mackor, Anne Ruth, 'Explanatory Non-Normative Legal Doctrine. Taking the Distinction Between Theoretical and Practical Reasoning Seriously' in Mark Van Hoecke (ed), *Methodologies of Legal Research. Which Kind of Method for What Kind of Discipline?* (Hart Publishing 2011) 45.

Mackor, Anne Ruth, 'Legal Doctrine As a Non-Normative Discipline' [2012] Recht en Methode in Onderzoek en Onderwijs 22.

Macrory, Richard, 'Reforming Regulatory Sanctions – Designing a Systematic Approach' in Dawn Oliver, Tony Prosser and Richard Rawlings (eds), *The Regulatory State: Constitutional Implications* (Oxford University Press 2010) 22.

Maes, Tom, 'The Energy Regulators' Competence: Network Tariff Setting' in Bram Delvaux, Michael Hunt and Kim Talus (eds), *EU Energy Law and Policy Issues* (Intersentia 2012) 123.

Maggetti, Martino, 'Legitimacy and Accountability of Independent Regulatory Agencies: A Critical Review' (2010) 2 Living Reviews in Democracy 1.

Magnette, Paul, 'The Politics of Regulation in the European Union' in Damien Geradin, Rodolphe Muñoz and Nicolas Petit (eds), *Regulation through Agencies in the EU. A New Paradigm of European Governance* (Edward Elgar Publishing 2005) 3.

Majone, Giandomenico, 'Regulatory Legitimacy' in Giandomenico Majone and Pio Baake (eds), *Regulating Europe* (Routledge 1996) 284.

Majone, Giandomenico, *Temporal Consistency and Policy Credibility: Why Democracies Need Non-Majoritarian Institutions*, EUI Working Paper RSC No. 96/57 (European University Institute, Robert Schuman Centre 1996).

Majone, Giandomenico, 'The Agency Model: The Growth of Regulation and Regulatory Institutions in the European Union' (1997) 3 Eipascope 1.

Marcou, Gérard, 'La notion juridique de régulation' [2006] AJDA 347.

Marique, Yseult, 'The Rule-Making Powers of Independent Administrative Agencies ('QUANGOs')' (2007) 11(3) Electronic Journal of Comparative Law.

Martin, Sébastien, 'Les autorités publiques indépendantes: réflexions autour d'une nouvelle personne publique' [2013] RDP 53.

McHarg, Aileen, 'Devolution in the Regulatory State: Constraints and Opportunities' in Dawn Oliver, Tony Prosser and Richard Rawlings (eds), *The Regulatory State: Constitutional Implications* (Oxford University Press 2010) 5.

McHarg, Aileen, 'Evolution and Revolution in the British Energy Network Regulation: from RPI-X to RIIO' in Martha Roggenkamp et al. (eds), *Energy Networks and the Law* (Oxford University Press 2012) 314.

Mehdi, Rostane, 'L'autonomie institutionnelle et procédurale et le droit administratif' in Jean-Bernard Auby and Jacqueline Dutheil de la Rochère (eds), *Droit Administratif Européen* (Bruylant 2007) 685.

Menuret, Jean-Jacques, 'Bientôt des autorités administratives indépendantes (AAI) territoriales' [2013] La Semaine Juridique Edition Générale 2231.

Ministerie van Justitie, Directie Wetgeving (ed), *Aanwijzingen voor de regelgeving, Aanwijzingen voor convenanten, Praktijkvoorschriften voor ontwerpers van regelingen en convenanten van de Rijksoverheid* (Sdu Uitgevers 1996).

Mitnick, Barry M, 'Capturing "Capture": Definition and Mechanisms' in David Levi-Faur (ed), *Handbook on the Politics of Regulation* (Edward Elgar Publishing 2011) 34.

Moran, Michael, *The British Regulatory State. The Modernism and Hyper-Innovation* (Oxford University Press 2003).

Moran, Michael, 'The Rise of the Regulatory State' in David Coen, Wyn Grant and Graham Wilson (eds), *The Oxford Handbook of Business and Government* (Oxford University Press 2010) 383.

Mulgan, Richard, *Holding Power to Account: Accountability in Modern Democracies* (Palgrave Macmillan 2003).

Murray, Rachel, 'National Human Rights Institutions. Criteria and Factors for Assessing Their Effectiveness' (2007) 25(2) Netherlands Quarterly of Human Rights 189.

Nesti, Giorgia, 'Strengthening the Accountability of Independent Regulatory Agencies: From Performance Back to Democracy' [2016] Comparative European Politics 1.

Nicolaïdes, Phedon, 'Regulation of Liberalised Markets: A New Role for the State?' in Damien Geradin, Rodolphe Muñoz and Nicolas Petit (eds), *Regulation through Agencies in the EU. A New Paradigm of European Governance* (Edward Elgar Publishing 2005) 23.

Nihoul, Pierre, Marc Joassart and Vinciane Franck, 'Le Conseil d'Etat, Chronique de jurisprudence 2007' [2008] RBDC 237.

Norton, Philip (Lord Norton of Louth), 'Regulating the Regulatory State' (2004) 57(4) Parliam Aff 785.

van Nus, J G L, *Overheidstoezicht op afstand. Verzelfstandiging van toezichthoudende taken naar zelfstandige bestuursorganen verkend* (Maklu 1995).

Oliver, Dawn, 'Law, Politics and Accountability' [1994] Public Law 238.

Oliver, Dawn, 'Regulation, Democracy and Democratic Oversight in the UK' in Dawn Oliver, Tony Prosser and Richard Rawlings (eds), *The Regulatory State: Constitutional Implications* (Oxford University Press 2010) 243.

Olsen, Johan P, 'Democratic Government, Institutional Autonomy and the Dynamics of Change' (2009) 32(3) West European Politics 439.

van Ommeren, Frank Julius, *De verplichting verankerd. De reikwijdte van het legaliteitsbeginsel en het materiële wetsbegrip* (W.E.J. Tjeenk Willink 1996).

Ooms, Anne, 'De uitvoerende bevoegdheid van de Koning: van conforme proclamatie tot eerste staatsmacht. Een historische analyse van artikel 108 Grondwet' [2009] CDPK 195.

Osborne, David and Ted Gaebler, *Reinventing Government: How the Entrepreneurial Spirit Is Transforming the Public Sector* (Addison-Wesley 1992).

Ossege, Christoph, *European Regulatory Agencies in EU Decision-Making – Between Expertise and Influence* (Palgrave MacMillan 2016).

Ottow, Annetje, *Telecommunicatietoezicht. De invloed van het Europese en Nederlandse bestuurs(proces)recht*, doctoral thesis in law, University of Amsterdam, 2006, http://dare.uva.nl/document/2/41206.

Ottow, Annetje, 'The Different Levels of Protection of National Supervisors' Independence in the European Landscape' in Suzanne Comtois and Kars J de Graaf (eds), *On Judicial and Quasi-judicial Independence* (Boom Juridische Uitgevers 2013) 139.

Ottow, Annetje and Margot Aelen, 'Commission v. Federal Republic of Germany' [2010] European Human Rights Cases 679.

Papadopoulos, Yannis, 'Problems of Democratic Accountability in Network and Multilevel Governance' (2007) 13(4) European Law Journal 469.

Paulus, Andreas L, 'The International Legal System as a Constitution' in Jeffrey L Dunoff and Joel P Trachtman (eds), *Ruling the World? Constitutionalism, International Law and Global Governance* (Cambridge University Press 2008) 69.

Pegram, Thomas, 'Diffusion Across Political Systems: The Global Spread of National Human Rights Institutions' (2010) 32 Human Rights Quarterly 729.

Perroud, Thomas, 'L'indépendance des autorités de régulation au Royaume-Uni' [2012] RFAP 735.

Piwnica, Emmanuel, 'La dévolution d'un pouvoir de sanction aux autorités administratives indépendantes' [2010] RFDA 915.

Poésy, René, 'La nature juridique de l'Autorité de la concurrence' [2009] AJDA 347.

Pollit, Christopher, Karen Bathgate, Janice Caulfield, Amanda Smullen and Colin Talbot, 'Agency Fever? Analysis of an International Policy Fashion' [2001] Journal of Comparative Policy Analysis: Research and Practice 271.

Popelier, Patricia, *Rechtszekerheid als beginsel voor behoorlijke regelgeving* (Intersentia 1997).

Popelier, Patricia, *Democratisch regelgeven* (Intersentia 2001).

Popelier, Patricia, *De wet juridisch bekeken* (die Keure 2004).

Popelier, Patricia, 'De verhouding tussen de Belgische Grondwet en het internationale recht' in *En hommage à Francis Delpérée. Itinéraires d'un constitutionnaliste* (Bruylant 2007) 1231.

Popelier, Patricia and Jeroen Van Nieuwenhove, 'Decentralisering en privatisering van wetgeving' in Jef De Mot (ed), *Liber Amicorum Boudewijn Bouckaert* (die Keure 2012) 261.

Przeworski, Adam, Susan C Stokes and Bernard Manin (eds), *Democracy, Accountability, and Representation* (Cambridge University Press 1999).

Prosser, Tony, 'Models of Economic and Social Regulation' in Dawn Oliver, Tony Prosser and Richard Rawlings (eds), *The Regulatory State: Constitutional Implications* (Oxford University Press 2010) 34.

Prosser, Tony, *The Regulatory Enterprise – Government, Regulation and Legitimacy* (Oxford University Press 2010).

Prosser, Tony, 'Regulation and Legitimacy' in Jeffrey Jowell and Dawn Oliver (eds), *The Changing Constitution* (7th edn, Oxford University Press 2011) 312.

Prosser, Tony, 'The Powers and Accountability of Agencies and Regulators' in David Feldman (ed), *English Public Law* (Oxford University Press 2011) 241.

Prosser, Tony, *The Economic Constitution* (Oxford University Press 2014).

Pyle, A J, *Locke* (Polity 2013).
Quilichini, Paule, 'Réguler n'est pas juger: Réflexions sur la nature du pouvoir de sanction des autorités de régulation économique' [2004] AJDA 1060.
Rawlings, Richard, 'Introduction: Testing Times' in Dawn Oliver, Tony Prosser and Richard Rawlings (eds), *The Regulatory State: Constitutional Implications* (Oxford University Press 2010) 1.
Renaud, Sébastien, 'Les autorités de régulation et le démembrement du pouvoir central' (2001) 16 Revue de la recherche juridique. Droit prospectif 2203.
Richards, David and Martin Smith, 'The Tensions of Political Control and Administrative Autonomy: from NPM to a Reconstituted Westminster Model' in Tom Christensen and Per Lægreid (eds), *Autonomy and Regulation, Coping with Agencies in the Modern State* (Edward Elgar Publishing 2006) 181.
Rimanque, Karel, *De grondwet toegelicht, gewikt en gewogen* (Intersentia 2005).
Rochet, Claude, Marc Cabane and Simon Formery, 'France' in OECD, *Distributed Public Governance* 71.
Rose-Ackerman, Susan, 'The Regulatory State' in Michel Rosenfeld and András Sajó (eds), *The Oxford Handbook of Comparative Constitutional Law* (Oxford University Press 2012) 671.
Rose-Ackerman, Susan and Thomas Perroud, 'Policymaking and Public Law in France: Public Participation, Agency Independence, and Impact Assessment' [2013] Colum. J. Eur. L. 225.
Ross, Cathryn, 'Independent Economic Regulation: A Tale of Two Paradoxes', Oxera Agenda November 2013.
Rouyère, Aude, 'La constitutionnalisation des autorités administratives indépendantes: quelle signification?' [2010] RFDA 887.
Rowe, Gerard C, 'Administrative Supervision of Administrative Action in the European Union' in Herwig C H Hofmann and Alexander H Türk (eds), *Legal Challenges in EU Administrative Law: Towards an Integrated Administration* (Edward Elgar Publishing 2009) 179.
de Ru, H J, 'Publiekrechtelijke of privaatrechtelijke rechtspersonen' [2002] NJB 1099.
de Ru, H J, 'Toezicht moet geen nieuwe staatsmacht worden. Commentaar op de preadviezen voor de VAR 2003 over: Toezicht op markten' [2003] M&M 178.
Rubinstein Reiss, Dorit, 'Administrative Agencies as Creators of Administrative Law Norms: Evidence from the UK, France and Sweden' in Susan Rose-Ackerman and Peter Lindseth (eds), *Comparative Administrative Law* (Edward Elgar Publishing 2010) 373.

A. R.-T., 'Une juridictionnalisation rampante, mais incomplète, des autorités administratives indépendantes' [2013] RFDA 144.

A. R.-T., 'Les exigences constitutionnelles d'indépendance et d'impartialité appliquées à l'Autorité de régulation des communications électroniques et des postes' [2013] RFDA 1262.

Sacreas, Yves, 'De politieke ministeriële verantwoordelijkheid' [2001] TBP 624.

Saiz Arnaiz, Alejandro and Carina Alcoberro Llivina (eds), *National Constitutional Identity and European Integration* (Intersentia 2013).

van Schaaijk, Geertje A F M, 'Praktijkgericht juridisch onderzoek' [2011] Recht en Methode in Onderzoek en Onderwijs 85.

Schick, Allen, 'Agencies in Search of Principles' in OECD, *Distributed Public Governance: Agencies, Authorities and Other Government Bodies* 33.

Schillemans, Thomas, 'Verantwoording na verzelfstandiging – Continuïteit, verwarring en vernieuwing' in Wieger Bakker and Kutsal Yesilkagit (eds), *Publieke verantwoording* (Boom 2005) 71.

Schmidt, Vivien A, 'Democracy and Legitimacy in the European Union Revisited: Input, Output *and* "Throughput"'[2013] Political Studies 2.

Schneider, Jens-Peter, 'A Common Framework for Decentralized EU Agencies and the Meroni Doctrine' in Herwig C H Hofmann and Russell L Weaver (eds), *Transatlantic Perspectives on Administrative Law* (Bruylant 2011) 203.

Scholten, Miroslava, 'Independent, Hence Unaccountable? – The Need for a Broader Debate on Accountability of the Executive' [2011] Review of European Administrative Law 5.

Scholten, Miroslava, 'Democratic Input Legitimacy of IRAs: Proposing an Assessment Framework' [2015] Utrecht Law Review 64.

Scott, Colin, 'Accountability in the Regulatory State' (2000) 27(1) Journal of Law and Society 38.

Scott, Colin, 'Regulatory Governance and the Challenge of Constitutionalism' in Dawn Oliver, Tony Prosser and Richard Rawlings (eds), *The Regulatory State: Constitutional Implications* (Oxford University Press 2010) 15.

Shapiro, Sidney A and Richard W Murphy, 'Eight Things Americans Can't Figure Out About Controlling Administrative Power' in Herwig C H Hofmann and Russel L Weaver (eds), *Transatlantic Perspectives on Administrative Law* (Bruylant 2011) 7.

Simoncini, Marta, 'The Erosion of the *Meroni* Doctrine. The Case of the European Aviation Safety Agency (EASA)' [2015] European Public Law 309.

Slautsky, Emmanuel, 'Droit Européen, constitution et autorités administratives indépendantes (noot onder GwH 18 November 2010), nr. 2010/130' [2012] APT 104.

Smith, Anne, 'The Unique Position of National Human Rights Institutions: A Mixed Blessing?' [2006] Human Rights Quarterly 904.

Smullen, Amanda Jane, *Translating Agency Reform: Rhetoric and Culture in Comparative Perspective*, PhD thesis, Rotterdam, 2007.

De Somer, Stéphanie, 'The Europeanisation of the Law on National Independent Regulatory Authorities from a Vertical and Horizontal Perspective' [2012] Review of European Administrative Law 93.

De Somer, Stéphanie, 'International and European Impulse with Regard to the Creation of Autonomous Public Bodies: An Emerging Trend' [2014] UCL Journal of Law and Jurisprudence 58.

Sordi, Bernardo, '*Révolution*, *Rechtsstaat*, and the Rule of Law: Historical Reflections on the Emergence of Administrative Law in Europe' in Susan Rose-Ackerman and Peter L Lindseth (eds), *Comparative Administrative Law* (Edward Elgar Publishing 2010) 23.

Spyrelli, Christina, 'Regulating the Regulators? An Assessment of Institutional Structures and Procedural Rules of National Regulatory Authorities' [2003–04] International Journal of Communications Law and Policy 1.

Stott, Tony, '"Snouts in the Trough": the Politics of Quangos' (1995) 48(2) Parliam Aff 323.

Strauss, Peter L, 'Rule-making and the American Constitution' in Dawn Oliver, Tony Prosser and Richard Rawlings (eds), *The Regulatory State: Constitutional Implications* (Oxford University Press 2010) 50.

StrØm, Kaare, 'Parliamentary Democracy and Delegation' in Kaare StrØm, Wolfgang C. Müller and Torbjörn Bergman (eds), *Delegation and Accountability in Parliamentary Democracies* (Oxford University Press 2008) 55.

Swanson, Claude-Albane, 'The Agency for the Cooperation of Energy Regulators – A Regulatory Perspective' in Martha M Roggenkamp and Ulf Hammer (eds), *European Energy Law Report VI* (Intersentia 2009) 37.

Talbot, Colin, 'The Agency Idea: Sometimes Old, Sometimes New, Sometimes Borrowed, Sometimes Untrue' in Christopher Pollit and Colin Talbot (eds), *Unbundled Government. A Critical Analysis of the Global Trend to Agencies, Quangos and Contractualisation* (Routledge 2004).

Teitgen-Colly, Catherine, 'Les autorités administratives indépendantes: histoire d'une institution' in Claude-Albert Colliard and Gérard Timsit (eds), *Les autorités administratives indépendantes* (Presses Universitaires de France 1988) 21.

Teitgen-Colly, Catherine, 'Les instances de régulation et la constitution' [1990] RDP 153.
Thatcher, Mark, 'Delegation to Independent Regulatory Agencies: Pressures, Functions and Contextual Mediation' (2002) 25(1) West European Politics 125, 127.
Thatcher, Mark, 'The Third Force? Independent Regulatory Agencies and Elected Politicians in Europe' (2005) 18(3) Governance 347, 352.
Thatcher, Mark and Alec Stone Sweet, 'Theory and Practice of Delegation to Non-Majoritarian Institutions' 25(1) (2002) West European Politics 1.
Van Thiel, Sandra, 'Comparing Agencies across Countries' in Koen Verhoest, Sandra Van Thiel, Geert Bouckaert and Per Lægreid (eds), *Government Agencies Practices and Lessons from 30 Countries* (Palgrave Macmillan 2012) 18.
Van Thiel, Sandra, Koen Verhoest, Geert Bouckaert and Per Lægreid, 'Lessons and Recommendations for the Practice of Agencification' in Koen Verhoest, Sandra Van Thiel, Geert Bouckaert and Per Lægreid (eds), *Government Agencies. Practices and Lessons from 30 Countries* (Palgrave Macmillan 2012) 413.
Tomkins, Adam, 'The Struggle to Delimit Executive Power in Britain' in Paul Craig and Adam Tomkins (eds), *The Executive and Public Law. Power and Accountability in Comparative Perspective* (Oxford University Press 2006) 16.
Troper, Michel, 'Sovereignty' in Michel Rosenfeld and András Sajó (eds), *The Oxford Handbook of Comparative Constitutional Law* (Oxford University Press 2012) 350.
Turpin, Colin, 'Ministerial Responsibility' in Dawn Oliver and Jeffrey Jowell (eds), *The Changing Constitution* (Clarendon Press 1994) 109.
Turpin, Colin and Adam Tomkins, *British Government and the Constitution* (7th edn, Cambridge University Press 2011).
Tushnet, Mark, 'Comparative Constitutional Law' in Mathias Reimann and Reinhard Zimmermann (eds), *The Oxford Handbook of Comparative Law* (Oxford University Press 2006) 1225.
Vandendriessche, Frederik, *Publieke en private rechtspersonen – Naar een graduele, meerduidige en evolutieve benadering van het onderscheid in de wetgeving en de rechtspraak* (die Keure 2004).
Vandernoot, Pierre, 'Regards du Conseil d'Etat sur une disposition orpheline: l'article 34 de la Constitution' in *En hommage à Francis Delpérée. Itinéraires d'un constitutionnaliste* (Bruylant 2007) 1599.
Velaers, Jan, *De Grondwet en de Raad van State, Afdeling wetgeving* (Maklu 1999).
Velaers, Jan, 'Over de politieke verantwoordelijkheid van ministers' in Maurice Adams, Renate Barbaix, Herman Braeckmans et al. (eds),

Verantwoordelijkheid en recht: eerste facultair congres Faculteit Rechten Universiteit Antwerpen, 14 November 2008 (Kluwer 2008) 361.
Verhey, Luc F M, 'British Agencies: Surveying the Quango State' in Tom Zwart and Luc Verhey (eds), *Agencies in European and Comparative Law* (Intersentia 2003) 19.
Verhey, L F M and N Verheij, 'De macht van marktmeesters, markttoezicht in constitutioneel perspectief' [2005] Toezicht, Handelingen Nederlandse Juristenvereniging 135.
Verhoest, Koen, Frederik Vandendriessche and Jan Rommel, 'Verzelfstandiging in Vlaanderen: theorie en praktijk' in Pierre Jadoul, Bruno Lombaert and François Tulkens (eds), *Le paraétatisme. Nouveaux régards sur la décentralisation fonctionnelle en Belgique et dans les institutions européennes* (la Charte 2010) 369.
Verhoest, Koen, Sandra Van Thiel, Geert Bouckaert and Per Lægreid, 'Introduction' in Koen Verhoest, Sandra Van Thiel, Geert Bouckaert and Per Lægreid (eds), *Government Agencies. Practices and Lessons from 30 Countries* (Palgrave Macmillan 2012) 3.
Verschuere, Bram, Koen Verhoest, Falke Meyers and B Guy Peters, 'Accountability and Accountability Arrangements in Public Agencies' in Tom Christensen and Per Lægreid (eds), *Autonomy and Regulation, Coping with Agencies in the Modern State* (Edward Elgar Publishing 2006) 268.
Voermans, Wim, *Toebedeling van bevoegdheid. Rede uitgesproken bij de aanvaarding van het ambt van hoogleraar op het gebied van het staats- en bestuursrecht op de universiteit Leiden op 12 september 2003* (Boom Juridische Uitgevers 2004).
Vranken, J, 'Exciting Times for Legal Scholarship' [2012] Recht en Methode in Onderzoek en Onderwijs 48.
Warmelink, H G, 'Ministeriële verantwoordelijkheid voor ambtelijk handelen' in D J Elzinga (ed), *Ministeriële Verantwoordelijkheid in Nederland* (W.E.J. Tjeenk Willink 1994) 103.
Webley, Lisa, 'Qualitative Approaches to Empirical Legal Research' in Peter Cane and Herbert M Kritzer (eds), *The Oxford Handbook of Empirical Legal Research* (Oxford University Press 2010) 926.
Weigel, Wolfgang, *Economics of the Law: A Primer* (Routledge 2008).
Weir, Stuart, 'Quangos: Questions of Democratic Accountability' (1995) 48(2) Parliam Aff 306.
Wettenhall, Roger, 'Agencies and Non Departmental Public Bodies' (2005) 7(4) Public Management Review 615.
Wilding, Richard, 'A Triangular Effect: Quangos, Ministers, and MPs' in Anthony Barker (ed), *Quangos in Britain. Government and the Networks of Public Policy-Making* (Palgrave Macmillan 1982) 34.

Wilhelm, Pascal, '3 QUESTIONS Le Pouvoir de sanction de l'ARCEP annulé par le Conseil constitutionnel sur QPC' [2013] La Semaine Juridique Entreprise et Affaires 608.

Williams, Howard, 'Kant on the Social Contract' in David Boucher and Paul Kelly (eds), *The Social Contract from Hobbes to Rawls* (Routledge 1994).

Wilson, David, 'Quangos in the Skeletal State' (1995) 48(2) Parliam Aff 181.

Wraight, Christopher D, *Rousseau's The Social Contract: A Reader's Guide* (Continuum 2008).

Zijlstra, Sjoerd E, *Zelfstandige bestuursorganen in een democratische rechtsstaat – een onderzoek naar democratisch-rechtsstatelijke en positiefrechtelijke aspecten van het gebruik van zelfstandige bestuursorganen, meer in het bijzonder op gemeentelijk niveau* (VUGA 1997).

Zijlstra, Sjoerd E, 'Weg met de zelfstandige bestuursorganen?' (2004) 38 NJB 1980.

Zijlstra, Sjoerd E, 'Zbo's, marktautoriteiten en regelgevende bevoegdheid' [2005] Tijdschrift voor Ondernemingsbestuur 2.

Zijlstra, Sjoerd E, *Bestuurlijk Organisatierecht* (Kluwer 2009).

Zijlstra, Sjoerd E, 'De maakbare overheid. Nieuw beleid inzake zelfstandige bestuursorganen' [2014] Nederlands Tijdschrift voor Bestuursrecht 279.

Zijlstra, Sjoerd E and Kirsten Wilkeshuis, 'Verantwoordelijkheid: bevoegdheid en publieke taak' in J L W Broeksteeg, J Th J van den Berg and L F M Verhey (eds), *Ministeriële verantwoordelijkheid opnieuw gewogen* (Kluwer 2006) 9.

Ziller, Jacques, 'Les autorités administratives indépendantes entre droit interne et droit de l'Union Européenne' [2010] RFDA 901.

Zivy, Fabien, 'La séparation des fonctions d'instruction et de décision au sein de l'Autorité de la concurrence' [2012] La Semaine Juridique Entreprise et Affaires 1142.

Zwart, Tom, 'Independent Regulatory Agencies in the US' in Tom Zwart and Luc Verhey (eds), *Agencies in European and Comparative Law* (Intersentia 2003) 3.

Zwart, Tom, 'Judicial Review of Agency Action: The Scope of Review' in Tom Zwart and Luc Verhey (eds), *Agencies in European and Comparative Law* (Intersentia 2003) 171.

Zwart, Tom, 'Overseeing the Executive: Is the Legislature Reclaiming Lost Territory from the Courts?' in Susan Rose-Ackerman and Peter Lindseth (eds), *Comparative Administrative Law* (Edward Elgar Publishing 2010) 148.

Index